A Research Agenda for Sustainable Ocean Governance

Elgar Research Agendas outline the future of research in a given area. Leading scholars are given the space to explore their subject in provocative ways, and map out the potential directions of travel. They are relevant but also visionary.

Forward-looking and innovative, Elgar Research Agendas are an essential resource for PhD students, scholars and anybody who wants to be at the forefront of research.

For a full list of Edward Elgar published titles, including the titles in this series, visit our website at www.e-elgar.com.

A Research Agenda for Sustainable Ocean Governance

Edited by

JUSTIN ALGER

School of Social and Political Sciences, University of Melbourne, Australia

U. RASHID SUMAILA

Institute for the Oceans and Fisheries and the School of Public Policy and Global Affairs, University of British Columbia, Canada

Elgar Research Agendas

Edward Elgar PUBLISHING

Cheltenham, UK · Northampton, MA, USA

Published by
Edward Elgar Publishing Limited
The Lypiatts
15 Lansdown Road
Cheltenham
Glos GL50 2JA
UK

Edward Elgar Publishing, Inc.
William Pratt House
9 Dewey Court
Northampton
Massachusetts 01060
USA

Authorised representative in the EU for GPSR queries only: Easy Access System Europe – Mustamäe tee 50, 10621 Tallinn, Estonia, gpsr.requests@easproject.com

A catalogue record for this book
is available from the British Library

Library of Congress Control Number: 2024952768

This book is available electronically in the **Elgar**online
Political Science and Public Policy subject collection
https://doi.org/10.4337/9781035325757

Printed on elemental chlorine free (ECF)
recycled paper containing 30% Post-Consumer Waste

ISBN 978 1 0353 2574 0 (cased)
ISBN 978 1 0353 2575 7 (eBook)

Printed and bound in the USA

Contents

PART III GOVERNING FISHERIES

PART IV OCEAN GOVERNANCE AND INTERNATIONAL REGIMES

PART V ADVANCING PRACTICE

Figures

Tables

Boxes

Contributors

Denis Worlanyo Aheto, Professor, Africa Centre of Excellence in Coastal Resilience (ACECoR), University of Cape Coast, Ghana.

Shehu Latunji Akintola, Professor of Fisheries, Department of Fisheries, Lagos State University, Nigeria, and Africa Centre of Excellence in Coastal Resilience (ACECoR), University of Cape Coast, Ghana.

Justin Alger, Senior Lecturer in International Relations, School of Social and Political Sciences, University of Melbourne, Australia.

Rafael Almeida Magris, Environmental Analyst, Instituto Chico Mendes de Conservação da Biodiversidade, Brazil.

Fernando Aranceta-Garza, Investigador, México CONAHCYT (Consejo Nacional de Humanidades, Ciencias y Tecnologías), Centro de Investigaciones Biológicas del Noroeste, Department of Fisheries Ecology, Mexico.

Natalie C. Ban, Professor, Environmental Studies, University of Victoria, Canada.

J. Samuel Barkin, Professor of Global Governance and Human Security, Department of Conflict Resolution, Human Security and Global Governance, University of Massachusetts Boston, USA.

Dyhia Belhabib, Principal Investigator, I-Sea Fisheries, Ecotrust Canada, Canada.

Nathan J. Bennett, Adjunct Professor, Institute for the Oceans and Fisheries, University of British Columbia, Canada.

Tomas Chaigneau, Senior Lecturer of Social Sciences for Our Environment, Environment and Sustainabiltiy Institute, University of Exeter, United Kingdom.

Andrés Cisneros-Montemayor, Assistant Professor, School of Resource & Environmental Management, Simon Fraser University, Canada.

Joachim Claudet, Director of Research, Centre National de la Recherche Scientifique (CNRS), Centre de Recherches Insulaires et Observatoire de l'Environnement (CRIOBE), France.

Ilyass Dahmouni, Postdoctoral Research Fellow, Fisheries Economics Research Unit, University of British Columbia, Canada.

Peter Dauvergne, Professor of International Relations, Department of Political Science, University of British Columbia, Canada.

Elizabeth R. DeSombre, Professor of Environmental Studies, Environmental Studies Department, Wellesley College, USA.

Rodolphe Devillers, Senior Research Scientist, UMR 228 Espace-Dev, Institut de Recherche pour le Développement (IRD), France.

Isa Olalekan Elegbede, Lecturer, Department of Fisheries, Lagos State University, Nigeria.

Irmak Ertör, Assistant Professor, Atatürk Institute for Modern Turkish History, Boğaziçi University, Turkey.

Natalie Fiertz, Research Associate, Environmental Security, Stimson Center, USA.

Iria García-Lorenzo, Postdoctoral Fellow, Department of Applied Economics, University of Vigo, Spain.

Babet de Groot, PhD candidate, School of Social and Political Sciences, University of Sydney, Australia.

Carolyn Gruber, Fellow and Deputy Director, Environmental Security, Stimson Center, USA.

John Hannigan, Professor of Sociology, Department of Sociology, University of Toronto Scarborough, Canada.

Ibrahim Issifu, Postdoctoral Research Fellow, Fisheries Economics Research Unit, University of British Columbia, Canada.

Peter J. Jacques, Rechnitz Family/UCI Endowed Chair in Marine and Environmental Law and Policy, Political Science and Sociology, Monmouth University, USA.

Chris T. Langevin, PhD candidate, Department of Conflict Resolution, Human Security and Global Governance, University of Massachusetts Boston, USA.

Philippe Le Billon, Professor, Department of Geography, University of British Columbia, Canada.

Rocío López de la Lama, Postdoctoral Fellow, School of Public Policy and Global Affairs, University of British Columbia, Canada.

Elizabeth Mendenhall, Associate Professor, Department of Marine Affairs, University of Rhode Island, USA.

Elisa Morgera, Professor of Global Environmental Law, Strathclyde Law School, University of Strathclyde, United Kingdom.

Umi Muawanah, Director, Research Center for Economics of Industry, Services and Trade, Badan Riset dan Inovasi Nasional, Indonesia.

Agus Eko Nugroho, Chairman of Research Organization of Governance, Economy and People Welfare, Badan Riset dan Inovasi Nasional, Indonesia.

Akinkunmi Sunday Ojo, Graduate Assistant, Department of Fisheries, Lagos State University, Nigeria.

Olanrewaju Femi Olagunju, PhD candidate, Faculty of Economics, University of Iceland, Iceland, and Federal Department of Fisheries and Aquaculture, Federal Ministry of Agriculture & Rural Development, Nigeria.

Isaac Kofi Osei, Postdoctoral Fellow, Africa Centre of Excellence in Coastal Resilience (ACECoR), University of Cape Coast, Ghana.

Daniel Pauly, Professor, Institute for the Oceans and Fisheries, University of British Columbia, Canada.

Laura M. Pereira, Professor, Global Change Institute, University of the Witwatersrand, South Africa.

Julie M. Reimer, Senior Policy Advisor, Fisheries and Oceans Canada, Canada.

Greg Richards, Professor of Leisure Studies, University of Tilburg, Netherlands.

Tracy Rouleau, Nonresident Fellow, Environmental Security, Stimson Center, USA.

Lina M. Saavedra-Díaz, Professor, Biology Program, Universidad del Magdalena, Colombia.

Abdulwakil Olawale Saba, Assistant Lecturer, Department of Fisheries, Lagos State University, Nigeria, and Department of Biology, University Putra Malaysia, Malaysia.

Zamroni Salim, Director, Research Center for Macroeconomics and Finance, Badan Riset dan Inovasi Nasional, Indonesia.

Paula Satizábal, Honorary Fellow, Geography, Earth and Atmospheric Sciences, University of Melbourne, Australia.

U. Rashid Sumaila, Professor of Fisheries Economics, Institute for the Oceans and Fisheries and School of Public Policy and Global Affairs, University of British Columbia, Canada.

Maxine Westhead, Director, Marine Affairs Program, Dalhousie University, Canada.

Margaret A. Young, Australian Research Council Future Fellow and Professor, Melbourne Law School, University of Melbourne.

Oran R. Young, Distinguished Professor Emeritus, Bren School of Environmental Science and Management, University of California Santa Barbara, USA.

Sally Yozell, Senior Fellow and Director, Environmental Security, Stimson Center, USA.

PART I

Setting the stage

1 Future research for a healthy ocean

Justin Alger and U. Rashid Sumaila

Introduction

Research on the sustainable governance of our ocean has been growing steadily in the 21st century as humanity's impact on it has become increasingly clear. Overfishing, plastic pollution, shifting biodiversity baselines, and warming and acidification, among other threats, are all fundamentally reshaping ocean ecosystems and threatening their capacity to support life. In recognition of this threat, the United Nations (UN) proclaimed the period from 2021 to 2030 the Decade of Ocean Science for Sustainable Development. The health of our ocean is on the agenda like never before. This growing attention to ocean issues from governments, non-governmental organizations (NGOs), businesses, and citizens alike provides an opportunity. We are at a critical juncture at which researchers can shape the institutions governing our oceans more so than ever before.

This ocean decade coincides with other governance breakthroughs to better protect the ocean. This includes the historic 2023 Treaty on Biodiversity Beyond National Jurisdiction (BBNJ) to finally provide a framework for states to better protect the high seas. The 2022 World Trade Organization (WTO) Agreement on Fisheries Subsidies was the first WTO agreement in history with sustainability at its core, and the only agreement reached by WTO member states of any kind in a decade. At the UN Climate Change Conference COP27 in 2022, states finally reached an agreement on a loss and damage fund for vulnerable countries, many of which will suffer from the impact of climate change on the ocean. The 2022 Kunming-Montreal Agreement codified the increasingly prominent 30 x 30 target to protect 30 percent of terrestrial and marine spaces by 2030. These agreements are merely a starting point for the more substantive governance arrangements we need to better protect our ocean, but they each represent a crucial step.

At the same time, the growing emphasis on an ocean or blue economy model—relying on ocean resources for economic growth while preserving healthy ocean ecosystems—engages more stakeholders in ocean governance. Businesses large and small are increasingly shaping ocean governance, risking exacerbating environmental harm as they seek new ways to extract more value from ocean ecosystems, including through artificial intelligence to target fish stocks or with deep-sea minerals extraction poised to begin sometime this decade. Local communities and traditional resource users must often compete with these enterprises to protect their access to ocean resources and ensure their longevity. The question of not only how to govern ocean resources, but for whom, looms large in ongoing efforts to better manage ocean resources for current and future generations.

The twenty chapters in this volume will reflect on these governance challenges, among others, from a variety of disciplinary perspectives, including political science, economics, law, geography, and the natural sciences. They explore issues ranging from biodiversity protection to ocean justice to fisheries management to plastics to deep-sea exploration, and more. They are not exhaustive of the manifold challenges we face in the pursuit of a healthy ocean, nor our approaches to addressing those challenges, but they highlight the diversity of this collective enterprise. The volume features 49 scholars from around the world, from different disciplines and outside of academia, and at various stages of their careers. It is an effort to gather in one place the diversity of these perspectives, so that we might all be better informed about the efforts of like-minded people across disciplinary and geographical boundaries to preserve the health of our ocean. Its goal is to outline potential avenues for high-impact, practical research for early-career scholars and graduate students interested in contributing to shaping ocean governance.

This chapter highlights what we see as some of the most important themes for future research emerging from this volume. We identify the following seven themes: (1) centering ecology, (2) justice and equity, (3) closing loopholes in ocean governance, (4) the design and impact of global institutions and regimes, (5) power and politics, (6) the imperative of ambitious thinking, and (7) the interdisciplinary coproduction of knowledge in partnership with public and private sector actors. Each theme draws from the contributions of the scholars in this volume, providing additional context and analysis of our own. The caveat is that the authors of this chapter are a political scientist and an economist, respectively, so these themes reflect our own disciplinary lenses on the chapters to follow. Our hope is that this chapter can provide some useful ideas about how future research for a healthy ocean can be as impactful as possible at a time of unprecedented collective ambition.

Centering ecology

Advancing research to improve ocean governance requires the dedication of scholars across many disciplines to make sense of its myriad institutions, rules, and principles, and to understand their impact. These scholars are unified across disciplines by a shared normative commitment to healthier oceans, but there can be considerable divergence on what the object of study is. An ocean biologist may focus on variables such as biomass in an ecosystem, food webs, spawning grounds, or the myriad other ways in which species interact with their ecosystem. An economist may be interested in catch numbers, values and valuation, and the distribution of benefits (and harms) from fishing. A legal scholar may examine how international law evolves as new treaties, rulings, and cases emerge. A political scientist may be concerned with how various international institutions and regimes shape how we govern oceans, or with the role of powerful corporate and state actors in undermining stronger governance. All these approaches, among others, are needed to navigate the complexity of ocean governance so that we might better attempt to steer it going forward.

It is crucial, however, that ocean health be the primary baseline that we use for identifying progress in ocean governance. Any new institution, rule, or principle is only progress insomuch as it contributes to healthier ecosystems and, going further, that it does so as urgently as possible. Incremental steps or symbolic victories for the ocean can contribute to momentum toward meaningful action, but they are not enough. The UN Ocean Decade, BBNJ Agreement, WTO Fisheries Subsidies Agreement, Kunming-Montreal Agreement, and other multilateral agreements are important diplomatic victories that establish collective responsibility for the ocean, but our evaluation of them should depend on whether they will meaningfully contribute to improving the health of the ocean. Whether they do remains to be seen and will undoubtedly be the focus of future research. This is not to say that their impact is easy to measure—the determinants of ecosystem health are multitudinous and complex—but rather that ocean health should underlie how we think about ocean governance across disciplines. As Pauly (Chapter 2) reminds us, the story of the decline in global fish biomass is the story of humanity's impact on the Earth. It is important not to lose sight of the goal of a lasting and healthy ocean environment.

Disciplinary approaches in the social sciences are still essential. How humanity impacts the ocean is fundamentally about people and social structures, and solutions will be too. Centering ecology can often just mean taking a more critical lens to social structures and reflecting on the ways in which they might detract from a healthier ocean. For example, the Food and Agricultural Organization's (FAO) maximum sustainable yield (MSY) approach to ocean sustainability has consistently prioritized short-term economic growth over ocean health, contributing to normalizing a global culture of overfishing (Jacques and Lobo 2018). Looking forward, the Kunming-Montreal Agreement's 30 x 30 target, if realized, is only meaningful if marine protected areas (MPAs) are well protected and not just paper parks (see Alger in Chapter 13). Scholarship that examines governing institutions, rules, and principles is needed to understand not only the social forces leading to ocean decline but also the social forces that could lead to solutions.

Finally, centering ecology means taking a critical eye to the term "sustainable," despite its appearance in the title of this volume. Too often, the language of sustainability is used to justify ongoing extraction and exploitation at the expense of the environment, rather than to the benefit of it. Centering ecology is one way to ensure that "sustainability" still refers to the longevity of healthy ecosystems and the conditions that we hand down to future generations.

Justice and equity

Centering ecology does not mean neglecting the needs of people, especially the marginalized. The same overextraction and pollution that degrade ecosystems also disproportionately impact marginalized groups. Justice and equity are essential in ocean governance not only to protect people from ocean decline and attempts to address it, but because injustice and inequity drive ecosystem decline. A super trawler not only contributes to decimating fish populations in an area but also threatens food security and livelihoods for coastal populations. Overfishing in West African waters, including by these super trawlers, has led to fish stock decline and increased malnutrition and poverty in coastal states (Belhabib et al. 2015). When the Canadian Atlantic cod fishery—a fishery that had provided for local communities for 500 years—collapsed in the 1990s, 30,000 jobs were lost and the population of the province of Newfoundland dropped by 10 percent. Promoting justice and equity means challenging elite interests, usually to the benefit of both people and the planet.

But what about when there are inherent justice trade-offs in ocean governance? Pereira et al. (Chapter 5) stress that justice must be explicit in decision-making for truly transformative ocean governance, but decisions require inherent justice trade-offs. Foregrounding justice does not mean there are no winners and losers nor varying implications for intergenerational or interspecies justice. Pereira et al. call for transparency on the values and philosophies underpinning the compromises that must be made. We would echo this call for transparency, especially since decisions about trade-offs are too often made behind closed doors and to the benefit of short-term commercial interests (Alger 2021, 2023). Transparency is especially important to ensure development is inclusive and equitable as governments increasingly look to blue economy models, as Muawanah et al. (Chapter 18) highlight in Indonesia. The longevity of healthy ecosystems and their ability to support current and future generations should, we would argue, remain paramount in ocean governance decisions (Sumaila 2021).

Further progress to promote the health of the ocean critically depends on the efforts of people fighting for change. Too often, Le Billon et al. (Chapter 3) lament, efforts by community activists to defend ocean spaces lead to harsh repression and violence from corporations and governments. Ocean governance scholarship can do more to foreground human rights in political resistance to unjust or inequitable ocean practices. While treaties are being negotiated in conference facilities in Geneva or New York to shape the future of ocean governance, ocean defenders are engaged in acts of resistance to shape it now. Le Billon et al. call for collaborative research with ocean defenders based on mutual trust to ensure that it reflects their concerns, aspirations, and well-being. Such research recognizes not only the centrality of human rights and justice in ocean governance, but that we cannot attain healthy oceans without political resistance. A future of ocean governance absent a justice and equity frame is bleak—the collective enterprise of a healthy ocean for people and planet requires advocacy, resistance, and the defense of community livelihoods and values.

Closing loopholes

One of the first practical steps to enhancing ocean governance is to work to close loopholes in existing governance arrangements, some of which are obvious and others less so. Loopholes can range from notable omissions from existing arrangements to the need to better consider the implications of existing concepts and practices. In some cases, these loopholes are by design but create considerable uncertainty about the impact of new governance initiatives. The 2022 WTO Agreement on Fisheries Subsidies, for example, excluded measures to address capacity-enhancing subsidies—subsidies that lead to larger fishing fleets than would otherwise be viable (Sumaila et al. 2010)—because agreement was too politically difficult (Alger et al. 2023). States have a limited window to reach an agreement on these subsidies, or the existing agreement will expire. Moreover, the impact of the current agreement will be limited, so these more comprehensive subsidies are needed to meaningfully combat overfishing (Sumaila et al. 2024a). Many international agreements include compromises that reduce their effectiveness in promoting healthy oceans, but the longer-term objective should be to continue to ratchet up ambition and commitments through these agreements over time.

While the WTO Agreement loophole is a clear gap and acknowledged as one by negotiating states, identifying loopholes, which can often require reconceptualizing how we think of the array of institutions and mechanisms governing the ocean, can itself be a challenging task. Barkin and Langevin (Chapter 8) argue that collectively referring to the failures of international fisheries governance as illegal, unreported, and unregulated (IUU) fishing contributes to ineffective governance (Sumaila et al. 2020). This is not a benign category, but rather one that tends to lead to certain kinds of problem framings and solution types, notably by emphasizing fishers not following rules rather than the inadequacies of the rules themselves (see Chapter 8). In some cases, identifying loopholes is difficult because of new and emerging activities in the ocean. Hannigan and Richards (Chapter 19) note the lack of regulation for deep-sea exploration and tourism, interest in which has recently grown despite safety risks, as the implosion of OceanGate Expeditions' *Titan* submersible highlighted all too well when it captured the news cycle in 2023. Closing loopholes, then, also means thinking carefully about how we conceptualize existing governance failures, our ability to identify emerging challenges, and how well we critically reflect on the types of solutions that we prioritize and where they may be falling short.

Many loopholes exist at the level of defining and implementing best practices. For example, international efforts toward combating harmful fisheries subsidies must also be supported by domestic subsidies reform. Aranceta-Garza and Cisneros-Montemayor (Chapter 9) examine Mexico's elimination of capacity-enhancing subsidies, noting some early signs of its success in reducing fishing effort, though further long-term study of ecological and social impacts will be needed. Yozell et al. (Chapter 16) call for holistic, locally tailored climate risk assessment and action to better insulate small island developing states (SIDS) and coastal least developed countries (LDCs) from the impacts of climate disasters. Better risk assessments can ensure that the tools that do exist to combat climate impacts on island and coastal communities can be deployed properly, addressing a disconnect between best practices and their on-the-ground implementation. The same is true for marine spatial planning (MSP), which Reimer et al. (Chapter 14) highlight is not as transformative as it could be due to a disconnect between research and practice. Researchers too often adopt an idealized version of MSP removed from political and economic processes in local contexts. For researchers, closing loopholes can mean more research that works to bridge research and practice in MSP and other contexts.

Global regimes and institutions

We are in an era of unprecedented progress in the development of global regimes and institutions to better govern our ocean. The BBNJ Treaty, the WTO Agreement on Fisheries Subsidies, and the Kunming-Montreal Agreement, among other developments, are the result of the coordinated efforts of states, NGOs, scientists, and others to put ocean health on the international agenda and to create instruments to empower states to govern it better. But to what extent is more global governance of our ocean amounting to better governance? Do these various governing arrangements complement one another or compete? Will they contribute to a healthier ocean?

The underlying agreement upon which most other international ocean agreements are built is the UN Convention on the Law of the Sea (UNCLOS)—colloquially the so-called constitution for our ocean. It sets territorial boundaries and establishes regulatory authority for ocean space. More recent agreements build upon the rules established by UNCLOS to expand states' ability to govern biodiversity beyond national boundaries, better regulate harmful fisheries subsidies, and establish more ambitious marine conservation targets. While these agreements are all welcome developments that expand the tools states have available to govern the ocean, they create challenges. Ocean governance is a crowded space with many interacting institutions and rules, which has made questions about regime interaction central to political scientists and legal scholars (see Oran R. Young in Chapter 10, Margaret A. Young in Chapter 11, and Mendenhall in Chapter 12). These interactions can create some unintuitive outcomes. For example, the BBNJ Treaty does not seem to provide states with many tools for managing fisheries in international waters, which means the agreement is unable to address even this most fundamental of ecosystem impacts. This is because providing that ability would undermine the authority of regional fisheries management organizations (RFMOs), which on balance have proven insufficient for preventing the overexploitation of fisheries (Cullis-Suzuki and Pauly 2010, DeSombre in Chapter 7). More positively, the recent International Tribunal for the Law of the Sea (ITLOS) found that UNCLOS contains specific obligations with respect to climate change, which may enhance the authority of institutions governing the ocean to address environmental impacts (see Chapter 11). This decision suggests potential regime interactions that can bolster the tools states have available to better protect the ocean. Much of this is evolving over time in response to new agreements and decisions.

One consistent feature of multilateral environmental agreements is that they must reflect compromises between states with varying interests, some of which will oppose meaningful limitations on economic activities that they benefit from or rely on. They are, as a result, rarely as ambitious as they need to be to effectively address the drivers of ocean decline (see DeSombre in Chapter 7 and Mendenhall in Chapter 12). The BBNJ Treaty does not allow states to directly manage fisheries. The WTO Subsidies Agreement so far does not include measures to address subsidies that lead to overcapacity, and two subsequent efforts to bolster the agreement in 2024 failed. The Kunming-Montreal Agreement provides states with considerable flexibility to decide what counts as protected in their pursuit of the 30 x 30 target. These shortcomings are included by design, and they are exploited by wealthy nations to ensure the continued benefits of exploiting ocean resources, often at the cost of long-term ecosystem decline. Moreover, the scope of these governing institutions is rarely as big as it needs to be to effectively address not just ocean decline but environmental decline. We would echo Oran R. Young's call in Chapter 10 for measures to address planetary governance that properly link atmospheric, marine, and terrestrial systems. Scholars and practitioners must do the necessary work to identify the gaps and shortcomings of these agreements in the pursuit of more effective governing regimes and institutions. But we should avoid viewing any multilateral agreement as a fait accompli. They provide the foundation upon which more ambitious action can emerge, but they will rarely be enough.

Power and politics

As with any other area of governance, power is fundamental to how governments make decisions about the ocean. It may be tempting to think about ocean governance as relatively benign, with fishing fleets operating far out at sea away from the power and politics of nation-states. But it is powerful interests that are fundamentally reshaping the ocean through overexploitation and the externalities of otherwise unrelated economic activities. The main opponents of a more ambitious BBNJ Treaty or WTO Agreement on Fisheries Subsidies were, unsurprisingly, states with large high seas fishing fleets or states reliant on providing considerable industry subsidies, respectively. While care needs to be taken that a transition to a more sustainable world is just and that it protects the economic interests of communities, opposition to more robust environmental governance usually comes in the form of wealthy nations and powerful commercial interests trying to lock in their advantage. Marine conservation through the establishment of MPAs provides a telling example. These processes often reflect compromises that allow commercial stakeholders to continue business-as-usual activity, creating "paper parks" that privilege short-term economic interests at the expense of long-term economic interests (Weitzman 2001, Sumaila 2004), ecosystem health, and intergenerational and interspecies justice (Sumaila and Walters 2005, Alger in Chapter 13). Faced with governance and management approaches that are proving insufficient to protect and restore ocean health, Reimer et al. (Chapter 14) call for researchers and practitioners to speak truth to power by both asserting scientific facts as well as values and policy recommendations. It is important that scholarship and researchers be engaged with practice, so that collectively some of the political barriers to more ambitious action might be overcome (Sumaila et al. 2024b).

One of the greatest challenges in strengthening governance for a healthy ocean is that some of the most impactful activities deteriorating the ocean are terrestrial. The fossil fuel and petrochemical sectors impact ocean health, including through ocean warming and acidification caused by climate change and the diffusion of plastics throughout the ocean. In both instances, the degradation of ocean ecosystems is an externality of economic activity that occurs elsewhere. No amount of strengthening ocean-specific governance will solve the climate or plastics crises. As de Groot et al. (Chapter 20) argue, initiatives to address ocean plastics once they have entered ocean ecosystems are not enough. Instead, we need to target the upstream production and dissemination of plastics, which is especially challenging given the ubiquity of plastics throughout global supply chains and the diverse and extensive network of decentralized actors contributing to the problem. Closing loopholes or strengthening governing institutions for the ocean cannot address some of the most potent threats to ocean ecosystems. Ocean scholarship instead must also recognize the political and economic power of state and corporate actors with a vested interest in continuing harmful activities, especially those of the fossil fuel and petrochemical industries.

The imperative of ambitious thinking

The existing suite of institutions, rules, and principles for ocean governance is failing both people and the planet. It is going to take more than incremental improvements to remedy their shortcomings. In any discipline, it can be easy to become lost in the specifics of a given case study, ecosystem dynamic, institution, regime, or any other unit of study. This is, in fact, often required to generate new knowledge—phenomena must be broken down into manageable, component parts to study further. We would encourage broad reflection with a view to generating ambitious ideas for strengthening ocean governance. Imagining a future characterized by "Infinity Fish"—global fisheries that are sustainable forever—can generate ambitious ideas, such as closing the high seas to fishing (see Sumaila in Chapter 6). Ideas like this seem radical. States are unlikely to agree to it. But proposing bold ideas raises the ceiling of what is possible. It can lead to a ratcheting up of existing efforts once it becomes clear just how far from this radical ideal we might be. It encourages higher levels of ambition, shapes ocean norms, and might just change the minds of critical decision-makers. Before 2006, Australia's Great Barrier Reef Marine Park was the only MPA in the world greater than 200,000 sq km, and designating more MPAs of that size or larger seemed radical. Now there are over two dozen MPAs in the world larger than this, with the Ross Sea Region being the world's largest at over 2 million sq km. The BBNJ Treaty creates the potential for many more. Closing the high seas to fishing might seem radical now, but ambitious ideas are necessary in the face of planetary crisis.

More ambitious thinking also means challenging the underlying assumptions of Western, neoliberal governance mechanisms. It seems unlikely that these rationalist approaches alone, with their emphasis on economic gains, will be enough to effectively address the drivers of ocean decline. There are important questions to ask about the values that we prioritize in developing new institutions, rules, and principles. Peter Jacques (Chapter 4) reminds us of the relative consistency of Indigenous approaches to the world ocean, with emphasis on creating and maintaining good relations with the planet. Such approaches can shift our thinking away from an extractive mindset toward one that recognizes the violations in how we interact with the ocean. Other worldviews similarly challenge the extractivism of Western economic liberalism, such as *Buen Vivir and Pachamama* from the Andes region, or *Ubuntu* from the Zulu. Relative to how we govern the ocean today, the ideas in these worldviews are radical, and by extension, wholesale adoption at a substantial scale is at odds with current priorities. But they serve the essential purpose of drawing attention to the interactions between people and planet that are exploitive of the latter, rather than symbiotic. It is more radical, we would argue, to think that incrementally improving on the existing institutions, rules, and principles dominating ocean governance will be enough to prevent ongoing ocean decline.

Conclusion: the coproduction of knowledge

Research for a healthy ocean is a collective enterprise that requires interdisciplinarity (Sumaila 2024). Our understanding of certain ocean ecosystem dynamics is exceptional, but there are other areas where biologists can enhance our understanding to better detect ecological and anthropogenic stressors (see Akintola et al. in Chapter 17). At the same time, economic analysis of certain marine spaces has been robust but lacking in many others (see Issifu et al. in Chapter 15). Each marine space also has a distinct politics, with an array of government, commercial, and community stakeholders all vying for potentially different environmental and social outcomes (see Pereira et al. in Chapter 5). In many of these spaces, local communities and activists face oppression and violence from powerful states and corporations (see Le Billon et al. in Chapter 3). Structuring all of this is a global ocean governance complex that shapes who makes the rules and how (see Oran R. Young in Chapter 10). We require all these contributions—from biology, economics, political science, geography, law, and more—to address the myriad barriers we face in the pursuit of a healthy ocean (Sumaila et al. 2024b).

This volume contains contributions from all these disciplines to provide a well-rounded, but by no means comprehensive, research agenda for more robust ocean governance. One of the most challenging aspects of ocean governance research is that it can be difficult to know what institutions, rules, and principles to promote in the face of such complexity. No discipline alone has a clear view of this. Understanding ecosystem dynamics and stressors is essential but does not tell us much about the cultural, economic, social, and political pathways to potential solutions. A hard-fought and politically viable environmental agreement only matters insofar as it improves ecological conditions overall. There are countless examples like these, but the message is that the coproduction of knowledge is not only good for stronger ocean governance but is an essential element of it. There is no desirable path forward other than one that incorporates the insights of all these disciplines. Our hope is that this book can contribute to inspiring future research for a healthy ocean that is interdisciplinary, diverse, and engaged. There has never been as much momentum on ocean governance as there is now. Equally, there has never been this big of an opportunity for researchers to shape ocean governance.

References

Alger, Justin. 2021. *Conserving the Oceans: The Politics of Large Marine Protected Areas*. New York: Oxford University Press.

Alger, Justin. 2023. The Political Economy of Protected Area Designations: Commercial Interests in Conservation Policy. *Global Environmental Politics* 23 (2): 54–73. https://doi.org/10.1162/glep_a_00690.

Alger, Justin, Philippe Le Billon, Eric Leinberger, and U. Rashid Sumaila. 2023. What Would Article 5.1 of the 2022 WTO Ministerial Agreement on Fisheries Subsidies Accomplish? *Marine Policy* 153. https://doi.org/10.1016/j.marpol.2023.105641.

Belhabib, Dyhia, U. Rashid Sumaila, and Daniel Pauly. 2015. Feeding the Poor: Contribution of West African Fisheries to Employment and Security. *Ocean & Coastal Management* 111: 72–81. https://doi.org/10.1016/j.ocecoaman.2015.04.010.

Cullis-Suzuki, Sarika, and Daniel Pauly. 2010. Failing the High Seas: A Global Evaluation of Regional Fisheries Management Organizations. *Marine Policy* 34 (5): 1036–1042. https://doi.org/10.1016/j.marpol.2010.03.002.

Jacques, Peter, and Rafaella Lobo. 2018. The Shifting Context of Sustainability: Growth and the World Ocean Regime. *Global Environmental Politics* 18 (4): 85–106. https://doi.org/10.1162/glep_a_00480.

Sumaila, U. Rashid. 2004. Intergenerational Cost–Benefit Analysis and Marine Ecosystem Restoration. *Fish and Fisheries* 5 (4): 329–343. https://doi.org/10.1111/j.1467-2679.2004.00166.x.

Sumaila, U. Rashid. 2021. *Infinity Fish: Economics and the Future of Fish and Fisheries*. Cambridge: Academic Press.

Sumaila, U. Rashid. 2024. Reflections on Breaking Down Silos in Fisheries Science. *Fisheries* 49 (5): 207–210. https://doi.org/10.1002/fsh.11076.

Sumaila, U. Rashid, Lubna Alam, Patrizia R. Abdallah, Denis Aheto, Shehu L. Akintola, Justin Alger, Vania Andreoli et al. 2024a. WTO Must Complete Ambitious Fisheries Subsidies Agreement. *npj Ocean Sustainability* 3 (6). https://doi.org/10.1038/s44183-024-00042-0.

Sumaila, U. Rashid, Derek Armitage, Megan Bailey, and William W.L. Cheung (Eds.). 2024b. *Sea Change: Charting a Sustainable Future for Oceans in Canada*. Vancouver: University of British Columbia Press.

Sumaila, U. Rashid, Ahmed Khan, Louise Teh, Reg Watson, Peter Tyedmers, and Daniel Pauly. 2010. Subsidies to High Seas Bottom Trawl Fleets and the Sustainability of Deep-Sea Demersal Fish Stocks. *Marine Policy* 34 (3): 495–497. https://doi.org/10.1016/j.marpol.2009.10.004.

Sumaila, U. Rashid, and Carl Walters. 2005. Intergenerational Discounting: A New Intuitive Approach. *Ecological Economics* 52 (2): 135–142. https://doi.org/10.1016/j.ecolecon.2003.11.012.

Sumaila, U. Rashid, Dirk Zeller, Lincoln Hood, M.L. Deng Palomares, Yu-Jun Li, and Daniel Pauly. 2020. Illicit Trade in Marine Fish Catch and its Effects on Ecosystems and People Worldwide. *Science Advances* 6 (9). https://doi.org/10.1126/sciadv.aaz3801.

Weitzman, Martin L. 2001. Gamma Discounting. *American Economic Review* 91 (1): 260–271.

2 The human conquest of the Earth and oceans

Daniel Pauly

Introduction: African beginnings and our first expansions

Anatomically modern humans (*Homo sapiens*) emerged in Africa about 300,000 years ago from a succession of earlier primate species, originally separated from the ancestors of chimpanzees and bonobos between 6 and 7 million years ago. By combining language and symbolic thinking with the manual dexterity inherited from their apish ancestors, modern humans could bring down any animal that walked. Indeed, except in Africa itself, where the potential prey animals had co-evolved with, and thus were wary of, bipedal primates holding pointed sticks, hunting caused hecatombs in all the lands that they migrated into after some humans—the ancestors of all non-African people—left the continent some 70,000 years ago.

Thus, in Europe, dozens of genera and even more species of large mammals were exterminated, including mammoths, woolly rhinoceros, and the Neanderthals as well, shortly after *Homo sapiens* migrated into that continent and similarly in Asia, where other hominins, the descendants of earlier migrations out of Africa, were still occurring. As for the Americas, which humans invaded either across the now submerged Beringia, which connected Asia and North America, or by boats along the coastlines of the North Pacific, or both, its fauna was drastically reduced in what was described as a blitzkrieg lasting less than 1000 years that extirpated almost all large herbivores (40 genera), notably mammoths, mastodons, camelids, giant sloths, and horses (yes, horses!) from North America, and a similar number of large herbivores from South America (Martin 1984).

The agricultural expansion and some consequences

A few thousand years later, the invention and rapid spread of agriculture from several 'Vavilov Centers' (Harris 1990) enabled a massive increase in human populations, resulting in further loss of biodiversity, now involving plants as well as the animals that had survived the onslaught by newly arrived modern humans. The biodiversity losses were due, this time, to habitat loss and the salinization of soils that follow irrigation. This process is well documented for once-verdant Mesopotamia, where the vegetation is now reduced to patches of green dotting the desert landscape that is now Iraq. This desertification is continuing to this day in, for example, Pakistan and Northeastern Brazil; jointly with other forms of land degradation, it results in over 10 million hectares of arable land being removed from agriculture every year (Cury and Pauly 2021).

Before the European colonial expansion that was induced by the Portuguese forays around Africa and the Spanish conquest of the Americas, the last large-scale human expansion was that of the Austronesian people, who, starting in about 1500 BCE from what is now Taiwan, peopled both Southeast Asia and Madagascar in the southwest and the Pacific in the southeast. This latter expansion ended around 1300 CE with the peopling of Rapa Nui (Easter Island) and Aeteroa/New Zealand (Bellwood 1991). Here again, although the Polynesian and other descendants of the first Austronesians had a maritime culture, the peopling of the Indo-Pacific Islands resulted in massive terrestrial defaunation, especially of large birds, including 11 species of moas in Aeteroa and the 'roc' or elephant bird in Madagascar.

The expansion of European fisheries

In Europe, marine fishing expanded at the end of the 10th century, mainly because of overfishing and pollution of freshwater rivers, such as via tanneries (Pauly 2004). Marine fisheries also grew tremendously to satisfy an increasing demand for fish generated by the growing reach and power of the Catholic Church, which, at its peak, imposed nearly 150 meat-free days a year. Thus, the enormous development of the North Sea fisheries for herring and the import of vast amounts of 'stock fish' (i.e., dried cod) from Norway.

The insatiable European demand for fish, which grew even when the meatless days were reduced to the 40 days of Lent, drove French and English fisheries across the Atlantic, where, from the end of the 15th century, they exploited the immense cod population along the hotly contested eastern coast of what is now Canada (Schijns et al. 2021).

The European fleets grew, and in the 1880s, as a belated result of the Industrial Revolution, the first steam-driven trawlers were deployed around the British Isles (Roberts 2007). Though inefficient by today's standards, these trawlers, derived from the first steel-hulled steam-driven warships, were hugely more effective than rowed or sailed fishing vessels.

Within one decade, trawlers had liquidated the abundance of large fish in the inshore waters of the British Isles and then had to begin operating offshore in the open North Sea and later in the open North Atlantic. Their successors, now driven by diesel engines, were ranging all the way to Iceland, from which they had to be forcefully dislodged by the Icelandic Navy in three successive 'cod wars,' lasting from 1958 to 1976. The point was that these trawlers relied, for their operations, on the accumulation of millions of years of the sun's energy in the form of coal, then petroleum, which gave them a catching power from which no marine animal could escape.

This bulldozing approach to fishing quickly became the norm in Europe, North America, and Japan, from which it spread throughout the world. Bottom trawling is now associated with a catch of about 25 million tonnes of bottom fish and invertebrates annually, between one-fifth and one-quarter of the global catch from the world's marine ecosystems, as can be seen on the website of Sea Around Us (www.seaaroundus.org).

Other gear, such as purse seines, which are large nets, was developed to catch fish living in the open water column, notably pelagic fish. These fish can be small, such as sardines and anchovy, and are usually reduced to fishmeal and fish oil, or large, such as several tuna species, whose capture is enhanced using so-called fish aggregating devices (FADs), of which enormous numbers are now spread in the tropical zones of the oceans.

From wars to the war on fish

Modern trawlers and purse seiners use sophisticated electronic equipment to navigate and to locate fish, such as equipment developed for naval warfare, especially for locating submarines. This is why it can be said that we are conducting a war on fish and that the fish have lost, as could have been expected.

Thus, the abundance of large fish has been radically reduced worldwide, first around the wealthier countries of Europe, America, and Asia, then everywhere. One result is that despite the increasing sophistication of our methods for locating and catching fish, the global catch of marine fisheries, which peaked at nearly 120 million tonnes in 1996, has been declining since by about 300,000 tonnes per year.

What we have now is an enormous overcapacity to catch fish in the form of immense fleets of huge industrial vessels—trawlers and purse seiners—competing in inshore fishing grounds for declining resources with millions of artisanal fishers, particularly along the coasts of countries in the Global South.

This competition is intensifying as fish stocks decline, particularly on the West African coast, where artisanal fishers must 'share' the fish of their exclusive economic zone (EEZ) with European and Asian (often Chinese) vessels operating based on often dubious 'access agreements' that compensate coastal countries for only 3–4 percent of the first sale value of the fish caught (Belhabib et al. 2015). Illegal fishing must be added to this, as practiced by, for example, the Russian pelagic trawler *Oleg Naydenov*, which, instead of operating in Mauritania, where it was entitled to operate, was caught in flagrante delicto in Senegal's EEZ in 2012, resulting in its impoundment.

This competition is one reason why many desperate young West African men try to reach Europe in the rickety boats of people smugglers: they are looking for the fishing livelihoods that this unfair competition has destroyed for them.

Subsidies only make things worse

Since the early modern period, several European governments have subsidized their fishing fleets, mainly because trained sailors were required during a war (Janzekovič 2020, Poulsen 2008)—and there was always one war or another. This pernicious tradition has not only persisted but spread throughout the world, and thus massive government subsidies are nowadays awarded not only to the European distant-water fleets, such as the French and Spanish fleets, but also to Asian fleets, such as those of India and especially China. Indeed, this is the main reason why these fleets can operate in the first place. Without these subsidies, which cover almost all aspects of the deployment of fishing vessels, from their construction to the fuel they consume, they could not ruin the livelihoods and lives of artisanal fishers in countries far from their ports of origin.

The detrimental effect of subsidies on fisheries is well documented (e.g., Sumaila et al. 2010). Notably, government subsidies encourage overfishing. Without this assistance, fishing vessels exploiting a declining resource would have to cease operating as soon as the ex-vessel value of their catch drops below their operating costs (Sumaila et al. 2024). These operating costs, incidentally, include the returns on the capital investment that would be obtained by investments in a less risky alternative venture (i.e., the opportunity costs of capital).

Subsidies, at least in part, cover these costs, thus allowing vessels to continue exploiting declining or collapsed fish stocks. This is why subsidies are anathema to even ultraliberal economists, who view them as market distortions (as if markets were ever 'free'!).

However, given that the operators of subsidized fleets have no reason to follow management measures structured around society gaining the most benefits from well-managed fisheries, fisheries scientists would also like subsidies abolished. As for conservationists, they hate subsidies because they are a major cause of the decline of marine biodiversity, including the fish population, marine mammals, seabirds, and indeed the entire ecosystems that contain that biodiversity.

Thus, it is quite galling that the agreement on fisheries subsidies reached by the World Trade Organization (WTO) in June 2022 did not contain any serious limitation on the subsidies that its member governments could legally provide to their fishing fleets. Indeed, the only restriction that was agreed upon is that countries may not provide subsidies to fleets that exploit overfished stocks. However, as it was left to the subsidizing countries to determine whether the stocks they exploit are overfished, all they must do to circumvent the new agreement is to *not* assess the status of the stocks they exploit. Thus, the WTO restriction on subsidies amounts to precisely nothing, which was the purpose of its major proponents, notably India, whose national government recently issued a report according to which an impossible 91 percent of the exploited fish populations along the Indian coasts are in a 'healthy' state (CMFRI, Kochi 2023).

And now global warming…

The subsidization of fisheries is as absurd as the subsidization of fossil fuel companies, to which our governments continue to hand over hundreds of billions of dollars, the very money that would be needed to rapidly transition to renewable energies. Indeed, marine fisheries could be very profitable and generate the same catch that they do today if their aggregate fishing effort was reduced to about a third of its present size. Note, *en passant*, that the fishing industry also contributes 1 to 2 percent to global greenhouse emissions (Greer et al. 2019), which could also easily be reduced by two-thirds without reducing catches if fleet overcapacity were addressed—subsidies again!

Protecting and rebuilding marine fish populations

Besides the broad consensus among fisheries scientists, economists, and conservationists about the negative role of government subsidies to fisheries, there is also an emerging consensus that the emphasis nowadays should not be on the sustainability of fisheries—the maintenance of their present state—but rather on the rebuilding of fish populations, notably along the coasts of countries with distant-water fleets. This would allow these countries to deploy their fleets in their own waters, where they would burn less fuel to access them, pay no access fee, and not cause the international tensions that they do now. Such rebuilding can be straightforwardly achieved by fisheries management, as in the European Union (EU), by imposing a relatively low Total Allowable Catch (TAC), allowing exploited fish populations to bounce back.

After a few years, this would result in abundant populations that could provide fisheries with such high yields that no subsidies would be necessary. Also, abundant fish populations can sustain a vast array of marine mammals and seabirds, thereby helping to rebuild the full diversity of functioning marine ecosystems.

This is not a vain dream. Legislation supporting rebuilding of this type already exists in the United States. According to the Magnuson–Stevens Fishery Conservation and Management Act, when an exploited stock falls below a critical level, the government must impose a TAC low enough to rebuild to a prescribed, high level within a non-negotiable period of ten years. Similar legislation exists in the EU and in Canada. However, in these versions, ministers of fisheries can intervene in the process, which invariably results in high TACs and no stock rebuilding.

A consensus similar to that for rebuilding overexploited fish populations exists concerning marine protected areas (MPAs). MPAs help rebuild the abundance of exploited populations targeted by fishing and species not targeted but caught as unintended bycatch.

This consensus foresees that 30 percent of the oceans should be protected by 2030, and that the world's seas should benefit from such protection. However, it is too easy for governments to declare remote areas under their jurisdictions to be protected while doing nothing to protect them. These MPAs are referred to as 'paper parks.'

France has numerous paper parks; for example, the Parc Naturel de la Mer de Coral, which encompasses all the EEZ of New Caledonia, but has led to absolutely zero changes in the management of this vast zone (Relano et al. 2021). In particular, there are no limitations as to where in the 'parc' commercial fishing can occur. Unfortunately, the paper park problem is not limited to France (Relano and Pauly 2023). In EU waters, bottom trawling is permitted in MPAs. This is equivalent to using bulldozers to pick flowers in Paris' Jardin des Plantes. In fact, paper parks are common virtually everywhere in the world. According to MPAtlas, 8.2 percent of the global ocean is protected, but only 3 percent is fully or highly protected. That means 5.2 percent of the global ocean is protected by an MPA that has weak or non-existent restrictions.

Marine plastic pollution and ocean deoxygenation

However, if we did protect 30 percent of the oceans and rebuild exploited fish populations, then, in addition to rejuvenating our fisheries, we would increase the resilience of marine ecosystems, which are now confronted with other major challenges, notably a wave of plastic pollution and global warming that leads to the deoxygenation of the oceans.

Plastic pollution is highly visible and should, in principle, be easy to resolve, notably because brands label their bottles; thus, we know who the polluters are. We must reduce the number of single-use plastic objects in our lives, because a huge fraction of these objects will invariably end up in the ocean. However, picking up plastic trash on our beaches is not the solution. We must get rid of plastic at the source, at the level of production. Here, in addition to the purveyors of single-use plastic items, we encounter resistance from the very same lobbies that represent the fossil fuel industries because the production of plastic is, after the transportation industries, the main consumer of petroleum. The fight against plastic pollution will thus require defeating the same opponents: the fossil fuel industries.

If we do not defeat them, our forests will all burn out of existence as they have begun to do in Canada, and our air will become irrespirable and too hot for outdoor activities. As for the oceans, marine heatwaves will become more frequent and cover larger areas, most of whose inhabitants will be killed. The reason for this is that marine heatwaves are not analogous to heatwaves on land, which tend to kill only more susceptible organisms, including old people and infants. Rather, marine heatwaves are analogous to forest fires, which prevent animals from breathing even before the heat itself does them in (Pauly 2023). Both terrestrial and marine heatwaves are windows into our future—the future some of us will struggle in if we do not reduce our emission of greenhouse gases. Saving the oceans and the life within has therefore become a part of the struggle to reduce and save ecosystems on land so we can continue to live in our villages and cities.

And marine governance?

Solving the issues presented above will require that we deal seriously with the worst invasive species the world has ever known, *Homo* (supposedly) *sapiens*. This must be our last conquest: we must overcome our invasive nature, learn to control our numbers and the greed that consumes many of us, and invent the sustainable civilization that we need. Marine governance, as discussed in the book of which this chapter is a part, must be a key component of this redesign of our lives and address the rebuilding of the abundance we have lost.

References

Belhabib, Dyhia, U. Rashid Sumaila, Vicky W.Y. Lam, Dirk Zeller, Philippe Le Billon, Elimane Abou Kane, and Daniel Pauly. 2015. Euro vs. Yuan: Comparing European and Chinese fishing access in West Africa. *PLOS One* 10 (3): e0118351.

Bellwood, Peter. 1991. The Austronesian Dispersal and the Origin of Languages. *Scientific American* 265 (1): 88–93.

CMFRI, Kochi (2023) Marine Fish Stock Status of India, 2022. CMFRI Booklet Series No.32/2023 (32). ICAR- Central Marine Fisheries Research Institute, Kochi, pp. 1–22.

Cury, Philippe, and Daniel Pauly. 2021. *Obstinate Nature*. Paris: Odile Jacob.

Greer, Krista, Dirk Zeller, Jessika Woroniak, Angie Coulter, Maeve Winchester, M.L. Deng Palomares, and Daniel Pauly. 2019. Reply to Ziegler et al. 'Adding Perspectives to: Global Trends in carbon Dioxide (CO2) Emissions from Fuel Combustion in Marine Fisheries from 1950–2016.' *Marine Policy* 107: 103491.

Harris, David R. 1990. Vavilov's Concept of Centres of Origin of Cultivated Plants: Its Genesis and its Influence on the Study of Agricultural Origins. *Biological Journal of the Linnean Society* 39 (1): 7–16.

Janzekovič, Izidor. 2020. The Rise of State Navies in the Early Seventeen Century: A Historiographical Study. *Journal of Maritime Research* 22 (1–2): 183–208.

Martin, Paul S. 1984. Prehistoric Overkill: The Global Model. In *Quaternary Extinctions: A Prehistoric Revolution*, edited by Paul S. Martin and Richard G. Klein, 354–403. Tucson, AZ: University of Arizona Press.

Pauly, Daniel. 2004. Much Rowing for Fish. *Nature* 432: 813–814.

Pauly, Daniel. 2023. What are Marine Heat Waves? *Oceana Magazine*. Winter 2023: 22–23.

Poulsen, Bo. 2008. *Dutch Herring: An Environment History, c. 1600–1860 (Vol. 3)*. Amsterdam: Amsterdam University Press.

Relano, Veronica, and Daniel Pauly. 2023. The 'Paper Park Index': Evaluating Marine Protected Area Effectiveness Through a Global Study of Stakeholder Perceptions. *Marine Policy* 151: 105571.1. https://doi.org/10.1016/j.marpol.2023.105571.

Relano, Veronica, M.L. Deng Palomares, and Daniel Pauly. 2021. Comparing the Performance of Four Very Large Marine Protected Areas with Different Levels of Protection. *Sustainability* 13 (17): 9572. https://doi.org/10.3390/su13179572.

Roberts, Callum. 2007. *The Unnatural History of the Sea*. Washington, DC: Island Press.

Schijns, Rebecca, Rainer Froese, Jeffrey A. Hutchings, and Daniel Pauly. 2021. Five Centuries of Cod Catches in Eastern Canada. *ICES Journal of Marine Science* 78 (8): 2675–2683.

Sumaila U. Rashid, Lubna Alam, Patrizia R. Abdallah, Denis Aheto, Shehu L. Akintola, Justin Alger, Vania Andreoli, Megan Bailey, Colin Barnes, Abdulrahman Ben-Hasan, Cassandra M. Brooks et al. 2024. WTO Must Complete an Ambitious Fisheries Subsidies Agreement. *npj Ocean Sustainability* 3.

Sumaila, U. Rashid, Ahmed Khan, Louise Teh, Reg Watson, Peter Tyedmers, and Daniel Pauly. 2010. Subsidies to High Seas Bottom Trawl Fleets and the Sustainability of Deep-Sea Demersal Fish Stocks. *Marine Policy* 34 (3): 495–497.

PART II

Ocean justice

3 Ocean governance and the protection of ocean defenders

Philippe Le Billon, Dyhia Belhabib, Nathan J. Bennett, Irmak Ertör, Rocío López de la Lama, Elisa Morgera, Lina M. Saavedra-Díaz and Paula Satizábal

Ocean defenders

The expansion of large-scale and industrialized economic development activities in marine and coastal environments poses a growing threat to coastal communities and ecosystems (Bennett et al. 2021, Jouffray et al. 2020). Whereas "Blue Growth" policies supposedly offer the promise of more sustainable ocean governance and economic benefits for society, coastal populations around the world continue to grapple with rampant overexploitation of natural resources, exclusionary conservation, spatial displacement due to development, and management regimes undermining their lives, livelihoods, and ecosystems. They often face multiple threats and stressors at once, increasing the level of complexity they must deal with to protect and defend their ways of life (Defeo and Elliott 2021).

Confronted by these mounting pressures, individuals, groups, and communities, including women and young people, in all regions of the world are mobilizing, advocating, or taking action to protect their coastal and oceanic territories and associated human and environmental rights (Bennett et al. 2022, Ertör 2023, World Forum of Fisher Peoples 2021). In response, many of these "ocean defenders" are facing marginalization, intimidation, criminalization, threats, violence, and even murder (Bennett et al. 2023). These attacks come from a wide range of actors, including governments, military and paramilitary forces, corporate hires, and criminal mafias (Alliance for Land, Indigenous and Environmental Defenders, 2022, Le Billon and Lujala 2020), with ocean defenders in the Global South facing different challenges than those in the Global North.

Even though some recent research in the ocean governance literature has stressed the importance of ocean defenders (Bennett et al. 2022, Bennett et al. 2023), the historical and ongoing repression and violence they face has rarely been systematically documented or theorized (but see Alexander 2019, Ertör 2023), and international guidance on the protection of environmental human rights defenders still tends to focus on land defenders (Morgera 2023, United Nations 2023). Coastal communities are often subjected to long histories of socio-economic marginalization (Ommer 2007), and the significant systemic challenges and political exclusion they face—along with the concept of maritime spaces as devoid of people—might explain the limited attention given to ocean defenders. This, in turn, hinders opportunities for recognition of tenure rights and the protection of the social, cultural, environmental, economic, civil, and political rights of communities in coastal and maritime spaces (Allison et al. 2012), and interferes with their pursuit of justice in defending these rights (Blythe et al. 2023, Ertör 2023, Jentoft et al. 2022).

There is an urgent need to understand and address the failure to protect ocean defenders at local, national, and international levels and across different sectors. Adequate recognition and protection for ocean defenders is imperative in sustaining marine territories and ways of living and in denouncing and resisting harmful projects. In this chapter, we identify key research areas and methodologies to support ocean defenders, advancing human-rights-based approaches that contribute to socio-environmental justice in marine and coastal environments (Morgera and Nakamura 2022).

Ocean defenders and marine-related human rights

International human rights frameworks extend to the oceans, providing broad protection for fundamental human rights (i.e., social, cultural, economic, civic, political, environmental) and recognition of unique entitlements for traditional coastal and ocean-dependent populations over their marine territories and resources (Allison et al. 2012, Bennett et al. 2024). Despite the fact that all groups of rights holders should be able to meaningfully participate in environmental decisions that will impact them, historically marginalized groups, including small-scale fishing communities, often lack representation in ocean governance and decision-making processes (Sunde and Erwin 2020), having been left out of or pushed aside from decision-making spaces by industrial economic interests and corrupt practices of governmental authorities (Cánovas-Molina and García-Frapolli 2022). The consequences of a growing ocean economy without sufficient social or environmental safeguards for coastal communities include physical displacement, dispossession, erosion of customary tenure and rights, and environmental destruction (Bennett et al. 2021, Das 2023). Furthermore, coastal communities are among the most vulnerable to climate change impacts, being directly affected by sea level rise, changing weather patterns, and migration of marine species (Gill et al. 2023). Hence, these cumulative impacts directly compromise the right to a clean, healthy, and sustainable marine environment (Bennett et al. 2024).

Small-scale fisher coalitions, civil society groups, and broader community alliances and networks resist various interventions framed as development projects that threaten marine and coastal ecosystems, together with existing customary tenure arrangements, livelihoods, and culture (Bennett et al. 2023, Ertör 2023, Scheidel et al. 2020). Such resistance is often met with rights violations to silence or marginalize these groups. The criminalization of defenders is particularly insidious as the state systematically undermines their rights, including through prosecution without clear charges and the instrumentalization of the judicial system, thereby stifling public participation and creating a context of impunity for other forms of abuses (Forst 2024). Indigenous peoples and other customary rights-holders are particularly exposed to criminalization (Scheidel et al. 2020), with state authorities repressing demands for the recognition of traditional territories and modes of life (Menton and Le Billon 2021). In some cases, resistance evolves into broader civil disobedience movements that are criminalized, as in the hanging of the leaders of the Movement for the Survival of the Ogoni People in the Gulf of Guinea in the 1990s (UN Office on Drugs and Crime 2021).

Several key insights have already emerged from research on and with ocean defenders. First, marginalized coastal communities—including small-scale fishers—are crucial actors in stewarding and defending marine and coastal living beings and their environments (Bennett et al. 2023). While allied individuals and organizations can support these efforts, it is those actors who hold customary rights and tenure to coastal areas and depend on oceans for sustenance and cultural continuity who are at the forefront and should be recognized as such. Second, ocean defenders intervene not only locally but globally, reflecting the widespread growth of the ocean economy, the global nature of environmental injustice in marine environments, and extensive solidarity networks between ocean defenders and their allied organizations (Environmental Justice Foundation 2023, Mills 2021). Solidarity networks can emerge at various scales among or between small-scale fishers, non-governmental organizations, and academics, providing an invaluable space for reflection, action, and defense (Mills 2021, Pereira and Erwin 2023). Examples of such networks include the World Forum of Fisher Peoples (WFFP), World Forum of Fish Harvesters & Fish Workers (WFF), the International Collective in Support of Fishworkers, the Too Big to Ignore Network, and the Coastal Justice Network. Third, defenders mobilize against diverse threats to the ocean, ranging from activities at sea (mostly near-shore in Exclusive Economic Zones [EEZs], but also on the seabed and in the high seas) or involving coastal lands and intertidal margins, as well as against diverse actors across scales promoting and profiting from capitalist interventions (e.g., local elites, governmental authorities, national and transnational corporations, and exclusionary conservation organizations) (Belhabib and Le Billon 2022, Ertör 2023, Morgera and Lily 2022). Fourth, ocean defenders seek to advance and protect basic human rights, including the right to participate in environmental decisions, a healthy ocean environment, livelihoods, cultural rights, and ultimately human dignity. Fifth, ocean defenders deeply care about the sea, with Indigenous perspectives often integrating nature's rights, thereby not only advocating for themselves but also for non-human beings (Bender et al. 2022). In turn, these rights are essential to more inclusive forms of sustainable ocean governance (Buchan et al. 2023). Last, ocean defenders employ various strategies, from public protests and demonstrations to legal interventions, forming organizations, and engaging with social movements despite a context of low agency, high complexity, and violence (Bennett et al. 2023, Ertör 2023, Figueroa et al. 2024).

Overall, a growing body of research points to the challenges facing ocean defenders, emphasizing the triple threat arising from the evolving destructive impacts of capitalist interventions, structural marginalization, and various forms of violence (Bennett et al. 2022, Bennett et al. 2023, Satizábal et al. 2021). More attention is required from the research community, governments, civil society, and the private sector to address these issues comprehensively. Efforts should focus on confronting processes that promote and sustain the expansion of extractivist and exclusionary ocean economies; addressing corrupt practices or ineffective legal frameworks that allow corporations to go unpunished when the human rights of coastal communities are violated; challenging power asymmetries; positioning marginalized groups at the center of decision-making processes; acknowledging colonial legacies and intersections of class, race, and gender; and ensuring access to justice and the protection of human rights. Researchers, especially when working in collaboration with ocean defenders, can help advance these goals.

A research agenda for ocean defenders and ocean governance

Already often at the margins of society, many coastal communities are seeking to secure recognition and protection of, or regain access to, stewardship of their customary waters (Said and MacMillan 2020). These communities are victimized, violently targeted, or criminalized as they mobilize against new enclosures privatizing and overexploiting marine commons, or fall into illegal fishing, forced labor, or smuggling (Belhabib et al. 2020, Okafor-Yarwood 2020). This victimization even occurs when communities have been able to maintain access or (re)assert their rights and authority through strategies such as cooperatives or court cases (Christoffels-DuPlessis et al. 2022). As the global demand for marine commodities and spaces drives exponential growth in the global ocean economy, it is crucial to understand the interconnected issues impacting those advocating for environmental justice and human rights. Here we outline three themes and main avenues for future research.

Theme 1: ocean governance and defenders

Ocean governance frameworks significantly impact environmental sustainability, the well-being of coastal communities, and socio-economic equity. Further research can critically examine whether *governance processes* promote development or conservation activities that harm the environment or lead to dispossession and ocean grabbing. Differing narratives, such as those surrounding environmental scarcity, ocean wealth, or the blue economy, shape these frameworks, often inclusively or exclusively, thereby affecting coastal communities. The extent of *civil society engagement and the protection of ocean defenders* are key factors, as is the recognition of customary rights of Indigenous peoples and small-scale fishers, which are sometimes limited or criminalized by these frameworks or their biased implementation. Understanding *governance gaps and compliance issues* is also crucial; this includes investigating local, national, and international mechanisms that contribute to environmental and human rights issues, assessing the effectiveness of regulations in protecting human rights within ocean economies, and analyzing state compliance with laws aimed at marine environment protection, ensuring non-retrogressive and non-discriminatory measures.

Theme 2: human rights and ocean defenders

Procedural rights and inclusive decision-making in ocean governance involve evaluating the incorporation of access to information, participatory decision-making, and access to justice within legal and policy frameworks, while assessing the effectiveness of these processes in addressing power imbalances and inequalities. This includes investigating the implementation and impact of Free, Prior, and Informed Consent (FPIC) for Indigenous peoples and effective consultation with other affected groups. *Recognition and protection of marine-related human rights* requires assessing public authorities' commitment to safeguarding the rights of coastal communities, evaluating state measures to protect these rights from negative marine policy impacts, and investigating the recognition and protection of customary tenure and access rights of small-scale fishers and Indigenous peoples. *Business responsibilities in ocean governance* necessitate analyzing the effectiveness of national regulations and businesses' adherence to international human rights standards, assessing the need for ocean-specific guidelines, examining the impact of international investment law on human rights and environmental protection, and exploring state–corporate relations in the criminalization of ocean defenders.

Theme 3: experiences and protection of ocean defenders

The *struggles of ocean defenders* amidst an expanding ocean economy and increasing conservation efforts are critical for just and sustainable ocean governance, including advocacy for food sovereignty and small-scale fisheries. Ocean defenders face numerous *threats and violence from governments and the private sector*, including silencing and criminalization tactics, necessitating research efforts to document and address these abuses, while facilitating conflict resolution processes to increase their protection and advocacy. Supporting the *political autonomy and agency of ocean defenders* is key to ensuring their effective participation in ocean governance. This means further exploring ways to empower defenders in shaping their agendas, exercising legal rights over coastal and marine territories, and increasing public attention to their causes through civil society organizations. In turn, this implies assessing the *risks and benefits of allyship with external entities* and ensuring alignment with ocean defenders' priorities. Further research can also better evaluate *protection strategies and methods* against the criminalization of ocean defenders, and investigate the effectiveness of state and non-state actors in supporting defenders, corrupt relations between states and corporations, non-judicial grievance mechanisms, and strategies to ensure perpetrators of human rights abuses are held accountable.

Ethics and methods

Normative commitments to knowledge co-production suggest that transdisciplinary, qualitative, and participatory approaches such as community-based and action research methods are best suited to align research with the priorities of ocean defenders. Yet, legal reviews, comparative studies, and quantitative analyses can also be used to provide a broader picture of the challenges they are facing, identify some of the main factors at play in their criminalization, and gain more policy traction for their effective protection. Finally, special consideration should be given to gender, age, and intersectional approaches.

Participatory methods

Careful methods informed by strong ethical considerations are critical for studies of the criminalization of and solutions to the issues facing ocean defenders. Satizábal et al. (2021) highlight the ethical challenges faced by researchers regarding small-scale fishers, emphasizing the need to navigate complexities responsibly. This calls for the cultivation of reciprocal relationships and careful attention to the contexts in which researchers and ocean defenders operate, with frequent risk evaluations. Research topics and questions should be defined or at least validated by ocean defenders to fit their needs or priorities. Research methods should integrate storytelling from ocean defenders, avoid reductionism, and involve a careful representation of people and practices. Collaborative approaches are key and should draw from anti/decolonial methodologies, feminist political ecology, Indigenous scholarship, and Black and Latinx geographies. Consideration should not only be given to the legal and policy implications of the research, but also to practical "on-the-ground" implications given the vulnerability and risks faced by many ocean defenders in their everyday lives. This notably requires adherence to communication ethics that will avoid greater exposure to potential harm. Researchers should be attentive to the emotional dimensions of interviews and their impacts on potential interviewees, and provide for the well-being of and self-care opportunities for defenders.

More fundamentally, academic researchers should recognize ocean defenders as knowledge holders and knowledge co-producers. Researchers should consider how to genuinely involve defenders in the earliest stages of research co-design and iteratively throughout the research project, and meaningfully reward their time and contributions. This approach, in turn, requires that researchers negotiate and/or influence research funders to create flexibilities in research budgets and conditions to allow for such preliminary co-design processes and iterative research collaborations. Collaborative research based on the co-creation of knowledge is needed to support resistance efforts. Participatory methods help shield leaders by supporting them in their struggles, going from individual to collective.

Ethical considerations should permeate research methodologies, team dynamics, discursive constructions, and the communication of outcomes. The aim of collaborative research should be to support struggles by ocean defenders and contribute to policies promoting human rights and ocean sustainability.

Legal reviews

Reviews of legislation, regulation, and case law can help assess the relative effectiveness of protection of ocean defenders, legal barriers to their recognition, and opportunities to enhance their protection, and identify the legal tools and processes used to criminalize defenders. Such reviews can also assess factors influencing relative access to legal support for ocean defenders. In a systematic analysis of human rights violations of small-scale/artisanal fishing communities analyzed by the Colombian Constitutional Court, Figueroa et al. (2024) reveal the role of the state in favoring the economic interests of powerful economic sectors, while promoting the expansion of the ocean economy at the expense of the lives, basic needs, and ways of living of marginalized coastal communities. Beyond reviews, proactive legal and quasi-legal processes can also be initiated. For example, civil society organizations hosted a participatory International Tribunal on the Impacts of Blue Economy in Indian Ocean Countries in five countries. The tribunal revealed how the blue economy narrative was excluding coastal populations, leading to dispossession, undermining rights, and producing conflict (WFFP 2021). To these ends, it is important to bring together different areas of expertise to conduct legal reviews, including national and international law expertise, history, human geography, environmental justice, and anthropology, as well as diverse knowledge systems (McGarry 2023).

Comparative analyses and mapping

Comparing case studies and countries can help better identify common patterns and differences, including in terms of threats, challenges, and potential for effective actions to protect defenders (Hines 2022, Scheidel et al. 2020). Comparative analyses of ocean governance frameworks and their impact on human rights and ocean defenders in different countries can yield insights into the relative risks faced by ocean defenders. Cross-country case studies, as well as exchanges of experiences among leaders from different communities, can also help identify best practices, challenges, and lessons learned in supporting ocean defenders and promoting inclusive and sustainable ocean governance. Quantitative methods can help analyze a large number of cases, yet be mindful of biased data sources and skewed statistical analysis (e.g., spotlight effect) (Belhabib and Le Billon 2022). Mapping, at diverse scales, can serve as a powerful tool for visualizing, connecting, understanding, and analyzing a broad spectrum of socio-environmental conflict cases where ocean defenders have become part of or led the struggles against capitalist industrial development projects. The Environmental Justice Atlas (EJAtlas), for example, has mapped and collected systematic information on more than 4000 conflicts (see https://ejatlas.org; Scheidel et al. 2020), including where fisher communities and organizations have been at the forefront of struggles for Blue Justice (Ertör 2023). Community-led counter-hegemonic mapping should also be considered as a specific methodology for knowledge co-production with ocean defenders, and as a way to directly support them in engaging in marine spatial planning and other forms of ocean governance based on their customary rights and Indigenous or local knowledge (Sunde 2023).

Gender and intersectional approaches

Women are central in defending oceans. For example, women play a key role in protecting near-shore fisheries that are often the most exposed to pollution and access restrictions. Although women encompass a sizable proportion of fish trading and processing workers exposed to stock decline, their work and contributions are undervalued and subjected to historical patriarchal violence and socio-economic marginalization (Sall

2024). Many women are also affected by the growing incarceration of fishers and fish workers, and the militarization of fisheries management and conservation, which also contributes to gender-based violence (Castillo 2019). Women have historically been excluded from state-led decision-making spaces and governance interventions, despite their major importance in fisheries and coastal communities (Macusi et al. 2023). Governments, businesses, and community organizations frequently limit the autonomy of women and tend to exert multiple forms of retaliation—including sexual violence—when their mobilization defies gendered forms of oppression (Mangubhai et al. 2023, Tran and Hanaček 2023). Yet, women ocean defenders are often the prime actors in denouncing abuses and advocating for change. Critical feminist approaches and research are central to understanding the risks faced by women, and by trans and gender-diverse persons, unpacking the power relations and the intersections of gender, race, and class in the context of the growing criminalization of small-scale fishers, and supporting their struggles, redistributing power, and pursuing gender equality (Golo and Erinosho 2023).

Given growing movements of ocean and ocean-climate defenders that are involving children and young people (Morgera and Lily 2022) and increased "threats, intimidation, harassment and other serious reprisals" against them (Committee on the Rights of the Child 2023), it is important for researchers to familiarize themselves with (and/or receive training on) the UN Convention on the Rights of the Child and the 2023 UN General Comment on Children's Human Rights and a Healthy Environment (Morgera and Shields 2024, Shields and Morgera 2023a) and methodologies for knowledge co-production with children (Shields et al. 2023). In addition, research on ocean defenders should consider specifically child defenders as "agents of change" whose "demands for urgent and decisive measures to tackle global environmental harm should be realized" (Committee on the Rights of the Child 2023). Child and youth defenders face specific challenges, including a limited understanding and awareness of the negative impacts of ocean degradation on their human rights (Strand et al. 2023). This often results in a limited range of allies to support them and their rights (Shields and Morgera 2023b). Equally, it is necessary for research on ocean defenders to specifically consider how to address "entrenched ageism in the human rights movement" (Lawlor 2024: 2) and ensure heightened levels of protection for specific age groups (Lundy 2020). To that end, researchers should promote intergenerational collaboration and mentorship, support and collaborate with child- or youth-led defender initiatives, collect age-disaggregated data, extend well-being and self-care opportunities to child and youth human rights defenders, and create safe and enabling spaces for child and youth defenders (Lawlor 2024).

Conclusions

The rapid and unchecked expansion of the ocean economy is producing environmental injustices and human rights issues around the world. Globally, ocean defenders, including women and young people, are at the forefront of efforts to resist these threats, yet they are being marginalized, silenced, stigmatized, threatened, criminalized, and even murdered. Threats and harm to their families and communities are a common occurrence. Recognizing, supporting, and protecting ocean defenders is thus essential for advancing socio-environmental justice and human rights in ocean governance. However, our knowledge of the situation facing ocean defenders and how to address these issues is limited. This chapter outlines key research areas to better understand interactions between ocean governance, human rights, and ocean defenders. While methodologies should be adapted to the research questions being asked, they should also reflect the concerns and aspirations of ocean defenders and therefore be co-developed with them. Ethical considerations in this regard should not only promote the co-creation of knowledge with ocean defenders to ensure relevance but also guarantee the security and well-being of ocean defenders and their communities through iterative research co-design and meaningful benefit-sharing. Equally, attention needs to focus specifically on preventing discriminatory practices in these research endeavors. Translation of research findings, innovative knowledge co-production, and solidarity practices integrated into policy and practice should be priorities to ensure that ocean defenders benefit from greater agency and more effective protection.

Acknowledgements

NJB and RLL acknowledge support via a grant from the David and Lucile Packard Foundation and the Coastal Renewal Society to the Ocean Defenders Project; PLB, DB, NJB, LMSD, and PS acknowledge support from the Social Sciences and Humanities Research Council via the Fishy Crimes Project.

References

Alexander, Karen A. 2019. *Conflicts over Marine and Coastal Common Resources: Causes, Governance and Prevention*. Routledge.

Alliance for Land, Indigenous and Environmental Defenders. 2022. *Supporting Environmental Human Rights Defenders*. Available at: https://www.universal-rights.org/urg-policy-reports/supporting-environmental-human-rights-defenders-developing-new-guidance-for-donors-and-civil-society-organisations-2/.

Allison, Edward H., Blake D. Ratner, Bjorn Åsgård, Rolf Willmann, Robert Pomeroy, and John Kurien. 2012. Rights-Based Fisheries Governance: From Fishing Rights to Human Rights. *Fish and Fisheries* 13 (1): 14–29. https://doi.org/10.1111/j.1467-2979.2011.00405.x.

Belhabib, Dyhia, and Philippe Le Billon. 2022. Fish Crimes in the Global Oceans. *Science Advances* 8 (12): eabj1927. https://doi.org/10.1126/sciadv.abj1927.

Belhabib, Dyhia, Philippe Le Billon, and David J. Wrathall. 2020. Narco-Fish: Global Fisheries and Drug Trafficking. *Fish and Fisheries* 21 (5): 992–1007. https://doi.org/10.1111/faf.12483.

Bender, Michelle, Rachel Bustamante, and Kelsey Leonard. 2022. Living in Relationship with the Ocean to Transform Governance in the UN Ocean Decade. *PLOS Biology* 20 (10): e3001828. https://doi.org/10.1371/journal.pbio.3001828.

Bennett, Nathan J., Jessica Blythe, Carole S. White, and Cecilia Campero. 2021. Blue Growth and Blue Justice: Ten Risks and Solutions for the Ocean Economy. *Marine Policy* 125: 104387. https://doi.org/10.1016/j.marpol.2020.104387.

Bennett, Nathan J., Philippe Le Billon, Dyhia Belhabib, and Paula Satizábal. 2022. Local Marine Stewardship and Ocean Defenders. *npj Ocean Sustainability* 1 (3): 1–5. https://doi.org/10.1038/s44183-022-00002-6.

Bennett, Nathan J., Rocío López de la Lama, Philippe Le Billon, Irmak Ertör, and Elisa Morgera. 2023. Ocean Defenders and Human Rights. *Frontiers in Marine Science* 9: 1089049. https://doi.org/10.3389/fmars.2022.1089049.

Bennett, Nathan J., Elisa Morgera, and David Boyd. 2024. The Human Right to a Clean, Healthy and Sustainable Ocean. *npj Ocean Sustainability* 3 (19): 1–8. https://doi.org/10.1038/s44183-024-00057-7.

Blythe, Jessica L., David A. Gill, Joachim Claudet, Nathan J. Bennett, Georgina G. Gurney, Jacopo A. Baggio, and Natalie C. Ban et al. 2023. Blue Justice: A Review of Emerging Scholarship and Resistance Movements. *Cambridge Prisms: Coastal Futures* 1 (e15): 1–12. https://doi.org/10.1017/cft.2023.4.

Buchan, Pamela M., Louisa S. Evans, Margherita Pieraccini, and Stewart Barr. 2023. Marine Citizenship: The Right to Participate in the Transformation of the Human-Ocean Relationship for Sustainability. *PLOS One* 18 (3): 1–23. https://doi.org/10.1371/journal.pone.0280518.

Cánovas-Molina, Almudena, and Eduardo García-Frapolli. 2022. A Review of Vulnerabilities in Worldwide Small-Scale Fisheries. *Fisheries Management and Ecology* 29 (5): 491–501. https://doi.org/10.1111/fme.12538.

Castillo, Tessie. 2019. The Ecuadorian Fishermen Snatched Away by US Drug Warriors. *Filter.* October 28. Available at: https://filtermag.org/ecuador-fishermen-drug-war/.

Christoffels-DuPlessis, Anthea, Bola Erinosho, Laura Major, Elisa Morgera, Jackie Sunde, and Saskia Vermeylen. 2022. Navigating a Sea of Laws: The Quests of Small-Scale Fishing Communities in Ghana and South Africa for Protecting Their Customary Rights. In *The Palgrave Handbook of Blue Heritage*, edited by Rosabelle Boswell, David O'Kane, and Jeremy Mills, 325–356. Palgrave. https://doi.org/10.1007/978-3-030-99347-4_18.

Committee on the Rights of the Child. 2023. General Comment No. 26 on Children's Rights and the Environment, with a Special Focus on Climate Change. CRC/C/GC/26. Available at: https://www.ohchr.org/en/documents/general-comments-and-recommendations/crccgc26-general-comment-no-26-2023-childrens-rights.

Das, Jewel. 2023. Blue Economy, Blue Growth, Social Equity and Small-Scale Fisheries: A Global and National Level Review. *Studies in Social Science Research* 4 (1): 38. https://doi.org/10.22158/sssr.v4n1p38.

Defeo, Omar, and Michael Elliott. 2021. The "Triple Whammy" of Coasts under Threat: Why We Should Be Worried! *Marine Pollution Bulletin* 163: 111832. https://doi.org/10.1016/j.marpolbul.2020.111832.

Environmental Justice Foundation. 2023. *A Manifesto for Our Ocean.* Available at: https://ejfoundation.org/resources/downloads/EJF-Ocean-Manifesto-2023.pdf.

Ertör, Irmak. 2023. "We Are the Oceans, We Are the People!" Fisher People's Struggles for Blue Justice. *The Journal of Peasant Studies* 50 (3): 1157–1186. https://doi.org/10.1080/03066150.2021.1999932.

Figueroa, Isabela, Lina M. Saavedra-Díaz, Paula Satizábal, Gina Noriega-Narváez, and Yulibeth Velásquez-Mendoza. 2024. Justice in Fishing Territories: Human Rights Violations in Artisanal Fisheries Analyzed by the Colombian Constitutional Court. *Journal of Political Ecology* 31 (1): 98–115. https://doi.org/10.2458/jpe.6026.

Forst, Michel. 2024. *State Repression of Environmental Protest and Civil Disobedience: A Major Threat to Human Rights and Democracy.* UNECE Position Paper. Available at: https://unece.org/sites/default/files/2024-02/UNSR_EnvDefenders_Aarhus_Position_Paper_Civil_Disobedience_EN.pdf.

Gill, David A., Jessica Blythe, Nathan Bennett, Louisa Evans, Katrina Brown, R. Adger Turner, Jacopo A. Baggio et al. 2023. Triple Exposure: Reducing Negative Impacts of Climate Change, Blue Growth, and Conservation on Coastal Communities. *One Earth* 6 (2): 118–130. https://doi.org/10.1016/j.oneear.2023.01.010.

Golo, Harrison K., and Bolanle Erinosho. 2023. Tackling the Challenges Confronting Women in the Elmina Fishing Community of Ghana: A Human Rights Framework. *Marine Policy* 147: 105349. https://doi.org/10.1016/j.marpol.2022.105349.

Hines, Ali. 2022. Decade of Defiance: Ten Years of Reporting Land and Environmental Activism Worldwide. Global Witness. Available at: https://www.globalwitness.org/en/campaigns/environmental-activists/decade-defiance/.

Jentoft, Svein, Ratana Chuenpagdee, Alicia B. Said, and Moenieba Isaacs. 2022. *Blue Justice: Small-Scale Fisheries in a Sustainable Ocean Economy.* Springer International.

Jouffray, Jean-Baptiste, Robert Blasiak, Albert V. Norström, Henrik Österblom, and Magnus Nyström. 2020. The Blue Acceleration: The Trajectory of Human Expansion into the Ocean. *One Earth* 2 (1): 43–54. https://doi.org/10.1016/j.oneear.2019.12.016.

Lawlor, Mary. 2024. *"We Are Not Just the Future": Challenges Faced by Child and Youth Human Rights Defenders.* Report of the Special Rapporteur on the Situation of Human Rights Defenders, United Nation General Assembly, A/HRC/55/50.

Le Billon, Philippe, and Päivi Lujala. 2020. Environmental and Land Defenders: Global Patterns and Determinants of Repression. *Global Environmental Change* 65: 102163. https://doi.org/10.1016/j.gloenvcha.2020.102163.

Lundy, Laura. 2020. *The Rights of Child Human Rights Defenders: Implementation Guide.* Child Rights Connect. Available at: https://wedocs.unep.org/bitstream/handle/20.500.11822/34574/RCHRD.pdf.

Macusi, Edison D., Imee S. Maynawang, Robert E. Katikiro, Jee G. Suyo, and Erna S. Macusi. 2023. Women Lead Small-Scale Fisheries to Sustainability in Surigao del Sur, Philippines. *Marine Policy* 155: 105768. https://doi.org/10.1016/j.marpol.2023.105768.

Mangubhai, Sangeeta, Kate M. Barclay, Sarah Lawless, and Natalie Makhoul. 2023. Gender-Based Violence: Relevance for Fisheries Practitioners. *Fish and Fisheries* 24 (4): 582–594. https://doi.org/10.1111/faf.12747.

McGarry, Dylan. 2023. When Ancestors Are Included in Ocean Decision-and Meaning-Making. In *Hydrofeminist Thinking With Oceans*, edited by Tamara Shefer, Vivienne Bozalek, and Nike Romano, 15–32. Routledge.

Menton, Mary, and Philippe Le Billon. 2021. *Environmental Defenders: Deadly Struggles for Life and Territory.* Routledge.

Mills, Elyse N. 2021. The Politics of Transnational Fishers' Movements. *The Journal of Peasant Studies* 50 (2): 665–690. https://doi.org/10.1080/03066150.2021.1975271.

Morgera, Elisa. 2023. Contributing to the 2025 UN Call for Action on Human Rights with a Focus on Defenders. One Ocean Hub. Available at: https://oneoceanhub.org/contributing-to-the-un-call-for-action-on-human-rights-with-a-focus-on-ocean-defenders/.

Morgera, Elisa, and Hannah Lily. 2022. Public Participation at the International Seabed Authority: An International Human Rights Law Analysis. *Review of European, Comparative & International Environmental Law* 31 (3): 374–388. https://doi.org/10.1111/reel.12472.

Morgera, Elisa, and Julia Nakamura. 2022. Shedding a Light on the Human Rights of Small-Scale Fisherfolk: Complementarities and Contrasts between the UN Declaration on Peasants' Rights and the Small-Scale Fisheries Guidelines. In *Commentary on the Declaration on the Rights of Peasants*, edited by Mariagrazia Alabrese, Adriana Bessa, Margherita Brunori, and Pier Filippo Giuggioli, 62–87. Routledge.

Morgera, Elisa, and Sophie Shields. 2024. *Integrating the General Comment 26 on Children's Rights and a Healthy Environment in the Implementation of the FAO Guidelines on*

Small-Scale Fisheries. One Ocean Hub policy brief. Available at: https://oneoceanhub.org/wp-content/uploads/2024/02/Policy-Brief-integrating-the-general-comment.FAO-Guidelines-on-Small-scale-Fisheries_12.02.24_1.pdf.

Okafor-Yarwood, Ifesinachi. 2020. The Cyclical Nature of Maritime Security Threats: Illegal, Unreported, and Unregulated Fishing as a Threat to Human and National Security in the Gulf of Guinea. *African Security* 13 (2): 116–146. https://doi.org/10.1080/19392206.2020.1724432.

Ommer, Rosemary E., with the Coasts Under Stress Research Project Team. 2007. *Coasts under Stress: Restructuring and Social-Ecological Health*. McGill-Queen's Press.

Pereira, Taryn, and Kira Erwin. 2023. Surfacing Solidarity Praxis in Transdisciplinary Research for Blue Justice. *Ecosystems and People* 19 (1): 2260502. https://doi.org/10.1080/26395916.2023.2260502.

Said, Alicia, and Douglas C. MacMillan. 2020. "Re-grabbing" Marine Resources: A Blue Degrowth Agenda for the Resurgence of Small-Scale Fisheries in Malta. *Sustainability Science* 15 (1): 91–102. https://doi.org/10.1007/s11625-019-00769-7.

Sall, Aliou. 2024. Diambari Sine: Women's Fish Processing Organization Leads the Resistance Against Industrial Fisheries and Fishmeal Factories in Senegal. The Ocean Defenders Project. Available at: https://oceandefendersproject.org/case-study/diambari-sine-womens-fish-organization/.

Satizábal, Paula, Philippe Le Billon, Dyhia Belhabib, Lina M. Saavedra-Díaz, Isabel Figueroa, Gina Noriega, and Nathan J. Bennett. 2021. Ethical Considerations for Research on Small-Scale Fisheries and Blue Crimes. *Fish and Fisheries* 22 (6): 1160–1166. https://doi.org/10.1111/faf.12590.

Scheidel, Arnim, Daniela Del Bene, Juan Liu, Grettel Navas, Sara Mingorria, Federico Demaria, and Sofía Avila et al. 2020. Environmental Conflicts and Defenders: A Global Overview. *Global Environmental Change* 63: 102104. https://doi.org/10.1016/j.gloenvcha.2020.102104.

Shields, Sophie, Andrea Longo, Mia Strand, and Elisa Morgera. 2023. Children's Human Right to be Heard at the Ocean-Climate Nexus. *The International Journal of Marine and Coastal Law* 38 (3): 545–580. https://doi.org/10.1163/15718085-bja10140.

Shields, Sophie, and Elisa Morgera. 2023a. Calling Attention to Children Defenders. One Ocean Hub. Available at: https://oneoceanhub.org/calling-attention-to-children-ocean-defenders/.

Shields, Sophie, and Elisa Morgera. 2023b. *What Child Environmental Human Rights Defenders Need to Know to Defend and Protect a Healthy Ocean*. One Ocean Hub policy brief. Available at: https://oneoceanhub.org/wp-content/uploads/2023/12/Policy-Brief-What-child-environmental-human-rights-defenders-need-to-know.12.12.23.pdf.

Strand, Mia, Sophie Shields, Elisa Morgera, Dylan McGarry, Alana S.N. Lancaster, Lyndy Brown, and Bernadette Snow. 2023. Protecting Children's Rights to Development and Culture by Re-Imagining "Ocean Literacies". *The International Journal of Children's Rights* 31 (4): 941–975. https://doi.org/10.1163/15718182-3104000.

Sunde, Jackie. 2023. Mapping for Justice: Towards an Accessible, Transparent Database of Mining along the West Coast of South Africa. One Ocean Hub. Available at: https://oneoceanhub.org/mapping-for-justice-towards-an-accessible-transparent-database-of-mining-along-the-west-coast-of-south-africa/.

Sunde, Jackie, and Kira Erwin. 2020. *Cast Out: The Systematic Exclusion of the Kwazulu-Natal Subsistence Fishers from the Fishing Rights Regime in South Africa*. The KNZ Substance Fishers Forum and South Durban Community Environmental Alliance. Available at: https://static.pmg.org.za/201027Cast_Out-_Policy_Document-2020.pdf.

Tran, Dalena, and Ksenija Hanaček. 2023. A Global Analysis of Violence Against Women Defenders in Environmental Conflicts. *Nature Sustainability* 6 (9): 1045–1053. https://doi.org/10.1038/s41893-023-01126-4.

United Nations. 2023. United Nations Guidance Note on Environmental Human Rights Defenders. UNEP. Available at: https://www.unep.org/resources/policy-and-strategy/united-nations-guidance-note-environmental-human-rights-defenders.

UN Office on Drugs and Crime. 2021. *Pirates of the Niger Delta: Between Brown and Blue Waters*. Available at: https://www.unodc.org/documents/Maritime_crime/UNODC_GMCP_Pirates_of_the_Niger_Delta_Part_2.pdf.

World Forum of Fisher Peoples. 2021. International Conference on "Impacts of Blue Economy: Response of the Affected Peoples". Available at: https://wffp-web.org/wffp-international-conference-on-impacts-of-blue-economy-response-of-the-affected-peoples-23rd-february-2021-4pm-to-630pm-indian-time-ist/.

4 Original Instructions for the World Ocean: an Indigenist research agenda

Peter J. Jacques

The current dominant vision and operation of ocean governance is better at creating commodities than it is relationships. Research on ocean governance can help create alternatives by asking different questions than those we normally ask in global environmental politics (GEP). GEP is dominated by questions that ask something like "What arrangements can nation-states make to maximize resource use without undermining said resource?" This is the main direction in "sustainable development," but in United Nations (UN) ocean documents, notions of "sustainability" and "sustainable development" function as substitutes for economic growth and it appears that the oceans are governed by a non-codified economistic regime (Lobo and Jacques 2017, Jacques and Lobo 2018). This is not surprising because the dominant view of the world is still intoxicated by Enlightenment Liberalism.

Mainstream GEP, and even more so international relations in general, takes some form of rationality for granted; that is, there are principal actors (states) who will maximize their own benefits and avoid costs at the expense of the collective welfare. Thus, mainstream international thinking is "rationalist." Rational actors will take what they can, and our research agendas and pedagogy have trained generations of diplomats to internalize this logic—and dream that world into existence. Realists might say it is naïve to think otherwise. However, it is equally naïve to think that a system that undermines the critical life supports that states and every living thing on Earth depends on to survive can last. We need to dream a different world, one that would come from an entirely distinct set of questions, and an Indigenist perspective provides just that: a question that can alter the direction of a world on fire. And, as Leroy Little Bear (2000) reminds us, "No matter how dominant a worldview is, there are always other ways to interpret the world" (p. 77).

An Indigenist perspective, as noted by Shawn Wilson and colleagues (Adams et al. 2015, Rix et al. 2019, Wilson 2007), starts with respectful relations, and the question is "How do we create and maintain good relations?" An Indigenist perspective is more interested in the question "How do I be a good ancestor?"—or "How do I be a good relative?" (Hausdoerffer et al. 2021). This is because we are all related, and not just to other humans. We are related to the four-legged, the winged, the finned, the land and water (or Country as it is referred to by Aboriginal Australians) … We are inescapably related to the mountains, rivers, and certainly the ocean, none of which are considered alive, let alone afforded personhood, in Western minds. We govern the World Ocean as if it were a dead "dull heap of matter that Nature could not bring to perfection" (Selden 1972 [1635], p. 127), which would be wasted without human conquest, exhaustion, and then ruin (see, for example, Van der Pijl 2001).

If we take these questions and points of departure seriously, it would be socially unacceptable to be irresponsible fishers, to allow entire non-human societies to go extinct, or to permit untold volumes of pollutants, like plastic, into a living ocean relative. What would the ocean be like if we respected these norms as law, just as Indigenous traditions demand (see Jackson 1993, Lyons 2008, Black 2010, Cajete 2000)? I expect that some would still violate this natural law, but these would be socially intolerable criminal acts, instead of an internalized norm.

This chapter will explain what an Indigenist ocean research agenda might look like. First, however, I am obligated to explain my relationship to aspects of some Indigenous knowledge. I am not Indigenous, and what I relate here comes from immersing myself in what Indigenous authors have communicated to the world, but which is often ignored, totally in international relations. So, I claim none of this Indigenous knowledge as my own, but I find the perspective extremely compelling. Further, I have a long-time relation to different elements of Indigenous thought, first coming from associations with Indigenous peoples. This was strongest when I was in graduate school at Northern Arizona University, where American Indian thought was part of every class and a good amount of my cohort were from Dinéland (Navajo) and Hopiland, as well as some other tribes in the region. For some time, I went to the Western Social Science Association, where the towering Standing Rock Lakota sage Vine Deloria set up shop for himself and his students and I had the privilege to hear him and other key figures in the American Indian Studies section. I have since created college classes on Indigenous thought and politics. I have also worked personally in Indigenous Amazigh villages in the High Atlas Mountains around Marrakech, Morocco—the Amazigh are one of the oldest people on the planet. This is my relation. I come with respect and intend to emphasize ignored voices, hoping that relating this ignored literature will be of some benefit to Indigenous peoples themselves, as well as the world which needs to hear a different story and dream a different dream. This is my intention.

Old coastal cultures

Original peoples remember "Original Instructions" (Lyons 2008, Nelson 2008), and ocean research should attend to the multitudes of Indigenous voices and authors that have communicated a vast literature. These instructions worked, and Indigenous "old coastal cultures" governed themselves in a sustainable manner (Acheson and Wilson 1996, Jacques 2017). Old coastal cultures emphasize the "three Rs": respect, reciprocity, and responsibility.

These instructions invariably described requirements for a good life and how to be a good ancestor. This did not include the Western mantra of "take everything you can." A good life requires the three Rs, which will produce balance and harmony (Tinker 1996, Wilson 2008). Good research, Indigenous scholars add, also must be relevant to authentic welfare. According to Cree elders, showing respect or *kihceyihtowin* is a basic law of life:

> 'Respect regulates how we treat Mother Earth, the plant, the animals, and our brothers and sisters of all races ... Respect means that you listen intently to other's ideas, that you do not insist that your idea prevails. By listening intently you show honour, consider the wellbeing of others, and treat others with kindness and courtesy'. (Steinhauer 2002, p. 73, quoting elders in a Blue Quills First Nations College manual)

Notice that respect is a law that requires you to care about the "wellbeing of others," and if you observe this law, you cannot remove an entire society, like the oysters that had been off the coast of contemporary New York, from existence. It also means that any kind of colonial or settler condition is against Original law, and the self-determination of Native people must be respected, making Indigenist approaches anti-colonial. An Indigenist research agenda takes decolonizing approaches, and it is important to note that across the history of colonialism, academics and academic research have been enablers of the oppression of Aboriginal people (Nelson 2020, Smith 2021).

Reciprocity

> begins with an understanding that anything and everything that humans do influences the rest of the world around us. Even when we cannot clearly know what that effect is in any act, we know that there is an effect ... Knowing that every action has its unique effect has always meant that there had to be some sort of built-in compensation for human actions, some act of reciprocity ... The value of reciprocity, which is a hallmark of Indian ceremonies, goes to the heart of issues of sustainability, which is maintaining a balance and tempering the negative effects of basic human survival techniques. Moreover, as far as I know, there is no ceremony for clear-cutting an entire forest. (Tinker 1996, pp. 160, 162)

Ceremony takes time, sometimes days, like in some Diné *Hozhoni* (walk in beauty) ceremonies. If there is no ceremony for clear-cuts, there certainly is no ceremony that covers wanton destruction of entire marine habitats or the elimination of entire finned relatives. As such, this second "R" implies a syllogism:

1. Modern ocean governance prioritizes a neoliberal capitalist structure.
2. The neoliberal political economy actively avoids reciprocal relations with the ocean.
3. Modern ocean governance is incompatible with a healthy, sustained World Ocean, which will therefore collapse.

The third "R," responsibility, refers to mutual accountability for keeping good relations. Under a rationalist framework, expecting people to be responsible is considered naïve, but without responsibility we cannot expect to survive. In fact, this relates to what Daniel Wildcat (2009) calls Indigenous realism:

> to know 'it'—reality—requires respect for the relationships and relatives that constitute the complex web of life. I call this Indigenous realism, and it entails that we, members of humankind, accept our inalienable responsibilities as members of the planet's complex life system. (p. 9)

Contemporary ocean norms

What are our relationships to the World Ocean? How do we create a resilient relationship with the World Ocean?

The normal rationalist approach is to maximize utility. In the social sciences, this has even been proposed as the fundamental human nature; that is, to think this way is essential to being human. Urbina and Ruiz-Villaverde (2019) explain five elements to this model, also known as *Homo economicus*: (1) individualism, (2) optimizing behavior, (3) full rationality, (4) universality, and (5) exogenous preferences. Individualism means "Individuals only think, decide, and act according to their own interests," and can only consider the "welfare of others *as far as it affects their own welfare*" (pp. 65–66, emphasis in original). We are said to optimize behavior in as much as we are supposed to instantly calculate the best options given our means. We are fully rational in that we can properly process all available information. Universality means that this model applies "to all kinds of events in every time and place. There would be no society or individual that can escape from this scheme" (p. 66), thus making it human nature for all human beings across all time. Preferences are exogenous when they are consistent, transitive, complete, and monotonic (always non-decreasing or non-increasing). While this model of humanity is a core assumption in neoclassical economics, it has been influential across the social sciences in general despite decades of criticism and discovery. This imperial epistemology implies that humans cannot adhere to Original Instructions, where, for example, we are said to be incapable of thinking of future generations only so much as it affects our own welfare, and this is locked into all people across all time. In addition, instead of the ecological systems around us co-constituting society, "Neoclassical economics conceptualizes the environment as fundamentally 'external' to the individual who perceives it in terms of the logic of consumption (utility) or production (exploitation)" (Urbina and Ruiz-Villaverde 2019, p. 77). Neoclassical economics is not alone here, but in agreement with Western thinking that separates ecology from humanity in the ubiquitous term, "nature," which is always "other" (see Latour 2004).

As a central tenet of Western thinking, the model of rationality has deeply influenced the dominant relationship of humans to the ocean. For example, our dominant approach to marine fishing is to maximize our catch (maximum sustainable yield, or

MSY), to take as much as possible without undermining future fish generations. Not maximizing the catch is considered "waste."

This means that, among other things, the dominant relation actively avoids savings, critical to resilience. The criticisms of MSY are as old as the idea of MSY (Larkin 1977) but it remains a dominant approach. MSY rests on Western mythology, including a sense that the natural world can be controlled. MSY delusionally proposes that we can identify the amount of a population that is renewable without considering the dependence of other populations and habitats. In keeping with Beck's (1992) risk society, modernity's assumption that the natural world can be controlled simply ends in a total lack of control (crisis) where world fisheries are at the brink of demise (Jacques 2015). Further, "widespread application of single-species MSY policies would in general cause severe deterioration in ecosystem structure" (Walters et al. 2005, p. 558). MSY also consistently fails for political reasons. We might set limits to the catch of tuna that would not undermine the tuna population, but fishing interests often push for a catch allotment that is beyond the agreed limit (Eagle and Thomson 2003). The problems with MSY have been widely agreed upon, and routinely dismissed at the policy level, and it "forms the heart of most international fisheries agreements and treaties to this day" (Finley and Oreskes 2013, p. 247). Maximizing what we take leaves truly little buffer to handle disturbances, and I have argued elsewhere that there are signs that we have positioned global fisheries for collapse and disorganization (Jacques 2015). Specifically, the signs are that, globally, we spend 10 times more energy to capture half of the fish now compared to the 1950s; and, despite this extra energy, global marine capture fish catch has plateaued. No wonder. As Narvaez et al. (2019) put it, "Most societies in the history of the world would consider individual 'self-interest'—assumed to be normal human nature in most of the West—to be profoundly destructive and even a sign of insanity" (p. 5).

Another major dominant relationship with the ocean is one that is often described as the freedom of the seas, *mare liberum*, as opposed to a relation of responsibility. "Freedom," since the days of Grotius (1916 [1609]), has meant an absence of responsibility to anything or anyone, where countries have taken this freedom to mean they can do whatever they want on the high seas where sovereignty is absent. Both notions—freedom of the seas and sovereignty—are a defense against non-interference from others, and both reject responsibility to the planet, to the ocean, and to marine life. This is quite different from Indigenous notions, such as that of a deep responsibility to other people (both human and non-human). Jackson (1993) describes a Maori *law* of responsibility to the ocean and to all who depend on it. Likewise, in Hawaiian Indigenous culture, there is *lawa pono*, or "taking just enough in accordance with pono—in a balanced, right way" (Gould et al. 2019, p. 1223). In the Hawaiian traditional worldview, there is no binary distinction between land and ocean; it is all one continuous spectrum of space where one finds 'aumākua: "'Aumākua, ancestors embodied in animals and other more-than-human entities, … are part of one's 'ohana (family)" (Gould et al. 2019, p. 1224). Under *mare liberum*, there are no 'aumākua. Under the UN Law of the Sea (UNCLOS), which affirmed *mare liberum* in the first conference (1958) to negotiate the umbrella treaty, the most important part is the demarcation of space, allocating resources to be maximized. Unfortunately, expectations of conservation (see Borgese 1998) under UNCLOS have been severely disappointed; under the new protections for biodiversity beyond national jurisdictions (BBNJ), there are still too many questions to evaluate its potential (Harden-Davies et al. 2024).

Under a Hawaiian worldview, *kuleana* are rights that are inherently tied to responsibilities: "rights are earned only by first fulfilling responsibilities and every right or privilege comes with increasing levels of responsibility" (Blaich, quoted in Gould et al. 2019, p. 1227). This makes sense in a relational worldview where our goal is to create good relations, and this includes being responsible for what is taken. Reciprocity demands that everything taken be compensated back, usually through ceremony and time, among other things.

Indigenous thought comes to ocean relations very differently from Western rationality. Ken Paul (2019) of the Wolastoqey First Nation, and the former Director of Fisheries for the Atlantic Policy Congress of First Nations Chiefs, was at an international ocean governance meeting, and he recounts the closing comments of Charlie Labrador, a Mi'kmaq elder:

> He addressed the crowd by saying, 'I have been watching you all this week and listening to your presentations. What I have learned is that you really don't know how to fish.' I was shocked when he said this. He went on to say that he is a simple Mi'kmaw man from a small community a couple of hours away and that he has spent his life fishing, hunting, and gathering plants for medicine. He said that the key to his existence was to respect the natural resources and only take what was needed. He followed this with a closing prayer. (p. 47)

Paul adds, "His message was simple (as opposed to simplistic, which eliminates relevant factors). His message of only using what you need and respecting the natural world as you would a relative is a deep-rooted value amongst all Indigenous tribes that I have encountered over my lifetime" (2019, p. 47).

Thus, the dominant Western relationship with the World Ocean is one of a taker; the living World Ocean is merely a container of marine commodities. This approach lacks reciprocity, responsibility, and respect and has allowed for unbridled exploitation that, if collapse or collapses occur, leaves us with little left to allow reorganization, to say nothing of the empty moral code that abuses other people (human and non-human). The dominant relationship with the ocean is patently, explicitly, not sustainable. Our exploitative relationship has set a human–ocean crisis that could have been avoided had we thought differently and asked different questions. Paul sees reason for optimism: "I believe deeply that if First Nations were given any voice in the management of ocean resources, there would be much healthier fish stocks and less destructive impacts on the ocean from human activity" (2019, p. 51). There are important research agendas that reside in this statement, and we should be compelled to act on them.

Further, embedded in this situation is one of inflexible commitment, much like the 1970s Atlantic cod build-up. Scientifically, we continue to learn so much about ocean and marine life, but politically we refuse to allow for a different relationship, one that allows for savings, flexibility, and restraint—one that views the World Ocean as a living, powerful relation. Can a new research agenda make room for revision? If we ask different questions and listen to and involve people who have 10,000 years of knowledge about the dynamism and changes the World Ocean exhibits, we might make different collective decisions.

One final dominant relationship organized by the current world order, found both in MSY and *mare liberum*, is anthropocentric hubris. In the approach of MSY, there is an assumption that human removal is the only factor affecting fish populations, and while there are counterexamples like the minority of regional fishery management organizations (RFMOs) that use ecosystem-based management (Webster 2013), this assumption remains dominant. There are few considerations for interactions in the food web, climate, or habitat changes, such as those changes being experienced in "cold pools." In one case, the reduction of a cold pool off the Bering Strait increased the caloric needs of Alaskan snow crabs, starving 10 billion—*billion*—crabs to death and collapsing the snow crab population (Szuwalski et al. 2023). Now, to the extent that this change in habitat is related to human-caused climate change, humans with deep greenhouse gas emission legacies are responsible for this massacre. But we are focused only on human concerns, and the fact that we have lost a multitude of crabs in the Bering Sea is seen as simply unfortunate for snow crab *fleets* as opposed to an unspeakable planetary loss.

Mare liberum also carries with it an anthropocentric hubris because it assigns humans freedom—human benefits without any reciprocal relations to the living ocean. It is hubris because this model assumes that we know enough about the marine world that only our actions matter. Indeed, the Selden comment above about the ocean as only a "dull heap" is in the context of debate about *mare liberum*, and the anthropocentric element of the debate was never contested. The centrality of that debate was whether the ocean could be controlled by nations. Selden said yes because it is just another space on the planet, and Grotius believed it was simply too vast. No European said it was a living Country of its own with infinite living relations across time and space that require respect and human restraint.

Anthropocentrism and hubris go together. Human-centeredness *requires* an inappropriate confidence that the rest of the world does not matter, or matter enough to consider as another source of understanding, wisdom, and importance. Anthropocentrism is the dominant Western value system (Hay 2002) which socially constructs and legitimizes a hierarchy of value where human beings are the only important concern and, in this way are the only "people" and the only legitimate, inherent locus of value. Hubris is a blind confidence that intoxicates with power, where sense of importance outpaces the reality of actual capability. Think of just about any colonial narrative:

> The tale is such a familiar one that it has assumed the quality of a parable: A white man, driven by hubristic dreams, sets off on an uncharted river to an unknown destination in

> an unfamiliar land inhabited by mysterious, usually dark-skinned, peoples (Kennedy 2024, p. 10).

How does this end?

> His journey steadily descends into madness, murder, and self-destruction (Kennedy 2024, p. 10).

It also very often ends with the destruction of so many others and Country, and long histories of dislocation and spiraling generations of misery for Indigenous people who have lost their ancestors found in the land and ocean, the two-legged, four-legged, winged, and finned.

If there are other Earth others, other non-human people, and Country that participate in a living universe in a way that co-constitutes connected identities; and, if everything is connected, then Anthropocentrism denies human inquiry into the world, and the ocean, on questions that are not only about the qualities of the world but the interdependent conditions of human identity. This involves, then, the nature of human and non-human prospects into the future. If we do not recognize non-human others as important while allowing ourselves permission to act in such a way that the world loses 10 billion snow crabs, and all non-human others and Countries are related to humans across the globe, then our existence is threatened as well.

Conclusion

We began with a critique of current and historical thought about the dominant research agenda in global environmental politics regarding ocean and marine worlds. This scholarship has focused on international (state-based) regimes or institutions surrounding specific problems, which work to solve collective action problems. This is important. However, it is also not the only way to think about the world. It operates from the privilege of Enlightenment Liberalism, a Western perspective that takes for granted the legitimacy and importance of the state, an epistemology of Western Enlightenment, and an ontological perspective that international relations are lived through the diplomatic corps of countries that will always act in rational ways to maximize their utility. This rationalist perspective has dominated international relations in general, let alone the study of environmental problems in international relations.

We then marked out a new line of inquiry away from an epistemology and ontology of rationalist "take all you can" informed by a vast literature of Indigenous voices who communicate "Original Instructions" on how to be a good ancestor and how to live on Earth, our collective Country. These instructions are law, and we abandon law to the detriment of all our relations. These interdependencies are vast because we are all related. These instructions are simple (not simplistic): live with respect for all your relations, take what you need with reciprocity and give back, and be responsible for your actions.

Finally, we compared these original laws to the dominant relations fostered by mainstream thinking. This dominant approach dreams worlds into existence, imaginaries that walk around and which others follow. In the mainstream, principal relations to the ocean have guided our research agendas around things like the anarchism of *mare liberum*, where states treat the seas as an unsupervised playground and the main question is how to get the unsupervised kids to act in a way that does not undermine the playground. One related tool in ocean relations has been managing ourselves via maximum sustainable yield. Under MSY, there is some theoretical maximum yield of any population, and in fisheries this is normally a percentage of the young that are assumed to recruit into adulthood. Then, actors are assigned an allotment of this percentage and are supposed to be limited to that percentage. However, the framework itself treats the fish people as simple commodities, and any percentage within MSY not captured is "waste." Again, it is a rationalist perspective in which the goal is to take as much as possible. All of this is confounded by the fact that humans are not the only factor in something like the maturity or number of fish people in any fish society. Other things, like climate and changing habitat, not to mention the interactions with the rest of the food web, also condition the lives of fish societies.

Mare liberum and MSY, however, are a function of anthropocentric hubris at the very least, where human groups give themselves permission to think only about themselves—and even then, only some human groups matter and can afford an increasingly scarce "commodity." It is hubris to think that humans are the only people that matter, and it is disastrous for human societies and the rest of a living planet. Working our way out of this will require us to ask different questions and dream of a different world, and this is imperative because if the Original Instructions are true, then the current ocean regime is inconsistent with a long, good future in which we are good ancestors.

References

Acheson, James M., and James A. Wilson. 1996. "Order out of chaos: The case for parametric fisheries management." *American Anthropologist* 98 (3): 579–594.

Adams, Dawn Hill, Shawn Wilson, Ryan Heavy Head, and Edmund W. Gordon. 2015. *Ceremony at a Boundary Fire: A Story of Indigenist Knowledge*. Longmont, CO, and Sydney: Sydney eScholarship Repository.

Beck, Ulrich. 1992. *The Risk Society: Towards a New Modernity*. Newbery Park, CA: Sage.

Black, Christopher F. 2010. *The Land Is the Source of the Law: A Dialogic Encounter with Indigenous Jurisprudence*. London: Routledge.

Borgese, Elisabeth Mann. 1998. *The Oceanic Circle: Governing the Seas as a Global Resource*. New York, NY: United Nations University Press.

Cajete, Gregory. 2000. *Native Science: Natural Laws of Interdependence*. Santa Fe, NM: Clear Light Publishers.

Eagle, J., and B.N. Thomson. 2003. "Answering Lord Petty's question: Dissecting regulatory overfishing." *Ocean and Coastal Management* 46: 649–679.

Finley, Carmel, and Naomi Oreskes. 2013. "Maximum sustained yield: A policy disguised as science." *ICES Journal of Marine Science / Journal du Conseil* 70 (2): 245–250. https://doi.org/10.1093/icesjms/fss192.

Gould, Rachelle K., Māhealani Pai, Barbara Muraca, and Kai M.A. Chan. 2019. "He 'ike 'ana ia i ka pono (it is a recognizing of the right thing): How one indigenous worldview informs relational values and social values." *Sustainability Science* 14 (5): 1213–1232. https://doi.org/10.1007/s11625-019-00721-9.

Grotius, Hugo. 1916. *The Freedom of the Seas or The Right Which Belongs to the Dutch to Take Part in the East Indian Trade*, edited by James Brown Scott. New York, NY: Carnegie Endowment for International Peace/Oxford University Press. Original edition, 1609.

Harden-Davies, Harriet, Vanessa Ferreira Lopes, Luciana Fernandes Coelho, Gemma Nelson, Julia Schutz Veiga, Sheena Talma, and Marjo Vierros. 2024. "First to finish, what comes next? Putting capacity building and the transfer of marine technology under the BBNJ Agreement into practice." *npj Ocean Sustainability* 3 (1): 3. https://doi.org/10.1038/s44183-023-00039-1.

Hausdoerffer, John, Brooke Parry Hecht, Melissa K. Nelson, and Katherine Kassouf Cummings. 2021. *What Kind of Ancestor Do You Want to Be?* Chicago, IL: University of Chicago Press.

Hay, Peter R. 2002. *Main Currents in Western Environmental Thought*. Bloomington, IN: Indiana University Press.

Jackson, Moana. 1993. "Indigenous law and the sea." In *Freedom for the Seas in the 21st Century: Ocean Governance and Environmental Harmony*, edited by Jon M. Van Dyke, 41–48. Washington, DC: Island Press.

Jacques, Peter J. 2015. "Are world fisheries a global panarchy?" *Marine Policy* 53: 165–170. http://dx.doi.org/10.1016/j.marpol.2014.11.024.

Jacques, Peter J. 2017. "The origins of coastal ecological decline and the Great Atlantic Oyster Collapse." *Political Geography* 60: 154–164. https://doi.org/10.1016/j.polgeo.2017.07.010.

Jacques, Peter J., and Rafaella Lobo. 2018. "The shifting context of sustainability: Growth and the world ocean regime." *Global Environmental Politics* 18 (4): 85–106.

Kennedy, Dane. 2024. *Mungo Park's Ghost: The Haunted Hubris of British Explorers in Nineteenth-Century Africa*. Cambridge: Cambridge University Press.

Larkin, P.A. 1977. "Epitaph for the concept of maximum susteined yield." *Transactions of the American Fisheries Society* 106 (1): 1–11.

Latour, Bruno. 2004. *The Politics of Nature: How to Bring the Sciences into Democracy*. Cambridge, MA: Harvard University Press.

Little Bear, Leroy. 2000. "Jagged worldviews colliding." In *Reclaiming Indigenous Voice and Vision*, edited by Marie Battiste, 77–85. Vancouver: University of British Columbia Press.

Lobo, Rafaella, and Peter J. Jacques. 2017. "SOFIA'S choices: Discourses, values, and norms of the World Ocean Regime." *Marine Policy* 78: 26–33. http://dx.doi.org/10.1016/j.marpol.2016.12.023.

Lyons, Oren. 2008. "Listening to natural law." In *Original Instructions: Indigenous Teachings for a Sustainable Future*, edited by Melissa Nelson, 21–24. Rochester, VT: Bear & Co.

Narvaez, Darcia, Four Arrows, Eugene Halton, Brian Collier, and Georges Enderle. 2019. *Indigenous Sustainable Wisdom: First-Nation Know-How for Global Flourishing*. New York, NY: Peter Lang.

Nelson, Melissa K., ed. 2008. *Original Instructions: Indigenous Teachings for a Sustainable Future*. Rochester, VT: Inner Traditions/Bear & Co.

Nelson, Melissa K. 2020. "Decolonizing conquest consciousness." Center for Humans & Nature. https://humansandnature.org/decolonizing-conquest-consciousness/.

Paul, Ken. 2019. "First Nations, Oceans Governance and Indigenous Knowledge Systems." In *The Future of Ocean Governance and Capacity Development: Essays in Honor of Elisabeth Mann Borgese (1918–2002)*, edited by International Ocean Institute, 46–52. Leiden: Brill.

Rix, Elizabeth F., Shawn Wilson, Norm Sheehan, and Nicole Tujague. 2019. "Indigenist and decolonizing research methodology." In *Handbook of Research Methods in Health Social Sciences*, edited by Pranee Liamputtong, 253–267. Singapore: Springer Singapore.

Selden J. Mare Clausum: The Right and Dominion of the Sea in Two Books. Andrew Kembe and Edward Thomas Publishers. https://www.google.com/books/edition/Mare_Clausum/2dhIAQAAMAAJ?hl=en&gbpv=1&dq=%22Of+the+Dominion,+Or,+Ownership+of+the+Sea%22&pg=PA1&printsec=frontcover.

Smith, Linda Tuhiwai. 2021. *Decolonizing Methodologies: Research and Indigenous Peoples*. London: Bloomsbury Publishing.

Steinhauer, Evelyn. 2002. "Thoughts on an Indigenous research methodology." *Canadian Journal of Native Education* 26 (2).

Szuwalski, Cody S., Kerim Aydin, Erin J. Fedewa, Brian Garber-Yonts, and Michael A. Litzow. 2023. "The collapse of eastern Bering Sea snow crab." *Science* 382 (6668): 306–310.

Tinker, George. 1996. "An American Indian theological response to eco-justice." In *Defending Mother Earth: Native American Perspectives on Environmental Justice*, edited by Jace Weaver, 153–176. Maryknoll, NY: Orbis Books.

Urbina, Dante A., and Alberto Ruiz-Villaverde. 2019. "A critical review of Homo economicus from five approaches." *The American Journal of Economics and Sociology* 78 (1): 63–93. https://doi.org/10.1111/ajes.12258.

Van der Pijl, Kees. 2001. "International relations and capitalist discipline." In *Phases of Capitalist Development: Booms, Crises and Globalizations*, edited by Robert Albritton, Makoto Itoh, Richard Westra, and Alan Zuege, 1–16. London: Palgrave Macmillan UK.

Walters, Carl J., Villy Christensen, Steven J. Martell, and James F. Kitchell. 2005. "Possible ecosystem impacts of applying MSY policies from single-species assessment." *ICES Journal of Marine Science* 62 (3): 558–568. https://doi.org/10.1016/j.icesjms.2004.12.005.

Webster, D.G. 2013. "International fisheries: Assessing the potential for ecosystem management." *Journal of Environmental Studies and Sciences* 3 (2): 169–183. https://doi.org/10.1007/s13412-013-0123-2.

Wildcat, Daniel. 2009. *Red Alert! Saving the World with Indigenous Knowledge*. Golden, CO: Fulcrum.

Wilson, Shawn. 2007. "Guest editorial: What is an Indigenist research paradigm?" *Canadian Journal of Native Education* 30 (2).

Wilson, Shawn. 2008. *Research Is Ceremony: Indigenous Research Methods*. Halifax: Fernwood Publishing.

5 Making justice explicit in decision-making for transformative ocean governance

Laura M. Pereira, Tomas Chaigneau and Rafael Almeida Magris

Justice for ocean sustainability

The ocean faces not only a sustainability crisis as the blue acceleration gets underway (Jouffray et al. 2020), but also an equity crisis (Österblom et al. 2023) as concerns emerge regarding fair access to fisheries (Prellezo et al. 2023), genomes (Blasiak et al. 2020), and resources in Areas Beyond National Jurisdiction (ABNJ) (Claudet et al. 2021) like the seabed (Feichtner 2019). The United Nations Convention on the Law of the Sea (UNCLOS) is the primary legal mechanism for governing the ocean at the international level, but other global environmental agreements like the Paris Agreement under the UN Framework Convention on Climate Change (UNFCCC) and the Kunming-Montreal Global Biodiversity Framework under the Convention on Biological Diversity (CBD) have specific relevance to the ocean. The recently agreed Biodiversity Beyond National Jurisdiction Treaty (BBNJ) also has an important role to play in ensuring that the vision for an "equitable and efficient" use of resources and protection of the marine environment is realized once it is ratified. However, implementing these agreements in practice will require different governance strategies in different jurisdictions. Furthermore, the kind of transformations required to enable a more sustainable and equitable ocean will undoubtedly lead to winners and losers, but who those winners and losers are is a matter of governance and ethics (Pereira et al. 2024). Some governance choices that correct for historical inequities and allow for equitable resource allocation can lead to more just outcomes, whereas those that perpetuate the status quo, no matter how sustainable for the environment, will never be just (Pereira et al. 2024, Blythe et al. 2023).

We argue that justice should be a core tenet of any ocean governance intervention. However, the concept of justice is disputed. We refer to the Earth system justice approach, which includes multiple dimensions of justice, including procedural, recognitional, and distributive dimensions linked to intragenerational justice (the relationships between humans right now), intergenerational justice (relationships with people across generations), and interspecies justice (including the rights of nature and other species to co-exist on Earth) (Gupta et al. 2023). Acknowledging these diverse forms of justice helps unpack the differential impacts that interventions may have on already vulnerable populations.

We aim to tackle this governance dilemma more concretely in the context of marine protected areas (MPAs). We explore theoretical examples of how interventions could be applied to help achieve the 30 x 30 agenda[1]. By drawing on a recent Marine Planning Trade-off Analysis (MaPTA) tool, we unpack potential trade-offs and key social and ecological thresholds to ensure such interventions could lead to a sustainable and just ocean.

The harsh reality of trade-offs

It is now increasingly recognized in both terrestrial and, more recently, marine systems that well-meaning sustainable development interventions can have unintentional, negative impacts on vulnerable people or ecosystems, or create tensions among groups who feel that they are losing out. This failure to consider how gains come at the expense of other system components can risk widening inequalities, failure to meet conservation and/or development objectives or expectations, and the most vulnerable and marginalized being left behind or, worse, driven unintentionally into serious harm. The fact that win–wins in sustainable development are proving elusive has been acknowledged by researchers, and the academic literature on the prevalence of trade-offs in environmental decision-making has expanded in recent years, pointing to diverse ecological, social, and well-being trade-offs occurring across spatial and temporal scales (Gill et al. 2019). This literature has also demonstrated that negotiating, promoting, and undertaking conservation development initiatives is a value-centered endeavor: the desirability of different objectives, processes, and outcomes is subjective and varies according to the perspectives, needs, aspirations, and motivations of different stakeholders (Manfredo et al. 2017). Trade-offs, therefore, prioritize certain values over other values (Vucetich et al. 2021), which can result in disagreement and conflict (Schaafsma et al. 2021).

If trade-offs are to be the norm rather than the exception in sustainable development, then not only is it critical to identify and anticipate such trade-offs, but equally there is a need to find ways to respond to them. What is done to mitigate, compensate, or prevent certain trade-offs from occurring will depend on whether some trade-off outcomes are deemed "acceptable" or not. In turn, this has been found to be dependent on contextually defined power relations that shape principles of acceptability, and thus whose values are voiced and prioritized in decision-making processes (Fortnam et al. 2023).

Recently developed tools such as MaPTA can help make decisions based on open dialogue and negotiation about potential trade-offs (Fortnam et al. 2022). MaPTA highlights synergies and co-benefits from interventions and reveals negative, harmful, or unintended impacts arising from interventions, which can alienate partners and reduce levels of stakeholder support if left unaddressed. Assessing the acceptability of trade-offs can help to reveal the reasons why different groups may support or oppose the intervention. This, in turn, can help to improve the legitimacy of an intervention and prevent ecosystem features and stakeholders from becoming harmed and/or disenfranchised. MaPTA aims to ensure that management interventions have more sustainable and equitable outcomes for the stakeholders and marine environments affected by them.

Below we apply an adapted MaPTA process to hypothetical examples of MPA interventions to achieve the 30 x 30 target to identify potential trade-offs that can arise from these interventions. Our adapted MaPTA steps are: (1) defining the intervention, (2) identifying impact on people and the environment, (3) assessing the future status and the degree of impact of the intervention, and (4) discussing the trade-offs and implications for inter-species, intragenerational, and intergenerational justice.

Examples of potential interventions to achieve 30 x 30

Intervention 1: no-take, strict small-scale MPAs, close to shore

Step 1: define the intervention

No-take MPAs are locations where extractive activities are prohibited, with the goal of conserving biodiversity and preventing the degradation of seascapes.

Step 2: identify the status of impacted ecosystem features and stakeholders

Key environmental components involve different marine species and habitats, while impacted stakeholders include the fishery and tourism industries. It is important to disaggregate stakeholders within communities, for instance differentiating between small-scale fishers and industrial fishers with access to larger boats and more destructive gear. Some of the primary stakeholder groups supporting MPAs are those that represent or profit from non-extractive human activities in the area (e.g., diving, contemplative ecotourism).

Step 3: future status and degree of impact

Although MPAs can vary in their effectiveness, small-scale no-take MPAs usually achieve positive outcomes for species with small spatial scales of larval and adult movement and can have positive impacts on habitat preservation by protecting reefs from tourists and fishers, thereby allowing fish stocks to regenerate (Di Lorenzo et al. 2020, Ferreira et al. 2022). However, the potential positive benefits for species are also contingent upon what happens outside MPAs, including extraction rates and other anthropogenic disturbances (Edgar et al. 2014, Lester et al. 2009). These changes do not always occur and are often marginal in the short term, but positive impacts on the environment can be observed after ten years (Edgar et al. 2014, Ferreira et al. 2022). Most local communities are highly dependent on the state of the sea, and therefore any ecological improvements arising from the MPA should have knock-on positive impacts on those affected communities. But, since fishers do not anticipate increased fish catch in the short term, and due to coastal development restrictions, the enactment of this type of MPA tends to lead to low social acceptability.

Step 4: discuss potential trade-offs and implications for justice

Interspecies justice

These MPAs will have ramifications for interspecies justice. Evidence of impacts is mixed and context-dependent. In many cases, these small-scale MPAs can effectively protect habitats and species and build up biomass and biodiversity. However, this is far less effective for small MPAs compared to large ones and takes time to be effective (Claudet et al. 2008).

Intergenerational justice

A key aim of such interventions is to protect critical ecosystem services so that future generations may benefit from otherwise overharvested and damaged coastal ecosystems. The benefits of small-scale MPAs can be hard to perceive and can take time (Chaigneau and Brown 2016), so preventing fishers from accessing traditional fishing grounds when fish stocks are in many cases dwindling can threaten their livelihoods. Striking the balance between protecting current generations versus future generations becomes a very complicated scenario—what is acceptable here will be determined by the current status of those affected (will a restriction of fishing grounds put them into serious harm?), of the environment (is an MPA critical for ensuring future ecosystem services for the affected communities?), and the values and priorities of those involved in making the decisions.

Intragenerational justice

The situation becomes more complex when considering intragenerational justice. The implementation of a small-scale MPA can significantly alter the pattern of winners and losers. First, establishing an MPA can clash with industry activity such as nearshore mining, fossil fuel development, and wind farms. While fishers may be hoping for a boost to their catch in the near term, an MPA will reduce the size of their fishing grounds. Nearshore MPAs also mean that fishers without motor boats or larger vessels will need to expend energy, effort, and cost to circumvent the MPA to access new grounds. Studies have also shown that a spatial trade-off can occur as fishing effort is displaced to neighboring communities and could negatively impact yields (Iacarella et al. 2023). This could come at a cost to small-scale fishers, especially since larger-scale fishers often fish in deeper waters and may stand to benefit from potential fishery spillover and larval export without being impacted by a reduced fishing ground near shore. At times, this may push small-scale fishers into poverty as fishing in times of need may no longer be an option, especially during rough weather conditions.

Another trade-off occurs between the tourism industry and fishers. An MPA that is more likely to generate environmental benefits could be a huge asset for tourism, especially diving and potentially recreational fishing. In this case, certain stakeholders may benefit greatly (i.e., guesthouse and hotel owners, restaurants), bolstering the local economy, but at the expense of the local fishing industry.

In this example, it is the intragenerational trade-offs that are the most complex and highlight that there may be no clear "right" or "just" way to establish, design, and implement a no-take MPA. Identifying such trade-offs and considering their impacts and whether they push individuals or the ecosystem into serious harm may help us foresee unacceptable outcomes. Mitigating factors could be put in place to circumvent such outcomes, such as placing MPAs in ways that allow small-scale fishers to access traditional fishing grounds, compensating fishers with boats, or providing social security for those affected.

Intervention 2: multiple-use MPAs, with offshore wind

Step 1: define the intervention

Multiple-use MPAs are intended to protect biodiversity while promoting the sustainable use of the marine environment by a wide variety of actors. Usually, various extractive activities are permitted but are regulated, spatially and temporally, to a greater extent than areas outside these MPAs. Ideally, they are designed to meet local management objectives and not only biodiversity conservation. For example, fishing resource use can be controlled through a diversity of mechanisms, including customary governance and tenure systems, bans on sectors or users extracting certain species, restrictions on certain gear types, and spatial and temporal closures located over specific fishing grounds.

Step 2: identify the status of impacted ecosystem features and stakeholders

The ecosystems and stakeholders are the same here as in the previous example, but also involve the wind power industry, as well as citizens receiving energy from wind farms.

Step 3: future status and degree of impact

The ecological benefits of these MPAs partially depend on their size and fishing mortality inside and outside of the protected area. Species targeted by fisheries inside MPAs are, in theory, partially protected from fishing mortality (since some fishing will typically remain), but fish are often exploited more heavily outside the MPA as fishers relocate, which may even increase overall yield at the expense of population viability (Moffitt et al. 2011). Multiple-use protected areas can be effective in conserving biodiversity and are more likely to be under equitable governance arrangements than their strict counterparts (Adams et al. 2023). However, in high-pressure areas, they might not perform as well as strict protected areas, and as with all protected areas, their performance depends on good management and appropriate use regulations being applied (Gill et al. 2024).

Step 4: discuss potential trade-offs and implications for justice

Interspecies justice

There are inherent trade-offs in mixed-use MPAs as they have multiple competing objectives, particularly biodiversity conservation and fisheries management. Protection effects on biodiversity (such as an increase in species size or abundance) might be negligible or take longer than in no-take MPAs, particularly for species targeted by fisheries (Edgar et al. 2014, Ferreira et al. 2022). Full protection provides stronger biodiversity and fish biomass benefits than partial protection, but all benefits only occur when well-enforced (Giakoumi et al. 2017). The establishment of wind farms is potentially bad for certain mammal species and birdlife in terms of sound, collision, and displacement, but is generally good for climate change mitigation globally (Virtanen et al. 2022). Offshore wind farms can also impact benthic habitats and contribute to the dispersion of non-indigenous species (Bergström et al. 2014). On the other hand, they can positively benefit biodiversity by providing new habitat, protection, and food resources for marine life (Inger et al. 2009). There are potential ways to mitigate some harms; for example, by putting these in areas where affected species are not found and avoiding migration corridors.

Intergenerational justice

Intergenerational justice, in the case of mixed-use MPAs, depends on the extent to which the implementation process is inclusive of diverse stakeholders, especially youth, and whether stakeholders were given genuine decision-making power in the management plan formulation and implementation (Zuercher et al. 2022). Research shows that the benefits of MPAs accrue over longer periods of time, assuming effective and inclusive management (Claudet et al. 2008).

Intragenerational justice

A co-designed and well-enforced multiple-use MPA can have significant positive impacts on intragenerational justice, as it should, in theory, take into account all local stakeholder needs and customs. While offshore wind contributes to renewable energy production, it can disadvantage some fishers. Since wind farms tend to be far from shore, they can interfere with larger boats, such as trawlers. This means that nearshore fishers may benefit more (from spillover and larval export) or, at the very least, suffer less in the short term from wind farms. Monitoring and evaluation programs should be co-developed by all social actors to ensure that all needs are incorporated into the objectives.

In this example, it is the interspecies justice that has the highest trade-offs as the MPA is not necessarily designed with biodiversity conservation as the highest priority. For such MPAs not to become "paper parks," it is vital to ensure effective monitoring and enforcement to maintain conservation goals.

Intervention 3: close the high seas to fishing and restrict other activities

Step 1: define the intervention

The world's oceans are governed as a system of over 150 sovereign exclusive economic zones (EEZs)—approximately 42 percent of the ocean—and one large high seas commons (approximately 58 percent of the ocean) with essentially open access. Many high-valued fish species such as tuna, billfish, and shark migrate around these large oceanic regions, which, as a consequence of competition across EEZs and a global race to fish on the high seas, have been over-exploited (White and Costello 2014). Completely closing the high seas to fishing (Sumaila et al. 2015) and banning seabed mining (Jaeckel et al. 2023, Cassotta and Goodsite 2024) are proposed interventions to enable a more sustainable ocean.

Step 2: identify the status of impacted ecosystem features and stakeholders

The main features affected are high seas ecosystems, the seabed, and species that are found in these regions, including, importantly, transboundary and migratory species. Stocks of some highly migratory species, such as tuna, have dropped precipitously since the 1950s (Juan-Jordá et al. 2011). Oceanic sharks and rays have also declined globally by 71 percent since 1970 (Pacoureau et al. 2021). The stakeholders that operate in the high seas are industrial fishers, shipping companies, mining companies, and companies using marine genetic resources.

Step 3: future status and degree of impact

Completely closing the high seas to fishing would simultaneously give rise to large gains in fisheries' profit, fisheries' yield, and fish stock conservation (White and Costello 2014). It is estimated that a negligible quantity and value of commercial fish taxa are obtained from catch taken exclusively in the high seas, and if the catch of straddling taxa increases by 18 percent on average following closure because of spillover, there would be no loss in global catch (Sumaila et al. 2015). Thus, closing the high seas could be catch-neutral while inequality in the distribution of fisheries benefits among the world's maritime countries could be reduced by 50 percent.

Step 4: discuss potential trade-offs and implications for justice

<u>Interspecies justice</u>
The benefits of closing the high seas to fishing go to transboundary species and those in the deep ocean and on the seabed. They benefit from less exposure to pollution, overexploitation, and other interference in high seas environments. A ban on deep-sea mining would further protect these habitats. This management strategy would also benefit small-range species inhabiting seamounts and other oceanographic features that promote their existence, such as vents and cold seeps.

<u>Intergenerational justice</u>
Although protecting the high seas from fishing may be controversial, it has been suggested that collective action can benefit the current generation while maintaining high seas resources for the benefit of future generations too (Sumaila et al. 2007). Closing the high seas to fishing could provide some insurance against extinction and biodiversity loss in the high seas, while also promoting more sustainable fisheries for current and future generations. A ban on deep-sea mining is sometimes said to be a trade-off against long-term climate mitigation as rare earth minerals are needed for batteries in the renewable energy sector, though this is debated.

<u>Intragenerational justice</u>
Industrialized fishers and big business are likely to be losers if the high seas are closed to fishing. It could also impact global food security if it affects which countries have access to fish, notably those without their own EEZ but where fish is still consumed.

A major obstacle to protecting the high seas is that different nations and fisheries will face different costs and benefits. Countries already active on the high seas will incur losses if the high seas are protected. These countries have, however, been benefiting from a global commons resource for many years, and it could be argued that this is an acceptable loss. Complete closure of the high seas would increase global stock levels by removing the race to fish in international waters, which would boost stock spillover into nearshore and ideally better-managed territorial waters, generating net increases in global fisheries' yield and profit (White 2023). Furthermore, two-thirds of the world's maritime countries would benefit because their artisanal fisheries would have enhanced access to stocks (White 2023). It is also projected that closing the high seas to fishing would decrease the global Gini[2], a key measure of inequality, from 0.66 to 0.33 (Sumaila et al. 2015). A second major challenge for the proposal is that short-term annual losses may be too large for many nations relative to long-term future benefits (Sumaila and Walters 2005).

In this example, it is again the intragenerational trade-offs that are the clearest, but unlike in the first example where these played out in local areas, here it is global actors that are affected. In this instance, it seems that the overall losers would be big industrial actors and rich nations that are benefiting disproportionately from the current system, and so it could be seen as acceptable for them to be the losers in this instance.

Conclusions: making imperfect decisions that are better

Our argument is that to enable effective ocean governance, it is important that different forms of justice and equity are made explicit. There are often irreconcilable justice trade-offs, which makes transparent decision-making essential in conservation governance. Transparency enables an open discussion of the value systems and philosophies underlying decision-making; for example, by calling out explicitly utilitarian approaches. It is impossible to be agnostic to value systems when making decisions, so transparency is needed to ensure more equitable outcomes.

Sometimes there is not a perfectly "safe" (operating within critical planetary boundaries) and perfectly "just" (ensuring nobody is harmed) outcome for an MPA. Very often, compromises would need to be reached, depending on each context. Different interventions to meet the 30 x 30 target, such as those examined in this chapter, highlight explicit trade-offs across justice dimensions. Identifying acceptable rather than perfect decisions, and then having an open discussion as to why an intervention is still acceptable based on a holistic understanding of justice, should be at the heart of ocean governance.

Note

1. The 30x30 agenda for ocean conservation, part of the post-2020 global biodiversity framework under the Convention on Biological Diversity (CBD), aims to protect 30%

of the world's ocean by 2030 through the establishment of marine protected areas (MPAs) or other area-based conservation measures (OECMs).

References

Adams, Vanessa M., Alienor L.M. Chauvenet, Natasha Stoudmann, Georgina G. Gurney, Dan Brockington, and Caitlin D. Kuempel. 2023. Multiple-Use Protected Areas Are Critical to Equitable and Effective Conservation. *One Earth* 6 (9): 1173–89. https://doi.org/10.1016/j.oneear.2023.08.011.

Bergström, Lena, Lena Kautsky, Torleif Malm, Rutger Rosenberg, Magnus Wahlberg, Nastassja Åstrand Capetillo, and Dan Wilhelmsson. 2014. Effects of Offshore Wind Farms on Marine Wildlife: A Generalized Impact Assessment. *Environmental Research Letters* 9 (3): 034012. https://doi.org/10.1088/1748-9326/9/3/034012.

Blasiak, Robert, Rachel Wynberg, Kirsten Grorud-Colvert, Siva Thambisetty, Narcisa M. Bandarra, Adelino V.M. Canário, João da Silva et al. 2020. The Ocean Genome and Future Prospects for Conservation and Equity. *Nature Sustainability* 3 (8): 588–96. https://doi.org/10.1038/s41893-020-0522-9.

Blythe, Jessica L., David A. Gill, Joachim Claudet, Nathan J. Bennett, Georgina G. Gurney, Jacopo A. Baggio, Natalie C. Ban et al. 2023. Blue Justice: A Review of Emerging Scholarship and Resistance Movements. Cambridge Prisms: *Coastal Futures* 1: e15. https://doi.org/10.1017/cft.2023.4.

Cassotta, Sandra, and Michael Goodsite. 2024. Deep-Seabed Mining: An Environmental Concern and a Holistic Social Environmental Justice Issue. *Frontiers in Ocean Sustainability* 2 (March). https://doi.org/10.3389/focsu.2024.1355965.

Chaigneau, Tomas, and Katrina Brown. 2016. Challenging the Win-Win Discourse on Conservation and Development: Analyzing Support for Marine Protected Areas. *Ecology and Society* 21 (1). https://www.jstor.org/stable/26270340.

Claudet, Joachim, Diva J. Amon, and Robert Blasiak. 2021. Transformational Opportunities for an Equitable Ocean Commons. *Proceedings of the National Academy of Sciences* 118 (42): e2117033118. https://doi.org/10.1073/pnas.2117033118.

Claudet, Joachim, Craig W. Osenberg, Lisandro Benedetti-Cecchi, Paolo Domenici, José-Antonio García-Charton, Ángel Pérez-Ruzafa, Fabio Badalamenti et al. 2008. Marine Reserves: Size and Age Do Matter. *Ecology Letters* 11 (5): 481–89. https://doi.org/10.1111/j.1461-0248.2008.01166.x.

Di Lorenzo, Manfredi, Paolo Guidetti, Antonio Di Franco, Antonio Calò, and Joachim Claudet. 2020. Assessing Spillover from Marine Protected Areas and Its Drivers: A Meta-Analytical Approach. *Fish and Fisheries* 21 (5): 906–15. https://doi.org/10.1111/faf.12469.

Edgar, Graham J., Rick D. Stuart-Smith, Trevor J. Willis, Stuart Kininmonth, Susan C. Baker, Stuart Banks, Neville S. Barrett et al. 2014. Global Conservation Outcomes Depend on Marine Protected Areas with Five Key Features. *Nature* 506 (7487): 216–20. https://doi.org/10.1038/nature13022.

Feichtner, Isabel. 2019. Sharing the Riches of the Sea: The Redistributive and Fiscal Dimension of Deep Seabed Exploitation. *European Journal of International Law* 30 (2): 601–33. https://doi.org/10.1093/ejil/chz022.

Ferreira, Harildon M., Rafael A. Magris, Sergio R. Floeter, and Carlos E.L. Ferreira. 2022. Drivers of Ecological Effectiveness of Marine Protected Areas: A Meta-Analytic Approach from the Southwestern Atlantic Ocean (Brazil). *Journal of Environmental Management* 301 (January): 113889. https://doi.org/10.1016/j.jenvman.2021.113889.

Fortnam, Matt, Tomas Chaigneau, and Louisa Evans. 2022. *A Participatory Tool for Assessing the Acceptability of Trade-Offs in Marine Management*. GCRF Blue Communities Programme. Exeter: University of Exeter.

Fortnam, Matt, Tomas Chaigneau, Louisa Evans, and Liliana Bastian. 2023. Practitioner Approaches to Trade-off Decision-Making in Marine Conservation Development. *People and Nature* 5 (5): 1636–48. https://doi.org/10.1002/pan3.10530.

Giakoumi, Sylvaine, Claudia Scianna, Jeremiah Plass-Johnson, Fiorenza Micheli, Kirsten Grorud-Colvert, Pierre Thiriet, Joachim Claudet et al. 2017. Ecological Effects of Full and Partial Protection in the Crowded Mediterranean Sea: A Regional Meta-Analysis. *Scientific Reports*, 7 (1): 8940. https://doi.org/10.1038/s41598-017-08850-w.

Gill, David A., Samantha H. Cheng, Louise Glew, Ernest Aigner, Nathan J. Bennett, and Michael B. Mascia. 2019. Social Synergies, Tradeoffs, and Equity in Marine Conservation Impacts. *Annual Review of Environment and Resources* 44: 347–72. https://doi.org/10.1146/annurev-environ-110718-032344.

Gill, David A., Sarah E. Lester, Christopher M. Free, Alexander Pfaff, Edwin Iversen, Brian J. Reich, Shu Yang et al. 2024. A Diverse Portfolio of Marine Protected Areas Can Better Advance Global Conservation and Equity. *Proceedings of the National Academy of Sciences*, 121(10): e2313205121. https://doi.org/10.1073/pnas.2313205121.

Gupta, Joyeeta, Diana Liverman, Klaudia Prodani, Paulina Aldunce, Xuemei Bai, Wendy Broadgate, Daniel Ciobanu et al. 2023. Earth System Justice Needed to Identify and Live within Earth System Boundaries. *Nature Sustainability*, March: 1–9. https://doi.org/10.1038/s41893-023-01064-1.

Iacarella, Josephine C., Lily Burke, Georgia Clyde, Adam Wicks, Tyler Clavelle, Anya Dunham, Emily Rubidge, and Paul Woods. 2023. Monitoring Temporal and Spatial Trends of Illegal and Legal Fishing in Marine Conservation Areas across Canada's Three Oceans. *Conservation Science and Practice* 5 (6): e12919. https://doi.org/10.1111/csp2.12919.

Inger, Richard, Martin J. Attrill, Stuart Bearhop, Annette C. Broderick, W. James Grecian, David J. Hodgson, Cheryl Mills et al. 2009. Marine Renewable Energy: Potential Benefits to Biodiversity? An Urgent Call for Research. *Journal of Applied Ecology* 46 (6): 1145–53. https://doi.org/10.1111/j.1365-2664.2009.01697.x.

Jaeckel, Aline, Harriet Harden-Davies, Diva J. Amon, Jesse van der Grient, Quentin Hanich, Judith van Leeuwen, Holly J. Niner, and Katherine Seto. 2023. Deep Seabed Mining Lacks Social Legitimacy. *npj Ocean Sustainability* 2 (1): 1–4. https://doi.org/10.1038/s44183-023-00009-7.

Jouffray, Jean-Baptiste, Robert Blasiak, Albert V. Norström, Henrik Österblom, and Magnus Nyström. 2020. The Blue Acceleration: The Trajectory of Human Expansion into the Ocean. *One Earth* 2 (1): 43–54. https://doi.org/10.1016/j.oneear.2019.12.016.

Juan-Jordá, Maria José, Iago Mosqueira, Andrew B. Cooper, Juan Freire, and Nicholas K. Dulvy. 2011. Global Population Trajectories of Tunas and Their Relatives. *Proceedings of the National Academy of Sciences* 108 (51): 20650–55. https://doi.org/10.1073/pnas.1107743108.

Lester, Sarah E., Benjamin S. Halpern, Kirsten Grorud-Colvert, Jane Lubchenco, Benjamin I. Ruttenberg, Steven D. Gaines, Satie Airamé, and Robert R. Warner. 2009. Biological Effects within No-Take Marine Reserves: A Global Synthesis. *Marine Ecology Progress Series* 384 (May): 33–46. https://doi.org/10.3354/meps08029.

Manfredo, Michael J., Jeremy T. Bruskotter, Tara L. Teel, David Fulton, Shalom H. Schwartz, Robert Arlinghaus, Shigehiro Oishi et al. 2017. Why Social Values Cannot Be Changed for the Sake of Conservation. *Conservation Biologyhelp_outlineAQ: Please check if the journal name is just Conservation Biology*31 (4): 772–80. https://doi.org/10.1111/cobi.12855.

Moffitt, Elizabeth A., J. Wilson White, and Louis W. Botsford. 2011. The utility and limitations of size and spacing guidelines for designing marine protected area (MPA) networks. *Biological Conservation* 144 (1): 306–318. https://doi.org/10.1016/j.biocon.2010.09.008.

Österblom, Henrik, Colette C.C. Wabnitz, Dire Tladi, Edward H. Allison, Sophie Arnaud-Haond, Jan Bebbington, Nathan Bennett et al. 2023. Towards Ocean Equity. In *The Blue Compendium: From Knowledge to Action for a Sustainable Ocean Economy*, edited by Jane Lubchenco and Peter M. Haugan, 485–521. Cham: Springer International. https://doi.org/10.1007/978-3-031-16277-0_13.

Pacoureau, Nathan, Cassandra L. Rigby, Peter M. Kyne, Richard B. Sherley, Henning Winker, John K. Carlson, Sonja V. Fordham et al. 2021. Half a Century of Global Decline in Oceanic Sharks and Rays. *Nature* 589 (7843): 567–71. https://doi.org/10.1038/s41586-020-03173-9.

Pereira, Laura M., Ignacio Gianelli, Therezah Achieng, Diva Amon, Sally Archibald, Suchinta Arif, Azucena Castro et al. 2024. Equity and Justice Should Underpin the Discourse on Tipping Points. *Earth System Dynamics* 15 (2): 341–66. https://doi.org/10.5194/esd-15-341-2024.

Prellezo, Raul, José María Da-Rocha, M.L. Deng Palomares, U. Rashid Sumaila, and Sebastian Villasante. 2023. Building Climate Resilience, Social Sustainability and Equity in Global Fisheries. *npj Ocean Sustainability* 2 (1): 1–7. https://doi.org/10.1038/s44183-023-00017-7.

Schaafsma, Marije, Felix Eigenbrod, Alexandros Gasparatos, Nicole Gross-Camp, Craig Hutton, Fiona Nunan, Kate Schreckenberg, and Kerry Turner. 2021. Trade-Off Decisions in Ecosystem Management for Poverty Alleviation. *Ecological Economics* 187 (September): 107103. https://doi.org/10.1016/j.ecolecon.2021.107103.

Sumaila, U. Rashid, Vicky W.Y. Lam, Dana D. Miller, Louise Teh, Reg A. Watson, Dirk Zeller, William W.L. Cheung et al. 2015. Winners and Losers in a World Where the High Seas Is Closed to Fishing. *Scientific Reports* 5 (1): 8481. https://doi.org/10.1038/srep08481.

Sumaila, U. Rashid, and Carl Walters. 2005. Intergenerational Discounting: A New Intuitive Approach. *Ecological Economics* 52 (2): 135–42. https://doi.org/10.1016/j.ecolecon.2003.11.012.

Sumaila, U. Rashid, Dirk Zeller, Reg Watson, Jackie Alder, and Daniel Pauly. 2007. Potential Costs and Benefits of Marine Reserves in the High Seas. *Marine Ecology Progress Series* 345: 305–10. https://doi.org/10.3354/meps07065.

Virtanen, Elina A., Juho Lappalainen, Marco Nurmi, Markku Viitasalo, Maria Tikanmäki, Jaakko Heinonen, Evgeny Atlaskin, Meri Kallasvuo, Hannu Tikkanen, and Atte Moilanen. 2022. Balancing Profitability of Energy Production, Societal Impacts and Biodiversity in Offshore Wind Farm Design. http://hdl.handle.net/10138/342902.

Vucetich, John A., Jeremy T. Bruskotter, Lily M. van Eeden, and Ewan A. Macdonald. 2021. How Scholars Prioritize the Competing Values of Conservation and Sustainability. *Biological Conservation* 257 (May): 109126. https://doi.org/10.1016/j.biocon.2021.109126.

White, Crow. 2023. Full Closure of High Seas Would Triple the Benefits. *Nature* 616 (7958): 661. https://doi.org/10.1038/d41586-023-01394-2.

White, Crow, and Christopher Costello. 2014. Close the High Seas to Fishing? *PLOS Biology* 12 (3): e1001826. https://doi.org/10.1371/journal.pbio.1001826.

Zuercher, Rachel, Natalie C. Ban, Wesley Flannery, Anne D. Guerry, Benjamin S. Halpern, Rafael Almeida Magris, Shauna L. Mahajan et al. 2022. Enabling Conditions for Effective Marine Spatial Planning. *Marine Policy* 143 (September): 105141. https://doi.org/10.1016/j.marpol.2022.105141.

PART III

Governing fisheries

6 Managing the high seas to achieve Infinity Fish

U. Rashid Sumaila

Introduction

The concept of "Infinity Fish" was introduced in my 2021 book *Infinity Fish: Economics and the Future of Fish and Fisheries*, which provocatively claims that "fish is more valuable than diamonds" (Sumaila 2021:1). The argument is that fish, as a renewable resource, can provide perpetual nutritional benefits if managed sustainably, making it "forever." Conversely, diamonds, being finite, do not offer the same perpetual value. Fish also holds more direct value to a broader population, unlike diamonds, which are valuable to a select few.

A central tenet of the Infinity Fish concept is the obligation of each generation to pass on a healthy, life-rich ocean to future generations, ensuring they too can benefit from it. I discuss in the book the sustainable management of global fish stocks, addressing the economic and ecological aspects of fisheries, and propose strategies for long-term sustainability. The book examines challenges such as overfishing, the illegal and illicit trade in fish, climate change, and economic pressures, advocating for transformative policy and management changes.

The United Nations Convention on the Law of the Sea (UNCLOS) of 1982 defines the high seas as areas beyond the 200-nautical mile Exclusive Economic Zones (EEZ) of coastal nations. Covering 45 percent of Earth's surface and 58 percent of the ocean, the high seas are the largest living space on the planet. However, human activities like overfishing (Belhabib et al. 2019), pollution (Abbott and Sumaila 2019; Issifu and Sumaila 2020), climate change (Sumaila et al. 2020; Cheung et al. 2021), and emerging issues such as seabed mining (Sumaila et al. 2023) threaten these essential ecosystems. The high seas represent the largest geopolitical feature and management unit, yet lack integrated global policies and management.

Fish stocks, such as tuna, do not recognize human-imposed boundaries, migrating across national borders and into the high seas. This interconnectivity means actions in the high seas impact EEZs (Figure 6.1).

This chapter highlights proposals to transform the high seas into a global fish bank by closing them to fishing, arguing that such a move would yield significant benefits at

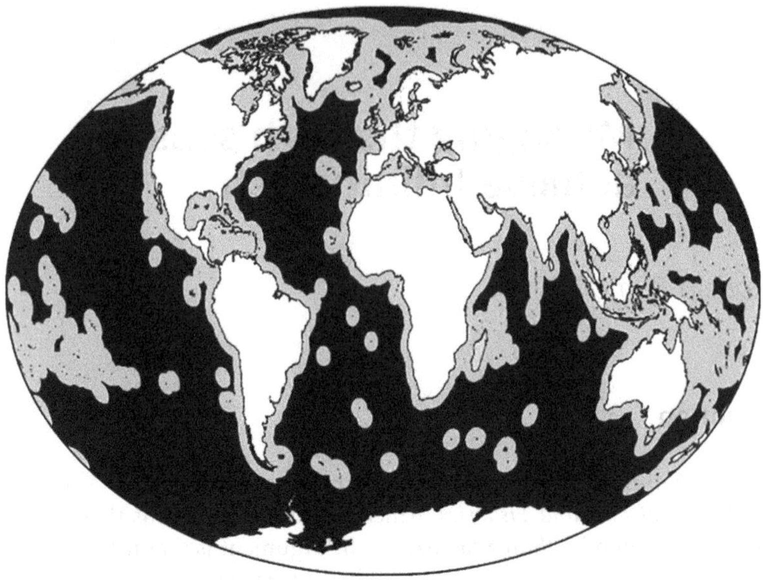

Source: Author's own.

Figure 6.1 Depicts the global ocean showing Exclusive Economic Zones in gray and the high seas in black

minimal cost (Sumaila et al. 2015). Closing the high seas to fishing could enhance the resilience and capacity of the global ocean to sustain Infinity Fish, biodiversity, and other benefits indefinitely.

Weak governance of the high seas

The high seas are attractive because of the natural resources in their waters and on the seabed. Fishing has been the most recognized ocean economic activity in the high seas to date, and bioprospecting (genetic resources) is an example of an emergent activity. These resources are public goods; hence, nobody owns them, but they belong to everybody. This makes the management of exploitative activities such as fishing complicated.

A crucial point to note is that, on balance, fisheries operating in EEZs are managed better than those in the high seas or areas beyond national jurisdictions (Sumaila et al. 2007, White and Costello 2014) notwithstanding the fact that regional fisheries management organizations (RFMOs) are trying to fill the void with varying degrees of success (Cullis-Suzuki and Pauly 2010).

I use migratory tuna to illustrate how complicated the management of high seas fisheries can be. These tuna species may spend part of their lifetime in the EEZ of coastal countries or island nations, and it is the responsibility of these countries to manage the fisheries within their EEZs. But when the tuna enter international waters, they belong to no one—until they enter the EEZ of another country. The lack of effective international management results in overexploitation (Bailey et al. 2010), with no incentives for countries to manage these fisheries sustainably within their EEZs (Munro 1979, Sumaila 1999). RFMOs were established to mitigate this by, among other things, determining global quotas for these highly migratory species that spend an important part of their lives in the high seas. Unfortunately, RFMOs are in many instances ineffective (Cullis-Suzuki and Pauly 2010).

Thus, the search for better high seas fisheries management continues, with several encouraging international agreements; for example, the COP 27 Agreement on Climate Change, the World Trade Organization Fisheries Subsidies Agreement, the 2022 UN High Seas Treaty, and the 2023 Kunming-Montreal Agreement on 30 x 30. These agreements are likely to increase the effectiveness of high seas management. However, the contention of my co-authors and me is that closing the high seas to fishing would make the greatest contribution to the conservation and sustainable and equitable use of ocean life (Sumaila et al. 2015, Sala et al. 2018).

Potential benefits of closing the high seas to fishing

It will stop bottom fishing in the high seas, which consists mainly of deep-sea trawling on seamounts, targeting chiefly slow-growing, long-lived fish such as the orange roughy (*Hoplostethus atlanticus*), which can live up to 150 years (Norse et al. 2012). Trawling the seamounts is the most destructive fishing method in the world, because the trawl nets virtually clear-cut the fragile bottom ecological community composed of long-lived corals, sponges, and bryozoans, as well as mobile invertebrates such as deep-sea starfishes and squat lobsters (Stocks and Hart 2007). Because of their vulnerable life histories (long living, slow growth, long time to maturity, small reproductive rates), seamount species are prone to quick depletion, and bottom trawling is causing the extinction of a large yet unknown number of species. In addition, many of these seamount fisheries would not be profitable without subsidies provided out of public funds (Sumaila et al. 2010, Sala et al. 2018).

It will eliminate pelagic fishing in the high seas, which targets mostly high-value species with large migratory ranges (Collette et al. 2011) that are caught both within EEZs and in the high seas (Block et al. 2011). Target species include several tuna species, swordfish, and sharks; incidental or illegally caught species include endangered sea turtles and sharks. This is putting some species at risk of collapse or extinction (Norse et al. 2012).

Pelagic fisheries in the high seas are highly inequitable. Although high seas fish are a public good, ten countries alone account for 70 percent of the total high seas catch (Sumaila et al. 2015, Sala et al. 2018). This means that developing countries with reduced possibilities to develop a high seas fleet are at a clear disadvantage. They are not only unable to develop a high seas fleet but catch of migratory species is reduced within their EEZs because of the intensive exploitation in the high seas by these ten nations. Food security in developing coastal countries is thus diminished because of the disproportionate exploitation of the high seas by a few countries. Pelagic fishing in the high seas is also heavily subsidized both through public funds and via the exceptionally low compensation to fishers on these fishing fleets, which has led many to (rightfully) describe these operations as modern slavery (Tickler et al. 2018).

Closing the high seas to fishing will also build marine biodiversity, including fish biomass in the high seas, by protecting marine life once they are in that part of the ocean. This would, in turn, generate higher catches within EEZs, thereby supporting fisheries economics and jobs (White and Costello 2014). Other benefits of closing the high seas to fishing are: (i) it can result in a fairer distribution of benefits among fishing nations (Sumaila et al. 2015, Sala et al. 2018); and (ii) increase benefits from the high seas' carbon sequestration (Sumaila and Tai 2020).

A high seas fish bank also increases resilience to climate change, which is transforming high seas biodiversity and productivity through warming, acidification, and increased hypoxia. Seawater warming means that tropical species are migrating to higher latitudes and expanding their distribution range, while polar species are contracting because they have nowhere to go. We are already detecting changes in catch composition due to warming (Cheung et al. 2010). Closing the high seas to fishing could protect high seas ecosystems from extractive activities (e.g., fishing and other destructive activities such as deep-sea mining), habitat transformation (e.g., trawling, cable laying), and other disturbances (e.g., harmful shipping, local pollution), but cannot directly protect against climate change and atmospheric and long-range pollution. It can, however, contribute to making marine ecosystems more resilient, and therefore more resilient to climate impacts (Sumaila and Tai 2020). Table 6.1 summarizes the ecological and socioeconomic benefits of closing the high seas to fishing.

Table 6.1 Benefits of closing the high seas to fishing

Ecological benefits	Socioeconomic benefits
• Preserve irreplaceable, fragile ecosystems • Preserve genetic diversity • Reduce species extinction risk • Ensure ecosystem function • Improve ecosystem resilience • Recovery of populations and ecosystem structure	• Enhance commercial fish stocks in EEZs • Increase fishery profits and reduce costs (e.g., subsidies) in EEZs • Increase sustainable employment in EEZs • Increase carbon storage potential • Achieve global ocean conservation targets • Improve equity among fishing countries

Source: Author's own.

Conclusion

In conclusion, closing the high seas to fishing offers several significant benefits. First, it would eliminate an unprofitable industry. Sumaila et al. (2010) demonstrated that high- and deep-sea bottom trawlers collectively receive subsidies amounting to 15 percent of their gross revenues while only achieving a 10 percent profit margin. Similarly, Sala et al. (2018) found that 54 percent of high seas fishing grounds would be unprofitable without subsidies and the use of modern slave labor.

Second, closing the high seas to fishing would increase fish populations in these areas, potentially spilling over into EEZs and enhancing the profitability of fishing within national waters (White and Costello 2014). An increase in biomass would also bolster the ocean's resilience to shocks such as climate change and enhance its carbon sequestration capabilities (Sumaila and Tai 2020).

Additionally, by reducing overfishing, this policy would decrease the fishing effort and the associated CO_2 emissions from the fishing sector, thereby contributing to climate change mitigation.

The beauty of closing the high seas to fishing is that it can generate these benefits without significant sacrifices in terms of catch, jobs (Sumaila et al. 2007, White and Costello 2014), or food and nutritional security (Schiller et al. 2018). This policy presents a viable and sustainable solution for preserving marine ecosystems and ensuring the long-term sustainability of global fish populations—in other words, it could help us to achieve Infinity Fish.

References

Abbott, Josh K., and U. Rashid Sumaila. 2019. Reducing Marine Plastic Pollution: Policy Insights from Economics. *Review of Environmental Economics and Policy* 13: 167–341.

Bailey, Megan, U. Rashid Sumaila, and Markos Lindroos. 2010. Application of Game Theory to Fisheries over Three Decades. *Fisheries Research* 102 (1–2): 1–8.

Belhabib, Dyhia, U. Rashid Sumaila, and Philippe Le Billon. 2019. The Fisheries of Africa: Exploitation, Policy, and Maritime Security Trends. *Marine Policy* 101: 80–92.

Block, Barbara, Ian D. Jonsen, Salvador Jorgensen, Arliss Winship, Scott Shaffer, Steven Bograd, Elliott Lee Hazen et al. 2011. Tracking Apex Marine Predator Movements in a Dynamic Ocean. *Nature* 475 (7354): 86–90.

Cheung, William W., Thomas L. Frölicher, Vicky W. Lam, Muhammed A. Oyinlola, Gabriel Reygondeau, U. Rashid Sumaila, Travis C. Tai et al. 2021. Marine High Temperature Extremes Amplify the Impacts of Climate Change on Fish and Fisheries. *Science Advances* 7 (40): eabh0895.

Cheung, William W., Vicky W. Lam, Jorge L. Sarmiento, Kelly Kearney, Reg Watson, Dirk Zeller, and Daniel Pauly. 2010. Large-Scale Redistribution of Maximum Fisheries Catch Potential in the Global Ocean Under Climate Change. *Global Change Biology* 16 (1): 24–35.

Collette, Bruce B., K.E. Carpenter, Beth Polidoro, Maria José Juan-Jordá, Andre Boustany, David J. Die, C. Elfes et al. 2011. High Value and Long Life: Double Jeopardy for Tunas and Billfishes. *Science* 333 (6040): 291–292.

Cullis-Suzuki, Sarika, and Daniel Pauly. 2010. Failing the High Seas: A Global Evaluation of Regional Fisheries Management Organizations. *Marine Policy* 34 (5): 1036–1042.

Issifu, Ibrahim, and U. Rashid Sumaila. 2020. A Review of the Production, Recycling and Management of Marine Plastic Pollution. *Marine Science and Engineering* 8: 945.

Munro, Gordon R. 1979. The Optimal Management of Transboundary Renewable Resources. *Canadian Journal of Economics*, 12 (3): 355–76.

Norse, Elliott A., Sandra Brooke, William Cheung, Malcolm R. Clark, Ivar Ekeland, Rainer Froese, Kristina M. Gjerde et al. 2012. Sustainability of Deep-Sea Fisheries. *Marine Policy* 36 (2): 307–320.

Sala, Enric, Juan Mayorga, Cristopher Costello, David Kroodsma, M.L. Deng Palomares, Daniel Pauly, U. Rashid Sumaila, and Dirk Zeller. 2018. The Economics of Fishing the High Seas. *Science Advances* 4 (6): p.eaat2504.

Schiller, Lauren, Megan Bailey, Jennifer Jacquet, and Enric Sala. 2018. High Seas Fisheries Play a Negligible Role in Addressing Global Food Security. *Science Advances* 4 (8): p.eaat8351.

Stocks, Karen I., and Paul J.B. Hart. 2007. Biogeography and Biodiversity of Seamounts. In *Seamounts: Ecology, Fisheries & Conservation*, edited by Tony J. Pitcher, Telmo Morato, Paul J.B. Hart, Macolm R. Clark, Nigel Haggan, and Ricardo S. Santos, 252–281. Hoboken, NJ: Blackwell Publishing.

Sumaila, U. R., Juliano Palacios-Abrantes, and William W.L. Cheung. 2020. Climate Change, Shifting Threat Points, and the Management of Transboundary Fish Stocks. *Ecology & Society*, 25 (4).

Sumaila, U. Rashid. 1999. A Review of Game-Theoretic Models of Fishing. *Marine Policy* 23 (1): 1–10.

Sumaila, U. Rashid. 2021. *Infinity Fish: Economics and the Future of Fish and Fisheries.* Cambridge: Academic Press.

Sumaila, U. Rashid, Lubna Alam, Kumara P. Pradhoshini, Temi. T. Onifade, Selma T. Karuaihe, Pradeep Singh, Lisa A. Levin, and Raphaelle Flint. 2023. To Engage in Deep-Sea Mining or Not to Engage: What do Full Net Cost Analyses Tell Us? *npj Ocean Sustainability* 2 (1): 19.

Sumaila, U. Rashid, Ahmed Khan, Louise Teh, Reg Watson, Peter Tyedmers, and Daniel Pauly. 2010. Subsidies to High Seas Bottom Trawl Fleet and the Sustainability of Deep Sea Benthic Fish Stocks. *Marine Policy* 34 (3): 495–497.

Sumaila, U. Rashid, Vicky W. Lam, Dana Miller, Louise Teh, Reg A. Watson, Dirk Zeller, William W.L. Cheung et al. 2015. Winners and Losers in a World Where the High Seas is Closed to Fishing. *Scientific Reports* 5 (1): 8481.

Sumaila, U. Rashid, and Travis Tai. 2020. End Overfishing and Increase the Resilience of the Ocean to Climate Change. *Frontiers in Marine Science* 7: 523.

Sumaila, U. Rashid, Travis C. Tai, Vicky W.Y. Lam, William W.L. Cheung, Megan Bailey, Andrés M. Cisneros-Montemayor, Oai Li Chen et al. 2019. Benefits of the Paris Agreement to Ocean Life, Economies, and People. *Science Advances* 5 (2): eaau3855.

Sumaila, U. Rashid, Dirk Zeller, Reg Watson, Jackie Alder, and Daniel Pauly. 2007. Potential Costs and Benefits of Marine Reserves in the High Seas. *Marine Ecology Progress Series* 345: 305–310.

Tickler, David, Jessica J. Meeuwig, Katharine Bryant, Fiona David, John A.H. Forrest, Elise Gordon, Jacqueline Joudo Larsen et al. 2018. Modern Slavery and the Race to Fish. *Nature Communications* 9 (1): 1–9.

White, Crow, and Christopher Costello. 2014. Close the High Seas to Fishing? *PLOS Biology* 12 (3): e1001826.

7 Governance of high seas fisheries

Elizabeth R. DeSombre

High seas fisheries are difficult to manage. The oceans are vast and opaque, leading to difficulties in making collective management decisions and ensuring that those who fish are not transgressing international rules. These rules are created collectively by governments because the high seas are one of the few areas of the globe over which no states have sovereign authority. The rules that are created to manage these fisheries are patchwork and incomplete, covering different areas and species across many different management organizations with only loose levels of communication or coordination. These regulatory decisions are made by governments, which face pressure from fishing interests in their own countries that are sometimes at odds with long-term management strategies. While some ocean fish species have been successfully managed at sustainable levels, overall, ocean fisheries are not well protected.

For scholars, these difficulties present research opportunities. There are structural aspects of the global governance of fisheries that offer both puzzles about, and potential solutions for, fisheries management. These structures include many different institutions, operating in similar ways with some variations, involving different sets of states, enabling comparative analysis of institutional structures, processes, or state characteristics. Actions governing fisheries can also be compared to other efforts to govern ocean resources or pollution or to efforts to manage land-based renewable resources, to ascertain what difference the ocean context makes for resource management, or what effect the difference between renewable resources and other types of ocean environmental problems has.

There are also opportunities for interdisciplinarity (Sumaila 2024): even among the social sciences, political scientists, economists, and sociologists, as well as those who focus on international relations, study global fishing from slightly different academic traditions. It may be possible to leverage insights from one field for use in another and bring them together in conceptual conversation. That is true beyond the social sciences. Creative scholars are examining the role of ecological factors in fisheries management. Among the innovative approaches are those that examine the connection between sociological and ecological systems in fisheries (e.g., Leslie et al. 2015, Schiller et al. 2024), especially in the context of climate change (e.g., Vogel et al. 2023).

The difficulties of managing fisheries

There are some advantages, compared to other environmental issues, that should benefit fisheries. Because fish are a renewable resource, they are good candidates for sustainable management: if enough of a fish species remains in the ocean to reproduce, the stock can last indefinitely. This sustainability is, however, subject to the broader conditions in the ecosystem remaining hospitable, something that climate change (Bryndum-Buchholz et al. 2019) and other forms of ocean pollution, especially by plastics (Jacob et al. 2020), have more recently challenged. For that reason, those who catch fish *should* want shorter-term catch restrictions to promote longer-term management successes and their ability to continue to catch fish.

But several structural aspects of fisheries management challenge this incentive. First, the temporal trade-off presupposes that fishers can accept short-term losses (of catches) to achieve long-term catch opportunities. For some, it may not be economically possible to forego the benefits of fishing in the present for the benefits of future sustainability. Fishers who rely on fish catches for subsistence or even basic income, however, may not be able to plan for the long term (Clark 1973, Sumaila 2004). Subsidies, discussed below (and in other chapters of this volume), can lead to overcapitalization (Sumaila et al. 2021), in which fishers have taken on debt to finance bigger and more technologically advanced vessels (Cisneros-Montemayor et al. 2016). If a lack of sufficient income causes them to lose their vessels, they cannot prioritize the long-term benefit that shorter-term restrictions can allow. In some fisheries, the normal supply and demand relationship can even be upended, and decreasing fish stocks (and decreasing income per effort, because of the difficulty of finding any fish to catch) can cause an increase in fishing effort (Barkin and Mansori 2001). Schaap and Richter (2019) also find that the technological advances that subsidies drive can decrease cooperation in fisheries.

In addition, structural characteristics of the international system can add to the risk to fishers and the difficulty of making and enforcing collective agreements to protect fish stocks for the long term. One of these is the collective action problem of management. Fishers benefit from short-term restrictions only if they are collectively implemented well enough to protect a stock. They run the risk of what game theorists refer to as "the sucker's payoff" if they act (either by individual choice, or because their governments require it) in a restrained manner but others continue to fish as usual, thus failing to protect the stock. The restrained fisher thus loses twice: by being able to catch fewer fish in the short term, and in the long term because the fishery declines. The reverse incentive is a powerful reason why collective action problems are pervasive: "free-riders" (those who fail to take environmentally beneficial action) benefit from being able to catch as much as they want in the short term, and, if others do act in a restrained manner, also benefit from the long-term health of the fishery that comes because most fishers decrease their catches.

While collective action problems in environmental management should not be overstated (Freeman et al. 2020, Ostrom 1990), they can definitely be found in fisheries management on the high seas. There are fishing states that do not belong to regulatory organizations for regions in which they fish and are therefore not technically bound by the rules of those organizations. Because of the ease of registering ships in scofflaw states (or even those without oversight capacity) (DeSombre 2005), vessel owners may intentionally choose to register in places that allow them to escape collective regulation (DeSombre 2006). For those ships that are bound by rules on the high seas, non-compliance is also possible. Again, something that is not a major problem in many resource-based international agreements (Bodansky and Van Asselt 2024) is much more of a problem on the open ocean: there is a meaningful amount of non-compliance with international rules on fishing (Lindley 2023, Rayfuse 2004), and the vast spaces of the ocean make detecting or preventing it difficult.

Another structural difficulty is that international fisheries management is what Robert Putnam (1988) refers to as a two-level game. Any management that takes place on the high seas requires negotiation among states (both to set up management organizations and to make specific regulatory decisions within them). But in engaging in these decisions, representatives of states are facing two audiences: the other states with which they are making regulatory decisions and their home populations. Domestic populations may constrain the positions states take at regional fisheries management organization (RFMO) negotiations; in particular, fishers would prefer not to be tightly regulated and, especially if they are a key political constituency, may constrain the ability of negotiators to agree to strict management. When this set of constraints is combined with potential collective action problems, it can result in a situation in which states may prefer cooperative management to succeed but seek the ability to free-ride on international management either by being less regulated than others or by getting around what regulation exists (Barkin et al. 2018). This could even include the possibility that states may not strongly oversee the compliance of their domestic fishers with international rules.

How high seas fisheries are managed

There are several regulatory contexts for addressing high seas fisheries. First is the broader framework of the United Nations Convention on the Law of the Sea (UNCLOS), sometimes referred to as UNCLOS III, to account for earlier efforts to create laws of the sea. UNCLOS completed its decade-long negotiation in 1982 and became legally binding in 1994. This agreement attempts to govern every aspect of the oceans and, as such, often involves general obligations that frame the context of an issue but do not engage in the finer details of ongoing management. UNCLOS nevertheless has several important implications for fisheries management in the high seas.

The most important effect of UNCLOS is that the agreement enclosed much of what had previously been the high seas. It formalized Exclusive Economic Zones (EEZs) in a uniform way, allocating to each country an area 200 nautical miles beyond its territorial sea in which it has the authority to control access to resources, including fish. Although some states had claimed varying degrees of management zones (or even dramatically extended territorial seas) before this, these were contentious and inconsistent. Since most ocean fish caught exist within these zones (Gelchu and Pauly 2007), UNCLOS removed many fish species from potential international management. States can agree collectively to internationally manage fish species that fall within their EEZs, which has been done with tuna species. UNCLOS also has a provision requiring that states join the regional fishing bodies in areas where vessels they flag fish (UNCLOS 1982, Articles 63–64).

A separate agreement with the unwieldy name of the Agreement for the Implementation of the Provisions of the United Nations Convention on the Law of the Sea of 10 December 1982 relating to the Conservation and Management of Straddling Fish Stocks and Highly Migratory Fish Stocks (known more colloquially as the Fish Stocks, or Straddling Stocks, Agreement), was negotiated under the auspices of UNCLOS in a context of conflict over access to and regulation of fish stocks (Henriksen et al. 2006). It specifies the obligation of states to conduct their high seas fishing within the rules of existing management organizations for species and locations where their vessels are fishing, and, if such agreements do not exist, to create them.

The most recent UNCLOS-related agreement that has implications for high seas fisheries management is the Agreement Under the United Nations Convention on the Law of the Sea on the Conservation and Sustainable Use of Marine Biological Diversity of Areas Beyond National Jurisdiction (2023), most frequently referred to as the BBNJ Treaty. It is new enough that its implications for high seas fisheries management are unclear, but it has some important components that are likely to matter.

One of these is the provision for the creation of what are called "area-based management tools," which include such things as marine protected areas (MPAs) on the high seas. MPAs in primarily nationally controlled spaces have been valuable tools for fisheries protection and management. They work in part by restricting access to fisheries or vulnerable ecosystems (though not all MPAs fully restrict fishing activity), which, on their own, can increase fish populations. But when MPAs are designed well, they can dramatically increase the available fish stocks nearby. Studies have shown increased fish catches over the long term near MPAs that restrict fishing (Stobart et al. 2009). Models may even undercount the benefits of MPAs on fish stocks because these areas often allow protected fish to grow larger, enabling them to bear more offspring (Marshall et al. 2019). A crucial element of this BBNJ process is that, while the agreement aims for consensus, these management areas can be created with the support of only three-quarters of the member states of the agreement (BBNJ Treaty, Part III), increasing the likelihood that they will be used as a conservation tool.

Another aspect of the BBNJ agreement that could have implications for fisheries management on the high seas is provisions that require environmental impact assessment for activities on the high seas (or even in EEZs) that could affect the biodiversity of the high seas. Even those actions that have a small prospect of causing harm need to go through a screening process to determine whether a full environmental impact assessment is required (BBNJ Treaty, Part IV). As of this writing, the treaty has not yet entered into force and is only just setting up the processes it will follow. Though some scholars have followed the negotiation process (e.g., Clark 2020, Mendenhall et al. 2023), there is still much to be analyzed about a negotiation that accomplished what has the potential to be major innovations in high seas governance, and more to be studied as the regulatory processes get underway.

The second, and primary, way that catches of fish on the high seas (and, in some cases, those highly migratory fish stocks that straddle the high seas and the EEZs of states) is managed is by RFMOs. These organizations are formally and practically independent of each other. They are created by separately negotiated agreements and focus on managing by species, region, or a combination of the two.

These agreements have differences. Further study to ascertain the effects these differences have on fisheries governance is warranted. Nevertheless, they share broad similarities in how they operate. These agreements are open to—and encourage membership by—any states whose vessels fish in the regions or for the species under management, though there is variation in membership rules. Most RFMOs decide on rules about catches, equipment, and other factors (such as size or season limits, and provisions for bycatch) on a regular basis, updating rules usually every year or two. Most RFMOs have scientific commissions that gather information on the health of the fish stocks and make recommendations about fishing-related regulations.

Those regulations themselves are created by the Fisheries Commission of the organization, which is made up of its member states, usually each having one vote. Comparisons between the recommendations from scientific commissions and the actual catch limits imposed by fisheries commissions suggest that the political process is rarely as precautionary as scientists recommend (Barkin and DeSombre 2013), though this phenomenon is worthy of further study to ascertain the conditions under which—in institutional structures, stock health or other species characteristics, and member states—scientific advice is more or less likely to be followed.

The voting rules in these RFMOs are important and differ from many other environmentally-focused international organizations. Historically, most fisheries commissions have had a process that allows decisions by non-unanimous voting. However, because states would be reluctant to join agreements whose rules can be made later without their support, the agreements that allow for non-unanimous voting give states the option of "objecting" (or opting out) of rules that are passed that they would prefer not to be bound by. That option is not as permissive as it may seem: states are only allowed to object during a time-limited period immediately following the passage of a rule. Furthermore, to avoid collective action problems in which a few states find themselves as the only ones bound by a rule, there are often subsequent periods during which, if a state has objected, other states have a renewed opportunity to do so. States that object are not bound by the rule.

In some RFMOs, there are additional limitations put on the ability to object. In some RFMOs (such as the General Fisheries Commission for the Mediterranean, or

GFCM), states need to provide a justification for an objection, or outline a comparably stringent management practice they will follow in lieu of the regulation to which they have objected (as in the South Pacific Regional Fisheries Management Organization, or SPRFMO). Some RFMOs that did not have these kinds of requirements for objections are adding them through amendments or renegotiations (Leroy and Morin 2018). It is also increasingly common to specify that if a certain number of states object to a measure, it ceases to bind any states (as is the case in the International Commission for the Conservation of Atlantic Tunas, or ICCAT). States are also able—and encouraged—to remove objections. Although there are exceptions, the actual use of objections procedures seems to function as intended—as a release valve to reassure states that provisions they oppose will not bind them against their will—and thus as a means of encouraging more stringent regulation rather than the "least common denominator" rules. It is nevertheless an open question whether this approach works better than the alternative. The trend is nevertheless away from this decision-making process altogether, with newer RFMOs more likely to require unanimous voting or put more limits on what objections are allowed.

Other aspects of decision-making vary across RFMOs. Apart from the issue of whether regulatory decisions are unanimous or not (and the extent to which objection procedures are regularly used), what types of activities are regulated, and how, can differ. Most RFMOs restrict catches and gear, but some, such as the Western and Central Pacific Fisheries Commission, regulate effort. Membership rules differ as well; some RFMOs allow any state to join, and others limit membership (and in any context, new members have implications for how catch limits are allocated across a greater number of fishing states).

The central question for RFMOs is how they manage the fish stocks they are created to oversee. This question is more difficult to answer than it might seem, at least if the goal is to ascertain which aspects of the regulatory process contribute to success or failure. One approach to studying RFMO effectiveness is to look at the health of fish stocks under management (Cullis-Suzuki and Pauly 2010). There have also been numerous studies, some of these by consultants or think tanks as well as by scholars, of the "best practices" among RFMOs (e.g., Lodge et al. 2007, Haas et al. 2020); enough of these have been produced that they could be evaluated against each other to determine commonalities or differences.

Management difficulties

Despite the plethora of regulatory structures governing high seas fisheries, their protection faces many difficulties. There are many ways for fishing vessels to escape regulation altogether. The academic literature often refers to the wide variety of problematic fishing activities by the name "Illegal, Unregulated, and Unreported," or IUU. Since each of the letters in this abbreviation refers to diverse ways that fish are problematically caught on the high seas, it is more productive to disaggregate the elements.

First, ships can avoid being bound by RFMO rules. When states opt out of RFMO rules through the legal processes within the organization, their ships are not bound by these rules, leaving them functionally unregulated. More consequentially, despite the general obligation within UNCLOS and its fish stocks agreement for states to join management organizations for the areas in which their ships are fishing, states sometimes remain outside of RFMOs.

A more problematic approach to the same issue is the decision by owners of fishing vessels to intentionally register their ships in states that have not joined these agreements. Some states offer open registration, in which they register ships that do not have ties to the registry state; these states are sometimes derisively referred to as providing "flags of convenience." States that draw major economic benefit from their ship registries want to encourage registration and may even court ships by promising low fees and lax regulation (DeSombre 2005).

Even fishing vessels whose states fully participate in RFMO regulations can nevertheless sometimes escape regulatory oversight or fish illegally. The ocean is vast, and it is difficult to keep track of what every vessel catches and where, even involving states that are interested in upholding international rules. Vessels may fish in closed areas or at closed times, catch fish that are undersized or otherwise restricted, use illegal gear, or, in the worst cases, disguise their catches through illegal holds or false logbooks (Joyner and von Gustedt 1996).

Finally, there are broader gaps created by the management system as implemented. RFMOs coordinate less than might be ideal, and although the species they manage are often regional, many of the vessels (as well as the market for fish) are global—fishing effort can shift from one region to another when seasons or catches are closed (Berkes et al. 2006, Barkin and DeSombre 2013). Fish species move from one area to another (shifting their ranges more dramatically under climate change, posing additional management problems), and swim in and out of EEZs. The existing patchwork of management approaches, even if it worked within its own terms, could not address all the difficulties with the management of high seas fisheries.

Creative solutions

RFMOs and other regulatory bodies have responded in creative ways to the structural difficulties their regulatory processes face. When invitations to non-member states whose vessels were fishing in their regulatory areas to join the RFMOs failed, some RFMOs developed innovative approaches to entice membership. ICCAT initiated what was initially a catch-documentation scheme to track catches within the regulatory process, and it eventually became a policy in which ICCAT member states only allowed landing, transhipment, or trade in fish caught within the regulatory process. Other RFMOs adopted similar regulations. These approaches do not prevent fishing vessels from catching managed fish outside of the regulatory process, but they decrease the opportunities for selling those fish internationally. If the biggest fish-consuming states are part of the RFMOs, these approaches can create an incentive for fishing vessels to operate within international regulation rather than try to escape it (DeSombre 2005).

Most RFMOs also keep what they refer to as IUU lists, listing the name and registry of specific vessels that are suspected of fishing in problematic ways in their regulatory areas; more recently, they have started sharing these lists across organizations (Hutniczak 2019), though much more coordination in both tracking and response would be useful. It is also becoming more common to require vessel monitoring systems (and/or observers) on member state vessels, which can increase the ability to monitor whether these vessels are complying with RFMO rules (Ewell et al. 2020, Orofino et al. 2023).

MPAs are another way to protect fisheries (and other marine resources). These have been shown to improve the health of fisheries (Gell and Roberts 2003, Halpern et al. 2010, Lester et al. 2009) by allowing fish safe areas to grow and reproduce. These have been established within EEZs, but there are now MPAs that overlap or exist entirely outside of state-controlled areas. The BBNJ Treaty and the process it creates for establishing "area-based management tools" is likely to facilitate the establishment of MPAs on the high seas, where they will be most beneficial for the species considered here.

More radical (and less politically likely) solutions propose different regulatory structures to fundamentally change the management of global fishing. These include a call for a Global Fisheries Organization to collectively manage all high seas stocks (Barkin and DeSombre 2013) or closing the high seas to fishing (Sumaila et al. 2015, Green and Rudyk 2020). Neither of these types of proposals seems especially politically viable, and the functioning of international relations means that states are always free to remain outside of international regulatory arrangements they do not want to join. But they represent an acknowledgment that the current system of fisheries management has serious problems.

Contribution to sustainable ocean governance

Successful management of fisheries is key to sustainable ocean governance more broadly. Fish are central parts of ocean ecosystems, so they are needed to keep biogeochemical systems in check. That also means that when the broader ocean system is in trouble, via climate change, pollution, or other environmental harms, fish are likely to suffer. Fisheries are thus an indicator of the sustainability of ocean governance and a contributor to it. Efforts to protect them may be able to contribute more broadly to our understanding of how to govern other marine systems and address non-oceanic biodiversity.

References

Barkin, J. Samuel, and Elizabeth R. DeSombre. 2013. *Saving Global Fisheries: Reducing Fishing Capacity to Promote Sustainability*. Cambridge, MA: MIT Press.

Barkin, J. Samuel, Elizabeth R. DeSombre, Atsushi Ishii, and Isao Sakaguchi. 2018. Domestic Sources of International Fisheries Diplomacy: A Framework for Analysis. *Marine Policy* 94: 256–263.

Barkin, J. Samuel, and Kashif Mansori. 2001. Backward Boycotts: Demand Management and Fishery Conservation. *Global Environmental Politics* 1 (2): 30–41.

BBNJ Treaty. The Agreement Under the United Nations Convention on the Law of the Sea on the Conservation and Sustainable Use of Marine Biological Diversity of Areas Beyond National Jurisdiction. 2023.

Berkes, Fikret, Terry P Hughes, Robert S Steneck, James A Wilson, David R Bellwood, Beatrice Crona, Carl Folke et al. 2006. Globalization, Roving Bandits, and Marine Resources. *Science* 311 (5767): 1557–1558. https://doi.org/10.1126/science.1122804.

Bodansky, Daniel, and Harro van Asselt. 2024. *The Art and Craft of International Environmental Law*. Oxford: Oxford University Press.

Bryndum-Buchholz, Andrea, Derek P. Tittensor, Julia L. Blanchard, William W.L. Cheung, Marta Coll, Eric D. Galbraith, Simon Jennings et al. 2019. Twenty-First-Century Climate Change Impacts on Marine Animal Biomass and Ecosystem Structure Across Ocean Basins. *Global Change Biology* 25 (2): 459–472.

Cisneros-Montemayor, Andrés M., Enrique Sanjurjo, Gordon R. Munro, Víctor Hernández-Trejo, and U. Rashid Sumaila. 2016. Strategies and Rationale for Fishery Subsidy Reform. *Marine Policy* 69: 229–236.

Clark, Colin W. 1973. The Economics of Overexploitation: Severe Depletion of Renewable Resources May Result from High Discount Rates Used by Private Exploiters. *Science* 181: 630–634.

Clark, Nichola A. 2020. Institutional Arrangements for the New BBNJ Agreement: Moving Beyond Global, Regional, and Hybrid. *Marine Policy* 122: 104143.

Cullis-Suzuki, Sarika, and Daniel Pauly. 2010. Failing the High Seas: A Global Evaluation of Regional Fisheries Management Organizations. *Marine Policy* 34 (5): 1036–1042.

DeSombre, Elizabeth R. 2005. Fishing Under Flags of Convenience: Using Market Power to Increase Participation in International Regulation. *Global Environmental Politics* 5 (4): 73–94.

DeSombre, Elizabeth R. 2006. *Flagging Standards: Globalization and Environmental, Safety, and Labor Regulations at Sea*. Cambridge, MA: MIT Press.

Ewell, Christopher, John Hocevar, Elizabeth Mitchell, Samantha Snowden, and Jennifer Jacquet. 2020. An Evaluation of Regional Fisheries Management Organization At-Sea Compliance Monitoring and Observer Programs. *Marine Policy* 115: 103842.

Freeman, Jacob, Jacopo Alessandro Baggio, and Thomas R. Coyle. 2020. Social and General Intelligence Improves Collective Action in a Common Pool Resource System. *Proceedings of the National Academy of Sciences* 117 (14): 7712–7718.

Gelchu, Ahmed, and Daniel Pauly. 2007. Growth and Distribution of Port-Based Global Fishing Effort within Countries' EEZs from 1970 to 1995. *Fisheries Center Research Reports* 15 (4), University of British Columbia.

Gell, Fiona R., and Callum M. Roberts. 2003. Benefits Beyond Boundaries: The Fishery Effects of Marine Reserves. *Trends in Ecology and Evolution* 18 (9): 448–455.

Green, Jessica F., and Bryce Rudyk. 2020. Closing the High Seas to Fishing: A Club Approach. *Marine Policy* 115: 103855.

Haas, Bianca, Jeffrey McGee, Aysha Fleming, and Marcus Haward. 2020. Factors Influencing the Performance of Regional Fisheries Management Organizations. *Marine Policy* 113: 103787.

Halpern, Benjamin S., Sarah E. Lester, and Julie B. Kellner. 2010. Spillover from Marine Reserves and the Replenishment of Fish Stocks. *Environmental Conservation* 36 (4): 268–276.

Henriksen, Tore, Geir Hønneland, and Are K. Sydnes. 2006. *Law and Politics in Ocean Governance: The UN Fish Stocks Agreement and Regional Fisheries Management Regimes*. Leiden: Martinus Nijhoff Publishers.

Hutniczak, Barbara. 2019. Coordination Between RFMOs on Mutual Recognition of IUU Vessel Lists. *Marine Policy* 107: 103596.

Jacob, Hugo, Marc Besson, Peter W. Swarzenski, David Lecchini, and Marc Metian. 2020. Effects of Virgin Micro-and Nanoplastics on Fish: Trends, Meta-analysis, and Perspectives. *Environmental Science & Technology* 54 (8): 4733–4745.

Joyner, Christopher C., and Alejandro Alvarez von Gustedt. 1996. The Turbot War of 1995: Lessons for the Law of the Sea. *The International Journal of Marine and Coastal Law* 11 (4): 425–458.

Leroy, Antonia, and Michel Morin. 2018. Innovation in the Decision-Making Process of the RFMOs. *Marine Policy* 97: 156–162.

Leslie, Heather M., Xavier Basurto, Mateja Nenadovic, Leila Sievanen, Kyle C. Cavanaugh, Juan José Cota-Nieto, Brad E. Erisman et al. 2015. Operationalizing the Social-Ecological Systems Framework to Assess Sustainability. *Proceedings of the National Academy of Sciences* 112 (19): 5979–5984.

Lester, Sarah E., Benjamin S. Halpern, Kirsten Grorud-Colvert, Jane Lubchenco, Benjamin I. Ruttenberg, Steven D. Gaines, Satie Airamé et al. 2009. Biological Effects within No-Take Marine Reserves: A Global Synthesis. *Marine Ecology Progress Series* 384: 33–46.

Lindley, J. 2023. *Fishing Non-Compliance and Culture.* Marine Policy 152: 05581.

Lodge, Michael W., David Anderson, Terje Løbach, Gordon Munro, Keith Sainsbury, and Anna Willock. 2007. *Recommended Best Practices for Regional Fisheries Management Organizations: Report of an Independent Panel to Develop a Model for Improved Governance by Regional Fisheries Management Organizations*. London: Chatham House.

Marshall, Dustin J., Steven Gaines, Robert Warner, Diego R. Barneche, and Michael Bode. 2019. Underestimating the Benefits of Marine Protected Areas for the Replenishment of Fished Populations. *Frontiers in Ecology and the Environment* 17 (7): 407–413.

Mendenhall, Elizabeth, Rachel Tiller, and Elizabeth Nyman. 2023. The Ship Has Reached the Shore: The Final Session of the "Biodiversity Beyond National Jurisdiction" Negotiations. *Marine Policy* 155: 105686.

Orofino, Sara, Gavin McDonald, Juan Mayorga, Christopher Costello, and Darcy Bradley. 2023. Opportunities and Challenges for Improving Fisheries Management through Greater Transparency in Vessel Tracking. *ICES Journal of Marine Science* 80 (4): 675–689.

Ostrom, Elinor. 1990. *Governing the Commons: The Evolution of Institutions for Collective Action*. Cambridge: Cambridge University Press.

Putnam, Robert D. 1988. Diplomacy and Domestic Politics: The Logic of Two-Level Games. *International Organization* 42 (3): 427–460.

Rayfuse, R. 2004. Countermeasures and High Seas Fisheries Enforcement. *Netherlands International Law Review* 51 (1): 41–76.

Schaap, Robbert, and Andries Richter. 2019. Overcapitalization and Social Norms of Cooperation in a Small-Scale *Fishery Ecological Economics* 166: 106438.

Schiller, Laurenne, Gregory L. Britten, Graeme Auld, and Boris Worm. 2024. Learning From Positive Deviants in Fisheries. *Fish and Fisheries* 25 (3): 409–428.

Stobart, B., Warwick, R., González, C., Mallol, S., Díaz, D., Reñones, O. and Goñi, R. 2009. Long-Term and Spillover Effects of a Marine Protected Area on an Exploited Fish Community. *Marine Ecology Progress Series* 384: 47–60.

Sumaila, U. Rashid. 2004. Intergenerational Cost-benefit Analysis and Marine Ecosystem Restoration. *Fish and Fisheries* 5 (4): 329–343. https://doi.org/10.1111/j.1467-2679.2004.00166.x.

Sumaila, U. Rashid et al. 2021. WTO must ban harmful fisheries subsidies. *Science* 374 (6567): 544–544. https://doi.org/10.1126/science.abm1680.

Sumaila, U. Rashid. 2024. Reflections on Breaking Down Silos in Fisheries Science. *Fisheries* 49 (5): 207–210.

Sumaila, U. Rashid, Vicky W.Y. Lam, Dana D. Miller, Louise Teh, Reg A. Watson, Dirk Zeller, William W.L. Cheung et al. 2015. Winners and Losers in a World Where the High Seas Is Closed to Fishing. *Scientific Reports* 5 (1): 8481.

United Nations Convention on the Law of the Sea (UNCLOS). 1982.

Vogel, Jacqueline M., Catherine Longo, Jessica Spijkers, Juliano Palacios-Abrantes, Julia Mason, Colette C.C. Wabnitz, William Cheung et al. 2023. Drivers of Conflict and Resilience in Shifting Transboundary Fisheries. *Marine Policy* 155: 105740.

8 Researching IUU: a fishy category?

J. Samuel Barkin and Chris T. Langevin

Introduction

The international community has created an array of institutions and mechanisms over the course of more than half a century to regulate and manage international fisheries. These have undoubtedly improved international fisheries governance. At the same time, nobody would argue that the system works perfectly (see Chapter 7 in this volume). The failures of international fisheries governance are often referred to as a category as IUU, or illegal, unreported, and unregulated fishing. IUU has become a common default category, within both the academic and regulatory communities, for all circumstances in which international fisheries are not managed as effectively as they might be or in which such management yields suboptimal results (United Nations Food and Agriculture Organization [FAO] 2001).

At first glance, having a general category for situations in which international fisheries governance needs improvement might seem benign. And in some circumstances, it is. But it poses real dangers as a generic research category. While it brings attention to issues that need further study, it also conflates a wide variety of different kinds of failures of governance. It risks suggesting to researchers both that they should look at the entire range of IUU behaviors if they want to study failures of international fisheries governance and that it makes sense to study illegal, unreported, and unregulated fishing as a single category of activity. It threatens to obscure links between specific fishing activities and the sorts of academic disciplinary approaches best suited to addressing those activities. It also allows policymakers to focus on certain kinds of IUU activities while suggesting that they are addressing IUU fishing more broadly. Studying IUU as an analytic construct rather than assuming it as a category helps to balance the tension faced by researchers between a holistic approach to addressing the challenges of international fisheries governance and the need to engage these challenges with the most effective analytical tools.

The central argument of this chapter is that effective research into international fisheries governance requires the disaggregation of IUU as a category. Only then can researchers and policymakers trace the causes of and identify effective policy responses to failures of governance. The chapter begins with definitions of IUU and its component elements. It discusses how these components represent distinct, and often non-overlapping, sets of behaviors. It then looks at the differential relationships between these behaviors and various disciplinary approaches to studying international fisheries governance, and the different sorts of solutions that are appropriate for the problems generated by these different behaviors. It also suggests a critique of the politics of IUU, and the utility of the general category for letting governments off the hook for their policy failures.

Definitions

The FAO defines IUU fishing as

> a broad term that captures a wide variety of fishing activity. IUU fishing is found in all types and dimensions of fisheries; it occurs both on the high seas and in areas within national jurisdiction. It concerns all aspects and stages of the capture and utilization of fish, and it may sometimes be associated with organized crime. (FAO n.d.)

It should also be noted that fishing activity, in the context of IUU, is not limited to fish species as a category but encompasses the capture of marine animals for human use and consumption. The category of IUU is a political construct designed to highlight the range of behaviors that threaten global efforts at sustainable fisheries management.

Within the broad ambit, *illegal fishing* refers to behaviors that break existing laws. This can mean fishing within national waters or in Exclusive Economic Zones (EEZs) of a state without the permission of or in contravention of the laws of that state. It can also mean fishing in international waters while flying the flag of a state without respecting the treaty obligations of that state, which in this circumstance usually means the state's responsibilities as a member of a regional fisheries management organization (RFMO). It may or may not include fishing in an area regulated by an RFMO while flying the flag of a non-member state, which might also be considered unreported or unregulated rather than illegal. This illustrates that the elements of IUU cannot always be clearly distinguished from each other, a caveat to some of the arguments made in this chapter. It also illustrates some of the complexities of the interaction of domestic and international law in fisheries regulation. The legality of what a fisher does may depend not just on where, how, or how many fish are caught, but also on the flag flown by the vessel at the time.

Unreported fishing refers to catches that are either not reported or are misreported to the relevant national fishing authorities, which may mean either the territorial state or the flag state, depending on the circumstances. It also refers to catches that should have been reported through the reporting mechanisms of relevant RFMOs, presumably either by the fishers or the territorial or flag state. Fishing can be unreported intentionally, because fishers are aware of the reporting rules and choose to break them (presumably to be able to catch more fish than a quota allows), or unintentionally, because fishers are unaware of the reporting requirements or reporting mechanisms may be inaccessible (language or procedural barriers and the like). Following a December 2023 bilateral agreement between Vietnam and Indonesia to resolve an EEZ boundary dispute, for example, illegal fishing numbers are largely unchanged. However, "neither Indonesia nor Vietnam has published a clear explanation or chart on where exactly the border line starts and ends, leaving analysts to make estimates based on UNCLOS [the UN Convention on the Law of the Sea] and continental shelf boundaries" (Tanamal 2023).

The category includes underreporting as well as nonreporting of catches; systematic underreporting of catches can be as damaging to fisheries management efforts as nonreporting. Not only does it provide cover for fishers to catch more than allowed by the rules, it generates inaccurate information for fisheries scientists, meaning that decisions on future quotas are made based on poor data. Underreporting can occur at the vessel level, leaving national authorities misinformed about national catches. It can also happen at the national level, where states intentionally and systematically underreport national catches to international regulators (see, for example, DeSombre 2022). As noted in the previous paragraph, it can be unclear at the margins when misreporting, when it is in breach of rules, shades into illegality.

Unregulated fishing refers to catches in areas or of species that are not governed by rules that bind the fishers. This could be because there are simply no rules governing that fishery, or because the relevant national authority or RFMO has not created rules. It could also be because there are international rules, but being international, they are only binding on states that sign on to them, and the vessel is flagged in a state that has not (DeSombre 2005). It might also be because legislatures and governing bodies are simply not able to respond immediately to species' migratory changes, an increasing issue for fisheries given ongoing water temperature changes. In all such cases, unregulated fishing is only considered part of IUU as a category by FAO definition if it is inconsistent with the ability of either a specific RFMO or of the community of states collectively to manage fisheries sustainably. But in a world in which a majority of fish stocks are either overfished or at risk thereof, this distinction is moot. Almost all unregulated fishing can threaten sustainability.

Differences

IUU, then, is a generic category for everything that undermines sustainable management of international fisheries, whatever the cause. The FAO argues that the broad category is both important and useful because "IUU fishing undermines national and regional efforts to conserve and manage fish stocks and, as a consequence, inhibits progress towards achieving the goals of long-term sustainability and responsibility" (FAO n.d.). In other words, the broad category is a useful rhetorical and political tool to highlight shortcomings in fisheries management processes and threats to sustainability. And it is the case that there is some overlap across categories. At the same time, it conflates a wide range of behaviors. For example, the general definition offered by the FAO, quoted above, notes that IUU may sometimes be associated with organized crime. This may be a useful frame through which to study illegal fishing. But it is a less useful frame through which to study unregulated fishing.

Illegal, unreported, and unregulated fishing in fact differ along a variety of different axes. One of these is that they are different problem types. The first, straightforwardly, is a problem of criminal activity, of people breaking existing laws. The second is an information problem; it is not that fish are being caught, but that the authorities do not know whether fish are being caught. This information problem can, but need not necessarily, mask illegal overfishing; the problem may undermine the science of fisheries management even if it does not mask illegality. The third is not a problem of laws being broken. It is a problem of laws not being made, being ineffective, or having loopholes.

These different problem types in turn point to different actors. Illegal fishing involves decisions by fishers or vessel owners to engage in illegal activity. The failure to report may involve decisions by the same people, but not necessarily; it can vary from case to case. For example, a decision to fish illegally may be made by a vessel owner and then implemented by a crew that does not know what it is doing is illegal. Like any work environment, there are opportunities for human error and breakdown in reporting at each link in a command or corporate chain, intentional or otherwise. Beyond the vessel, a decision to underreport might be undertaken by a vessel captain without the knowledge of the owner. Reporting of fishing results may fail at the vessel level, but it may also fail elsewhere in the reporting structure. Even limiting examination to a single vessel, misreporting can happen anywhere along a line of communication requiring the transfer of knowledge from and between crew members, the first mate, captain, and at times fishery observers. And while the decision to engage in unregulated fishing is taken at the vessel level, decisions about what to regulate and not regulate are taken at the political rather than industrial level. Industry representatives may be involved in such decisions, but most fishers individually are not (Barkin et al. 2018).

For example, the Indonesia Maritime Information Center (IMIC) provides regular reports of maritime security incidents. The data captures a wide range of activities, both at sea and within their IUU fishing category. Of the five IUU fishing incidents for February 2024, there were fishers with incomplete or expired documents and a lack of permits, foreign vessel fishers lacking proper Indonesian licensing, two separate groups using illegal methods (explosives) to catch fish, and one ship caught in possession of explosives (IMIC 2024). Each individual circumstance has a different catalyst for violating IUU regulations, with different ecological and maritime impacts.

Finally, these problems all operate at a range of different scales that cut across both problem and actor types. These scales range from the global to the individual. At one end of the spectrum are policymakers who represent states making international agreements to regulate fishing, national industry representatives lobbying (and sometimes becoming) those policymakers, and national and transnational corporations fishing on a heavy industrial scale. At the other end of the spectrum are artisanal fishers, indigenous fishing communities, and local authorities responsible for implementing fisheries policies operating in varied regulatory and legal environments. In the middle are a range of local and regional fishers, vessel owners, and fisheries authorities managing vessels representing investments ranging from thousands to hundreds of millions of dollars.

While IUU fishing can happen at any of these scales, the sustainability effects are likely to vary hugely. Capital-intensive overfishing, whether illegal, unreported, or unregulated (and all of these do happen), is likely to happen far from shore, often thousands of miles away, whereas the artisanal equivalent is likely to happen close to home. Warren and Steenbergen's (2021) examination of declining Indonesian fisheries shows how commercial vessels decimate juvenile sardine stocks via the use of illegally sized mesh nets, despite proper licensing, with a far more significant impact on the fish population than local artisanal fishers whose fishing may be unregulated. The more capital-intensive the vessel, the more likely it is that IUU behavior is intentional and systematic, because it is likely to involve corporate decision-makers and lawyers whose job it is to be versed in the rules. And the larger the scale, the more damage can be done by individuals. One artisanal fisher is unlikely to have a meaningful impact on a fish stock; the sustainability threat is from a group of fishers collectively. But one large trawler capable of catching hundreds of tons of fish a day can do real damage individually, which calls for both a different policy response and a different implementation strategy.

Disciplines

From a research perspective, the key upshot of the differences within the category of IUU fishing is that the individual components often need to be studied in distinct ways and from the perspectives of different disciplines. While a broad range of academic disciplines, ranging from ecology to criminology to economics to political science, can usefully inform the analysis of many aspects of IUU fishing, the balance of these disciplinary inputs across illegal, unreported, and unregulated fishing can vary greatly. Identifying the specific category within IUU fishing and understanding the applicable analytical lenses is an opportunity for especially new researchers and PhD students to chart a functional research agenda.

Criminology, for example, may be necessary to understand both decisions to engage in and methods of combating illegal fishing, especially when such activity involves criminal activities other than overfishing, such as trafficking in people. Reports from Interpol, non-governmental organizations, and other organizations examining IUU fishing and its nexus with other crimes find considerable overlap, including frequent trafficking of other illicit commodities such as animals, drugs, and arms, as well as money laundering (Interpol 2018, Phelps Bondaroff, Reitano, and Van der Werf 2015). A criminological lens allows scholars to see the concatenation of illegal activities on board particular vessels or by corporate actors in a way that a fishing-specific focus cannot. Some existing approaches that use this lens tend to examine IUU and state responses as a problem of organized transnational crime over fisheries management (see, for example, Telesetsky 2014). Within that lens, you can see similar tensions in categorization of "organized" and "transnational" crimes; like IUU fishing, these categories were created to capture many activities that require coordinated examination of illegal fishing and the networks of affiliated actors, but these broad categories are inadequate for precise analysis and response.

A criminology lens is less useful in addressing unregulated fishing. Criminology is especially helpful for understanding what effective regulation to address unregulated fishing might look like, but less so the processes through which it might be created. Similarly, it can contribute more effectively to a discussion of how to enforce reporting requirements than to one of unintentional or systematic underreporting. Furthermore, this lens risks emphasizing criminal activity in the study of fisheries management, when inadequate regulation may in fact be a greater enabler of unsustainable fishing.

Ecology, conversely, is likely to play a much greater role in the study of unregulated fishing rather than illegal fishing. In the former case, it can identify both those stocks and fishing areas that most need regulation and provide input into decisions about the details of regulation, such as quotas and equipment restrictions. It is less likely to play a key role in the study of patterns of illegality in fishing because such fishing activity is breaking established rules that already reflect the input of ecological study. Unreported and underreported fishing, meanwhile, is something that makes it more difficult to study the ecology effectively rather than something that an ecological lens can help fix.

A political science and international relations lens can be usefully applied across the various IUU problem types. Addressing the sustainability issues associated with unregulated fishing, for example, may benefit from the literature on international cooperation and negotiation. Issues of reporting may benefit from a focus more specifically on institutional design. Outright illegality in fishing behavior may call for a comparative and international law perspective. Artisanal IUU fishing, meanwhile, may benefit from the perspective of the political economy of development, while industrial-scale overfishing might benefit more from an analysis of state capture.

While it is certainly possible for researchers to figure out on a case-by-case basis what the most appropriate set of disciplinary lenses is for any given question about sustainable international fisheries management, putting so many kinds of behavior together in the category of IUU creates the risk that scholars will focus too much on some lenses in trying to develop a generic IUU methodology. Recall, for example, that the FAO's definition of IUU includes the mention of organized crime. On the one hand, it is indeed true that some cases of IUU fishing will involve organized crime. On the other hand, this is much more likely to be the case for illegal rather than for unreported or unregulated fishing, and on the industrial rather than artisanal scale. Highlighting the potential for organized crime in the definition, therefore, risks focusing general attention on a criminological rather than organizational or cooperative mode of analysis, without first addressing the question of how big a part of the IUU problem is traceable to organized crime in any particular fisheries management case.

Solutions

Not only do the component elements of IUU benefit from different disciplinary lenses, but they also demand diverse kinds of solutions. To the extent that scholars interested in international fisheries management are interested in addressing as well as understanding its failures, therefore, disaggregating IUU fishing is a necessary step. The general framing of IUU fishing, with illegality in the first slot and with its implication that it is what the fishers are doing that is the core of the problem, suggests solutions that focus on enforcement. But such a focus cannot be of much utility in addressing unregulated fishing and may well be of limited utility in addressing unreported and underreported fishing. It may even fail to successfully address some kinds of illegal fishing, particularly those at the artisanal end of the scale.

An enforcement lens will certainly be of some utility in cases of organized criminality, particularly when the criminality involves activities in addition to fishing, such as human trafficking (Belhabib and Le Billon 2022). But the best focus of enforcement efforts will vary across specific cases—sometimes it will be best focused on ships' captains and crews, at other times on owners or corporate decision-makers. In some circumstances, it might also be best focused on convincing national political and regulatory actors to enforce their own rules. Illegal fishing at an artisanal scale, conversely, may reflect either a lack of information or a lack of viable economic alternatives on the part of fishers, rather than organized criminality. To the extent that this is the case, helping fishing communities to understand the rules and providing incentives to make abiding by the rules economically tenable is likely to prove a more effective method of improving fisheries management outcomes.

Other problems of IUU fishing may require quite distinct kinds of solutions. Unreported or underreported fishing may in some cases be best approached as criminal behavior, with a focus on penalizing individuals breaking the rules, particularly when only a minority of fishers engage in it. At other times, when most fishers of a given stock engage in it, it may be better approached as a problem of institutional design, with a focus on fixing the rules. This may include reducing the administrative burden of reporting (perhaps by reducing the amount of bureaucracy the reports must go through before getting to an RFMO), improving monitoring (for example, through the use of observers or transponders), or creating catch labeling systems (which increase the value to fishers of fish caught within the rules). The labeling of a problem impacts how scholars think about solutions.

Finally, the logical solution to unregulated fishing is to regulate it. But regulation is not an activity undertaken either by fishers themselves or by the authorities that enforce regulation. It is undertaken by policy actors; in other words, representatives of states. While unregulated fishing may be similar in its ecological effects to illegal and unreported fishing, it is in important ways an entirely different kind of political and sociological issue. At the international level, it is a problem of both institutional design and political will facing states collectively rather than a problem of monitoring or enforcing behavior individually (Barkin et al. 2018). IUU as a category therefore makes more sense when studying issues like fish population levels or food supply management than it does when studying the politics of ocean governance.

This observation suggests an important critique of IUU as a category. It lets states off the hook for their failures of political will in international fisheries governance (Serdy 2016). The category is used by intergovernmental actors such as the FAO and RFMOs. It is also used by national regulators, such as the National Oceanic and Atmospheric Administration (NOAA) in the United States, particularly with respect to international cooperation on fisheries. IUU fishing as a category leads with illegal behavior and leaves regulatory failure for last. It emphasizes criminality, and more broadly misbehavior on the part of fishers, rather than misbehavior (or absence of behavior) on the part of states. NOAA's discussion of IUU fishing, for example, focuses entirely on negative behavior by fishers and positive activities undertaken by NOAA and other parts of the US government (NOAA n.d.).

In other words, the use of the category is led by states and international organizations that represent states, the same actors whose role in the failure of international fisheries governance is minimized by the category. The fusing together of the component parts of IUU into not just a category but a catchphrase has become a tool whereby states and the intergovernmental organizations they create focus attention on the misbehavior of the actors they regulate and away from their own failures to create regulation. It focuses efforts on the creation of mechanisms to enforce existing rules rather than the creation of the political will necessary to generate new rules. Scholars studying international fisheries governance therefore need to beware of IUU as a category in part because it focuses researcher attention on the behavior of fishers rather than the regulatory failures of states (see, for example, Barkin and DeSombre 2013).

Conclusion

IUU fishing as a category is not entirely unreasonable. It serves as a useful basket for much that researchers need to look at to understand the failures of international fisheries governance. And the component parts of IUU are not so clearly distinct that there is no logic to considering them together. There is considerable overlap at the margins among the categories within IUU. At the same time, uncritical adoption of IUU as a research frame is problematic. It nudges the researcher toward certain disciplinary lenses and ways of thinking about solutions, and away from others. It implies more continuity among the component parts of IUU than is necessarily there. And it focuses attention on the failures of fishers to follow the rules rather than the failure of states to make them.

Researchers of international fisheries governance, then, should be wary of IUU as a category, unless, of course, they research the history, politics, or effects of the categorization itself. Beginning with the category risks losing sight of various specific problems facing international fisheries governance, looking at specific problems through inappropriate disciplinary lenses, and prioritizing research focusing on criminality and enforcement over research focusing on political cooperation. Research that begins with specific questions about international fisheries governance rather than the broader category of IUU avoids these pitfalls.

References

Barkin, J. Samuel, and Elizabeth R. DeSombre. 2013. *Saving Global Fisheries: Reducing Fishing Capacity to Promote Sustainability.* Cambridge, MA: MIT Press.

Barkin, J. Samuel, Elizabeth R. DeSombre, Atsushi Ishii, and Isao Sakaguchi. 2018. Domestic Sources of International Fisheries Diplomacy: A Framework for Analysis. *Marine Policy* 94: 256–263.

Belhabib, Dyhia, and Phillipe Le Billon. 2022. Fish Crimes in the Global Oceans. *Science Advances* 8 (12).

DeSombre, Elizabeth R. 2005. Fishing Under Flags of Convenience: Using Market Power to Increase Participation in International Regulation. *Global Environmental Politics* 5 (4): 73–94.

DeSombre, Elizabeth R. 2022. Fisheries and Marine Mammals: The Complexities of Collective Management. In Paul G. Harris, ed., *Routledge Handbook of Global Environmental Politics*, 539–551. Routledge.

Food and Agriculture Organization. n.d. Illegal, Unreported and Unregulated (IUU) Fishing. https://www.fao.org/iuu-fishing/background/what-is-iuu-fishing/en/.

Food and Agriculture Organization. 2001. *International Plan of Action to Prevent, Deter, and Eliminate Illegal, Unreported and Unregulated Fishing.* Rome: FAO.

Indonesia Maritime Information Centre. 2024. *Indonesia Maritime Information Centre Monthly Report February 2024.* Jakarta: Bakamla. https://imic.bakamla.go.id/storage/publication-activity-reports/March2024/ycA6h4KyVUYRubTfvX5p.pdf.

Interpol. 2018. *International Law Enforcement Cooperation in the Fisheries Sector.* Lyon: Interpol.

National Oceanic and Atmospheric Administration. n.d. Understanding Illegal, Unreported, and Unregulated Fishing. National Oceanic and Atmospheric Administration, US Department of Commerce. https://www.fisheries.noaa.gov/insight/understanding-illegal-unreported-and-unregulated-fishing.

Phelps Bondaroff, Teale, Wietse Van Der Werf, and Tuesday Reitano. 2015. *The Illegal Fishing and Organized Crime Nexus: Illegal Fishing as Transnational Organized Crime.* Geneva: The Global Initiative Against Transnational Organized Crime.

Serdy, Andrew. 2016. *The New Entrants Problem in International Fisheries Law.* Cambridge: Cambridge University Press.

Tanamal, Yvette. 2023. Illegal Fishing Still Rife Despite Indonesia-Vietnam EEZ. *The Jakarta Post*, 20 April. https://asianews.network/illegal-fishing-still-rife-despite-indonesia-vietnam-eez/.

Telesetsky, Anastasia. 2014. Laundering Fish in the Global Undercurrents: Illegal, Unreported, and Unregulated Fishing and Transnational Organized Crime. *Ecology Law Quarterly* 41 (4): 939–998.

Warren, Carol, and Dirk J. Steenbergen. 2021. Fisheries Decline, Local Livelihoods and Conflicted Governance: An Indonesian Case. *Ocean & Coastal Management* 202: 105498.

9 Learning from the unexpected: informing better policies from a past reform of fisheries subsidies

Fernando Aranceta-Garza and Andrés Cisneros-Montemayor

Background

Fishery subsidies have been a key topic of discussion over the last two decades both for national policy and in international fora (see, for example, Milazzo 1998, Munro and Sumaila 2002). At the core of these discussions are key arguments from bioeconomic theory which hold that, after a fish stock is past effort at maximum sustainable yield, any further increases in effort will only lead to declining financial profits and a higher risk of serious overfishing and stock collapse (Clark et al. 2005). The World Bank estimated that this excess capacity in fisheries around the world already leads to annual lost profits totaling an estimated $80 billion (World Bank 2017). Nevertheless, recent data on global fishery subsidies suggest that some $27 billion per year are still granted, with the majority (60 percent) directly contributing to increased capacity (Sumaila et al. 2019).

These issues are central to the World Trade Organization's (WTO's) recent agreement to reduce capacity-enhancing subsidies, particularly when these are granted to fisheries that are engaging in illegal, unreported, and unregulated (IUU) fishing; vessels targeting overfished stocks; and/or vessels operating in unregulated areas of the ocean, mainly in the high seas (Sumaila et al. 2024). This can be challenging given the social importance of already exceptionally large fishing sectors and because capacity-enhancing subsidies have historically been used to grow and sustain fishing fleets (Skerritt et al. 2020). Indeed, institutional and policy inertia are partly to blame for the continued granting of such subsidies (Cisneros-Montemayor et al. 2020) even when there is much evidence that most countries are operating well beyond the capacity required for sustainable fisheries (Cisneros-Montemayor and Sumaila 2019). As discussions continue surrounding the ratification of this agreement, there are important questions about how countries will transition to new subsidy regulations, and these can guide future research that benefits fisherfolk and ecosystems.

This chapter presents a recent example of national-scale fishery subsidy reform implemented in Mexico in 2020. As we discuss below, this reform was not implemented to meet objectives related to bioeconomic targets or fisheries performance. However, there is an important opportunity to learn from this policy change and inform follow-up policies. This will depend on researchers quickly implementing monitoring and progress evaluations to see what the short-, medium-, and long-term effects of this large-scale policy are on fisheries economics, local ecosystems, and, most importantly, fishers and fish workers who depend on this sector for their livelihoods and food sovereignty.

Here, we highlight research questions that apply to similar cases throughout the world, but first provide a pre-reform context grounded in examples from some key Mexican fisheries, emphasizing legitimate bioeconomic and equity reasons for undertaking large-scale policy change. We then discuss the 2020 fisheries subsidy reform, using current available data to highlight current effects and future ones. Finally, we discuss key themes to guide future researchers in this field to address salient policy questions. These include the types of monitoring and assessment programs and indicators required to ensure that this policy change has meaningful positive impacts for the country and can inform future changes worldwide.

Pre-reform context

Like many other coastal nations throughout Latin America, fisheries in Mexico are fundamental for sustaining coastal communities throughout the country and make significant contributions to the overall national economy. This makes the overall fisheries sector quite important, but the majority of political attention and influence is often placed on a handful of high-value species that are particularly dominant in fisheries exports (Cisneros-Montemayor and Cisneros-Mata 2018). These include shrimp, tuna, and small pelagic fish such as sardines, all of which sustain economically important and vertically integrated industrial fisheries. Conversely, most fisheries employment and coastal food security and sovereignty needs are met through the work of artisanal fishers and fish workers in local value chains (Schuhbauer et al. 2019), all of which receive comparatively much less policy attention (Cisneros-Montemayor and Cisneros-Mata 2018).

The disparity in political and economic influence between the artisanal and industrial sectors in Mexico—as elsewhere in the world—is reflected in subsidies data. Whereas artisanal fisheries create more than 90 percent of fisheries employment throughout the country, in previous years industrial fisheries received almost 80 percent of total fishery subsidies (Schuhbauer et al. 2019). Subsidies for fisheries before the 2020–2021 reform included support for maintenance, gear, and vessel renewal and buybacks, income transfers, and processing capacity, but the largest portion (~25 percent) was granted for fuel (Cisneros-Montemayor et al. 2016). This subsidy was provided as a per-liter cash contribution at the pump, lowering the fuel price for artisanal and industrial vessels. This partly explains the much larger total granted to industrial fisheries that operate with much higher fuel costs; indeed, this form of subsidy provision reduces incentives for fuel efficiency.

A legitimate argument for granting more operating subsidies to industrial fisheries is that they are more efficient and produce higher overall catch despite their relatively smaller size in terms of vessels or employment. Data available for Mexico, however, suggest that this is not the case, as artisanal fisheries also contribute more than 50 percent of total fisheries catch (Schuhbauer et al. 2019). In ecosystems where species can be caught in shallow waters with artisanal gears, industrializing fisheries shifts catch from one fleet to another without increasing overall production and can bring significant negative impacts to habitat and bycatch species. In Panama, for example, discards by industrial fleets have caused some US$50 million in overall losses for artisanal fleets that could have benefited from catching discarded juveniles once they grew to commercial size (Cisneros-Montemayor et al. 2018). Similar observations have been made in other countries, all pointing to a general lack of transparency but also an obvious lack of efficiency, bioeconomic, or equity goals behind the types and distribution of subsidies being granted (Cisneros-Montemayor et al. 2020).

Shrimp fisheries are a good illustrative case because they target species with high commercial value and can be pursued both by artisanal and industrial fisheries. Shrimp also have a short lifespan that aids in sustaining catches yet are fished with gears that can have significant impacts on other species through bycatch and habitat damage. The shrimp industry in Mexico is the most important fishery in socioeconomic terms, ranking first in value and volume of exports, port infrastructure, number of industrial vessels, and generation of direct (40,000) and indirect jobs (CONAPESCA 2022). The fishery landed 55,000 tons in 2020–2021, 56 percent by the artisanal sector, with an approximate landed value of US$2 billion (CONAPESCA 2022).

Despite the significant expansion in fishing effort over the last several decades, shrimp catch in Mexico has shown interannual variability but remained mostly stable overall (Figure 9.1). This is likely in part because of a sequential adding of shrimp species and stocks as others became locally overexploited (Aranceta-Garza et al. 2021), though this is difficult to observe in official data because catch was not differentiated by species until very recently (Figure 9.1). On the other hand, the artisanal fleet operates under a poor data context. Fishery statistics show yield records with a positive trend, ranging from 15,000 tons in the 1990s to 35,000 tons in 2017 (CONAPESCA 2022). However, the total number of fishers and effective effort are unknown, as are effects of subsidies on fishing operations. This highlights issues of fisheries and subsidies data quality and transparency that will be further discussed below.

Shrimp are a good example of fisheries expansion leading not necessarily to stock collapse but to rapidly declining per-vessel profit; between the 1980s and 2021, the shrimp fishing fleet decreased from 1,700 to 647 vessels (CONAPESCA 2022). The historical effect of overcapacity and overexploitation made most industrial vessels, before 2019–2020, dependent on the diesel subsidy to operate with minimal profit margins (Cisneros-Montemayor and Clarke 2019). Economic data are often difficult to find in Latin American fisheries (and those of most other regions), owing to the broader lack of collection of bioeconomic data in most national monitoring programs and also to the (perhaps understandable) reluctance of private fishing firms to publicly disclose

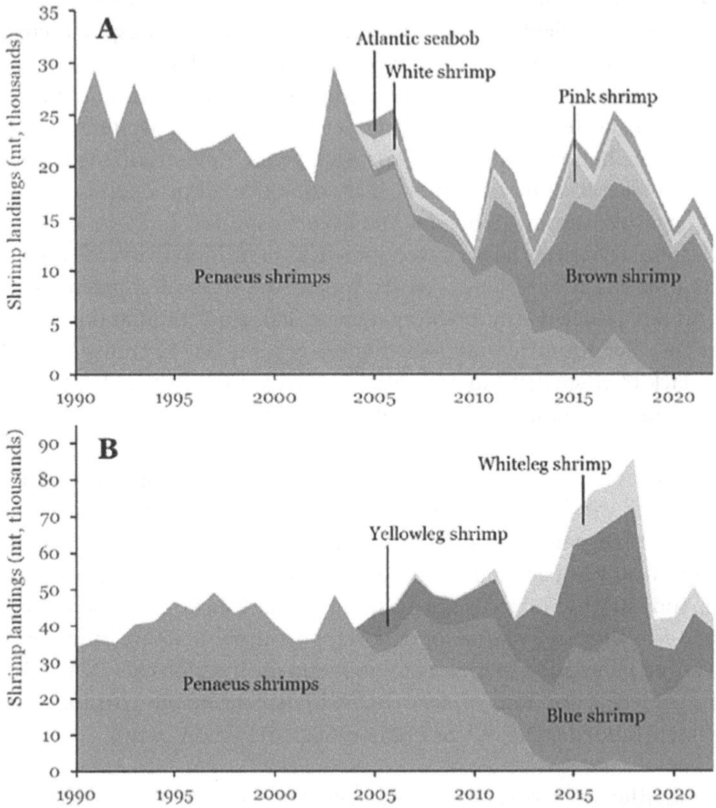

Source: Data from UN Food and Agriculture Organization (2024).

Figure 9.1 Official reported shrimp landings in the Mexican Atlantic (A) and Pacific (B), 1950–2022

their profit margins. However, available data for Mexican shrimp fisheries suggest that fleets in recent years have operated under very tight margins, with fuel making up the majority of variable costs (~40 percent) and labor another important portion (~25 percent) (Cisneros-Montemayor and Clarke 2019). Crucially, these data also show that subsidies were indeed the main source of profit for firms in this fishery, shifting operating profits from around -20 percent to +10 percent margins (Figure 9.2). These data do align with expected outcomes from the rapid historical expansion of fleets in Mexico (Cisneros-Montemayor et al. 2013) and observed subsequent reductions in catch and profit in the shrimp fishery (Aranceta-Garza et al. 2021). National-scale data for other fisheries show similar trends, where industrial fisheries become less profitable over time without accounting for subsidies (Schuhbauer et al. 2019).

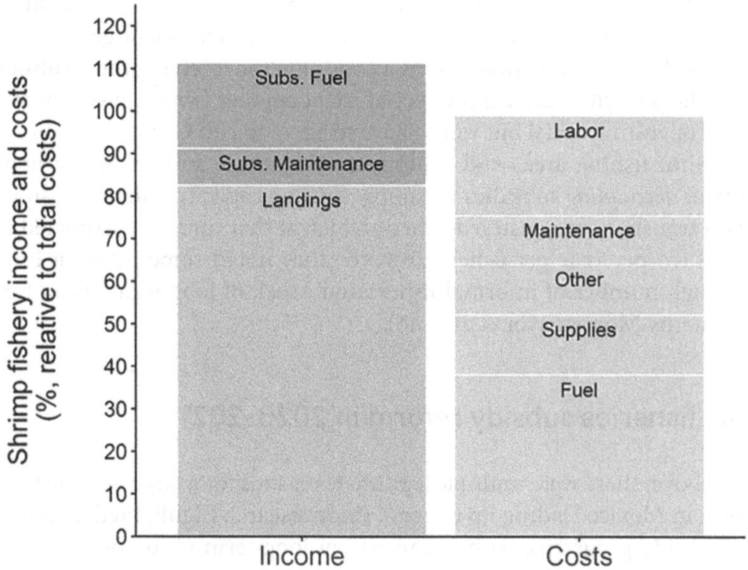

Source: Data from Cisneros-Montemayor and Clarke (2019).

Figure 9.2 Mexican shrimp fishery cost structure including subsidies, pre-2020 reform

An international context that is relevant here is the multilateral and binding WTO agreement on fisheries subsidies, corresponding to Sustainable Development Goal 14.6 (Sumaila et al. 2024). The agreement was adopted in 2022 and has not yet been ratified, but negotiations were well underway in 2020. Mexico publicly supported these reforms, and the Mexican Ambassador to the WTO, Roberto Zapata, served as the chair of the fisheries subsidies negotiations from 2017–2020.

The core rationale for international cooperation on subsidies reform is that capacity-enhancing subsidies are a key reason for widespread global overfishing and associated profit losses, and contribute to unfair competition between developed and developing nations. Thus, a multilateral agreement is necessary (Cisneros-Montemayor et al. 2020). Generally, the current regulations curtail the granting of subsidies for individuals or vessels: (1) found to be fishing illegally, (2) targeting overfished stocks, or (3) operating outside of their own country's waters (WTO 2024). These are important points to consider if Mexico's new subsidy policy should need to show alignment with international commitments.

In prior research on options to reform subsidy programs, Cisneros-Montemayor et al. (2016) found that reorienting and conditioning were particularly helpful strategies. *Reorienting* refers to the shifting of capacity-enhancing subsidies towards management enforcement, gear development, or other actions to directly support fisheries without increasing their capacity. *Conditioning* might retain some subsidies traditionally identified as capacity-enhancing (such as maintenance or gear switch-outs), but with strictly enforced regulations as a condition for receiving these subsidies. For example, fishers might receive more fuel-efficient engines (which lower emissions but also reduce operating costs) but would have to agree to run GPS devices on their vessels to monitor fishing areas and timing. Notably, these authors also proposed the possibility of *decoupling* subsidies by simply shifting capacity-enhancing subsidies to yearly cash transfers for registered fishers, which at that time was estimated to result in at least $470 per year per fisher. However, they noted some inherent limitations given the high number of informal fishers and a lack of long-term vision for such a policy (Cisneros-Montemayor et al. 2016).

Mexican fisheries subsidy reform in 2020–2021

As shown above, there were multiple legitimate reasons for a large-scale fisheries subsidy reform in Mexico leading up to 2020. Prior research highlighted a need for clear goals for subsidy programs, with a transparent long-term vision on social and ecological impacts and ongoing monitoring to evaluate and adapt to results (Cisneros-Montemayor et al. 2016). One important prior reform in the previous decade had provided a one-time increase in the percentage value of fuel subsidies per liter for fisheries, but with the corresponding absolute value per liter at the time held constant from that point onward (Sanjurjo and Arenas 2019). Given the increases in gasoline and diesel prices over time, this effectively resulted in a gradual decrease in the percentage contribution of fisheries subsidies to fuel costs, but still with some incentives to continue operating to receive such coupled subsidies.

Despite this ongoing increase in research into the bioeconomic effects of fisheries subsidies and reforms in Mexico and elsewhere, the most important trigger of large-scale reform was the emergence in 2020 of the Covid-19 pandemic. Like all other countries, Mexico's response included urgent and sweeping changes in fiscal, social, and public health policies. These changes were implemented with unprecedented speed and did not go through the planning, deliberation, and oversight processes that are normally mandated or at least encouraged in public policy.

Such ad hoc adaptations to unforeseen and urgent challenges are indeed common and sometimes unavoidable in the developing world. In Mexico, some 60 percent of national employment—including the vast majority of fishers and fishworkers—is in the informal sector, where it is exceedingly difficult to implement or monitor policies based on fiscal instruments (Pedroza-Gutiérrez and López-Rocha 2021). Fisheries were impacted almost immediately by the closure of both local and national seafood markets, many of which are open air and often crowded—and therefore subject to the strictest initial health regulations—leading to rapid decreases in demand and ex-vessel prices for all seafood products (Amos et al. 2022). This, combined with fear of infection in coastal rural communities without access to health facilities, de facto shut down most commercial fishing activities and sometimes entire communities.

Before the onset of the Covid-19 pandemic, the Mexican federal government had been following an overall strategy of centralization of decision-making but decentralization of social program implementation, and had emphasized individual cash transfers in national subsidy programs. Thus, the rapid policy changes undertaken as part of the response to the Covid-19 pandemic enabled a similarly sweeping reform of fishery subsidies that simultaneously aligned with overall government narratives. Under the new program, named *Bienpesca*, individual fishers registered in official lists receive approximately $420 in a one-time yearly cash deposit in an account within a nationalized bank. The program was announced and implemented in months, with all prior programs effectively ending immediately.

The remarkably rapid shift in the overall portfolio of fisheries subsidies in Mexico is clear in available data (Figure 9.3), where individual cash transfer programs grew from around 20 percent in 2020 to virtually 100 percent of all yearly fisheries subsidies provided by 2021 (Causa Natura 2024). It is particularly interesting from a fisheries policy standpoint that the shift towards individual cash transfers beginning in 2020 was enabled by reductions in subsidies across the board (Figure 9.3), including those for monitoring and enforcement, capacity building, and other types of support that are commonly identified as some of the most effective for achieving long-term goals for sustainable and equitable fisheries (Martini and Innes 2018, Cisneros-Montemayor et al. 2016).

It is important to note that the stated reasons for shifting subsidies to individual cash transfers in Mexico did not emphasize long-term environmental or economic goals for fisheries performance. First, the new subsidy regime would allow for the rapid disbursement of cash to individuals in communities throughout the country, a particularly timely feature given the near halting of fishing income at the time. Second,

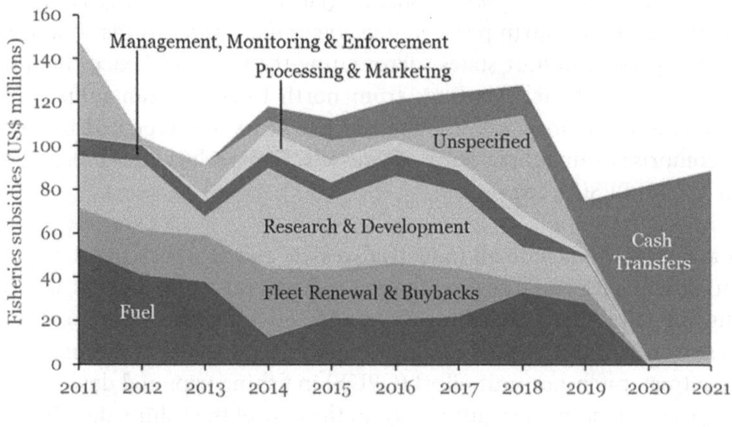

Source: Data from Causa Natura (2024).

Figure 9.3 Fisheries subsidies in Mexico by type, 2011-2021

the disbursement of cash directly to individuals allows the government to support them without intermediaries (aligning with decentralization), including large fishing companies in the case of industrial fisheries. Interestingly, however, this also bypasses fishing cooperatives, which have historically been the main form of social organization in fisheries throughout the country. These local cooperatives, sometimes organized within larger federations, have been shown to be key for supporting collective benefits, negotiating better prices for fish catch, and lobbying and resisting centralized political decisions (Espinosa-Romero et al. 2014, de la Torre et al. 2021). Some of these aspects are beyond the purview of fisheries bioeconomics per se, but they are important for providing context to the types of effects that might be expected and for the types of research and evaluation programs that would be necessary to appropriately monitor outcomes.

Individual-based subsidies are also controversial given that artisanal fisher registries are notoriously inaccurate. Fishing cooperatives had previously provided an important platform for collective action and an intermediary for subsidies that could serve locally-recognized fishers (Espinosa-Romero et al. 2014, de la Torre et al. 2021), though there have indeed been instances of corruption and abuse to misdirect subsidy funds. In any case, the current recipient list (i.e., 'officially' recognized fishers) includes 155,000 individuals out of a minimum estimated 300,000 fishers in the country (Cisneros-Montemayor et al. 2013), without even accounting for fishworkers, mostly women, throughout the value chain (Torre et al. 2019). An important future research question for many similar places is how policy implementation strategies could provide flexibility to facilitate informal arrangements that may address locally-recognized inequities.

Early effects of subsidy reform in Mexican fisheries

As a case study, we analyze the effect of the subsidy reform of 2019–2020 on the Gulf of Mexico shrimp fishery from 2017 to 2023. Briefly, this is a multi-species and multi-fleet fishery, mainly targeting brown shrimp (*Farfantepenaeus aztecus*) in the north-central region and pink shrimp (*Farfantepenaeus duorarum*) in the southern region. The fishery is present in four states surrounding the Gulf of Mexico that provide 30 percent of national shrimp landings from north to south: Tamaulipas, Veracruz, Campeche, and Quintana Roo. For the last five years, the reported industrial fleet per state comprises Tamaulipas with ~175 vessels, Campeche with ~100, and Veracruz with ~30 (CONAPESCA 2024).

For this analysis, we include all industrial vessels and all species as a single fishery. Results highlight a potential regime change and general decline across all effort indicators (fishing trips, effective fishing days, and active vessels; Figure 9.4) starting in the 2020 season, associated with, among other factors, the loss of marine diesel subsidies. In contrast, catch-per-unit-effort (CPUE) in fishing trips and days has shown an increasing trend since 2020 (Figure 9.4a). In the case of the fishing days indicator, the trend only shows a stabilization in the CPUE and a decline in effort for the analyzed period, showing that the vessel's catch-per-day indicator is more complex and variable than fishing trips. In the long run, however, there was a 40 percent decrease in industrial shrimp vessels in the Gulf of Mexico (~250 to ~150 vessels). Other studies in the Gulf of California shrimp fishery have shown a 70 percent fleet reduction to maximize the fishery's net present value, including the unregulated small-scale fleet (Aranceta-Garza et al. 2021).

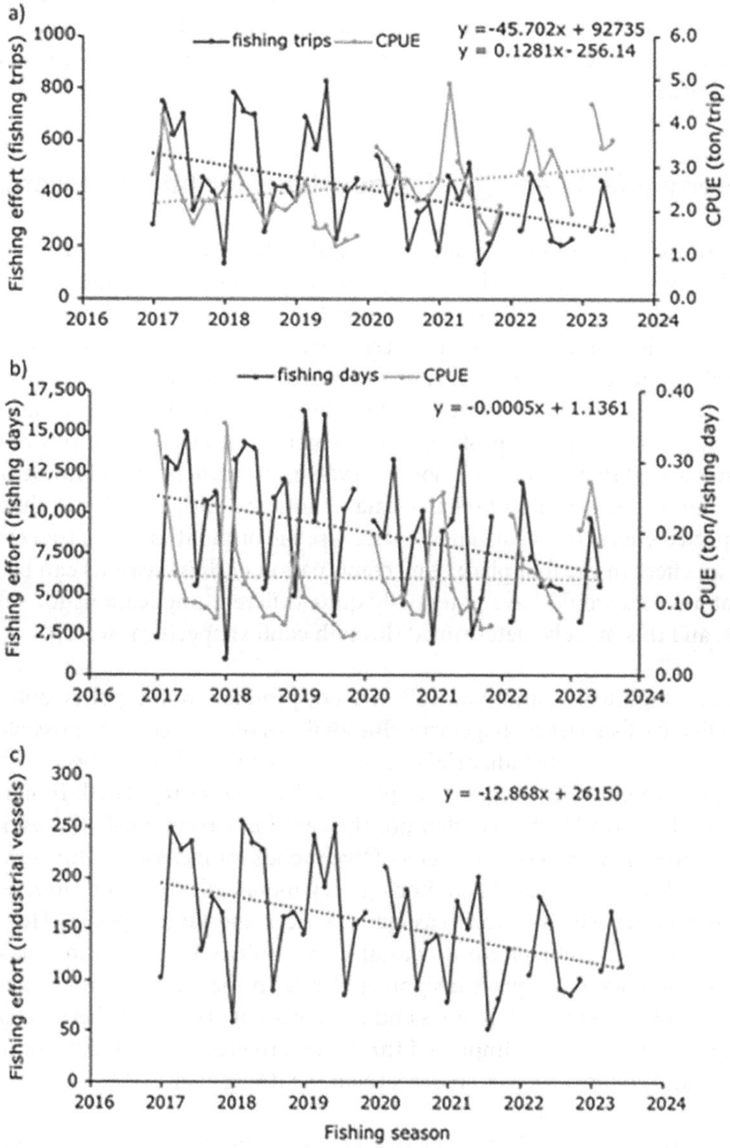

Source: Data from CONAPESCA (2024).

Figure 9.4 Mexican shrimp fishing effort and catch-per-unit-effort (CPUE) in the Gulf of Mexico in number of (a) trips, (b) days at sea, and (c) vessels

According to the case study results, the removal of fuel and vessel maintenance subsidies—regardless of the reform's policy goals—has indeed resulted in a reduction of effort within an overcapitalized fleet. Fishery managers could take advantage of the current state of the fishery fleet by establishing effort regulations to achieve maximum sustainable effort levels for the Gulf of Mexico. The remaining vessels have increased CPUE, which is expected to materialize more quickly for species with fast population growth rates, such as shrimp. Additional benefits of this fleet reduction for (mainly artisanal) fleets targeting shrimp bycatch species would also be expected but may take longer to observe.

Long-term effects and guiding questions for future research

Clearly, subsidy programs can have large-scale effects, and this is one of the main rationales for ensuring that these programs are aligned across and within nations (Sumaila et al. 2024). A first step in gauging the types and magnitude of these effects can be taken by using traditional fisheries data that, uncertainties aside, are most often included in national statistics and monitoring programs. As shown in this chapter, for example, CPUE and effort would be the first place where one would expect to see the effects of a change in profit and cost structure because of a subsidy reform (i.e., see Figure 9.4). If these effects are not observable, researchers should immediately ask whether this is due to a lack of reliable data, or to some mitigating factor that is offsetting expected effects from subsidies, or because the original subsidy program was not having an effect in the first place. Any combination of these reasons can be true, but different answers would have potentially quite different implications for subsequent policies, and this must be determined through context-specific research.

To be clear, monitoring and data collection of production and policy outcomes are key for effective fisheries management. The analyses shown here were possible because some fisheries—regularly industrial ones with more focused target species—have long and ongoing monitoring programs in place and are better regulated. In many countries around the world, this is often not the case for artisanal fisheries even though they comprise the vast majority of global livelihoods for fisherfolk. This is in part due to the technical challenges of monitoring very mobile, flexible, and diverse types of artisanal fisheries with variable seasonal practices and target species. However, the historic marginalization of rural coastal communities from decision-making and 'scientific' methodologies plays a significant role in the lack of appropriate ways to recognize and address the dynamics and challenges of artisanal fisheries (Finkbeiner et al. 2017), and this can be improved through a broader acknowledgment of current inequities and concrete steps to redress them (Spalding et al. 2023).

Future research into the effects of fisheries subsidy reform can benefit from considering an ideal policy cycle approach and interrogating the observed process at various stages. A classic model of a policy cycle (Edelmann and Albrecht 2023) comprises five different yet overlapping steps that are commonly followed in fisheries management yet not often researched as a whole. First, one must develop an overall agenda with specific, measurable, and attainable goals to be reached within a set period. Second, a range of policy options might be constructed based on inputs from a wide array of stakeholders, including fishers but also fishworkers who may often be ignored in management decisions (Crosman et al. 2022). Third, ideally within a similar multi-stakeholder process, a policy would be selected out of several options as the one most likely to effectively reach intended goals in the context in which it is to be deployed. Fourth, the implementation of a policy and its various programs and strategies should first ensure that the various organizations and institutions necessary are all aligned and understand their various roles, responsibilities, and interlinkages. This is crucial for fisheries that all operate within complex social-ecological systems and often ill-defined regulatory frameworks (Espinosa-Romero et al. 2014). Finally, a predetermined evaluation plan should follow throughout the entire process to enable real-time monitoring of outcomes to inform policy adaptation. As alluded to in the sections above, any of these steps yields many pertinent research questions that could inform future best practices, particularly if multiple researchers work to collectively address interlinked steps of the cycle.

In the context of social-ecological systems thinking, it is important to remember that fisheries are not only a profit-driven activity. While they indeed generate billions in global economic activity, they also underpin livelihoods, cultural practices, food security, and sovereignty in local communities throughout the world (Crosman et al. 2022). This means that it is essential to move beyond the first-order bioeconomic effects of subsidy reform to properly monitor its potential effects on social dynamics and well-being. This is true at national and international scales but is particularly important in places where fisheries may not be a large sector nationally but could be essential for local economies and livelihoods, as these situations increase the risk that local impacts might be lost within national overviews. This equity-focused approach recognizes that while better fisheries data and analyses are useful, they can also perpetuate colonial power dynamics that continue to marginalize fisherfolk (and many other communities) throughout the world. New policies must then integrate better data with equity goals that recognize and redress past harms and support local goals and perspectives (Croft et al. 2024).

In this sense, there are two types of indicators that might be collected and analyzed (Cisneros-Montemayor et al. 2023). First, total production indicators are those that account for overall catches, employment, effort, stock status, and so on. These are some of the most common indicators in national fisheries statistics and, as noted above, can be especially useful to observe overall trends. However, such indicators cannot shed light on inequities or group-specific effects of a national policy, which are more likely to impact already marginalized and often vulnerable groups. It is therefore important to move beyond these indicators into a second group of disaggregated indicators. As their name implies, these indicators may collect information on similar themes as those of the previous group, but with a particular emphasis on disaggregating between distinct groups. For example, this includes collecting data not just on overall landings or employment but on how employment has changed specifically for women, an ethnic group, migrants, or other types of social groups (keeping in mind intersectionality) that are relevant in a particular context.

Even the limited available data on the effects of this subsidy reform speaks to the importance of designing fisheries policy, including subsidy programs, in ways that will effectively meet societal goals. Indeed, one of the key gaps that we highlight in this chapter—and which has been identified in prior work—is the overall lack of long-term goals for such a program. It is possible that these goals do exist and have not been communicated publicly, yet this would also be an important problem given that there is much research showing that transparency in the thinking and assumptions behind policy decisions and their implementation is one of the most important aspects to providing legitimacy to the overall governance process (Jentoft 2004).

As shown in this chapter, there is empirical evidence to support the theoretical expectation that large-scale reforms to fisheries subsidies will have significant real-world impacts on fishing operations. This is particularly true for industrialized fisheries that primarily operate under a financial profit motive, though this also applies to artisanal fisheries that are fully integrated within local and often international value chains. Such reforms must be accompanied by equity-focused research efforts to ensure that any fisheries policies are truly serving well-being at national scales and especially for frontline coastal communities. The types of indicators and research themes that we highlight here are intended to be useful for a wide range of fisheries, but they need to be thoughtfully considered in the specific social contexts where they are to be applied. As more countries move towards a meaningful integration of long-term social goals in the ecological and economic management of natural resource sectors, we must learn from past experiences to ensure that our programs have the greatest chance of success.

References

Amos, Holly, Alfredo Giron-Nava, Tu Nguyen, Andrés M. Cisneros-Montemayor, Mathieu Colléter, Pedro C. González-Espinosa, and Wilf Swartz. 2022. Collapse and recovery of seafood wholesale prices in time of COVID-19. *Fish and Fisheries* 23(4): 963–976. https://doi.org/10.1111/faf.12665.

Aranceta-Garza, Fernando, Juan Carlos Seijo, and Francisco Vergara-Solana. 2021. Bioeconomics of technological interdependencies in a sequential shrimp fishery: Optimal size of the industrial fleet in southern Gulf of California. *CICIMAR Oceánides* 36(1–2): 1–18. https://doi.org/10.37543/oceanides.v36i1-2.254.

Causa Natura. 2024. Pescando datos. Subsidios pesqueros. Available at: https://pescandodatos.causanatura.org/subsidios-pesqueros.html

Cisneros-Montemayor, Andrés M., and Miguel A. Cisneros-Mata. 2018. A medio siglo de manejo pesquero en el noroeste de México, el futuro de la pesca como sistema socioecológico. Relaciones. *Estudios de historia y sociedad* 39(153): 99–127. https://doi.org/10.24901/rehs.v39i153.392.

Cisneros-Montemayor, Andrés M., Miguel A. Cisneros-Mata, Sarah Harper, and Daniel Pauly. 2013. Extent and implications of IUU catch in Mexico's marine fisheries. *Marine Policy* 39: 283–288. https://doi.org/10.1016/j.marpol.2012.12.003.

Cisneros-Montemayor, Andrés M., and Tayler M. Clarke. 2019. *Exploración de los Posibles Impactos de las Reglas de la OMC Sobre Subsidios a la Pesca: El Caso del Camarón en la Costa Oeste de América Latina*. International Institute for Sustainable Development. Available at: https://www.iisd.org/publications/subsidios-pesca-camaron-america-latina.

Cisneros-Montemayor, Andrés M., Sarah Harper, and Travis C. Tai. 2018. The market and shadow value of informal fish catch: A framework and application to Panama. *Natural Resources Forum* 42(2): 83–92.

Cisneros-Montemayor, Andrés M., Yoshitaka Ota, Megan Bailey, Christina C. Hicks, Ahmed S. Khan, Anthony Rogers, U. Rashid Sumaila et al. 2020. Changing the narrative on fisheries subsidies reform: Enabling transitions to achieve SDG 14.6 and beyond. *Marine Policy* 117: 103970. https://doi.org/10.1016/j.marpol.2020.103970.

Cisneros-Montemayor, Andrés M., Enrique Sanjurjo, Gordon R. Munro, Victor Hernández-Trejo, and U. Rashid Sumaila. 2016. Strategies and rationale for fishery subsidy reform. *Marine Policy* 69: 229–236. https://doi.org/10.1016/j.marpol.2015.10.001.

Cisneros-Montemayor, Andrés M., and U. Rashid Sumaila. 2019. Busting myths that hinder an agreement to end harmful fisheries subsidies. *Marine Policy* 109: 103699. https://doi.org/10.1016/j.marpol.2019.103699.

Clark, Colin W., Gordon R. Munro, and U. Rashid Sumaila. 2005. Subsidies, buybacks, and sustainable fisheries. *Journal of Environmental Economics and Management* 50(1): 47–58. https://doi.org/10.1016/j.jeem.2004.11.002.

CONAPESCA. 2022. *Anuario Estadístico de Acuacultura y Pesca*. September 09, 2022. Available at: https://www.gob.mx/conapesca/documentos/anuario-estadistico-de-acuacultura-y-pesca.

CONAPESCA. 2024. *Avisos de Arribo, Cosecha y Producción*. August 15, 2024. Available at: https://conapesca.gob.mx/wb/cona/avisos_arribo_cosecha_produccion, last accessed November 13, 2024.

Croft, Freya, Hugh Breakey, Michelle Voyer, Andrés Cisneros-Montemayor, Ibrahim Issifu, Makrita Solitei, Catherine Moyle et al. 2024. Rethinking blue economy governance: A blue economy equity model as an approach to operationalise equity. *Environmental Science & Policy* 155: 103710. https://doi.org/10.1016/j.envsci.2024.103710.

Crosman, Katherine M., Edward H. Allison, Yoshitaka Ota, Andrés M. Cisneros-Montemayor, Gerald G. Singh, Wilf Swartz, Megan Bailey et al. 2022. Social equity is key to sustainable ocean governance. *npj Ocean Sustainability* 1(1): 4. https://doi.org/10.1038/s44183-022-00001-7.

De la Torre, Diana A. Ramos, María C. Anaya-Corona, Juan L. Cifuentes-Lemus, and Jesús T. Ponce-Palafox. 2021. Historical background of fishing and cooperative fisheries in Mexico (1917–2018): Legal and institutional aspect. *IOSR Journal of Agriculture and Veterinary Science* 14: 31–37. Available at: https://www.iosrjournals.org/iosr-javs/papers/Vol14-issue2/Series-2/F1402023137.pdf.

Edelmann, Noella, and Valerie Albrecht. 2023. The Policy Cycle: A framework for knowledge management of practitioners' expertise and role in participatory processes. *Frontiers in Political Science* 5: 1223013. https://doi.org/10.3389/fpos.2023.1223013.

Espinosa-Romero, María Jose, Laura F. Rodríguez, Amy Hudson Weaver, Cristina Villanueva-Aznar, and Jorge Torre. 2014. The changing role of NGOs in Mexican small-scale fisheries: From environmental conservation to multi-scale governance. *Marine Policy* 50: 290–299. https://doi.org/10.1016/j.marpol.2014.07.005.

Finkbeiner, Elena M., Nathan J. Bennett, Timothy H. Frawley, Julia G. Mason, Dana K. Briscoe, Cassandra M. Brooks, Crystal A. Ng et al. 2017. Reconstructing overfishing: Moving beyond Malthus for effective and equitable solutions. *Fish and Fisheries* 18(6): 1180–1191. https://doi.org/10.1111/faf.12245.

Food and Agriculture Organization. 2024. FAO Fisheries and Aquaculture: Global Statistical Collections. FAO Fisheries and Aquaculture Division. https://www.fao.org/fishery/en/statistics.

Jentoft, Svein. 2004. Institutions in fisheries: What they are, what they do, and how they change. *Marine Policy* 28(2): 137–149. https://doi.org/10.1016/S0308-597X(03)00085-X.

Martini, Roger, and James Innes. 2018. *Relative effects of fisheries support policies.* Organisation for Economic Co-operation and Development.

Milazzo, Matteo. 1998. *Subsidies in world fisheries: A reexamination*, Vol. 23. World Bank Publications.

Munro, Gordon, & Sumaila, U. Rashid. 2002. The impact of subsidies upon fisheries management and sustainability: The case of the North Atlantic. *Fish and Fisheries*, 3(4): 233–250. https://doi.org/10.1046/j.1467-2979.2002.00081.x.

Pedroza-Gutiérrez, Carmen, and Jorge A. López-Rocha. 2021. Ungovernable systems: The strength of informal institutions in the sea cucumber fishery in Yucatan, Mexico. *PLOS One* 16(3): e0249132. https://doi.org/10.1371/journal.pone.0249132.

Sanjurjo, Enrique, and Esteban Arenas. 2019. *Reforming harmful fisheries subsidies: Making the economic case for Mexico.* WWF. https://wwfint.awsassets.panda.org/downloads/reforming_harmful_fisheries_subsidies__mexico_april_2019.pdf.

Schuhbauer, Anna, Andrés M. Cisneros-Montemayor, Ratana Chuenpagdee, and U. Rashid Sumaila. 2019. Assessing the economic viability of small-scale fisheries: An example from Mexico. *Marine Ecology Progress Series* 617: 365–376. https://doi.org/10.3354/meps12942.

Skerritt, Daniel J., Robert Arthur, Naazia Ebrahim, Valérie Le Brenne, Frédéric Le Manach, Anna Schuhbauer, Sebastián Villasante, and U. Rashid Sumaila. 2020. A 20-year retrospective on the provision of fisheries subsidies in the European Union. *ICES Journal of Marine Science* 77(7–8): 2741–2752. https://doi.org/10.1093/icesjms/fsaa142.

Spalding, Ana K., Kirsten Grorud-Colvert, Edward H. Allison, Diva J. Amon, Rachel Collin, Asha de Vos, Alan M. Friedlander et al. 2023. Engaging the tropical majority to make ocean governance and science more equitable and effective. *npj Ocean Sustainability* 2(1): 8. https://doi.org/10.1038/s44183-023-00015-9.

Sumaila, U. Rashid, Lubna Alam, Patrizia R. Abdallah, Denis Aheto, Shehu L. Akintola, Justin Alger, and Vania Andreoli. 2024. WTO must complete an ambitious fisheries subsidies agreement. *npj Ocean Sustainability* 3(1): 6. https://doi.org/10.1038/s44183-024-00042-0.

Sumaila, U. Rashid, Naazia Ebrahim, Anna Schuhbauer, Daniel Skerritt, Yang Li, Hong Sik Kim, Tabitha Grace Mallory et al. 2019. Updated estimates and analysis of global fisheries subsidies. *Marine Policy* 109: 103695. https://doi.org/10.1016/j.marpol.2019.103695.

Torre, Jorge, Arturo Hernández-Velasco, Francisco Fernández Rivera-Melo, Jaime López, and María Jose Espinosa-Romero. 2019. Women's empowerment, collective actions, and sustainable fisheries: lessons from Mexico. *Maritime Studies* 18(3): 373–384. https://doi.org/10.1007/s40152-019-00153-2.

World Bank. 2017. *The sunken billions revisited: Progress and challenges in global marine fisheries.* World Bank Publications.

World Trade Organization. 2024. *The WTO Agreement on Fisheries Subsidies: What it does and what comes next.* https://www.wto.org/english/tratop_e/rulesneg_e/fish_e/fish_e.htm.

PART IV

Ocean governance and international regimes

10 Institutional integration: addressing overlaps and gaps in ocean governance

Oran R. Young

Introduction: the state of ocean governance

Efforts to address needs for governance relating to marine issues and the oceans more generally start from a widely accepted point of departure articulated in the constitutive provisions of the 1982 United Nations Convention on the Law of the Sea (UNCLOS 1982). Whatever our feelings about the suitability or legitimacy of this point of departure in normative terms, it sets well-defined boundaries on our thinking about issues and options in the realm of ocean governance. At this stage, at least, there is no real debate about the status of this point of departure. In other words, there is no organized opposition to the core provisions of UNCLOS on the part of those calling for the introduction of some alternative approach to ocean governance. But the story is very different when we turn to operational regimes dealing with functional activities involving the oceans (e.g., fishing, mining, shipping, submarine cables, research) or with matters of environmental protection relating to the oceans (e.g., the conservation of marine mammals, the control of waterborne pollutants including plastics, the establishment of marine protected areas). Not only are there controversies regarding the terms of regimes dealing with specific issues; the growing density of issue-specific regimes is also generating a significant increase in complications arising from actual or potential interactions between or among regimes intended to deal with distinct issues.

The result is a rising concern about the challenge of meshing the elements of the expanding collection of operational regimes to maximize the capacity of individual regimes to achieve their own objectives, while minimizing the extent to which focused efforts to implement the provisions of individual regimes lead to interference with the operation of others. To take a current case in point, will efforts to implement the provisions of the newly emerging Agreement on the Conservation and Sustainable Use of Marine Biological Diversity create serious problems for those engaged in commercial fishing for stocks of fish located in or passing through the high seas (BBNJ Agreement 2023)? A major complicating factor arises from the fact that human activities in other issue domains are generating side effects that are increasingly disruptive to marine systems. The most dramatic example involves climate change arising from anthropogenic greenhouse gas emissions and producing many impacts on marine systems. But this is not the only case. Various land-based forces leading to the loss of biological diversity are affecting marine and terrestrial species. The Great Pacific Garbage Patch, a vast collection of marine debris including many types of plastics that originate from terrestrial sources, are not biodegradable, and are harmful to marine organisms, is a source of growing concern.

In this chapter, I seek to address the resultant challenges of institutional integration. To set the stage, I begin with a brief account of the contours of the ocean governance complex. I then turn to an assessment of the significance of what I call *overlaps*, or issues arising from interactions between or among operational regimes dealing with specific marine-related issues, and what I call *gaps*, or issues arising from the unintended side effects on marine systems of human activities subject to other governance complexes, such as the arrangements dealing with climate change. This provides a point of departure for an effort to identify and assess the merits of strategies that may prove helpful in coming to terms with the challenges arising from both overlaps and gaps. In a brief concluding section, I ask whether this analysis of institutional integration in the case of ocean governance suggests any broader insights that may be of interest to those concerned with parallel issues in other domains of international or global governance.

The ocean governance complex

The ocean governance complex includes two distinct, albeit related, components: (i) a constitutive core articulated in the provisions of UNCLOS and (ii) a sizable and growing collection of operational regimes encompassing a range of functionally defined or spatially delimited arrangements pertaining to marine concerns. The constitutive core rests squarely on the proposition that sovereign states are the principal subjects of ocean governance. UNCLOS is a legally binding instrument whose signatories are sovereign states. The principal provisions of UNCLOS set forth a system of rights and duties applicable to the actions of states. States are expected to comply with the requirements and prohibitions embedded in these provisions and to take responsibility for compliance on the part of those subject to their jurisdiction (including the personnel of ships at sea). Of course, it is understood that many users of marine resources, such as fishers and shippers, are non-state actors. But the activities of these actors are subject to the regulatory authority of states. To illustrate, signatories to UNCLOS that are flag states, port states, and coastal states are authorized to make and implement rules applicable to the owners, operators, and crews of vessels engaged in maritime activities in areas subject to their jurisdiction.

This does not mean that there are no unresolved issues pertaining to specific provisions of UNCLOS. States disagree, for example, regarding the applicability of the general provisions of Article 37 on transit rights in international straits to specific cases (e.g., the waters of the Northwest Passage in the Canadian Arctic or the Vilkitsky Strait connecting the Kara and Laptev Seas north of the Russian mainland). Coastal states continue to push their claims to jurisdiction over areas of the outer continental shelf beyond the limits of their Exclusive Economic Zones (EEZs) under the provisions of Article 76. It is far from clear how the recession of sea ice in the Arctic will affect the status of the provisions of Article 234 dealing with ice-covered areas. Nevertheless, these and other similar matters featuring conflicting interests do not pose fundamental challenges to the constitutive core of the ocean governance complex. States are prepared to devise workable responses to such issues on a case-by-case basis; they do not give rise to any organized efforts to restructure or overturn the constitutive core of the ocean governance complex.

Resting on this constitutive core is an expanding web of operational regimes dealing with a wide range of focused issues. Some of these regimes are spatially delimited in the sense that they address issues arising in parts of the world ocean. Prominent among these are Regional Seas Conventions and Action Plans operating under the auspices of the UN Environment Programme (UNEP) in some cases (e.g., the Caribbean Region, the Mediterranean Region) and administered in other cases (e.g., the Black Sea Region, Red Sea, and Gulf of Aden) by organizations operating outside the UN system. Other spatially delimited regimes are bilateral in nature (e.g., the Norwegian–Russian arrangements for the Barents Sea) or are products of efforts unrelated to the Regional Seas Programme (e.g., the OSPAR Convention dealing with matters of environmental protection in the Northeast Atlantic).

Other operational regimes deal with functionally defined matters. Prominent among these is the array of fisheries regimes ranging from arrangements dealing with highly migratory species (e.g., the International Convention on the Conservation of Atlantic Tunas) to arrangements dealing with matters of particular concern in specific areas (e.g., the Central Bering Sea Pollock Convention) and on to arrangements intended to anticipate needs for governance that may arise in the future (e.g., the Central Arctic Ocean Fisheries Agreement). A more integrated collection of functional regimes is the set of arrangements dealing with commercial shipping and developed under the auspices of the International Maritime Organization, or IMO (e.g., the Safety of Life at Sea Convention, the International Convention for the Prevention of Pollution from Ships). Beyond this lies a growing collection of stand-alone regimes addressing well-defined concerns. The London Dumping Convention (LDC) aims to control marine pollution resulting from the dumping of waste at sea. The International Convention on the Regulation of Whaling (ICRW), designed initially to ensure sustainable harvesting of great whales, now focuses on matters pertaining to the conservation of whales. The International Council on the Exploration of the Sea (ICES) is a treaty-based arrangement for promoting scientific research on marine living resources, particularly in the Northeast Atlantic. The Convention on the Conservation of Antarctic Marine Living Resources (CCAMLR) creates an unusual arrangement in the sense that it covers the full range of issues pertaining to living resources in the marine areas surrounding Antarctica and seeks to make use of the principles of ecosystem-based management in addressing these issues.

The Department of Ocean Affairs and the Law of the Sea (DOALOS) within the UN Secretariat plays the lead role in matters of administration relating to the constitutive core of the ocean governance complex. However, the situation is far more complex when it comes to the operational regimes dealing with maritime issues. Specialized agencies of the UN are in charge in some cases, including the IMO for regimes dealing with commercial shipping and the UNEP for some, but not all, regimes included in the Regional Seas Programme. Other operational regimes, such as ICRW, ICES, and CCAMLR, have administrative arrangements of their own, established *sui generis* to serve the needs of regimes. The result is a fragmented patchwork of arrangements focused on their own concerns rather than on the overall coherence of the ocean governance complex. Still, it is worth emphasizing that all these arrangements are rooted in agreements whose signatories are sovereign states. In the final analysis, states will need to take the lead in efforts to sort out issues pertaining to the coherence of the ocean governance complex.

Overlaps and gaps in ocean governance

Overlaps in ocean governance occur when activities taking place under the auspices of two or more operational regimes affect each other in significant ways. Two broad types of overlaps are worth differentiating at the outset. The most familiar type arises from interactions between or among human activities and the international regimes established to govern them. Commercial shipping may impact the activities of those engaged in commercial fishing. Deep seabed mining may have adverse consequences for both shipping and fishing. Efforts to establish marine protected areas may have results affecting the activities of users of marine living resources. A second type of overlap involves interactions between international regimes and regimes established by coastal states dealing with activities taking place within areas subject to their jurisdiction (e.g., EEZs). Such interactions are particularly prominent in cases where living resources, such as migratory fish and marine mammals, move in and out of areas subject to coastal state jurisdiction and areas beyond national jurisdiction and in cases where pollutants (e.g., spilled oil, plastic debris) released in areas subject to the jurisdiction of a coastal state migrate into areas beyond national jurisdiction or areas under the jurisdiction of other states.

There is a natural tendency to focus on adverse consequences of overlaps in ocean governance. Commercial shipping threatens the welfare of marine mammals and may prove disruptive to fishers' efforts. Mining may be a source of severe pollution affecting marine biota. Fishers may regard the establishment of marine protected areas as disruptive to fishing efforts. Yet it is worth bearing in mind that overlaps in ocean governance also may produce positive consequences. The establishment of seasonal shipping channels under the terms of regimes governing commercial shipping can protect marine mammals. Imposing speed limits on commercial vessels can limit emissions of pollutants and reduce the frequency of ship strikes on marine mammals. Bans on the combustion and carriage of heavy fuel oil can lower the environmental impacts of commercial shipping. A particularly interesting case in this regard concerns the effects of establishing marine protected areas on commercial fisheries. Much remains to be learned about this subject, but there is considerable evidence to suggest that well-designed and properly administered marine protected areas can increase the productivity of fisheries located in adjacent waters. Under the circumstances, we need to be alert to opportunities to create positive overlaps as well as to the importance of finding ways to alleviate negative overlaps.

In some respects, gaps in ocean governance pose challenges that are more severe than those arising from overlaps. Without a doubt, the most extreme gap arises from the impacts of climate change on marine systems. But there are others, including the role of human actions as drivers of the loss of biological diversity and land-based human activities giving rise to particularly severe forms of marine pollution (e.g., the diffusion of plastic debris throughout the world ocean). The constitutive core of the ocean governance complex, as articulated in the provisions of UNCLOS, does include expressions of concern regarding problems of environmental protection. Part XII deals with the protection and preservation of the marine environment. Article 194, for example, asserts that "States shall take ... all measures ... that are necessary to prevent, reduce and control pollution of the marine environment from any source ... and shall endeavor to harmonize their policies in this connection." But the provisions of this part of UNCLOS are general. They do not set forth explicit requirements and prohibitions that are compulsory for signatories and non-state actors operating under their jurisdiction. They focus on familiar sources of marine pollution. They have little to say about issues like climate change and the loss of biological diversity that were not prominent concerns during the 1980s when the provisions of UNCLOS were negotiated but that have become matters of great urgency under conditions prevailing today.

Of course, there are separate governance complexes dealing with issue domains like climate change and biological diversity. In an ideal world, the development of effective governance systems under the terms of the UN Framework Convention on Climate Change (UNFCCC 1992) and the UN Convention on Biological Diversity (CBD 1992) would serve to protect the oceans from the impacts of climate change and the loss of biological diversity. But the lack of progress in these areas has proven profoundly disruptive to the health of the world ocean and, as a result, to the performance of the various elements of the ocean governance complex. Some 25 percent of anthropogenic emissions of carbon dioxide and 90 percent of the heat generated by such emissions end up in the ocean; the deep ocean is the largest reservoir of carbon on Earth (World Ocean Review 2010). Though there are variations from place to place, sea levels are rising, ocean temperatures are increasing, and the acidification of marine systems is becoming more severe. Major marine currents are shifting, and atmospheric interactions with warmer waters are producing more intense hurricanes and typhoons. While we have been aware of the consequences of these changes for certain species (e.g., corals) for some time, we are just beginning to understand the far-reaching impacts of climate change on many forms of marine life.

Whereas overlaps present us with the challenge of integrating individual elements of the ocean governance complex, dealing with gaps requires a concerted effort to address interactions between the ocean governance complex and parallel complexes dealing with matters that are atmospheric or terrestrial in nature. Dealing with overlaps arising within a single governance complex is not easy. But such efforts do feature a mutually understandable discourse linked to a common constitutive core. Dealing with gaps, on the other hand, is a more challenging matter. It requires dealing with diverse sets of actors that may have little understanding of each other's concerns and that often lack a common discourse needed to communicate effectively with one another.

Integrating ocean governance

Institutional integration requires efforts to address both overlaps and gaps. However, there are crucial differences between the two sets of challenges affecting the efficacy of strategies needed to come to terms with them.

Sorting out overlaps

The good news from the perspective of those concerned with overlaps between or among operational regimes is that the relevant actors are all parties to the constitutive core of the ocean governance complex. Everyone agrees that states are the principal players in efforts to come to terms with overlaps. No one disagrees with the basic system of jurisdictional arrangements set forth in UNCLOS. Everyone accepts the provisions relating to innocent passage and transit passage for commercial ships and the principle that the deep seabed is to be regarded as the common heritage of humankind. What is more, there is a general sense that sorting out overlaps is a matter of adjusting to accommodate conflicting values and interests in such a way as to promote good ocean governance rather than excluding activities of interest to some actors in favor of the preferences of others. For example, it may seem reasonable to ask those engaged in maritime commerce to take steps to protect marine mammals or to minimize certain types of pollution but not to prohibit commercial shipping altogether. There is agreement that marine protected areas located beyond the boundaries of national jurisdiction should be designed in such a way as to minimize their disruptive impacts on commercial fisheries. There may even be cases in which overlaps between operational regimes produce positive side effects. For example, while science is far from definitive at this stage, there is considerable evidence to suggest that well-designed marine protected areas can have positive impacts on the productivity of fish stocks located in adjacent areas. Under the circumstances, it is understandable that environmental advocates have welcomed recent efforts on the part of the IMO to develop more stringent regulations dealing with environmental concerns relating to commercial shipping and that the IMO itself has issued a statement welcoming the recent opening of the new BBNJ Agreement for signature.

Still, there is no denying the existence of frictions between or among the interests of those whose activities are covered by the provisions of specific operational regimes dealing with marine issues. So, it is relevant to ask what factors account for the willingness of key actors to engage in pragmatic efforts to sort out their differences in the interest of promoting the integration of the overall ocean governance complex. An assessment of actual cases reveals several conditions relevant to thinking about this matter, though there is no basis for concluding that the outcomes generally will prove satisfactory to all parties concerned.

Sometimes, there is authoritative guidance from above that bears on the treatment of overlaps between operational regimes. For example, the 2017 UN General Assembly (UNGA) Resolution setting in motion the negotiations that produced the BBNJ Agreement not only reconfirms the constitutive provisions of UNCLOS, it also specifically commands the negotiators to craft the terms of the new agreement in such a way as to minimize interference with preexisting regimes dealing with other matters (UNGA 2017). The most prominent concern in this case centered on the interests of commercial fishers operating under the terms of international regimes covering fishing in various parts of the high seas. Coming to terms with this injunction was a source of considerable tension in the negotiations eventuating in the completion of the terms of the BBNJ Agreement in 2023. But at this juncture, the evidence suggests that the supporters of the key interests involved were able to arrive at mutually acceptable provisions. Going forward, much will depend on how the language of the agreement is interpreted during the process of implementation or moving the agreement from paper to practice.

It is also important to consider the roles of various actors prominent in the creation and implementation of operational regimes. States are the principal players in this realm. But states are not unitary actors when it comes to their engagement with operational regimes. This makes it important to think about what some analysts have described as two-level games (Putnam 1988). For example, while those favoring the interests of commercial shippers play prominent roles in national delegations at meetings of the IMO, the positions states adopt at such meetings are influenced as well by interactions with officials from agencies favoring the interests of other constituencies. In recent years, this has produced a rising sensitivity to environmental concerns in the deliberations of the IMO, as reflected in the operations of regimes the IMO supervises, such as the International Convention for the Prevention of Pollution from Ships (MARPOL 1973/1978). A particularly dramatic case involving two-level games involves the shift over time toward greater concern for conservation among members of national delegations to the International Whaling Commission (Friedheim 2001). The influence of two-level games affecting the positions member states adopt in the activities of operational regimes is discernible in a wide range of cases.

Recent years have also have witnessed a rise in the ability of non-state actors to exercise influence in ways that are relevant to sorting out overlaps between operational regimes. Sometimes, these actors can bring pressure to bear within the boundaries of individual regimes. The Antarctic and Southern Ocean Coalition (ASOC), for instance, has become a prominent player in the activities carried out under the terms of the CCAMLR (1982), supporting the principle of ecosystem-based management in contrast to the interests of commercial fishers and advocating for the establishment of large marine protected areas in the Southern Ocean. In recent years, environmental groups have found ways to amplify their voices in the deliberations of the IMO. More generally, the development of the idea of major groups within the UN system has heightened the legitimacy of non-state actors seeking to exert influence at the international level. Of course, these developments do not eliminate the occurrence of overlaps between or among operational regimes. But they do contribute to the rise of more complex bargaining processes in which progress requires a willingness on the part of all parties involved to find ways to accommodate the major concerns of a wider range of interest groups.

Beyond this, it is worth emphasizing that shifts in technology and the content of social discourses can make a difference when it comes to sorting out overlaps between or among operational regimes. Technological advances can be significant, especially in alleviating conflicts between commercial interests and the concerns of environmental groups. For example, the introduction of turtle-excluding devices helped to address the tension between harvesters of shrimp and those who argued that the bycatch of turtles associated with such activities violated the terms of national regulatory restrictions compatible with the environmental provisions of the World Trade Organization. Similarly, there is reason to believe that technological advances will lead to the development of cleaner fuels that reduce emissions of black carbon from the operation of commercial ships. The willingness on the part of commercial operators to adopt new technologies of this sort undoubtedly is influenced by shifts in the overarching social discourse regarding the importance of paying attention to environmental protection. In the past, whalers did not face determined opposition on the part of those dedicated to saving whales; commercial fishers were not subject to rising concerns about the problem of bycatch nor the damage caused by bottom trawling; operators of commercial ships were not subject to severe criticism regarding emissions of black carbon or other greenhouse gases as side effects of their operations. Today, all of these side effects are matters of intense concern to members of an attentive and increasingly vocal public. The result is growing pressure to find workable compromises between the concerns of those involved in regimes dealing with commercial activities like fishing, mining, and shipping and the concerns of those promoting regimes focused on environmental protection.

Dealing with gaps

Unlike overlaps, gaps involve interactions between different issue domains and the distinct governance complexes that emerge to address issues arising in these domains. Those concerned with minimizing the impact of commercial shipping on whales, for example, are all operating within a common constitutive framework set forth in the provisions of UNCLOS. The challenge is to produce workable adjustments that respect the interests of all parties concerned. Compare this case with the rapidly growing threats to marine systems posed by the spread of plastic debris originating from land-based sources but spread everywhere by ocean currents. The provisions of UNCLOS do not provide a straightforward basis for addressing these threats. There is an effort underway at this time to develop the terms of an international agreement designed to come to terms with environmental threats associated with the spread of plastic debris (Intergovernmental Negotiating Committee 2023). This effort may produce results beneficial to marine systems' health. But to the extent that it does, this will take the form of a positive side effect of efforts to address needs for governance in another setting.

What can we do to deal with such gaps in ocean governance? As the example of plastic debris suggests, there may be cases in which evidence pertaining to impacts on marine systems can be brought to bear in ways that make a difference to processes unfolding in other governance complexes. It is now clear that plastic debris is present throughout the world's oceans and that the impacts of this debris can be highly disruptive to marine ecosystems. Whether this evidence can be packaged and presented in such a way that it enhances the prospects of success in the negotiations designed to produce a legally binding agreement on the control of plastic debris remains to be seen. But this mechanism for achieving cross-domain influence may prove helpful as a response to gaps under some conditions.

Without a doubt, the most dramatic gap in ocean governance centers on the impacts of climate change on marine systems. Of course, there is a governance complex focused on addressing the problem of climate change (Keohane and Victor 2009). But this governance complex operates in its own domain, separate from the ocean governance complex. So far, at least, it has failed to prevent far-reaching impacts on marine systems arising from the onset of climate change. Sea levels are rising; ocean temperatures are increasing; ocean acidification is becoming more severe, especially in the high latitudes. The oceans are the greatest carbon sink on the planet. Several tipping elements in the Earth's climate system (e.g., the recession of Arctic Sea ice, major shifts in oceanic circulation systems) involve marine processes (Lenton et al. 2023). Yet the ocean governance complex and the climate governance complex operate on separate tracks. There is no straightforward way to create effective links between them in the interest of ensuring that responsible actors take steps to limit the disruptive impacts of climate change on marine systems.

Addressing problems of this sort is difficult. It is possible that dramatic developments, including the growing threat of sea level rise to the well-being of small island states and major coastal cities, the bleaching of corals due to rising water temperatures, and the disruption of marine organisms caused by acidification, will have some impact on efforts to strengthen the terms of the climate governance complex. But it would be unwise to count on the efficacy of this mechanism. The fundamental problem is that the voices of those concerned with the health of the oceans are not strong enough to make a real difference in efforts to strengthen the climate governance complex. In the absence of some way to overcome this limitation, it is likely that the impacts of climate change on the health of marine systems will not receive the attention needed to deal with them effectively.

Broader implications

Are there insights from this analysis of institutional integration in the realm of ocean governance that should and will be of interest to those concerned with other issue domains? In sorting out overlaps, the existence of an accepted constitutive framework is helpful. Consider the contrast between marine systems and atmospheric and terrestrial systems in this regard. The absence of a widely accepted constitutive framework is emerging as a major problem for those seeking to sort out a variety of needs for governance arising in conjunction with the dramatic growth in human activities in outer space (Byers and Boley 2023). In the case of terrestrial systems, the established practice of addressing needs for governance within the jurisdiction of spatially delimited states has made it difficult to address issues involving transboundary concerns (e.g., shared rivers and water bodies, transboundary air pollution) effectively. We deal with these issues in an ad hoc fashion with little concern for interactions between or among them (e.g., the impacts of acid precipitation on shared water bodies). While there is no shortage of specific overlaps relating to the oceans, there is much to be said in this regard for the benefits of the existence of the constitutive framework that forms the core of the ocean governance complex.

The most difficult problems involve needs for governance arising from interactions between and among atmospheric, marine, and terrestrial systems. We are used to separating these domains sharply in identifying relevant actors and devising institutional arrangements governing interactions among these actors in each of the three domains independently. Whatever the virtues of this approach in the past, it will not suffice in addressing matters of planetary governance in the future. For example, most anthropogenic emissions of greenhouse gases arise from land-based activities. But they have profound consequences for atmospheric systems, leading in turn to fundamental impacts on marine systems. And this is not the only case of governance needs arising from linkages among atmospheric, marine, and terrestrial systems. In dealing with gaps, there is no getting around the necessity of coming to terms with these linkages. Is it realistic to suppose this can be done without a critical transition in the existing system of global order? There is no simple or clear answer to this question. But it does serve to draw attention to the challenges that have given rise to the growing interest in what more of us now call planetary governance (Young 2021).

References

BBNJ Agreement. 2023. Agreement on the Conservation and Sustainable Use of Marine Biological Diversity. https://www.un.org/bbnj.

Byers, Michael, and Aaron Boley. 2023. *Who Owns Outer Space? International Law, Astrophysics, and the Sustainable Development of Space*. Cambridge, UK: Cambridge University Press.

CCAMLR. 1982. Convention on the Conservation of Antarctic Marine Living Resources. https://www.ccamlr.org/en/organisation/camlr-convention-text.

CBD. 1992. Convention on Biological Diversity. https://www.cbd.int.

Friedheim, Robert L., ed. 2001. *Toward a Sustainable Whaling Regime*. Seattle, WA: University of Washington Press.

Intergovernmental Negotiating Committee. 2023. International Negotiating Committee on Plastic Pollution. https://www.unep.org/inc-plastic-pollution/.

Keohane, Robert O., and David G. Victor. 2009. The Regime Complex for Climate. *Perspectives on Politics*, 9: 7–23.

Lenton, Timothy, David I. Armstrong McKay, Sina Loriani, Jesse F. Abrams, Steven J. Lade, Jonathan F. Donges, Joshua E. Buxton et al., eds. 2023. *The Global Tipping Elements Report*. Exeter, UK: University of Exeter.

MARPOL. 1973/1978. International Convention on the Prevention of Pollution from Ships. https://www.imo.org.

Putnam, Robert. 1988. Diplomacy and Domestic Politics: The Logic of Two-Level Games. *International Organization*, 42: 427–460.

UNCLOS. 1982. United Nations Convention on the Law of the Sea. https://www.un.org/depts/los/convention_agreements/texts/unclos/unclos_e.pdf.

UNFCCC. 1992. United Nations Framework Convention on Climate Change. https://unfccc.int.

UN General Assembly. 2017. Intergovernmental Conference on Marine Biodiversity, UN General Assembly Resolution 72/249 of 24 December 2017. https://www.un.org/bbnj/.

World Ocean Review. 2010. Living with the Oceans. https://worldoceanreview.com/en/wor-1/.

Young, Oran R. 2021. *Grand Challenges of Planetary Governance: Global Order in Turbulent Times*. Cheltenham, UK and Northampton, MA: Edward Elgar Publishing.

11

Systemic integration, the law of the sea, and courts: constraints and opportunities for ocean governance

Margaret A. Young

Introduction

International lawyers have much to offer a research agenda for sustainable ocean governance, as demonstrated by contemporary international advisory proceedings on climate change and the marine environment.[1] Public international law as a field of study marshals legal methods and techniques to analyze the law that governs the relations between states. In the first quarter of this century, these relations are increasingly focused on a 'blue economy,' with states turning their attention (unilaterally or jointly) to the resources of the oceans within and beyond national jurisdiction. The United Nations Convention on the Law of the Sea (UNCLOS 1982) provides a framework for this activity, amidst a set of additional and related treaty regimes that seek to govern shipping, fishing, trade, investment, environmental protection, climate change, and other issues. As plans for the blue economy proliferate, there is increasing evidence of the declining health of the ocean (UN 2019) and growing awareness of a triple planetary crisis of climate change, biodiversity loss, and pollution (UN Secretary-General 2023). Human activities on land and sea are the drivers of the crisis, and the research agenda for sustainable ocean governance to which this chapter contributes must be focused on solutions, or at least an understanding of how to better govern those drivers.

With its tradition of rulemaking and peaceful dispute settlement, scholars may turn to international law to lead the research agenda. We may ask if solutions lie in more law (such as the recently concluded UNCLOS implementing agreement on marine biological diversity beyond national jurisdiction; BBNJ 2023) and more litigation (which has led to such historic rulings as the 2024 advisory opinion by the International Tribunal for the Law of the Sea [ITLOS] on obligations in UNCLOS to prevent and address climate change impacts on the marine environment). Or does the existing international law need better implementation, through institutional integration (see Oran Young's chapter in this volume), domestic law, empowered state officials, or resilient communities? Or perhaps international law is due for criticism of its positivist foundations and a revolution of ideas such as rights for non-human animals and the heightened protection of the commons. Evaluating these trends depends upon legal theory and methods and an openness to other epistemic communities, ontologies, and disciplinary engagements that include anthropology, the design disciplines, history, science, social science, and international relations scholarship.

In this chapter, I aim to give the perspective of a legal scholar in identifying a research agenda for sustainable ocean governance in three sections. First, I engage with 'gaps' and 'overlaps' in ocean governance. I explore the constraints and opportunities of a principle of systemic integration, which provides a unifying influence in international law by presuming that states intend to act consistently with existing obligations (in treaty and custom) when entering into treaties. Second, I point to the role of international courts and tribunals, which have interpreted UNCLOS's 'open character', thus allowing this treaty to serve as a living instrument and adapt to external rules including the climate change treaties. Third, I reflect more broadly on the diversity of ideas for how to live well with the ocean, which reside in plural responses to competing demands for ocean science, ecosystem restoration, the blue economy, the protection of the commons, and sustainable development itself, and which resist convergence within a broader set of human–nature relations.

Systemic integration and ocean governance

A multidisciplinary volume addressing sustainable ocean governance provides a welcome opportunity for me to engage directly with a fellow contributor who is one of the leaders in the field. I have always enjoyed the coincidence of our identical surname and similar research interests, although Oran Young comes from a background in political science and international relations, while I am an international lawyer who came later to these issues and drew much guidance from his work. In this section, I endorse Oran Young's comments about institutional integration, while describing the different approaches and emphases that come from a field of study focused on international law.

Oran Young points to 'overlaps' and 'gaps' in ocean governance. Overlaps arise from 'interactions between or among operational regimes dealing with specific marine-related issues' (this volume, p. 110). To his examples of shipping and fishing and deep seabed mining, one could add interactions between regimes governing commercial fishing and the restriction of trade in marine species (Young 2011a, 134–188). Gaps arise from the 'unintended side effects on marine systems of human activities subject to other governance complexes, such as the arrangements dealing with climate change' (Oran Young, this volume, p. 110). One might add here arrangements protecting cultural and other human rights (which have been found to have been violated by a state's failure to support adaptation to sea level rise and other climate impacts; *Billy v Australia* 2022), or arrangements that liberalize trade (noting the gap sought to be filled by the World Trade Organization's (WTO's) recent and welcome Agreement on Fisheries Subsidies; Young 2022). Oran Young notes that addressing gaps 'requires dealing with diverse sets of actors that may have little understanding of each other's concerns and that often lack a common discourse' (this volume, p. 114).

There are several synergies with Oran Young's approach and the parallel literature within international law, including in terminology and diagnosis. The meaning of 'regimes' here is similar to my synthesis of approaches from international relations and international law (Young 2012, 11):

> regimes are sets of norms, decision-making procedures and organisations coalescing around functional issue-areas and dominated by particular modes of behaviour, assumptions and biases.

Oran Young's comment on the 'growing density of issue-specific regimes' (this volume, p. 109) is consistent with the general observation of international law's fragmentation and diversification (International Law Commission [ILC] 2006). This has generated studies on regime interaction by international lawyers, including in the context of the law of the sea (Young 2011a, Trevisanut et al. 2020, Matz-Lück et al. 2023). Oran Young observes correctly that states need to 'take the lead in efforts to sort out issues pertaining to the coherence of the ocean governance complex' (this volume, p. 112). Lawyers are left to wrestle with the intentions of states parties to new treaties, such as the recently drafted clause in the BBNJ Agreement that the treaty will 'not undermine relevant legal instruments and frameworks and relevant global, regional, subregional and sectoral bodies' (Article 4), and neither will its Conference of the Parties in establishing area-based management tools (Article 19(2)).

Yet there are differences in approach in international law to gaps and overlaps as compared to other disciplines, which rest on the character of law and the international legal system. International lawyers are necessarily preoccupied with legal relations (rights, duties, powers, freedoms, liabilities, immunities, etc.) and the will of states (expressed through custom or treaties). International lawyers must engage with state consent, the common intention of states parties to treaties, and the conditions under which certain norms (such as a right or a duty under UNCLOS) apply alongside other norms, including conflicting ones (such as a right, duty, or even freedom under the climate change regime). Dominant methods are doctrinal (dealing especially with primary sources such as treaties but also case-law and general principles including *pacta sunt servanda*, "agreements must be kept"), but also include empirical studies (including interviews with state officials and other actors), and historical, sociological, theoretical, and critical analysis.

I will return to this broader set of ideas in the third section, but for now I will continue the positivist account of how various international obligations sit together. International lawyers delve deeply into relational words and phrases such as treaty references to rules that are 'not incompatible' or are 'without prejudice', or do 'not undermine' (UNCLOS and BBNJ, respectively). They are concerned with giving priority to *lex specialis* (according to the maxim that holds that when two types of rules regulate the same matter, the specific rule takes precedence over the general one), or deploy other techniques to deal with the collision between norms (ILC 2006). When interpreting UNCLOS, they take account of external treaties, soft law instruments, or factual and technological developments by drawing on provisions which refer to 'generally accepted international rules and standards' (Paine 2020, 190–191, McLachlan 2024, 190–195).

Yet there is also significant restraint on the amalgamating forces from the rest of public international law. International lawyers must work within the constraints of a legal system that draws its legitimacy from sovereignty and the consent of states. According to the principle of systemic integration, parties are presumed to intend not to act inconsistently with generally recognized principles of international law or with their previous treaty obligations when entering into new treaty obligations (ILC 2006, 234; see also McLachlan 2005, 311). In the Vienna Convention on the Law of Treaties (VCLT) 1969, states have agreed upon a rule on the interpretation of treaties that takes into account other 'relevant rules … applicable in the relations between the parties' (Article 31(3)(c)). Anyone called upon to interpret UNCLOS – whether it be a state official, a scholar, or an adjudicator – according to this provision can consider normative developments in other treaties only if they are 'applicable in the relations between the parties [to UNCLOS]'. The 'parties' in this clause has proved to be a major hurdle in the quest for systemic integration. Unlike customary international law, which binds all states, treaty ratification is rarely universal. The principle of systemic integration is restricted if there is a lack of parallel membership between UNCLOS and another relevant treaty. The underlying reason for this is, of course, the wish for states parties to a treaty, like UNCLOS, to establish a type of contract upon ratification, which they can understand and control, and which has a certain sanctity (according to *pacta sunt servanda*) regardless of the proliferation of other treaties on similar or related issues. Stability, security, and even peace are linked to this prospect of legal certainty and respect for sovereignty.

While Oran Young might consider it good news that relevant actors are 'all parties to the constitutive core of the ocean governance complex' (this volume, p. 114), this is not always correct let alone determinative, and disputes have arisen about whether to allow surrounding legal developments to influence UNCLOS, or whether to restrict its interpretation. For example, lawyers have struggled to ensure UNCLOS's provisions relating to the protection and preservation of the marine environment are interpreted in light of the protection of listed sea turtles in the Convention on International Trade in Endangered Species of Wild Fauna and Flora (CITES), or that UNCLOS's provisions on freedom of navigation include protest at sea as derived from the freedom of expression and assembly in human rights treaties (Azaria 2023, 75–76). In those cases, the adjudicators upheld an interpretation of UNCLOS that drew upon other law. The Tribunal in the *South China Sea Arbitration 2016* emphasized the ratification of CITES by both the Philippines and China (para. 956), and the Tribunal in the *Arctic Sunrise Arbitration 2015* noted the ratification by both Russia and the Netherlands of relevant human rights treaties and ultimately had regard to rules of customary international law including international human rights standards (para. 198). Yet adjudicators are understandably reluctant to rest their interpretative tasks on VCLT Article 31(3)(c), when 'the parties' in that clause means *all parties to UNCLOS* (not the parties involved in a dispute), and there are significant non-ratifying countries, including the United States. Like previous tribunals before it, including the International Court of Justice (ICJ; McLachlan 2005) and the WTO (Young 2007), adjudicators defer to the will of states parties when building a systemic account of international law. The will of states parties might be found to include an acceptance of various systematizing objects and purposes, as interpreted according to VCLT Article 31(1) rather than Article 31(3)(c) (McLachlan 2024, 399). Moreover, the foundations of legitimacy in international law – resting on state consent – can be seen as extending to procedural values, deliberative credentials, and powers of international organizations that guarantee appropriate regime interaction (Young 2011a, 267–87).

Though a discussion about the general foundations of international law risks straying too far from the focus of this chapter, it is important to understand the link between authority and legitimacy in regime interaction. Examples from cases demonstrate the importance of the judicial function in this regard. The first example relates to the obligation for states to give 'due regard' to others' rights in several UNCLOS provisions; this means states must engage with their neighbors when declaring marine protected areas to minimize interference with others' rights (*Chagos Marine Protected Area Arbitration (Mauritius v UK), 2015*, paras 537–41). In this example, the arbitral tribunal established the necessity to consult by balancing competing rights, reviewing the availability of alternative actions, and engaging in other interpretative techniques. The finding was not a product of integrating UNCLOS with, say, treaties guaranteeing rights of access in environmental decision-making. In a second example, when the International Court of Justice ruled upon an alleged violation of the International Convention for the Regulation of Whaling (1946) in *Whaling in the Antarctic (Australia v Japan)* in 2014, it did not seek to interpret that treaty in the context of the Convention on Biological Diversity or other treaties, but rather drew on the duty of the disputing parties to cooperate and give 'due regard' to resolutions of the International Whaling Commission relating to non-lethal methods (Young and Rioseco Sullivan 2015). As a distinguished scholar of the field has observed, regimes are not 'billiard balls', but are open for re-definition and innovation (Koskenniemi 2009: 13). A third example is ITLOS's reference to UNCLOS's 'open character', as is described in the following section.

UNCLOS's 'open character' and the role of courts and tribunals

The United Nations Framework Convention on Climate Change (UNFCCC 1992) and the Paris Agreement (2015) have so far failed to address sea level rise, ocean acidification, and the devastating rise in ocean temperatures. As noted by Oran Young, the impacts of climate change on marine systems present an example of the most dramatic gap in ocean governance (this volume, p. 117). The interaction between the climate change treaties and other areas of international law is sporadic and stymied by legal uncertainty (Young 2011b), especially with respect to the law of the sea despite UNCLOS's continuing vitality (Barnes 2016). International lawyers have recognized the urgency of dealing with this gap and sought recourse through courts and tribunals. In this section, I first describe the 2024 ruling by ITLOS, before moving to the ongoing request before the ICJ. Both cases attest to the contribution of courts, the role of advocates within the scholarly discipline of law, and an expanded sense of agency for smaller states and civil society in sustainable ocean governance.

The ITLOS advisory opinion on climate change and international law

In 2022, the newly formed Commission of Small Island States and Climate Change and International Law (COSIS), which comprised six states parties to UNCLOS, requested an advisory opinion from ITLOS. Advisory opinions are not binding decisions but provide an opportunity for a court to hand down an interpretation on a legal question, thus providing legal certainty for the bodies that have requested the opinion, other international organizations, and states. The settled legal question may then give rise to contentious cases that lead to rulings that are binding on the disputing parties.

The question posed by COSIS to ITLOS was as follows (*Advisory Opinion 2024*, para. 102):

> What are the specific obligations of State Parties to the United Nations Convention on the Law of the Sea ("UNCLOS"), including under Part XII:
>
> (a) to prevent, reduce and control pollution of the marine environment in relation to the deleterious effects that result or are likely to result from climate change, including through ocean warming and sea level rise, and ocean acidification, which are caused by anthropogenic greenhouse gas [GHG] emissions into the atmosphere?
> (b) to protect and preserve the marine environment in relation to climate change impacts, including ocean warming and sea level rise, and ocean acidification?

In an opinion delivered on 21 May 2024, the Tribunal ruled that UNCLOS contains obligations concerning climate change, despite the submissions by many states that such obligations were within the sole realm of the Paris Agreement and UNFCCC. The specific obligations under UNCLOS would not be satisfied simply by states' compliance with obligations and commitments under the Paris Agreement (para. 223). In detailed interpretative steps, the Tribunal drew on the temperature goal and timeline for emission pathways set out in the Paris Agreement, in addition to other factors, to give meaning and application to the UNCLOS obligations. It confirmed that the objectives in Part XII of UNCLOS are consistent with the goal in Article 4 of the Paris Agreement relating to the global peaking of GHG emissions (para. 200). There is not the space here for me to discuss the many implications for sustainable ocean governance of the Tribunal's opinion, but I will point out three findings that are especially relevant to systemic integration.

First, in finding that anthropogenic GHG emissions fell within the definition of marine pollution under UNCLOS, ITLOS drew attention to the obligations of states parties to UNCLOS to take necessary measures to prevent, reduce, and control such pollution. ITLOS noted that cessation of marine pollution from GHG emissions may be less immediate than reduction and control, as consistent with the approach of the Paris Agreement. International rules and standards (especially the 1.5°C temperature target of Paris, which was emphasized by the Tribunal instead of 2°C) were deemed highly important in determining the necessity of measures. However, the Tribunal was careful to emphasize that the approach of the Paris Agreement does not 'supersede' UNCLOS (para. 223). In legal terms, the Paris Agreement was not *lex specialis*. The Tribunal's observation that UNCLOS was a living instrument (paras 130–137) that allowed for coordination and harmonization with other regimes while advancing its own goals represents a systemic understanding of obligations.

Second, the Tribunal ruled on the nature of obligations with respect to marine pollution, which requires states parties to act with 'due diligence'. The standard to act to prevent, reduce, and control marine pollution was found by the Tribunal to be 'stringent,' and the precautionary approach applies (paras 242–43). The standard to act to ensure that the activities of states parties are conducted so as not to cause damage can be even more stringent with respect to transboundary pollution (para. 258). In dealing with these obligations, the Tribunal was careful to emphasize that the standard of due diligence may differ among states parties in accordance with the availability of means and capabilities. This is not a direct application of the principle of 'common but differentiated responsibilities' (CBDR) that is found in various iterations within the climate treaties but is instead a recognition that due diligence obligations are contextual and may vary in relation to several factors. The Tribunal thus expertly navigated the need to integrate equity considerations in its interpretation of UNCLOS, notwithstanding that a specific concept of CBDR was not part of UNCLOS.

Third, the Tribunal emphasized that one of the means of addressing inequity in UNCLOS is to ensure the provision of 'scientific, technical, educational and other assistance to developing states that are particularly vulnerable to the adverse effects of climate change' (para. 327). Once again, coexisting provisions of the Paris Agreement, the UNFCCC, and UNCLOS were interpreted to support a finding of specific obligations to assist developing states, in particular vulnerable developing states, in their efforts to address marine pollution from anthropogenic GHG emissions. This finding is especially relevant given gaps in capacity in ocean governance and provides further imprimatur to international organizations and others who are engaged in these activities and whose work itself has a major impact on regime interaction (Young 2023). It parallels the recognition in the recent BBNJ Agreement of the centrality of building capacity of developing states in fulfilling the objectives of fair and equitable sharing of benefits arising from activities with respect to marine genetic resources.

The ITLOS opinion may have implications for sustainable ocean governance at the domestic level too, including in litigation before national courts. For example, the Tribunal found that states parties' 'due diligence' obligations included a requirement that states enforce national laws (para. 235). It also noted that measures by states to address pollution of the marine environment could be joint or individual, as appropriate. This is a significant statement that could be used in advocacy to pre-empt the dismissal of lawsuits. In climate litigation, domestic judges have sometimes found that action on climate change must be pursued internationally (due to the collective nature of the problem of global warming) and therefore is not appropriate to rule upon domestically (Young 2021a, 355–56). In contrast, the ITLOS opinion shows that unilateral domestic action to protect the marine environment is appropriate despite the global nature of the threats to ocean health.

The ICJ advisory opinion on obligations of states in respect of climate change

The request for an ITLOS opinion was made alongside efforts to build support for an opinion from the ICJ, the UN's primary judicial organ (International Court of Justice, Request for Advisory Opinion 2023). The initiative for this request started with law students from the University of the South Pacific and was propelled by the government of Vanuatu, which worked with lawyers and academics to generate the required majority support at the General Assembly (Wewerinke-Singh et al. 2023). The General Assembly's request of 29 March 2023 considers a broader range of issues than the UNCLOS-focused ITLOS request, due to the general nature of the ICJ's jurisdiction. The legal question draws the Court's attention, in its introductory paragraph, to the UN Charter, human rights treaties, the law of the sea, the duty of due diligence, and customary norms that have evolved from the duty to prevent transboundary harm. It asks the Court to rule on the obligations of states to ensure the protection of 'the climate system', which includes the hydrosphere and biosphere, and thus the oceans.

Although ITLOS's advisory opinion is not a formal legal precedent for the ICJ, it is likely that the ICJ will be guided by ITLOS's reasoning relating to UNCLOS obligations, and ITLOS's quest to accommodate a constructive relationship between the climate treaties and other areas of international law. The advisory opinion from the ICJ is likely to go much further than the ITLOS advisory opinion because it has been asked to consider obligations under international law (not just UNCLOS), and because it has been asked to consider legal consequences. Indeed, when COSIS asked for an advisory opinion from ITLOS, it expressed support for the initiative of Vanuatu (which is also one of the members of COSIS), and it later provided written statements to the ICJ along with many other organizations and states. Oral proceedings at the ICJ, which were conducted in December 2024, included references to the ITLOS opinion by multiple participating states and organizations. The careful and expansive reasoning of ITLOS, especially in rejecting *lex specialis* arguments, hardening the precautionary approach, raising the bar on due diligence, and dwelling on 1.5°C, is expected to be given close attention in the ICJ opinion, which is pending and expected to be delivered in 2025. The Tribunal's reasoning about UNCLOS's 'open character' may be replicated by the ICJ and also applied to other treaties, with far-reaching implications for sources of obligations to mitigate and adapt to climate change, including in the marine context.

This review of contemporary cases (which, due to space constraints, leaves out many other regional and bilateral disputes) might suggest that the concerns of Oran Young about gaps and overlaps, and the work of international lawyers on fragmentation and regime interaction, are answered by a research agenda that seeks convergence in international law, including through the advice or rulings of international courts and tribunals. This might be so when the common intentions of states are integrated in ways that support sustainable ocean governance. In the following section, however, I show that convergence is neither the best explanation nor the best normative guidepost, by adding a further set of issues for discussion.

Plural responses to sustainable ocean governance in the blue economy

Systemic integration helps address overlaps and gaps, ensuring more effective implementation of existing law. Yet the research agenda for international lawyers interested in sustainable ocean governance is much longer. The agenda must allow for the exploration of alternative conceptions of legal relations, which emerge not from synergies in existing law but from innovative ideas, creativity, and exploration. Moreover, the agenda includes the acknowledgment that sometimes differentiation and diversity in the law are preferable, that efforts to unify may detract or distract, and that the asymmetry of adjudication in international law can make integration far from systematic.

To take the last point first: this chapter has demonstrated the role of international courts and tribunals in systemic integration, but it is important to note the highly circumscribed nature of their jurisdiction. Compulsory dispute settlement is rare in international law, and even UNCLOS's Part XV has significant limitations. Often, the regimes that give rise to binding decisions are within functional areas that do not have sustainability as a primary focus, such as trade and investment law. For example, when countries complained about the United States' use of import bans to address turtle bycatch from shrimp harvesting, the United States had no choice as a WTO member but to appear before a WTO panel (*US-Shrimp 1998*). Legal submissions supporting environmental protection were raised as an exception to the General Agreement on Tariffs and Trade by the respondent state, rather than as a primary obligation (Young 2011a, 189–240). Multilateral environmental agreements, by contrast, are mostly outside of the purview of international courts and binding rulings, and litigation that centers on obligations to protect the environment is rare (Klein 2021, McLachlan 2024, 174–75).

The asymmetric nature of dispute settlement in international law has implications for the blue economy. States, international funding institutions, and corporations increasingly seek opportunities to yield economic potential within states' exclusive economic zones and areas beyond national jurisdiction while maintaining sustainability. Economic returns are anticipated from established activities such as fishing, shipping, aquaculture, and oil and gas exploitation alongside new growth sectors, including eco-tourism, off-shore renewable energy infrastructure, plastic recycling facilities in port areas, and ocean-related climate mitigation. For a research agenda in sustainable ocean governance, this suggests a need for scholarship that understands, critiques, and engages with international economic law. For example, alongside current efforts to develop a multilateral treaty on plastic pollution, states are inserting obligations to address marine plastic debris into their trade agreements (Young 2021b). Action to address illegal, unreported, and unregulated (IUU) fishing is taking place through market-related measures that restrict or ban certain imports. The new WTO Agreement on Fisheries Subsidies allows compulsory dispute settlement against WTO members alleged to have granted subsidies that contribute to IUU fishing or the fishing of overfished stocks, which could lead to trade panels adjudicating on standards and rules from fisheries management and the law of the sea.

The research agenda for sustainable ocean governance must also make clear the place in international law for collective decisions *not* to exploit or extract in the blue economy. Legal relations that are built around the protection of the commons or public goods contrast with the freedom to exploit the oceans. Legal precedents for marine reserves or restricted techniques or targets can be traced to certain limitations on fur sealing in the Bering Sea established by the 1893 arbitration (Young 2019), and even earlier in the marine governance practices of Indigenous peoples and local communities (Wilson 2021). As to the latter point, an awareness of the Eurocentric and Anthropocentric foundations of international law is worth our attention. Legal pluralism throws up many questions about whether legal systems and practices outside state-centric law provide lessons for living more harmoniously with the ocean. For example, if the perspective of non-human animals is brought to UNCLOS in the form of 'common heritage for kin-kind' (Jones et al. 2024), decisions to mine the deep seabed would give primacy to the habitat of organisms living there (pp. 124–5). Ideas about rights of nature, which have flourished in domestic settings relating to iconic mountains and rivers, and in the cosmologies of many Indigenous peoples, may bring a positive influence to the quest to live in better harmony with the ocean. Perhaps too will the call for planetary governance (Oran Young, this volume, p. 118) . A research agenda for sustainable ocean governance is enriched by speculative and historiographical study, a critical assessment of the limitations of international law, and a rigorous analysis of the valid yet competing justifications for stability and change.

I conclude this section by juxtaposing the UN Decade of Ocean Science for Sustainable Development (2021–30) with the concurrent United Nations Decade on Ecosystem Restoration (2021–30). Both are galvanizing ideas for better ocean health. Both demand support and engagement by states, international organizations, and civil society. Yet both can lead to harm, particularly in the context of a history of colonialism, extractivism, and global inequity. For example, the Ocean Decade may further the imaginary of the ocean as a 'final frontier' (Dela Cruz 2023) at odds with requests by some states for a moratorium on deep seabed mining, or at the very least a precautionary pause. Meanwhile, restoring ecosystems and achieving the Kunming-Montreal Global Biodiversity Framework's target of conserving or protecting at least 30 percent of marine and coastal areas by 2030 must be done with appropriate recognition of the rights of Indigenous peoples and local communities, a lesson learned from terrestrial carbon sequestration. The success of these activities within sustainable ocean governance relies on an openness by international lawyers – and by international law – to the diverse ways of relating to the ocean.

Conclusion

It is now trite to describe UNCLOS as a constitution for the oceans. Lawyers pay close attention to constitutions, which comprise frameworks supporting certainty and stability, while also allowing for adaptation to societal needs. Within international law, UNCLOS has near-universal ratification and structures collective decision-making about maritime zones and entitlements. As the triple planetary crisis escalates alongside competing demands in a blue economy, new agreements such as the BBNJ Agreement and the Agreement on Fisheries Subsidies express changing societal expectations, and existing agreements are interpreted in new ways. Systemic integration of international law and broader incorporation of developments in science and human values are needed. This chapter endorses the observations about institutional integration by Oran Young, while also showing the differences between the literature in international relations and international law. In particular, the chapter demonstrates the constraints of integrative techniques such as treaty interpretation, and the vital role of international courts and tribunals in filling gaps and ranking overlapping norms in international law.

The advisory opinion by ITLOS in 2024 is a striking development that endorses UNCLOS's 'open character'. This chapter has described the main findings of the Tribunal, which ruled on the specific obligations under UNCLOS to prevent, reduce, and control marine pollution caused by GHG emissions, and the related obligations to protect and preserve the marine environment in relation to climate change impacts. These obligations would not be satisfied simply by states' compliance with obligations and commitments under the Paris Agreement, yet their meaning and application drew on the 1.5°C temperature goal, a recognition of the precautionary approach, and a stringent standard of due diligence. The chapter points to the implications of these findings, which will influence the ICJ's pending advisory opinion on climate obligations , as well as future contentious cases.

Yet despite the significant contribution to ocean governance of the ITLOS opinion, the chapter shows why coordination and harmonization are not the only animating goals for the law of the sea. It points to plural responses to the ocean's needs and ailing health, which emerge from other disciplines, perspectives, and ontologies, including rights for nature and the protection of the commons. Whether these will better support the governance or regulation of the drivers of ocean ill-health, which include but are not limited to our uses of the ocean, remains an open question. A research agenda on ocean governance is well served by scholars whose recognition of the structures, methods, and constraints of international law co-exists with an openness to history, critical approaches, and innovative ideas.

Note

1. The author acknowledges the support of the Australian Research Council Future Fellowship (FT220100418). She notes that she was one of the legal counsel for IUCN

in proceedings at the International Court of Justice on the request for an Advisory Opinion on obligations of States in respect of climate change, and that none of the comments here can be attributed to IUCN or its submissions.

List of cases

Advisory Opinion of the International Tribunal for the Law of the Sea, Request for an Advisory Opinion Submitted by the Commission of Small Island States on Climate Change and International Law (International Tribunal for the Law of the Sea) 21 May 2024.

Arbitration regarding the Chagos Marine Protected Area between Mauritius and the United Kingdom of Great Britain and Northern Ireland, Award of 18 March 2015.

Arctic Sunrise Arbitration between the Kingdom of the Netherlands and the Russian Federation (Arbitral Tribunal constituted under Annex VII to the 1982 United Nations Convention on the Law of the Sea) 14 August 2015 https://pcacases.com/web/sendAttach/1438.

Billy v Australia UN Doc CCPR/C/135/D/3624/2019 (2022) (Views adopted by the Human Rights Committee concerning communication No. 3624/2019) 21 July 2022.

International Court of Justice, Request for Advisory Opinion transmitted to the Court pursuant to General Assembly resolution 77/276 on 29 March 2023, Obligations of States in Respect of Climate Change (Advisory Opinion pending). https://www.icj-cij.org/case/187.

South China Sea Arbitration (The Republic of Philippines v The People's Republic of China) (Arbitral Tribunal constituted under Annex XI to the 1982 United Nations Convention on the Law of the Sea) 12 July 2016. https://pca-cpa.org/en/cases/7/.

United States – Import Prohibition of Certain Shrimp and Shrimp Products (WTO Appellate Body Report) 12 October 1998.

Whaling in the Antarctic (Australia v Japan, New Zealand intervening) [2014] ICJ Rep 226.

References

Azaria, Danae. 2023. The Use of 'Other' Rules of International Law by the Law of the Sea Convention Tribunals. In *Peaceful Management of Maritime Disputes*, edited by James Kraska and Hee Cheol Yang, 55–79. London and New York: Routledge.

Barnes, Richard. 2016. The Continuing Vitality of UNCLOS. In *Law of the Sea: UNCLOS as a Living Treaty*, edited by Jill Barrett and Richard Barnes, 459–487. London: British Institute of International and Comparative Law.

BBNJ Agreement. 2023. Agreement under the United Nations Convention on the Law of the Sea on the Conservation and Sustainable Use of Marine Biological Diversity in Areas Beyond National Jurisdiction. https://un.org/bbnj/.

Dela Cruz, Alex. 2023. 'The Ocean We Want': Development and the Oceanic Future in International Law. In *The Oxford Handbook of International Law and Development*, edited by Ruth Buchanan, Luis Eslava, and Sundhya Pahuja, 601–616. Oxford: Oxford University Press.

International Convention for the Regulation of Whaling. 1946. https://legal.un.org/avl/ha/icrw/icrw.html.

International Law Commission (ILC) of the United Nations. 2006. *Fragmentation and Diversification of International Law, Report of the Study Group*. New York: UN.

Jones, Emily, Cristian van Eijk, and Gina Heathcote. 2024. The Common Heritage of Kin-Kind. In *International Law and Posthuman Theory*, edited by Matilda Arvidsson and Emily Jones, 105–135. Abingdon: Routledge.

Klein, Natalie. 2021. International Environmental Law Disputes before International Courts and Tribunals. In *Oxford Handbook of International Environmental Law*, edited by Jacqueline Peel and Lavanya Rajamani, 1038–1051. Oxford: Oxford University Press.
Koskenniemi, Martti. 2009. The Politics of International Law – 20 Years Later. *European Journal of International Law* 20(1): 7–19.
Matz-Lück, Nele, Øystein Jensen and Elise Johansen (editors). 2023. *The Law of the Sea: Normative Context and Interactions with other Legal Regimes*. Abingdon: Routledge.
McLachlan, Campbell. 2005. The Principle of Systemic Integration and Article 31(3)(c) of the Vienna Convention. *International and Comparative Law Quarterly* 54: 279
McLachlan, Campbell. 2024. *The Principle of Systemic Integration in International Law*. Oxford: Oxford University Press.
Paine, Joshua. 2020. The Judicial Dimension of Regime Interaction beyond Systemic Integration. In *Regime Interaction in Ocean Governance: Problems, Theories and Methods*, edited by Seline Trevisanut, Nikolaos Giannopoulos, and Rozemarijn Roland Holst, 184–221. Leiden: Brill.
Paris Agreement. 2015. https://unfccc.int.
Trevisanut, Seline, Nikolaos Giannopoulos, and Rozemarijn Roland Holst (editors). 2020. *Regime Interaction in Ocean Governance: Problems, Theories and Methods*. Leiden: Brill.
UNCLOS. 1982. United Nations Convention on the Law of the Sea. https://www.un.org/depts/los/convention_agreements/texts/unclos/unclos_e.pdf.
UNFCCC. 1992. United Nations Framework Convention on Climate Change. https://unfccc.int.
United Nations. 2019. World Ocean Assessment II. https://www.un.org/regularprocess/woa2launch.
United Nations Secretary General. 2023. Oceans and the Law of the Sea: Report of the Secretary-General (A/78/339) (1 September 2023).
Vienna Convention on the Law of Treaties. 1969. 1155 UNTS 331.
Wewerinke-Singh, Margaretha, Jorge E. Viñuales, and Julian Aguon. 2023. The Role of Advocates in the Conception of Advisory Opinion Requests. *AJIL Unbound* 117: 277–81.
Wilson, David. 2021. European Colonisation, Law, and Indigenous Marine Dispossession: Historical Perspectives on the Construction and Entrenchment of Unequal Marine Governance. *Maritime Studies* 20(4): 387–407.
Young, Margaret A. 2007. The WTO's Use of Relevant Rules of International Law: An Analysis of the Biotech Case. *International and Comparative Law Quarterly* 56: 907–929.
Young, Margaret A. 2011a. *Trading Fish, Saving Fish: The Interaction between Regimes in International Law*. Cambridge: Cambridge University Press.
Young, Margaret A. 2011b. Climate Change Law and Regime Interaction. *Carbon and Climate Law Review* 2: 147–157
Young, Margaret A. 2012. Introduction: The Productive Friction between Regimes. In *Regime Interaction in International Law: Facing Fragmentation*, edited by Margaret Young, 1–19. Cambridge: Cambridge University Press.
Young, Margaret A. 2019. International Adjudication and the Commons. *University of Hawai'i Law Review* 41(2): 353–383.
Young, Margaret A. 2021a. Climate Change and Law: A Global Challenge for Legal Education. *University of Queensland Law Journal* 40(3): 351–370.
Young, Margaret A. 2021b. Protection of the Marine Environment: Rights and Obligations in Trade Agreements. *Korean Journal of International and Comparative Law* 9: 196–211.
Young, Margaret A. 2022. Fisheries. In *The Oxford Handbook of International Trade Law*, edited by Daniel Bethlehem, Donald McRae, Rodney Neufeld, and Isabelle Van Damme, 817–837. Oxford: Oxford University Press.

Young, Margaret A. 2023. Strengthening Capacity in Ocean Governance. *Asia-Pacific Journal of Ocean Law and Policy* 8: 5–24.

Young, Margaret A., and Sebastian Rioseco Sullivan. 2015. Evolution through the Duty to Cooperate: Implications of the *Whaling* Case at the International Court of Justice. *Melbourne Journal of International Law* 16: 310–342.

12 Drivers and mechanisms of change in UNCLOS: an international relations research agenda

Elizabeth Mendenhall

The 21st-century ocean is highly dynamic.[1] The impact of human activity on the marine environment is "substantial, ubiquitous, and changing" (Halpern et al. 2019). Marine and coastal ecosystems are pressured and destabilized, as shifting patterns of human activity contribute to and respond to alterations in the material ocean. Marine resource extraction (especially fish, energy, and minerals) is being politicized in new ways, as the pursuit of strategic resources rubs against evolving norms of global justice and environmental stewardship. We are likely on the verge of massive defaunation and biodiversity loss (McCauley et al. 2015). New technologies such as autonomous vehicles are radically augmenting the possibilities for marine scientific research, maritime domain awareness, and military operations. All of this is occurring in the context of a shifting global balance of power, especially between China, Russia, the United States, and the European Union, all of whom have preferences in terms of the use of ocean space. Some states and regions continue to invest in multilateralism, while others act as spoilers, refusing to participate (or participate in good faith) in the shared implementation of the ocean governance regime. This overall situation is deeply concerning, as the ocean itself, ocean use activities, and the human relationship to the ocean are subject to potentially radical and long-lasting changes.

The ocean governance regime, centered on the United Nations Convention on the Law of the Sea (UNCLOS), is designed to help us manage the ocean and our relationship to it in ways that achieve our collective goals. UNCLOS reflects a broad set of aspirations, including conservation, sustainability, equity, and international cooperation. To achieve these goals in the context of a highly dynamic ocean, the regime must respond and adapt to new developments.

But UNCLOS faces many challenges. It was mostly constructed during the 20th century before climate change was a generally understood and acutely harmful phenomenon. The political geography UNCLOS creates—a suite of maritime zones with specific rights and duties—is generated from the "baseline," a legal concept whose foundations are undermined by sea level rise. UNCLOS relies on a jurisdictional framework (flag state jurisdiction) that facilitates non-compliance and rule avoidance. Regional and sectoral governance institutions are responsible for much of the implementation of UNCLOS and have very mixed track records. Overall, the relationship between the design of UNCLOS and its effectiveness is increasingly strained.

Despite these structural issues, UNCLOS is not going anywhere. The Convention represents a substantial "sunk cost" by the international community of states, because of the time and effort it took to negotiate, and the carefully balanced compromises it contains. Since its finalization in 1982, and its entry into force in 1994, UNCLOS has served as the framework institution for an expanding ocean governance regime, made up of international treaties, affiliated organizations, and normative frameworks that collectively govern ocean space. That regime is still growing, within the jurisdictional and territorial confines established by UNCLOS.

But as conditions change, so must UNCLOS. Change might include reinterpretation, modification, augmentation, or even replacement of parts of UNCLOS or the larger regime constructed under its framework. The capacity, conditions, and mechanisms of change within the ocean governance regime represent an important research agenda for political scientists, geographers, and others. This chapter argues that contemporary English-language UNCLOS scholarship is incomplete, as far as international relations (IR) theories, concepts, and approaches have been inadequately harnessed. More thorough and targeted IR research on UNCLOS and the ocean governance regime more broadly should draw on liberal, realist, and constructivist IR theory. A key motivation for this research agenda is to support the need for efficient and effective regime development, given planetary problems such as climate change and biodiversity loss. IR approaches are especially needed because of the geopolitical patterns shaping ocean governance. These include the limited investment of great powers in UNCLOS, the assertiveness of regional coalitions, and shifting patterns of strategic resource competition. IR is necessary because the ocean is a global commons, which must be governed by the international community of states.

This chapter outlines an IR agenda for UNCLOS research in three sections. The first section identifies gaps and biases in UNCLOS scholarship, demonstrating the need for broader approaches. The second outlines a research agenda focused on change in the global ocean governance regime. The last section considers the relationship between UNCLOS scholarship and effective ocean governance, connecting the research endeavor to normative goals.

UNCLOS scholarship

The patterns of UNCLOS scholarship are distinctive and uneven. While there is a large body of marine social science literature, it is difficult to identify strands that are distinctively political science. This is especially the case with IR (Carvalho and Leira 2022). The "law of the sea[2] would seem a natural fit with IR theories and concepts. The law of the sea is constructed by the international community of states through custom and treaty. But a closer look suggests that IR approaches to ocean governance, and especially UNCLOS, are under-utilized, siloed, or otherwise of low visibility. A recent "Manifesto for the marine social sciences," generated from engagement with the epistemic community of marine social scientists, includes a section on governance research needs that does not mention UNCLOS or international politics (Bavinck and Verrips 2020). There is both a dearth of research in this area and a lack of understanding that something is missing. This section unpacks that assessment through three observations: (1) law-of-the-sea scholarship is dominated by lawyers, (2) UNCLOS scholarship is particularly weak in the United States, and (3) the use of IR theory to study the law of the sea occurs primarily in security studies.

Law-of-the-sea scholarship is produced primarily by international legal experts and is concentrated in a small number of journals.[3] Book-length research is dominated by the publisher Brill, which traces its history back to 1683. Brill publishes the well-known *Virginia Commentaries*, which carefully document the UNCLOS III negotiations, and maintains an updated guide to international maritime boundaries. Brill also publishes the *International Journal of Marine and Coastal Law*, which has recently endeavored to assess the field through a new series of articles "that explore and reflect upon law of the sea scholarship" (Barnes 2023, 2). Three such articles have been published, and they collectively portray unity and coherence, with the law of the sea described as a "mature discipline" undertaken by an "epistemic community"[4] with a real impact on practitioners (Barnes 2023, 7; Ridings 2023, 9). Law-of-the-sea research is recognized as professionalized; "There are textbooks on the law of the sea, there are conferences on the law of the sea, there are law of the sea institutes" (Papanicolopulu 2023, 158). But this perspective on UNCLOS scholarship comes from international law. All three authors are lawyers, barristers, and/or professors of law. So is the Editor-in-Chief of the *International Journal of Marine and Coastal Law*.

It is not surprising that law-of-the-sea scholarship would be the purview of legal scholars—the boundaries between the law of the sea and private maritime law are often fuzzy. But international law perspectives are limited. Legal scholars typically take a positivist approach that is primarily descriptive and normative (Ridings 2023, 10). Their source material is "general principles of law, treaties or customary international law" (Ridings 2023, 10). They focus on what the law means, does, and should be. In contrast, the field of IR strives to be *explanatory*, drawing on and building theories of state behavior and concepts of world order that bring in the broader context of power, interests, and ideas. IR views international law as epiphenomenal to international politics. These two fields—international law and IR—are not well connected generally (Byers 2009, 612). This disconnect is especially troublesome in the context of UNCLOS, because while much of the ocean governance regime deals with non-state actors and private law, UNCLOS is the exception—it is a state-centric, public law, "Constitution for the Oceans" (Papanicolopulu 2023, 177; Roland Holst 2023, 284).

An IR perspective is critical to understanding the negotiation, design, implementation, and (in)effectiveness of UNCLOS and related institutions. UNCLOS is a product of international politics, and it succeeds only to the degree that it can shape the behavior of states. Indeed, its primary purpose is to order relations among sovereign states in shared ocean space. UNCLOS is a fundamental part of the contemporary world order, as one of the framework global commons treaties of the 20th century, alongside the Antarctic Treaty (1959) and Outer Space Treaty (1967). Its design and implementation have been deeply conditioned by trends in international politics, including the Cold War, decolonization and the New International Economic Order movement, and the emergence of global environmentalism. The ocean governance regime should therefore be fertile ground for IR theory and concepts.

There is a notable lack of UNCLOS scholarship produced in the United States. Anecdotally, it has been observed that there is a "generation gap" between the scholars who participated in the UNCLOS III negotiations and those getting into the field today.[5] Early UNCLOS scholarship in the United States was propelled by heavyweights such as John Norton Moore, Myron Nordquist, Lewis Alexander, Harry Scheiber, Bernard Oxman, and J. Ashley Roach, all of whom made careers in the law of the sea. No such cohort of UNCLOS scholars seems to exist today, with a very limited number of early- and mid-career law-of-the-sea researchers, especially at US universities. Only two members of the 25-person editorial board of the *International Journal of Marine and Coastal Law* are based at US institutions. Only one member of the 26-person advisory board of *Ocean Development & International Law* is from a US-based institution (the author). While there are many law-of-the-sea research institutes around the world (see Table 12.1 for a sample), the Law of the Sea Institute located at the UC Berkeley School of Law is significantly reduced in comparison to its heyday.

One exception to this trend is in security studies. Much of the UNCLOS-related scholarship produced in the United States comes from the institutions of professional military education, such as the US Naval War College. While such work is more attentive to power, hegemony, and incentive structures for states, it sometimes blurs the lines between IR and foreign policy (Paskal 2023, Pedrozo 2024) and tends to prioritize Realist perspectives. There is an overwhelming focus on freedom of navigation and "securing the global commons" (Dutton et al. 2013, Kraska and Pedrozo 2018, Kraska 2018). Topics related to maritime security, such as the South China Sea, illegal fishing, piracy, and trafficking, are commonly explored. But many other topics and perspectives are under-explored, and there are few who specialize in UNCLOS itself. The general lack of expert knowledge about UNCLOS is often reflected in small errors, such as the suggestion that 350 nautical miles is the farthest possible extent for a continental shelf, or the conflation of the high seas (the water beyond the Exclusive Economic Zone) and Area (the seabed beyond the continental shelf).

The low level of civilian UNCLOS expertise in the United States is a problem for the future of the Convention. Recurring debates over US ratification can be ill-informed. One common criticism made by opponents of UNCLOS is that the United States would be subject to international environmental litigation. However, UNCLOS Part XII (dealing with the marine environment) has rarely been used in dispute settlement, and only between neighboring states. Another common retort against ratification is the idea that the United States already gets the rights and follows the rules of the "good parts" of UNCLOS, especially those related to navigational freedoms. The

Table 12.1 Notable centers of UNCLOS research

Institute	Character/location
Law of the Sea Institute (LOSI)	University of California, Berkeley, USA
Stockton Center for International Law	US Naval War College, USA
IMO International Maritime Law Institute	University of Malta
National Center for the Sea and Maritime Law (DEHUKAM)	Ankara University, Turkey
Netherlands Institute for the Law of the Sea	University of Utrecht, Netherlands
Norwegian Centre for the Law of the Sea	Arctic University of Norway
Maritime and Oceanic Law Centre	University of Nantes, France
World Maritime University	IMO postgraduate university, Sweden
Institute of Maritime Law and International Law of the Sea	University of Hamburg, Germany
Australian National Centre for Ocean Resources & Security (ANCORS)	University of Wollongong, Australia
Center for International Law	National University of Singapore
National Maritime Foundation India	Think tank, India
Korea Institute of Ocean Science and Technology (KIOST)	Think tank, South Korea
Institute of Marine & Environmental Law	University of Cape Town
Institute of the Law of the Sea	Ocean University of China

Note: This list should be taken as a non-exhaustive list, especially because it excludes research centers that do not produce English-language literature and web material. The table also excludes research by individuals.
Source: Author's own.

US Freedom of Navigation Program is said to support the "rule of law" embedded in UNCLOS. US citizens and officials will have a tough time understanding other states' negative reactions to these assertions without the historical context of the UNCLOS III negotiations, or awareness of the differing interpretations held by other maritime powers (Bianco et al. 2023).

Researching change in UNCLOS

In some ways, the ocean governance regime *has* adapted to new circumstances and new understandings. While never formally amended, UNCLOS has been augmented and/or modified by three "implementing agreements." These agreements reflect evolving understandings of the object of governance, from species to ecosystems to biodiversity. Progress has also been driven by dispute settlement, including the development of a consistent approach to maritime boundary delimitation (Østhagen 2021). New interpretations of UNCLOS provisions have been generated by subsequent practice and subsequent agreement (Buga 2015). But in general, UNCLOS is slow to change, even in response to obvious needs for clarity and/or adjustment. A primary example is the need to clarify the rules for baselines in the face of sea level rise. Although the issue was flagged by UNCLOS scholars almost 35 years ago (Caron 1990, Soons 1990), it remains unresolved. Change does not happen automatically, and it cannot be assumed.

The first step to understanding when, how, and why UNCLOS changes is identifying the mechanisms through which change is possible. Because much of the law of the sea exists as both formal and customary international law, the mechanisms of change are diverse and can be difficult to trace. These include formal treaty negotiations, dispute settlement rulings, institutional decision-making, changes in treaty interpretation, the development of new legal ideas, and shifting patterns of state practice. Central research questions *about* mechanisms of change include: Whose interests, and which ideas, drive changes in the law of the sea? What factors influence the choice of one mechanism or forum over others? How do decision-making procedures affect regulatory possibilities? In what ways does the exercise of power influence change in the law of the sea? In what ways do shifts in the balance of power between states create new opportunities and obstacles for change? All these areas of research need sustained scholarly attention.

This section identifies under-explored research areas related to change in UNCLOS and the UNCLOS-centered ocean governance regime. But first, there are two areas where the literature on regime development is already quite active: the new Biodiversity Beyond National Jurisdiction (BBNJ) Treaty and the International Seabed Authority (ISA). Articles on both are commonly found in journals like *Marine Policy*, *Frontiers in Marine Science*, and *Ocean & Coastal Management*. This part of the literature focuses on international law *making* but is interdisciplinary. It is the continuation of a large literature produced around the UNCLOS III negotiations and their aftermath, which reports on the dynamics between states, coalitions, and institutional leadership, and proffers ideas and proposals for better governance. These are obvious and key areas of regime development, and scholarship strives to capture key dynamics in these legal evolutions. But the depth of research on the BBNJ and ISA processes is the exception, not the rule. Significant work remains to be done in other areas, including those outlined below.

Defining the ocean governance regime

UNCLOS sits at the core of the ocean governance regime because it establishes the basic framework for prescriptive and enforcement jurisdiction at sea and allocates rights and duties among maritime and coastal states. But the regime itself—the collection of principles, norms, rules, and procedures to govern the ocean—has grown significantly within this framework. It includes a web of regional and sectoral institutions that engage in rulemaking for particular places and activities. Recent "governance breakthroughs" for ocean management and protection include the BBNJ Treaty, the World Trade Organization Agreement on Fisheries Subsidies, and Sustainable Development Goal 14 on "Life Below Water." Other relevant developments include the addition of a "loss and damage" fund in the climate change regime (COP 27) and the "30 x 30" target and Global Biodiversity Framework produced through the Convention on Biological Diversity. In short, the ocean is a crowded governance space, and the architecture of ocean governance continues to expand.

Approaching UNCLOS and associated institutions as an ocean governance regime implies attention to how states engage with legalization and institutionalization to pursue their national and shared global interests. Although its core components are clear (Mendenhall 2019), there are many important research questions about changes in the boundaries of the regime. Topics include:

1. Regime complexes, which are overlapping and non-hierarchical institutions in the same issue area (Alter and Raustiala, 2018). Under what conditions do states create a hierarchy between institutions? Why and how do concepts of the object of governance constrain the boundaries of regime complexes?
2. Interfaces with other regimes, including international norms and laws for labor, trade, human rights, intellectual property, and others. To what degree, and in what ways, is the interface between UNCLOS and these other regimes (dys)functional? What explains the overall lack of attentiveness to regime interfaces?
3. Bad faith engagement, or when states engage in institution building to avoid changing their behavior in ways they consider too costly. Institution creation can be about establishing weaker forums and gaining domestic credibility, where the stated goals of diplomats are not their actual goals (Dimitrov 2019). Does the growth of the ocean governance regime always mean more conditioned, cooperative, and shared goal-oriented behavior?

Information theory of institutional adaptation

One theory of state behavior, rational choice, suggests that states update governance institutions in response to current information and new needs (Laurens et al. 2023, 2). Current information can affect interest formation and problem definition, both of which are important drivers for institutional change. Whether this is happening for UNCLOS is an interesting and important question, especially in the context of major shifts such as ocean acidification and sea level rise. We may be on the verge of a massive influx of knowledge about the mesopelagic zone (200–1000 meters below the surface), which will change our ideas about the value of this part of the ocean (Schadeberg et al. 2023, 1). But access to new knowledge is uneven. Because the mesopelagic is so distant, our ideas about it are mediated primarily by the scientific community, and relevant primarily to the interests of private commercial actors and environmental non-governmental organizations. To what degree, and how, do information brokers influence the uptake and response to the latest information about the marine environment? In what situations does new knowledge provoke, speed up, delay, or impede regime development?

The basis of rational choice theory is the assumption that states *want* the latest information to inform their choices. But this is not necessarily the case, as sometimes a lack of information supports status quo activities and interests. New scientific information is needed to animate the BBNJ Treaty through environmental impact assessments and marine protected areas, but new scientific data collection is not mandated and will not be sponsored through BBNJ mechanisms (Mendenhall and Helm 2024). What factors influence state investment, or lack of investment, in marine scientific research? Relevant data is often not available before decision-making occurs. How does decision-making under uncertainty work in ocean governance? To what degree does the involvement of industry actors in sectoral governance influence such decision-making? How are risk–risk trade-offs defined and accounted for? Such questions will be especially critical as the international community of states confronts the possibilities associated with marine geoengineering.

Alternative normative paradigms

Twenty-first-century problems and perspectives have prompted a substantial rethinking of the purposes of ocean governance. Three contrasting paradigms have emerged, which vary in their degree of departure from UNCLOS principles. The idea of the "Blue Economy" suggests that through effective technocratic management, the ocean can be a site of continued development and growth. The "Ocean Equity" paradigm asserts that the central goal of governance should be a redistribution of rights, authority, and access, which can improve outcomes for both society and the environment. The "Ocean Rights" paradigm draws on "Rights of Nature" approaches adopted in domestic jurisdictions as a model for recognizing that the ocean has "inherent rights" through international law. Each of these paradigms implies change in ocean governance, reinforcing and building on some aspects of the UNCLOS-centered regime and rejecting and/or replacing others. Each paradigm also has constituencies or interest groups and embodies different visions for the future of the human/ocean relationship. But do any of these paradigms correlate with normative development among maritime and coastal states, or ocean users?

Future scholarship should investigate the relationship between these paradigms and the UNCLOS-centered ocean governance regime. English School theories, which are attentive to the distinction between normative systems among states ("international society) and among people ("world society"), have been underused to study the norms of global environmental politics (Falkner 2024). Along with constructivist theory, the English School offers conceptual tools and frameworks that help scholars trace norm constitution, development, diffusion, and adoption. Areas of research might include how non-state actors promote normative shifts among the international community of states, shifts in the sources of legitimacy and authority in ocean governance, and the persistence and/or transmogrification of international social movements like the New International Economic Order.

Dispute settlement and great powers

One potential avenue for the progressive development of the ocean governance regime is dispute settlement. The compulsory dispute settlement system created by UNCLOS is remarkable for its degree of articulation and obligation. Through both contentious cases and advisory opinions, the International Court of Justice, the International Tribunal on the Law of the Sea (ITLOS), and ad hoc arbitral tribunals have contributed to the interpretation and implementation of parts of the law of the sea, especially, but not exclusively, those contained in UNCLOS. Dispute settlement has been most active in the areas of prompt release, maritime enforcement, and boundary delimitation. ITLOS has issued three advisory opinions related to UNCLOS. Yet there have also been high-profile rejections of the dispute settlement system, most notably by "great powers," including Russia and China. The credibility and future of the dispute settlement system are at risk, with their viability depending on states' willingness to use and abide by the rulings of international tribunals.

The contribution of dispute settlement to the development of UNCLOS needs additional investigation. Although there is a significant amount of English-language scholarship already, it is dominated by international lawyers (see: Jensen 2020). Critical IR research questions include: Under what conditions will states use the system? Under what conditions will they abide by rulings? Does the issuance of advisory opinions undermine or strengthen tribunals' normative authority? What factors shape "forum shopping" between dispute settlement bodies? Research is especially needed on the durability, credibility, and authority of UNCLOS Part XV, after rejections of rulings by maritime powers including China, Russia, and the United Kingdom, and the total non-participation of the United States.

Researching ocean governance forums

A wide range of ocean governance forums are under-researched.[6] The UNCLOS Meeting of State Parties (MOSP) is one such forum, although civil society organizations (and through them, researchers) can attend as accredited UN observers. The MOSP deals with a more restricted set of topics related to the administration of UNCLOS, such as the nomination and election of ITLOS judges and members of the Commission on the Limits of the Continental Shelf (CLCS). The Informal Consultative Process (ICP)[7] is a broader process, wherein the UN General Assembly reviews the progress in ocean affairs and the law of the sea, starting with a report from the Secretary-General. The ICP involves informal information sharing and discussion of emerging issues. Linked to, but separate from, the ICP are two annual resolutions passed by the General Assembly: the so-called "omnibus" resolution and a resolution on sustainable fisheries. These are intended in part to drive global policy, and sometimes they do (see, for example, the call for bans on bottom trawling). Other relevant forums include the "Regular Process," which involves international and interdisciplinary collaboration to produce a World Ocean Assessment, the UN Oceans Conference and Our Ocean Conferences, the UN Decade for Ocean Science, the Review Conference for the Fish Stocks Agreement, and committee work at the International Law Association and International Law Commission. Some elements of the regime cannot be directly accessed or observed, such as the CLCS, but most allow for some form of research access.

Many of these processes are facilitated by the Division for Ocean Affairs and the Law of the Sea (DOALOS) (Tarassenko and Tani 2013). DOALOS is the secretariat to UNCLOS and the Fish Stocks Agreement. It provides direct support to the CLCS and convenes the MOSP. It sponsors fellowships, provides training, and engages in outreach activities "with a view to promoting a better understanding of [UNCLOS] and related instruments, their wider acceptance, uniform and consistent application and effective implementation" (Tarassenko and Tani 2013, 691). DOALOS is only taking on more functions. The role of DOALOS in the definition and development of UNCLOS is under-studied. Secretariats are "typically discounted as political actors in their own right," and assumed to be neutral and apolitical functionaries (Jinnah and Young 2015, 21). But there is a "veiled aspect of secretariat politics," behind which they "perform key regime functions" that are "often informal, unacknowledged, undocumented, and/or obscured" (Jinnah and Young 2015, 21). Through filtering, framing, and drafting, secretariats like DOALOS can shape state preferences and problem definitions, two major drivers of regime development.

Scholarship as citizenship[8]

The research agenda described above can and should support the development of a more effective ocean governance regime. Scholarship can shape the interest formation and diplomatic strategies of states. As Richard Falk argues, states are locked into the pursuit of national interests and do not generally pursue the global public interest; "Governmental institutions are too embedded in the extremely uneven particularities of national experience and hampered by special interests and bureaucratic rigidities to have the energy and imagination needed to find solutions" (Falk 2016, 97). It will be critical to connect the formation of global public interests to a close understanding of the drivers and mechanisms of change in UNCLOS. The moment is coming when we will better understand "the pace of change in cumulative impact on ocean ecosystems from expanding human activities – and the patterns, locations and drivers of the most significant change" (Halpern et al. 2019). This new, and critical, information will not *necessarily* drive the development of UNCLOS in useful and functional directions. But the cumulative impact of humans on the ocean "may rapidly push many ocean regions past critical tipping points," and in doing so create new windows of political opportunity (Halpern et al. 2019).

Crises can serve as catalyzing events, enabling radical change. The ocean is already beginning to experience a cascading series of crises, including ocean warming, acidification, and biodiversity loss. Scholars who forward alternative paradigms for international governance often describe what they are doing as creating blueprints so that when windows of opportunity open, mobilization can readily latch onto and actualize alternative architectures. In this view, what matters are the "horizons of necessity," unconstrained by judgments about what is immediately possible, because what is possible might change (Falk 2016, 101). An example of this is Chris Armstrong's *Blue New Deal*, which essentially wishes to replace UNCLOS with a Global Ocean Authority (among other changes) (Armstrong 2023). This kind of scholarship supplements what is lacking in international legal scholarship, where "scholars often seem to be expending more effort on the detail than the grand ideas" (Barnes 2023, 4).

Another scholarly approach, well illustrated by the work of Oran Young, is attentive to "horizons of feasibility," keeping always in mind what is possible in the current economic, political, and cultural context (Falk 2016, 101). This kind of scholarship can be more influential in the current moment, as the interests and goals expressed are more likely to be shared with practitioners (Ridings 2023, 25). IR research that is directly useful for law-of-the-sea practitioners must take seriously the interests, ideas, and perspectives of other members of the international community, including state and non-state actors. Rather than simply providing advice or support to foreign policymakers, such scholarship can help to define the "horizons of feasibility" in terms of possible cooperative agreements and collaborative behavior among states.

Notes

1. The author would like to thank Slate Northington for her valuable research assistance in support of this chapter.
2. "Law of the sea" is a term of art that generally refers to the public international law governing the ocean. As a concept, it therefore overlaps with the IR concept of a "governance regime." UNCLOS is a core part of the law of the sea.
3. The academic journals *Marine Policy, Ocean Development & International Law, Ocean & Coastal Management*, and *International Journal of Marine and Coastal Law* consistently publish UNCLOS-related research.
4. Epistemic communities wield credible, authoritative, and salient expert knowledge to "identify cause-and-effect relationships, elucidate interlinkages among problems, help define the consulting state's or organization's interests, and help formulate policy" (Haas 2015, 9).
5. This insight is credited to Myron Nordquist, who shared his wisdom at the 2019 Rhodes Academy on the Law of the Sea.
6. The author would like to thank Valentina Germani for a helpful conversation sorting through the processes described in this paragraph.
7. The United Nations Open-Ended Informal Consultative Process on Oceans and the Law of the Sea.
8. Taken from Richard Falk (2016). Falk defines engaged citizenship as "an interest in affecting the public discourse relating to the New Earth agenda, encouraging radical critique of political, economic, cultural, and ideological structures" (Falk 2016, 98–99).

References

Alter, Karen J., and Kal Raustiala. 2018. The Rise of International Regime Complexity. *Annual Review of Law and Social Science* 14 (1): 329–49. https://doi.org/10.1146/annurev-lawsocsci-101317-030830.

Armstrong, Chris. 2023. *A Blue New Deal: Why We Need a New Politics for the Ocean*. New Haven, CT: Yale University Press.

Barnes, Richard. 2023. Reflections on the Waters: Law of the Sea Scholarship and Practice. *The International Journal of Marine and Coastal Law* 38 (1): 1–10. https://doi.org/10.1163/15718085-bja10114.

Bavinck, Maarten, and Jojada Verrips. 2020. Manifesto for the Marine Social Sciences. *Maritime Studies* 19 (2): 121–23. https://doi.org/10.1007/s40152-020-00179-x.

Bianco, Christine, Zenel Garcia, and Bibek Chand. 2023. What Is Innocent? Freedom of Navigation Versus Coastal States' Rights in the Law of the Sea. *Ocean Development & International Law* 54 (3): 349–74. https://doi.org/10.1080/00908320.2023.2267406.

Buga, Irina. 2015. Between Stability and Change in the Law of the Sea Convention: Subsequent Practice, Treaty Modification, and Regime Interaction. In *The Oxford Handbook of the Law of the Sea*, edited by Donald R. Rothwell, Alex G. Oude Elferink, Karen N. Scott, and Tim Stephens, 46–68. Oxford: Oxford University Press.

Byers, Michael. 2009. International Law. In *The Oxford Handbook of International Relations*, edited by Christian Reus-Smit and Duncan Snidal, 612–32. Oxford: Oxford University Press. https://doi.org/10.1093/oxfordhb/9780199219322.003.0035.

Caron, David D. 1990. When Law Makes Climate Change Worse: Rethinking the Law of Baselines in Light of a Rising Sea Level. *Ecology Law Quarterly* 17 (4): 621–54.

Carvalho, Benjamin de, and Halvard Leira, eds. 2022. *The Sea and International Relations*. Manchester: Manchester University Press.

Dimitrov, Radoslav S. 2019. Empty Institutions in Global Environmental Politics. *International Studies Review*. https://doi.org/10.1093/isr/viz029.

Dutton, Peter, Robert Ross, and Øystein Tunsjø. 2013. *Twenty-First Century Seapower: Cooperation and Conflict at Sea*. Hoboken, NJ: Taylor & Francis.

Falk, Richard A. 2016. Scholarship as Citizenship. In *New Earth Politics: Essays from the Anthropocene*, edited by Simon Nicholson and Sikina Jinnah. Earth System Governance. Cambridge, MA: MIT Press.

Falkner, Robert. 2024. The *Longue Durée* of International Environmental Norm Change: Global Environmental Politics Meets the English School of International Relations. *Global Environmental Politics* 24 (1): 124–37. https://doi.org/10.1162/glep_a_00718.

Haas, Peter M. 2015. *Epistemic Communities, Constructivism, and International Environmental Politics*. London: Taylor & Francis.

Halpern, Benjamin S., Melanie Frazier, Jamie Afflerbach, Julia S. Lowndes, Fiorenza Micheli, Casey O'Hara, Courtney Scarborough, and Kimberly A. Selkoe. 2019. Recent Pace of Change in Human Impact on the World's Ocean. *Scientific Reports* 9 (1). https://doi.org/10.1038/s41598-019-47201-9.

Jensen, Øystein, ed. 2020. *The Development of the Law of the Sea Convention: The Role of International Courts and Tribunals*. Cheltenham, UK and Northampton, MA: Edward Elgar Publishing.

Jinnah, Sikina, and Oran R. Young. 2015. *Post-Treaty Politics: Secretariat Influence in Global Environmental Governance*. Cambridge: MIT Press.

Kraska, James. 2018. The Strategic Foundation of the Law of the Sea. In *Ocean Law Debates*, edited by Harry N. Scheiber, Nilufer Oral, and Moon-Sang Kwon, 181–215. Leiden: Brill | Nijhoff. https://doi.org/10.1163/9789004343146_008.

Kraska, James, and Raul A. Pedrozo. 2018. *The Free Sea: The American Fight for Freedom of Navigation*. Annapolis, MD: Naval Institute Press.

Laurens, Noémie, James Hollway, and Jean-Frédéric Morin. 2023. Checking for Updates: Ratification, Design, and Institutional Adaptation. *International Studies Quarterly* 67 (3): sqad049. https://doi.org/10.1093/isq/sqad049.

McCauley, Douglas J., Malin L. Pinsky, Stephen R. Palumbi, James A. Estes, Francis H. Joyce, and Robert R. Warner. 2015. Marine Defaunation: Animal Loss in the Global Ocean. *Science* 347 (6219): 1255641. https://doi.org/10.1126/science.1255641.

Mendenhall, Elizabeth. 2019. The Ocean Governance Regime: International Conventions and Institutions. In *Climate Change and Ocean Governance*, edited by Paul G. Harris, 27–42. Cambridge: Cambridge University Press. https://doi.org/10.1017/9781108502238.002.

Mendenhall, Elizabeth, and Rebecca R. Helm. 2024. When the "Best Available Science" Is Not Good Enough: The Need for Supporting Scientific Research in the United Nations Treaty to Protect Biodiversity beyond National Jurisdiction. *Marine Policy* 161: 105940. https://doi.org/10.1016/j.marpol.2023.105940.

Østhagen, Andreas. 2021. Troubled Seas? The Changing Politics of Maritime Boundary Disputes. *Ocean & Coastal Management* 205: 105535. https://doi.org/10.1016/j.ocecoaman.2021.105535.

Papanicolopulu, Irini. 2023. The Law of the Sea in Past Scholarship. *The International Journal of Marine and Coastal Law* 39 (1): 157–78. https://doi.org/10.1163/15718085-bja10144.

Paskal, Cleo. 2023. Island-Hopping with Chinese Characteristics: What the PRC Is Doing in the Pacific Islands, Why It Matters, and Why the Time Has Come to "Block and Build." *Naval War College Review* 76 (4): 5.

Pedrozo, Raul. 2024. Another Missed Opportunity to Adopt a Universally Accepted Maritime Treaty. *International Law Studies* 103: 133–50.

Ridings, Penelope Jane. 2023. The Influence of Scholarship on the Shaping and Making of the Law of the Sea. *The International Journal of Marine and Coastal Law* 38: 1–27. https://doi.org/10.1163/15718085-bja10113.

Roland Holst, Rozemarijn J. 2023. Reflections on the Governance Function of Compulsory Dispute Settlement in the Legal Order for the Ocean. *The International Journal of Marine and Coastal Law* 38 (2): 283–301. https://doi.org/10.1163/15718085-bja10122.

Schadeberg, Amanda, Marloes Kraan, Rolf Groeneveld, Damian Trilling, and Simon Bush. 2023. Science Governs the Future of the Mesopelagic Zone. *npj Ocean Sustainability* 2 (1): 2. https://doi.org/10.1038/s44183-023-00008-8.

Soons, Alfred H.A. 1990. The Effects of a Rising Sea Level on Maritime Limits and Boundaries. *Netherlands International Law Review* 37 (2): 207. https://www.cambridge.org/core/journals/netherlands-international-law-review/article/abs/effects-of-a-rising-sea-level-on-maritime-limits-and-boundaries/145B75E446D762F24BFE9E61610367D6.

Tarassenko, Serguei, and Ilaria Tani. 2013. The Functions and Role of the United Nations Secretariat in Ocean Affairs and the Law of the Sea. In *The 1982 Law of the Sea Convention at 30*, edited by David Freestone, 9–25. Leiden: Brill | Nijhoff. https://doi.org/10.1163/9789004245044_003.

13 The global politics of marine protected areas

Justin Alger

Introduction

Overfishing, plastics, and climate change are putting extreme pressure on ocean ecosystems and species. Our ability to manage these threats has so far been limited. Fishing catch plateaued in the 1990s, not due to lack of fishing effort, but because of a global decline in fish stocks due to overexploitation (Pauly and Zeller 2016) and increasingly sophisticated technology (Barkin and DeSombre 2013). The proliferation of plastics poses a threat on par with climate change, with production growing each year and much of it ending up not only in the ocean (Abbott and Sumaila 2019, Lau et al. 2020), but throughout human and animal food systems (Dauvergne 2018). The 1.5°C warming target that the Paris Agreement aspires to is unachievable, with coral reef ecosystems already existentially threatened by ocean warming and acidification. These threats, among others, paint a bleak picture of the future of our ocean. In the case of plastics and climate change, the solutions are not specifically a matter of ocean governance but rather of the upstream extraction of fossil fuels and our use of them in energy systems and plastics production. Tools to combat these threats in ocean ecosystems are few.

Marine protected areas (MPAs) are perhaps the most common and important tool we have for bolstering the resilience of marine ecosystems. Australia established the world's first MPA in 1879, but Indigenous practices of spatial protection of course long predate this. As of 2024, there are nearly 17,000 MPAs in the world, covering 8 percent of the ocean (Marine Conservation Institute [MCI] 2024). They tend to be quite small, with a median MPA size of just 5 sq km. MPAs cannot curb plastic production or the burning of fossil fuels, but they can limit other forms of human impact, most notably fishing and mining. When MPAs are large enough and no-take—meaning they do not allow any extractive activity—they allow species to thrive, leading to much higher biomass levels than their smaller or mixed-use counterparts (Beattie et al. 2008, Edgar et al. 2014). They provide ocean ecosystems with the opportunity to build the resilience that they need to better absorb external pressures, including from plastics and climate (Pauly et al. 2002, McLeod et al. 2009). They are not a panacea, but they can help.

They are also not easy solutions. The decision to create an MPA is an inherently political one that establishes access rights to natural resources for various stakeholders (Alger 2021, 2023; Lubchenco and Grorud-Colvert 2015; Christie et al. 2017). Those stakeholders can often include entrenched commercial interests opposed to seeing their profitability threatened by environmental regulation. They can also include traditional and Indigenous communities whose rights have been eroded by overzealous governments using protected areas as a tool for political control (Peluso 1993, Bennett et al. 2015, De Santo 2020). Protected areas are therefore not a benign tool for protecting nature. They not only determine who has a right to resources, but the decision-making process itself adopts a commodification lens, through which states make cost–benefit decisions about the economic value of an area (Alger 2023). There is an inherent political trade-off in the siting and management of an MPA. Areas remote from commercial activity are politically easier to establish and manage effectively, but do not do much to limit immediate human impacts. Areas targeting the sites of commercial activity are more contested, and they often lead to 'paper parks' with very few protections.

This chapter outlines a research agenda for enhancing our understanding of the global politics of MPAs as a tool for protecting our oceans. It begins by documenting significant shifts in how states use MPAs that began in the mid-2000s. I then turn to a discussion of MPAs as sites of contestation and the political economy of their creation and management. The next section explores recent efforts by states in establishing MPAs in areas beyond national jurisdiction. I conclude by reflecting on the importance of new visions of a protected ocean.

The ocean governance transformation

In the mid-2000s, states began to increase their ambition about the scope of their MPAs. It was becoming clear by this point that the ocean was not as immune to human impacts as we once thought, despite its size, with scientific studies increasingly showing rapid decline (Pauly et al. 2002). Most MPAs are quite small, but from 2006 onward we have seen a proliferation of large MPAs exceeding 200,000 sq km that has led to a drastic increase in the extent of ocean protections. In 2000, about 2 million sq km totaling 0.7 percent of the global ocean was protected, but as of 2024 that total is now 29 million sq km, totaling 8 percent (Protected Planet 2024). The overwhelming majority of this growth is in these large MPAs: the 100 largest MPAs account for 89 percent of the total (MCI 2024). This shift was largely driven by the work of advocacy groups, who advanced a norm of large marine protection globally (Alger 2021, Alger and Dauvergne 2017). These large MPAs are in no way uniform, and each has its own unique politics as local forces—their unique customs, economics, and political institutions—interact with this global norm. Numerous studies document the politics of specific large MPAs, with useful insights into patterns of global ocean governance, and with room for more of this kind of locally informed research (e.g., Goncalves and De Santo 2021, Relano et al. 2021).

This progress toward more ambitious protections for national jurisdictions was a spark that contributed to the advancement of global ocean governance more generally. It led to invigorated efforts to create international agreements on issues ranging from fisheries subsidies to areas beyond national jurisdiction to plastics. In 2022, the World Trade Organization (WTO) reached its first agreement in 10 years, and the first ever with sustainability at its core. That agreement imposed some restrictions on fishery subsidies, which have not only distorted the market and disadvantaged small-scale fishers but have contributed to the overcapitalization of an industry already overexploiting fisheries. The agreement was limited to restrictions on subsidies to illegal, unreported, and unregulated (IUU) fishing; fishing overexploited stocks (as defined by a given state); and unregulated high seas fishing. In practice, the restrictions will do little, and negotiations are underway to strengthen them (Alger et al. 2023, Sumaila et al. 2024). Meaningful restrictions on fishing subsidies could impact how states manage their MPAs, perhaps even undermining the role of subsidies in contributing to paper parks. More importantly, though, the leadership that many states have shown in protecting their national ocean spaces likely contributes to momentum toward agreements such as this one. These kinds of regime interaction effects are under-studied. Research into how domestic efforts to protect oceans contribute to global leadership and ocean advocacy in related international negotiations—such as the WTO fisheries agreement, United Nations Framework Convention on Climate Change (UNFCCC), or negotiations for a global plastics treaty—would help to enhance our understanding of how we make progress in ocean governance across several issue areas simultaneously.

Two recent international developments could considerably bolster the prospects of MPAs as a tool for ocean governance. The first is the 2022 Kunming-Montreal Agreement, which codified the 30 x 30 target to protect 30 percent of terrestrial and marine space by 2030. The target was one long advocated by environmental organizations as necessary to ensure that we were doing enough at scale to protect nature. The politics of this campaign, states' follow-through on their commitments (or lack thereof), and whether it is effectively protecting ecosystems and species are all important research areas. States all too often do not comply with aspirational environmental targets such as the 30 x 30 target and, when they do, it is not necessarily a clear indication that domestic measures are effective (e.g., Young 2016). The second development is the recent agreement on the historic 2023 Treaty on Biodiversity Beyond National Jurisdiction (BBNJ), which provides a framework for states to establish MPAs on the high seas. I will turn to a discussion of high seas protections later, but for now, it is worth highlighting the significant political capital and effort that went into reaching this agreement. The desire to expand the scope of the large MPA norm beyond national jurisdictions played a role in this, but further study building on previous works into why and how states were able to reach this agreement could provide valuable insight into future international negotiations (e.g., Tiller et al. 2019, Mendenhall et al. 2023).

In recognition of both recent progress on and the need for stronger ocean governance, the UN declared the 2020s the UN Ocean Decade of Science for Sustainable

Development. The vision for this decade includes protecting and restoring ecosystems, reducing marine pollution, a sustainable and equitable ocean economy, and sustainable marine food systems. The goal is transformative, science-based solutions to ocean decline. While this platform reflects the UN's recognition of the imperative of addressing ocean issues, it also raises several questions. International relations scholars have mixed views about the efficacy of this kind of high-level goal setting, often exemplified by the shortcomings of the Millennium Development Goals (MDGs) or its successor the Sustainable Development Goals (SDGs) (e.g., Reinert 2020). The extent to which the UN Ocean Decade goals contribute to better ocean governance is unclear, though roadmaps do exist (Claudet et al. 2020). Sustainability language is also easily co-opted. While there is certainly a need for ecosystem protections that consider human needs, all too often the language of sustainability is used to legitimize an extractive agenda that is inherently unsustainable (Bernstein 2001). Ocean resource management practices are historically woefully inadequate; witness, for example, the failure of the maximum sustainable yield (MSY) model of fisheries management (Jacques and Lobo 2018). This model attempts to set limits on catch to maximize resource extraction while preserving the ability of a fish stock to sustain itself. Unsurprisingly, it fails because we are not very good at it and because it does not adequately allow for exogenous shocks, such as warming waters leading to migration (Sumaila 2022). It seems unlikely that the UN or its partners in this mission will deviate from this lacking vision of sustainability. Problematizing the concept of ocean sustainability is a fruitful avenue for potential research.

These developments in the global governance of our oceans have important implications for the global politics of MPAs. Ocean sustainability norms have the potential to erode what is considered appropriate within protected areas. An ocean sustainability model—increasingly referred to as a blue economy—can undermine efforts to protect ecosystems and species (Cisneros-Montemayor et al. 2019). It can promote a stakeholder model of environmental problem-solving that prioritizes meeting various stakeholder needs, with biodiversity outcomes epiphenomenal to the process itself (Cashore and Bernstein 2023). In other words, we should be asking questions about whether our marine governance initiatives, including the political processes in designating and managing protected areas, are helping to protect ecosystems and species. This is not to argue that human considerations should not matter, but rather that a sustainability approach too often leads to bolstering economic interests at the cost of poor environmental outcomes. Further research is needed into a politics of protected areas that prioritizes environmental outcomes, while still promoting equity, especially for marginalized peoples.

A critical political economy of MPAs

The express purpose of protected areas is to limit or prohibit human activity, which means that they inevitably face challenges from various sources of economic power. A fully protected area prohibiting commercial activity seemingly runs counter to the established liberal paradigm of environmentalism, which prioritizes economic growth and development over environmental goals (Bernstein 2001). Protected areas can suppress the economic growth of certain industries in the short term, which can be especially challenging in democratic societies in which specific communities of voters and workers might be disproportionately impacted. States have therefore become very good at making their protected area practices compatible with their economic goals, which, unfortunately, generally means diluting their environmental objectives (Alger 2021). This pattern is a global one and has led to a relatively patchwork network of protected areas that, according to one study, means we are designating protected areas no more effectively than if they were placed randomly (Kuempel et al. 2016). International relations scholars can contribute to our understanding of why the global MPA (and terrestrial protected area) network is falling short in several ways.

First, one of the challenges with the existing MPA network is that much of it is remote from commercial activity (Devillers et al. 2015). These remote MPAs still matter because they enshrine protections from future exploitation. For years, fishers have ventured farther into the open ocean as fish stocks closer to land decline. Climate change is changing the migratory patterns of fish, and new threats such as deep-sea mining are around the corner. Remote MPAs can act as a bulwark against ever-expanding commercial exploitation. But more needs to be done to address current and ongoing exploitation, which is already pushing the ocean beyond its capacity to sustain life. There is substantive international relations literature about the politics of contestation on land, including over deforestation, minerals extraction, agricultural production, and much more (e.g., Neville 2021). Applying the lessons from this literature to marine protections could yield useful insights. What does contestation look like in more remote spaces? How do we balance long-term, intergenerational concerns with the need for short-term profit? How can local communities fight back against better-coordinated and better-funded (and sometimes violent) industries over how often remote ocean spaces are used? If protected areas are going to be more effective, they need to be in areas in which they can better challenge ongoing exploitation.

Second, when MPAs are situated closer to commercial activity, there is a strong tendency for them to be paper parks. The stakeholder-driven process of designating many MPAs can lead governments to considerably compromise the environmental purposes of an MPA to meet the needs of businesses and local communities (Alger 2021). If strict regulations would force businesses to shut down or put people out of work, opposition to them can be quite powerful. Instead, governments often rely on mixed-use regulations, which permit some (or all) commercial activity to continue unabated. These can include zoning within an MPA, limitations on certain types of extraction (i.e., bottom trawling versus purse seine fishing), or catch limits, among others. Too often, these processes lead to business-as-usual outcomes in which a protected area is accomplishing virtually nothing—merely lines on a map. This pattern plays out globally with only 2.9 percent of the ocean fully or highly protected despite 8 percent global protected area coverage (Marine Conservation Institute [MCI] 2024). This problem is exacerbated by states' emphasis on area targets to meet their biodiversity goals rather than measures that more accurately reflect biodiversity outcomes (De Santo 2013). The global politics of the paper park problem offers several avenues for future research. Comparative or quantitative analysis of the ways in which states are working toward the Kunming-Montreal 30 x 30 goal could yield useful insights about state behavior and the reasons the protected area network is falling short. More analysis of corporate power and influence over biodiversity governance could also generate useful knowledge about the ways in which environmental goals become compromised. Similarly, examining success stories in which states did not compromise environmental goals despite resistance could provide models for future MPA advocacy work and policymaking.

Third, while each protected area has its own unique local politics, part of this story is a transnational one. Transnational advocacy campaigns deserve much of the credit for the upsurge in MPAs since the mid-2000s, but it is unclear whether they can sustain that momentum. These campaigns—such as the Global Ocean Legacy or Pristine Seas campaigns—helped to put large MPAs on the agendas of states, who have since made considerable progress on a range of ocean issues. The scope of what is possible for ocean protection was changed by those efforts, but it is still not enough. How can transnational activists continue to ratchet up ocean commitments? How can they call out and push back against weak implementation of protected areas that undermine them as a tool for ocean protection? How can they promote equity and effective ecosystem protections without promoting a faulty sustainability or blue economy approach? The future of our oceans depends on the ability of activists, community defenders, scientists, scholars, and others to think big about what is possible for the oceans and to successfully advocate for it. This is especially important with new frontiers of extraction emerging in ocean spaces, such as the ongoing rush to begin the deep-sea mining of critical minerals. Research that seeks to understand how this happens in the face of considerable resistance from powerful industries and often states can make an important contribution to the field.

There is an inherent tension between MPAs and economic priorities. It is not as simple as saying that MPAs undermine economic growth. They should, in fact, promote healthier, sustainable economies by ensuring the survival of the species and ecosystems that people depend on. But as with so many other environmental problems, the challenge is often to overcome entrenched, often powerful, parochial interests. Environmental regulations—even if overwhelmingly positive for the economy in the long run—have short-term distributive consequences that mean some stakeholders lose out. The challenge is to promote regulations that challenge unsustainable industrial extraction practices without undermining the rights and practices of local and Indigenous resource users. On this issue of power and equity in ocean spaces, too, scholars can contribute considerably (i.e., Bennett 2022).

Protecting biodiversity in the high seas

Areas beyond national jurisdiction—colloquially known as the high seas—are one of the final remaining frontiers for protected areas. The BBNJ Treaty for the first time creates an international process by which states can collectively designate MPAs in areas beyond national jurisdiction. There is some precedent for this, most notably the 2.09 million sq km Ross Sea Protected Area—the largest protected area on the planet as of 2024. The Commission on the Conservation of Antarctic Living Marine Resources (CCAMLR) created the Ross Sea Protected Area in 2016 after years of negotiations. The Ross Sea MPA required consensus from its members, which included China, Russia, and the US. It was a major multilateral achievement that protects a significant area of the Antarctic. The (geo)politics of this process are under-studied, with some exceptions (i.e., Brooks et al. 2020), and could provide further insight into the creation of future high seas MPAs, although relations between the major powers have since declined, limiting the potential for cooperation.

Nonetheless, with the BBNJ hopefully entering into force soon, multilateral MPA designations will become more common. The veracity of this process has considerable implications for the potential of the BBNJ to make a difference in protecting high seas biodiversity. Multilateral environmental decision-making rarely leads to robust agreements. Coupled with the prominence of paper parks in national waters, there is a high risk that high seas protected areas may not accomplish much. States—and even environmental organizations in many cases—often view the creation of an MPA as an end, but it is biodiversity outcomes that matter. Ensuring that the BBNJ process foregrounds biodiversity outcomes, and not just splashy MPA announcements, is essential. Research into how states employ and implement the BBNJ Treaty will be needed as it progresses. Will the decision-making rules allow for robust MPAs? What shape will noncompliance take, especially in cases in which dissenting states may not respect an MPA? Will social pressure dissuade these states from violating MPAs created by the majority? Most importantly, the BBNJ does not allow states to regulate fisheries, restricting states' ability to put limits on one of the primary extractive activities MPAs are intended to regulate. Will social norms surrounding conservation and overfishing matter, or are high seas MPAs destined to be paper parks? The potential for states to finally create high seas protected areas means that there is considerable demand for more traditional, state-centered forms of international relations scholarship to better understand the global politics of MPAs.

There are also more ambitious proposals for protecting the high seas. This includes a proposal to close the high seas to fishing, supported by a robust economic analysis of doing so by one of the editors of this volume (Sumaila et al. 2015). The political feasibility of doing so in the short term is low, but international relations scholars should not shy away from ambitious thinking. Ambitious thinking is the only thing that will allow us to bring species and ecosystems back from the brink. While future casting can be a risky way to generate and publish research in international relations, especially for early-career scholars, there is a nascent politics of opposition to greater ambition. The Sumaila et al. (2015) study identifies the states that would lose out were the high seas closed to fishing, and they are predominantly wealthier, Western nations with large commercial fishing industries. These are the same nations that frequently oppose stricter fisheries management through regional fishery management organizations (RFMOs) and who opposed the BBNJ giving any authority to regulate fisheries. Power and politics are at the heart of why our efforts to protect biodiversity are falling short, so it is important that international relations scholars ask questions about why our governance initiatives cannot be more ambitious, including about the interests, institutions, and norms that order global politics.

Conclusion: a better vision of a protected ocean

It is worth stepping back to remember and reflect on what protected areas are for. They are not just a policy tool, but at their best are recognition that nature is important and it has intrinsic value beyond its use to humanity. We need visions of a planet in which nature can thrive because the current model of liberal environmentalism is failing to prevent ecological and planetary collapse. There are different philosophies about the relationship between humanity and nature. Some feel that reserving space for nature is the answer, such as the late E.O. Wilson's call for a half-earth—a planet in which half is reserved for nature (Wilson 2016). The 30 x 30 goal is inspired by similar thinking. Others see a more symbiotic integration between humanity and the rest of the natural world, rejecting the notion that we can artificially separate the two (e.g., Büscher et al. 2017). Whatever the vision for a healthy ocean—and a healthy planet—the answer does not lie solely in existing institutions and practices.

There has been a recent shift to a more global international relations discipline that better integrates the voices, experiences, knowledge, and contributions of societies beyond its traditional Western focus (Acharya 2014). Global international relations scholarship can perhaps offer more than traditional scholarship to a discussion of a different vision for protecting the oceans. Many earth-centered worldviews have emerged from the Global South that international relations scholars can incorporate into their thinking. Worldviews such as *Buen Vivir and Pachamama* from the Andes region, and *Ubuntu* from the Zulu people all advance ideas of community and harmony with nature distinct from the extractivism of Western economic liberalism. International relations scholarship that takes these and other Indigenous ideas seriously as alternative ways of being may be what the discipline needs to better challenge failing environmental institutions, and to envision better solutions.

At the heart of the claim that we need a better vision for protecting our ocean is the observation that current practices are not working, at least not well enough or fast enough. But there is still optimism to be found in the progress states have made in recent years to better protect the ocean. The upsurge in MPAs, measures to introduce MPAs beyond national jurisdiction, and the more expansive 30 x 30 target constitute considerable progress in ocean governance. States' ambition to protect the ocean through MPAs is on the rise, but it can only produce results when they are well managed and not undermined by other policies, as studies of recently established large MPAs have already revealed (e.g., Relano et al. 2021). The science of conservation is sound—when species and ecosystems are untouched by humans, they thrive. MPAs can contribute to building ecosystem resilience to exogenous threats such as plastics and climate change, and they can allow species and ecosystems to rebound and thrive away from human activity. Achieving a more effective global biodiversity network on par with the threat to ocean ecosystems is a primarily political challenge. This chapter has identified just a few of the many ways in which the work of scholars of international relations and related fields can contribute to a better understanding of the role of MPAs in protecting our ocean.

References

Abbott, Joshua K., and U. Rashid Sumaila. 2019. Reducing Marine Plastic Pollution: Policy Insights from Economics. *Review of Environmental Economics and Policy* 13 (2). https://doi.org/10.1093/reep/rez007.

Acharya, Amitav. 2014. Global International Relations (IR) and Regional Worlds: A New Agenda for International Studies. *International Studies Quarterly* 58 (4): 647–659. https://doi.org/10.1111/isqu.12171.

Alger, Justin. 2021. *Conserving the Oceans: The Politics of Large Marine Protected Areas*. New York, NY: Oxford University Press.

Alger, Justin. 2023. The Political Economy of Protected Area Designations: Commercial Interests in Conservation Policy. *Global Environmental Politics* 23 (2): 54–73. https://doi.org/10.1162/glep_a_00690.

Alger, Justin, and Peter Dauvergne. 2017. The Politics of Pacific Ocean Conservation: Lessons from the Pitcairn Islands Marine Reserve. *Pacific Affairs* 90 (1): 29–50. https://doi.org/10.5509/201790129.

Alger, Justin, Philippe Le Billon, Eric Leinberger, and U. Rashid Sumaila. 2023. What Would Article 5.1 of the 2022 WTO Ministerial Agreement on Fisheries Subsidies Accomplish? *Marine Policy* 153: 105641. https://doi.org/10.1016/j.marpol.2023.105641.

Barkin, J. Samuel, and Elizabeth R. DeSombre. 2013. *Saving Global Fisheries: Reducing Fishing Capacity to Promote Sustainability*. Cambridge, MA: MIT Press.

Beattie, Alasdair, U. Rashid Sumaila, Villy Christensen, and Daniel Pauly. 2008. A Model for the Bioeconomic Evaluation of Marine Protected Area Size and Placement in the North Sea. *Natural Resource Modeling* 15 (4): 413–437. https://doi.org/10.1111/j.1939-7445.2002.tb00096.x.

Bennett, Nathan J. 2022. Opinion: Mainstreaming Equity and Justice in the Ocean. *Frontiers in Marine Science* 9. https://doi.org/10.3389/fmars.2022.873572.

Bennett, Nathan J., Hugh Govan, and Terre Satterfield. 2015. Ocean Grabbing. *Marine Policy* 57: 61–68. https://doi.org/10.1016/j.marpol.2015.03.026.

Bernstein, Steven. 2001. *The Compromise of Liberal Environmentalism*. New York, NY: Columbia University Press.

Brooks, Cassandra M., Larry B. Crowder, Henrik Österblom, and Aaron L. Strong. 2020. Reaching Consensus for Conserving the Global Commons: The Case of the Ross Sea, Antarctica. *Conservation Letters* 13 (1): e12676. https://doi.org/10.1111/conl.12676.

Büscher, Bram, Robert Fletcher, Dan Brockington, Chris Sandbrook, William M. Adams, Lisa Campbell, Catherine Corson et al. 2017. Half-Earth or Whole Earth? Radical Ideas for Conservation, and Their Implications. *Oryx* 51 (3): 407–410. https://doi.org/10.1017/S0030605316001228.

Cashore, Benjamin, and Steven Bernstein. 2023. Bringing the Environment Back In: Overcoming the Tragedy of the Diffusion of the Commons Metaphor. *Perspectives on Politics* 21 (2): 478–501. https://doi.org/10.1017/S1537592721002553.

Christie, Patrick, Nathan J. Bennett, Noella J. Gray, T'Aulani Wilhelm, Nai'a Lewis, John Parks, Natalie C. Ban et al. 2017. Why People Matter in Ocean Governance: Incorporating

Human Dimensions into Large-Scale Marine Protected Areas. *Marine Policy* 84: 273–284. https://doi.org/10.1016/j.marpol.2017.08.002.
Cisneros-Montemayor, Andrés M., Marcia Moreno-Báez, Michelle Voyer, Edward H. Allison, William W.L. Cheung, Margot Hessing-Lewis, Muhammed A. Oyinlola et al. 2019. Social Equity and Benefits as the Nexus of a Transformative Blue Economy: A Sector Review of Implications. *Marine Policy* 109: 103702. https://doi.org/10.1016/j.marpol.2019.103702.
Claudet, Joachim, Laurent Bopp, William W. L. Cheung, Rodolphe Devillers, Elva Escobar-Briones, Peter Haugan, Johanna J. Heymans et al. 2020. A Roadmap for Using the UN Decade of Ocean Science for Sustainable Development in Support of Science, Policy, and Action. *One Earth* 2 (1): 34–42. https://doi.org/10.1016/j.oneear.2019.10.012.
Dauvergne, Peter. 2018. Why is the Global Governance of Plastic Failing the Oceans? *Global Environmental Change* 51: 22–31. https://doi.org/10.1016/j.gloenvcha.2018.05.002.
De Santo, Elizabeth M. 2013. Missing Marine Protected Area (MPA) Targets: How the Push for Quantity Over Quality Undermines Sustainability and Social Justice. *Journal of Environmental Management* 124: 137–146. https://doi.org/10.1016/j.jenvman.2013.01.033.
De Santo, Elizabeth M. 2020. Militarized Marine Protected Areas in Overseas Territories: Conserving Biodiversity, Geopolitical Positioning, and Securing Resources in the 21st Century. *Ocean & Coastal Management* 184: 105006. https://doi.org/10.1016/j.ocecoaman.2019.105006.
Devillers, Rodolphe, Robert L. Pressey, Alana Grech, John N. Kittinger, Graham J. Edgar, Trevor Ward, and Reg Watson. 2015. Reinventing Residual Reserves in the Sea: Are We Favouring Ease of Establishment Over Need for Protection? *Aquatic Conservation: Marine and Freshwater Ecosystems* 25 (4): 480–504. https://doi.org/10.1002/aqc.2445.
Edgar, Graham J., Rick D. Stuart-Smith, Trevor J. Willis, Stuart Kininmonth, Susan C. Baker, Stuart Banks, Neville S. Barrett et al. 2014. Global Conservation Outcomes Depend on Marine Protected Areas with Five Key Features. *Nature* 506: 216–220.
Goncalves, Leandra, and Elizabeth M. De Santo. 2021. Unpacking the Process: How Agenda-Setting Theory Explains the Case of Creating Large Scale Marine Protected Areas in Brazil. *Environmental Politics* 31 (2): 205–225. https://doi.org/10.1080/09644016.2021.1915037.
Jacques, Peter, and Rafaella Lobo. 2018. The Shifting Context of Sustainability: Growth and the World Ocean Regime. *Global Environmental Politics* 18 (4): 85–106. https://doi.org/10.1162/glep_a_00480.
Kuempel, Caitlin D., Alienor L.M. Chauvenet, and Hugh P. Possingham. 2016. Equitable Representation of Ecoregions Is Slowly Improving Despite Strategic Planning Shortfalls. *Conservation Letters* 9 (6): 422–428. https://doi.org/10.1111/conl.12298.
Lau, Winnie W.Y., Yonathan Shiran, Richard M. Bailey, Ed Cook, Martin R. Stuchtey, Julia Koskella, Costas A. Velis et al. 2020. Evaluating Scenarios Toward Zero Plastic Pollution. *Science* 369 (6510): 1455–1461. https://doi.org/10.1126/science.aba9475.
Lubchenco, Jane, and Kirsten Grorud-Colvert. 2015. Making Waves: The Science and Politics of Ocean Protection. *Science* 350 (6259): 382–383: https://doi.org/10.1126/science.aad5443.
Marine Conservation Institute. 2024. The Marine Protection Atlas. Available at: https://www.mpatlas.org.
McLeod, Elizabeth, Rodney Salm, Alison Green, and Jeanine Almany. 2009. Designing Marine Protected Area Networks to Address the Impacts of Climate Change. *Frontiers in Ecology and the Environment* 7 (7): 362–370. https://doi.org/10.1890/070211.
Mendenhall, Elizabeth, Rachel Tiller, and Elizabeth Nyman. 2023. The Ship has Reached the Shore: The Final Session of the 'Biodiversity Beyond National Jurisdiction' Negotiations. *Marine Policy* 155. https://doi.org/10.1016/j.marpol.2023.105686.
Neville, Kate J. 2021. *Fueling Resistance: The Contentious Political Economy of Biofuels and Fracking.* New York, NY: Oxford University Press.

Pauly, Daniel, Villy Christensen, Sylvie Guénette, Tony J. Pitcher, U. Rashid Sumaila, Carl J. Walters, Reg Watson, and Dirk Zeller. 2002. Towards Sustainability in World Fisheries. *Nature* 418: 689–695.

Pauly, Daniel, and Dirk Zeller. 2016. Catch Reconstructions Reveal that Global Marine Fisheries Catches Are Higher than Reported and Declining. *Nature Communications* 7: 10244.

Peluso, Nancy L. 1993. Coercing Conservation? The Politics of State Resource Control. *Global Environmental Change* 3 (2): 199–217. https://doi.org/10.1016/0959-3780(93)90006-7.

Protected Planet. 2024. Marine Protected Areas. Available at: https://www.protectedplanet.net.

Reinert, Kenneth A. 2020. From Sustainable Development Goals to Basic Development Goals. *Ethics & International Affairs* 34 (2): 125–137. https://doi.org/10.1017/S0892679420000180.

Relano, Veronica, M.L. Deng Palomares, and Daniel Pauly. 2021. Comparing the Performance of Four Very Large Marine Protected Areas with Different Levels of Protection. *Sustainability* 13 (17): 9572. https://doi.org/10.3390/su13179572.

Sumaila, U. Rashid. 2022. *Infinity Fish: Economic and the Future of Fish and Fisheries.* San Diego, CA: Academic Press.

Sumaila, U. Rashid, Lubna Alam, Patrizia R. Abdallah, Denis Aheto, Shehu L. Akintola, Justin Alger, Vania Andreoli et al. 2024. WTO Must Complete an Ambitious Fisheries Subsidies Agreement. *npj Ocean Sustainability* 3 (6). https://doi.org/10.1038/s44183-024-00042-0.

Sumaila, U. Rashid, Vicky W.Y. Lam, Dana D. Miller, Louise The, Reg A. Watson, Dirk Zeller, William W.L. Cheung et al. 2015. Winners and Losers in a World Where the High Seas Is Closed to Fishing. *Scientific Reports* 5. https://doi.org/10.1038/srep08481.

Tiller, Rachel, Elizabeth De Santo, Elizabeth Mendenhall, and Elizabeth Nyman. 2019. The Once and Future Treaty: Towards a New Regime for Biodiversity in Areas Beyond National Jurisdiction. *Marine Policy* 99: 239–242. https://doi.org/10.1016/j.marpol.2018.10.046.

Wilson, Edward O. 2016. *Half-Earth: Our Planet's Fight for Life.* New York, NY: W.W. Norton.

Young, Oran R. 2016. The Paris Agreement: Destined to Succeed or Doomed to Fail? *Politics and Governance* 4 (3): 124–132.

PART V

Advancing practice

14 Five actions to close the gap between marine spatial planning research and practice

Julie M. Reimer, Rodolphe Devillers, Natalie C. Ban, Maxine Westhead and Joachim Claudet

Marine spatial planning (MSP) is a process for understanding and coordinating when, where, and how the ocean and its resources are used and managed, simultaneously responding to conflicting uses and ecosystem threats, to achieve ecological, economic, and social objectives (Collie et al. 2013, Ehler and Douvere 2009). It offers an alternative to traditionally siloed, single-sector, single-issue, and reactive approaches to ocean management, holding the potential to proactively support both ocean conservation and sustainable use or development goals (Kirkfeldt and Frazão Santos 2021). To achieve its full potential, effective MSP should reflect six principles: (1) ecosystem-based, (2) integrated, (3) place- or area-based, (4) adaptive, (5) strategic, and (6) participatory (Ehler and Douvere 2009); however, these principles have permeated MSP practice to varying extents (Reimer et al. 2023). Despite its promise, the implementation of MSP is stifled by insufficient regulatory policy and institutional frameworks, balancing economic development with biodiversity conservation, engaging stakeholders, integrating social data, and adapting to changing conditions, including those induced by climate change (Frazão Santos et al. 2021).

Case study analyses have revealed a gap between the idealized version of MSP described in the literature and the reality, where MSP is often driven by political processes and economic development (Clarke and Flannery 2020, Jones et al. 2016, Zuercher et al. 2022). This gap raises questions about the barriers and challenges associated with implementing guiding principles. For example, by following administrative and geopolitical boundaries, MSP may not effectively employ the ecosystem-based principle (Le Tissier 2020), though some marine spatial plans account for ecological considerations within administrative boundaries (Domínguez-Tejo et al. 2016). While MSP initiatives often engage stakeholders, they may not participate at all stages of the process (Collie et al. 2013), and a failure to acknowledge power and inequality in MSP may reduce inclusivity and the participatory principle (Flannery et al. 2018). MSP initiatives often reference monitoring intentions (Collie et al. 2013), though comprehensive evaluations of plans are rare and often under-prioritized and poorly funded (Zuercher et al. 2022), failing to uphold the adaptive principle (Reimer et al. 2023). MSP practitioners clearly continue to struggle with bringing theoretical principles and fundamental steps in the MSP process, like effective participation and adaptation (Ehler and Douvere 2009), to fruition.

At the same time, these persistent challenges may indicate that MSP researchers have fundamentally misunderstood, or opted not to engage with, the complex realities of ocean governance, planning, and management (Flannery et al. 2020). Alternatively, researchers may undertake studies aimed at transforming institutions that are exceedingly difficult and slow to change. Results from these studies may be critical for advancing fundamental and incremental change over time. Importantly, there are dual roles for researchers in MSP: one that focuses on shorter-term, implementable recommendations to catalyze MSP toward its full potential and another that continues to develop the longer-term, more theoretical foundations for MSP in an ever-changing world.

While MSP is envisioned as a more holistic, inclusive, and proactive alternative to piecemeal, issue-driven, and reactive approaches to ocean management (Flannery 2023), the challenges of implementing MSP have in practice failed to enable, or have not been enabled by, the necessary and foundational institutional and governance changes (Fairbanks et al. 2019). MSP involves fundamental governance transformations—reformation of existing governance systems to include approaches that reduce bureaucratic red tape, set transformative goals, and deepen participation far beyond tokenism (Flannery and McAteer 2020). Still, MSP often upholds the status quo in governance and hinders the necessary transformation of management practices that are unsustainable (Flannery 2023, Flannery and McAteer 2020). More transformative versions of MSP may be enabled by addressing key tensions between theory and reality, for example, between future orientation aimed at problem-solving and path dependency in existing governance structures (Flannery 2023).

MSP research has grown exponentially since the late 2000s, occurring in tandem with a growing practice of MSP by ocean nations (Ehler et al. 2019). During their simultaneous evolutions, a largely academic literature that shows little awareness of, or perhaps interest in, the complex socio-political and planning dimensions of MSP has emerged (Ehler et al. 2019, Flannery et al. 2020, Le Tissier 2020). This literature provides high-level goals for MSP that appear to be mirrored in the often vague objectives of marine spatial plans (Zuercher et al. 2022). MSP theory is likely haphazardly applied in practice to support often political and development-oriented objectives (Trouillet 2020). Though this literature frequently intends to inform decision-making and practice (see, for example, Fernandes et al. 2017, Said and Trouillet 2020, Wright et al. 2021), mismatches between MSP research and marine spatial plans indicate that an idealized version of MSP is diverging from, and potentially incompatible with, the realities of ocean governance (Zuercher et al. 2022). While there is value in science continuing to advance and advocate for an idealized version of what could be possible with MSP, additional focus from researchers on short-term needs and practical realities may be critical for realizing this more visionary version of MSP. For example, research that identifies or develops approaches for dispelling power dynamics in MSP, in a specific MSP initiative or more broadly, may address a current need in MSP practice. For MSP to achieve its full potential, the gap between theory and reality, between researchers and practitioners, must be narrowed.

As the gap between the science produced and the science needed and used by practitioners grows (Lemieux et al. 2021), both researchers and practitioners hold responsibility for taking action to work together to harness the transformative potential of MSP. Today, more than 75 countries are using MSP (Ehler 2021), relying on this process to deliver healthy ecosystems and sustainable blue economies (Voyer et al. 2018). At the same time, MSP is becoming increasingly central to international goals and commitments. For example, Target 1 of the Kunming-Montreal Global Biodiversity Framework requires all areas to be under participatory, integrated, and biodiversity-inclusive spatial planning and/or other effective management processes by 2030. The High-Level Panel for a Sustainable Ocean Economy requires the sustainable management of 100 percent of ocean areas under national jurisdiction, guided by Sustainable Ocean Plans, by 2025. The expectation for MSP to deliver its transformative promise is clear, and the time for uniting MSP research and practice is now.

In this chapter, we suggest five actions to bridge the gap between MSP research and practice: (1) find allies across research and government/management agencies, (2) better understand the realities of the researcher's and practitioner's day-to-day, (3) co-develop research that is fit-for-purpose to current MSP needs, (4) challenge barriers to transforming the status quo, and (5) speak truth to power by leveraging research outputs and recommendations (Figure 14.1). We describe these actions, their interrelations, and how they may help to catalyze MSP practice to better engage research and vice versa. With these actions, we aim to provide guidance to our colleagues to leverage their combined power and work together to right the story of MSP, amplifying its potential for ocean conservation and sustainability.

Find allies

Allies are the individuals or groups who share interests, and ideally values, or have the resources, capacity, or power to support progress toward a shared goal (University of Kansas 2023). Neither research nor practice are void of values, including those of honesty, objectivity, and accuracy, and this can be good for how both groups serve in their respective roles (Douglas 2023). Where the values of researchers and practitioners align, alliances may be formed that mobilize our goal: a healthy and sustainable ocean. Ocean researchers often aim to influence governance and management, leveraging the scientific process to produce relevant and useful results, guidance, and tools (see, for example, Claudet et al. 2020, Reimer et al. 2021, Wisz et al. 2020). Governments and their ocean agencies staff thousands of practitioners with the knowledge, skills, and passion for ensuring a healthy and sustainable ocean. These are enabling conditions for building alliances across groups to integrate science into decision-making while also advancing research that reflects complex governance realities and the needs of practitioners. As a first action toward bridging the gap between MSP research and practice, both groups must seek out allies in the other organization.

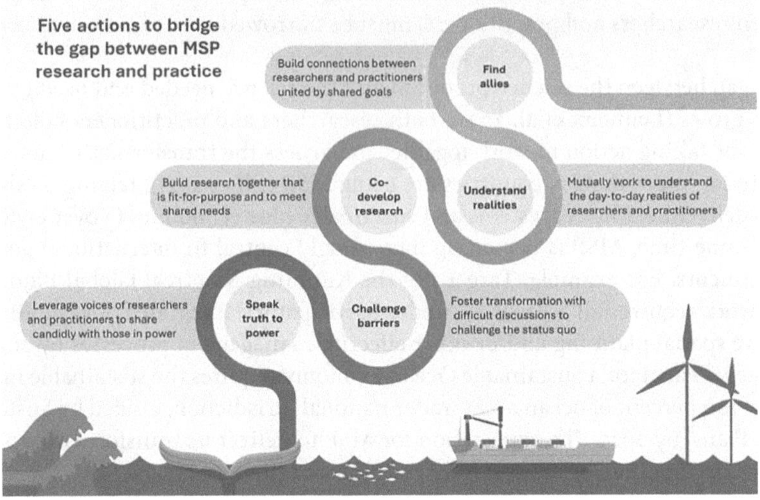

Source: Authors' own.

Figure 14.1 Five actions to bridge the gap between MSP research and practice

Practitioners can serve as "insider allies" to researchers by applying their skills, ability to navigate governance systems, and commitments to ocean conservation and sustainability within government agencies (London and Harrison 2021). They can help to bring MSP research closer to decision-makers and integrate research in developing initiatives that more strongly reflect MSP theory. For practitioners, researcher allies can help to build legitimacy, ensure accountability, overcome operational challenges, and engage rightsholders and stakeholders who practitioners otherwise might not be able to reach (Reed 2020). As partnerships between allies evolve over time, the collective understanding of an overarching problem deepens and becomes more nuanced, fostering stronger and more efficient problem-solving (Slawinski et al. 2023). Genuine partnerships involve a two-way exchange of information, resources or assets, and commitment to a common goal (Reed 2020), which may be best fostered by long-term alliances between researchers and practitioners. Exploring new avenues to find new allies could involve taking an interest in the work of individuals in the other organization, participating in opportunities to share knowledge or collaborate, and dedicating capacity or performance indicators in their working roles to this effort.

Understand realities

Mismatches between academic research and MSP practice may be producing recommendations that are incompatible with the complex realities of ocean governance (Zuercher et al. 2022). For example, recommendations that are too high-level, detached from complexity, or lacking operational guidance (e.g., a recommendation for MSP to integrate across ocean regulatory authorities, without recognizing the complexity of ocean authorities or describing how integration might be achieved) render them ill-suited to practical and short-term needs and potentially unlikely to be taken up in earnest by practitioners. As MSP gets closer to theoretical best practices, it also becomes more complex and results in plans that are likely to be more challenging to implement (Reimer 2022). For example, spatial management plans developed in New South Wales, Australia, were highly ambitious in their management objectives, but they suffered from ambiguous language, unclear planning hierarchies, and a lack of clear timelines that rendered plans effectively immeasurable (Domínguez-Tejo and Metternicht 2018). To bridge MSP research and practice, and better realize best practices, researchers must work to understand the governance system and operational environments of practitioners that influence how MSP initiatives are developed and implemented year over year, month over month, and day over day. Similarly, practitioners must work to understand how research systems operate—their limitations and timelines—to set realistic expectations for research.

In building strong partnerships, both researchers and practitioners should work to better understand their respective responsibilities, operating environments, and systemic barriers to implementing a more idealized version of MSP; for example, by asking questions about how projects or programs are funded, how decisions are made and by whom, and the procedural requirements of their operating systems. Further, understanding systemic barriers experienced by practitioners (e.g., the influence of political will, dual mandates in ocean agencies to support both the growth of marine industries and ocean protection) and by researchers (e.g., the high value placed on publications; conflict between short-term pressures, like publications, and long-term scientific needs, like ecological monitoring; less value placed on policy influence) can be critical in deepening the understanding of reality. While evidence-informed policy may be the ideal of both groups, scientists tend to define problems as something to technically solve, whereas practitioners, particularly those in policymaking, define problems in a much more social context, as a process for negotiating solutions with majority support (Sienkiewicz and Mair 2020). Research and practice are divided by mismatched timeframes, incompatible attention spans, and diverging attitudes about uncertainty (Sienkiewicz and Mair 2020). Working to understand the other's worldview may be central to building lasting and productive alliances. As insider allies, practitioners are doing challenging, vulnerable, and impactful work under significant pressures, operating in highly bureaucratic environments, with the potential to transform government agencies (London and Harrison 2021). With strong partnerships that value operational realities, we can produce MSP research that is more grounded in those realities and MSP practice that is more grounded in research, making the most strategic use of insider allies.

Co-develop research

The separation of science and policy, of research and practice, hinders complex problem-solving (Sienkiewicz and Mair 2020). For science to inform MSP, both researchers and government agencies must advance knowledge exchange, requiring two-way investments in individual, institutional, and financial capacities for accessing, interpreting, and integrating science into decision-making (Cvitanovic et al. 2016). In short, this will require co-developed research that is designed to meet the research needs of decision-makers and practitioners. Co-developed research goes further than applied research, which aims to address socially relevant research questions based on the researchers' idea of what is useful (Bednarek et al. 2018), by building research questions in partnership with research end-users to ensure its usefulness (Wall et al. 2017). Mutually valuable, collaborative research should consider the perspectives and realities of all partners; should use methods that enable collaboration with practitioners, rather than about practitioners; and should include opportunities for both parties to assess the quality of the research process and its outputs (Young and Freytag 2021).

As an act of bridging MSP research and practice, co-developing research projects will be essential to solving complex problems. The largely academic body of MSP research that exists today has been driven by largely scientific interests (Flannery et al. 2020), but practitioners also have significant research needs that may be difficult to fulfill in an operating environment that prioritizes other tasks or, for some, where the necessary skills or resources to undertake proper research are lacking. Further, the complexity of implementing MSP can be paralyzing for practitioners. Co-developing research that focuses on implementing specific elements of MSP and is fit-for-purpose for implementation challenges in the shorter term may be particularly important for aligning MSP with theoretical best practices. In the longer term, theoretical advancement of MSP continues to be an important contribution of science, providing an ambitious vision that ensures MSP can reach its full potential. While applied research that is co-developed might focus first on identifying solutions and developing tools, guidance, or products that serve MSP practice, co-design and collaborative transdisciplinary work are often poorly recognized and rewarded in the scientific system (Satterthwaite et al. 2022). Given this, co-developing research should be preceded by collective action among practitioners and researchers to find allies and understand realities.

Challenge barriers

MSP is commonly described firstly as a "public process" that seeks to achieve objectives "usually specified through a political process" (Ehler and Douvere 2009, 22), though it may be more apt to describe it firstly as political. As a political process, MSP may intrinsically favor large industrial sectors to the disadvantage of the general public and smaller stakeholders, especially those often neglected in ocean planning processes, such as Indigenous communities (though there are exceptions; see Diggon et al. 2022), small-scale fisheries, and coastal communities (Flannery et al. 2018, Gilek et al. 2021, Smith and Basurto 2019, Yet et al. 2022). Despite this, MSP processes often appear to be devoid of politics, diluting the complexity of the process and the diversity of perspectives that ought to be captured through inclusive MSP (Flannery et al. 2019). In theory, the comprehensive and integrated nature of MSP necessitates a level of collaboration, transparency, and flexibility that is well beyond today's predominant forms of ocean governance (Wright et al. 2021). In reality, many MSP initiatives appear to reinforce the status quo in governance systems, rather than address longstanding governance issues that hinder the transformative potential of MSP (Flannery 2023). To bridge the gap between theory and reality, practitioners and researchers should feel empowered to challenge barriers in bureaucratic systems that simply cannot harness the transformative potential of MSP in their current forms.

Leveraging the results and recommendations from co-developed research projects, practitioners and researchers should facilitate difficult conversations with decision-makers—asking why and why not when presented with barriers to transforming the status quo. For example, barriers to participatory ocean governance often emerge from the traditional role of governments, outdated practices, and centralized legislation (Werle et al. 2018); yet it is clear from MSP research that such practices are ineffective in establishing inclusive participatory governance (Flannery et al. 2018). The combination of scientific expertise among researchers and insider ally skills among practitioners can create a powerful voice that not only calls for governance transformation but articulates specific, evidence-based steps to operationalize transformative action.

Speak truth to power

It is clear that contemporary approaches to ocean governance and management are failing to restore ocean health, thereby failing global communities, industries, and economies that depend on the ocean (Claudet 2021, Laffoley et al. 2020). Researchers and practitioners have a responsibility to speak truth to power about these failures, while holding the collective knowledge and skills to strengthen and legitimize their message. Speaking truth to power not only means asserting scientific fact, but also asserting values and policy recommendations (Peterson 2018). Researchers and practitioners should be confident that their values and deep understanding of their organizational goals provide a solid foundation for their message and recommendations (Grossgold and Eich 2020). While important for bridging MSP research and practice, speaking truth to power is difficult, involves risk, and is an action that should be taken with strategic purpose (DellaSala 2021, Grossgold and Eich 2020). Speaking truth to power should leverage other actions to bridge MSP research and practice, making strategic use of allies, demonstrating an understanding of reality, highlighting the outputs of co-developed research, and articulating clear steps to overcome real or perceived barriers. While the voice of a single researcher or practitioner might be lost on decision-makers, the collective voice of researchers and practitioners working in partnership can be influential (Grossgold and Eich 2020).

Conclusions

Over a relatively brief period, MSP has emerged prominently as a process with the potential to transform contemporary ocean governance and management. In realizing its theoretical principles, MSP can address multiple objectives, integrate across jurisdictions and sectors, consider conflicts and compatibilities among ocean uses, plan in the face of uncertainty, enable evidence-based decision-making, foster stakeholder empowerment, and more (Reimer et al. 2023). Now more than ever, it is critical that we take action to close the gap between MSP research and practice if we are to see MSP achieve its full potential. We provide five such actions, though we recognize that these alone will not completely bridge this gap. Each action is influenced by external forces, such as the systemic barriers in government and scientific systems identified, and many more, such as power dynamics, lobbying, short-term priorities over long-term goals, and other political, social, economic, and environmental drivers. While researchers and practitioners can, in part, share responsibility for bridging this gap, governance systems must also invest in enabling conditions, including access to skilled personnel, that allow for science to be translated into specific MSP contexts. We also recognize that these actions are applicable to any challenge at the science–policy interface and encourage the use of these actions beyond MSP to bridge other gaps. Drawing from our collective experience as researchers and practitioners in ocean planning and management, we call on our colleagues to find allies, understand realities, co-develop research, challenge barriers, and speak truth to power.

References

Bednarek, A.T., C. Wyborn, C. Cvitanovic, R. Meyer, R.M. Colvin, P.F.E. Addison, S.L. Close et al. 2018. Boundary Spanning at the Science–Policy Interface: The Practitioners' Perspectives. *Sustainability Science* 13: 1175–1183. https://doi.org/10.1007/s11625-018-0550-9.

Clarke, Jane, and Wesley Flannery. 2020. The Post-Political Nature of Marine Spatial Planning and Modalities for its Re-Politicisation. *Journal of Environmental Policy and Planning* 22 (2): 170–183. https://doi.org/10.1080/1523908X.2019.1680276.

Claudet, Joachim. 2021. The Seven Domains of Action for a Sustainable Ocean. *Cell* 184 (6): 1426–1429. https://doi.org/10.1016/j.cell.2021.01.055.

Claudet, Joachim, Laurent Bopp, William W.L. Cheung, Rodolphe Devillers, Elva Escobar-Briones, Peter Haugan, Johanna J. Heymans et al. 2020. A Roadmap for Using the UN Decade of Ocean Science for Sustainable Development in Support of Science, Policy, and Action. *One Earth* 2 (1): 34–42. https://doi.org/10.1016/j.oneear.2019.10.012.

Collie, Jeremy S., W.L. (Vic) Adamowicz, Michael W. Beck, Bethany Craig, Timothy E. Essington, David Fluharty, Jake Rice and James N. Sanchirico. 2013. Marine Spatial Planning in Practice. *Estuarine, Coastal and Shelf Science* 117: 1–11. https://doi.org/10.1016/j.ecss.2012.11.010.

Cvitanovic, C., McDonald, J. and A.J. Hobday. 2016. From Science to Action: Principles for Undertaking Environmental Research That Enables Knowledge Exchange and Evidence-Based Decision-Making. *Journal of Environmental Management* 183: 864–874. https://doi.org/10.1016/j.jenvman.2016.09.038.

DellaSala, Dominick A. 2021. Scientists as Advocates: Advocacy Should Not Be a Four-Letter Word. In *Conservation Science and Advocacy for a Planet in Peril: Speaking Truth to Power*, edited by Dominick A. DellaSala, 3–23. Elsevier.

Diggon, Steve, John Bones, Charles J. Short, Joanna L. Smith, Megan Dickinson, Kelly Wozniak, Karen Topelko, and Kylee A. Pawluk. 2022. The Marine Plan Partnership for the North Pacific Coast – MaPP: A Collaborative and Co-Led Marine Planning Process in British Columbia. *Marine Policy* 142: 104065. https://doi.org/10.1016/j.marpol.2020.104065.

Domínguez-Tejo, Elianny, and Graciela Metternicht. 2018. Poorly-Designed Goals and Objectives in Resource Management Plans: Assessing Their Impact For an Ecosystem-Based Approach To Marine Spatial Planning. *Marine Policy* 88: 122–131. https://doi.org/10.1016/j.marpol.2017.11.013.

Domínguez-Tejo, Elianny, Graciela Metternicht, Emma Johnston, and Luke Hedge. 2016. Marine Spatial Planning Advancing the Ecosystem-Based Approach to Coastal Zone Management: A Review. *Marine Policy* 72: 115–130. https://doi.org/10.1016/j.marpol.2016.06.023.

Douglas, Heather. 2023. The Importance of Values for Science. *Interdisciplinary Science Reviews* 48 (2): 251–263. https://doi.org/10.1080/03080188.2023.2191559.

Ehler, Charles. 2021. Two Decades of Progress in Marine Spatial Planning. *Marine Policy* 132: 104134. https://doi.org/10.1016/j.marpol.2020.104134.

Ehler, Charles, and Fanny Douvere. 2009. *Marine Spatial Planning: A Step-by-Step Approach Toward Ecosystem-Based Management*. Intergovernmental Oceanographic Commission and Man and the Biosphere Programme. IOC Manual and Guides, No. 53, ICAM Dossier No. 6. UNESCO.

Ehler, Charles, Jacek Zaucha, and Kira Gee. 2019. Maritime/Marine Spatial Planning at the Interface of Research and Practice. In *Maritime Spatial Planning: Past, Present, Future*, edited by Jacek Zaucha and Kira Gee, 1–21. Palgrave Macmillan. https://doi.org/10.1007/978-3-319-98696-8.

Fairbanks, Luke, Noelle Boucquey, Lisa M. Campbell, and Sarah Wise. 2019. Remaking Oceans Governance: Critical Perspectives on Marine Spatial Planning. *Environment and Society: Advances in Research* 10 (1): 122–140. https://doi.org/10.3167/ares.2019.100108.

Fernandes, Maria da Luz, Tanya C. Esteves, Eduardo R. Oliveira, and Fatima L. Alves. 2017. How Does the Cumulative Impacts Approach Support Maritime Spatial Planning? *Ecological Indicators* 73: 189–202. https://doi.org/10.1016/j.ecolind.2016.09.014.

Flannery, Wesley. 2023. Making Marine Spatial Planning Matter. In *Ocean Governance*, edited by Stefan Partelow, Maria Hadjimichael, and Anna-Katharina Hornidge, 93–111. Springer. https://doi.org/10.1007/978-3-031-20740-2_5.

Flannery, Wesley, Jane Clarke, and Ben McAteer. 2019. Politics and Power in Marine Spatial Planning. In *Maritime Spatial Planning: Past, Present, Future*, edited by Jacek Zaucha and Kira Gee, 201–217. Palgrave Macmillan. https://doi.org/10.1007/978-3-319-98696-8_9.

Flannery, Wesley, Noel Healy, and Marcos Luna. 2018. Exclusion and Non-Participation in Marine Spatial Planning. *Marine Policy* 88: 32–40. https://doi.org/10.1016/j.marpol.2017.11.001.

Flannery, Wesley, and Ben McAteer. 2020. Assessing Marine Spatial Planning Governmentality. *Maritime Studies* 19 (3): 269–284. https://doi.org/10.1007/s40152-020-00174-2.

Flannery, Wesley, Hilde Toonen, Stephen Jay, and Joanna Vince. 2020. A Critical Turn in Marine Spatial Planning. *Maritime Studies* 19 (3): 223–228. https://doi.org/10.1007/s40152-020-00198-8.

Frazão Santos, Catarina, Tundi Agardy, Francisco Andrade, Larry B. Crowder, Charles N. Ehler, and Michael K. Orbach. 2021. Major Challenges in Developing Marine Spatial Planning. *Marine Policy* 132: 103248. https://doi.org/10.1016/j.marpol.2018.08.032.

Gilek, Michael, Aurelija Armoskaite, Kira Gee, Fred Saunders, Ralph Tafon, and Jacek Zaucha. 2021. In Search of Social Sustainability in Marine Spatial Planning: A Review of Scientific Literature Published 2005–2020. *Ocean and Coastal Management* 208: 105618. https://doi.org/10.1016/j.ocecoaman.2021.105618.

Grossgold, Paul, and Ritch Eich. 2020. Five Guidelines for Speaking Truth to Power. *Journal of Values-Based Leadership* 13 (1): 5. https://doi.org/10.22543/0733.131.1303.

Jones, Peter J.S., L.M. Lieberknecht and W. Qiu. 2016. Marine Spatial Planning in Reality: Introduction to Case Studies and Discussion of Findings. *Marine Policy* 71: 256–264. https://doi.org/10.1016/j.marpol.2016.04.026.

Kirkfeldt, Trine S., and Catarina Frazão Santos. 2021. A Review of Sustainability Concepts in Marine Spatial Planning and the Potential to Supporting the UN Sustainable Development Goal 14. *Frontiers in Marine Science* 8: 1–12. https://doi.org/10.3389/fmars.2021.713980.

Laffoley, Dan, John M. Baxter, Diva J. Amon, Duncan E.J. Currie, Craig A. Downs, Jason M. Hall-Spencer, Harriet Harden-Davies et al. 2020. Eight Urgent, Fundamental and Simultaneous Steps Needed to Restore Ocean Health, and the Consequences for Humanity and the Planet of Inaction Or Delay. *Aquatic Conservation: Marine and Freshwater Ecosystems* 30 (1): 194–208. https://doi.org/10.1002/aqc.3182.

Le Tissier, Martin. 2020. Unravelling the Relationship Between Ecosystem-Based Management, Integrated Coastal Zone Management and Marine Spatial Planning. In *Ecosystem-Based Management, Ecosystem Services and Aquatic Biodiversity*, edited by Timothy G. O'Higgins, Manuel Lago, and Theodore H. DeWitt, 403–413. Springer. https://doi.org/10.1007/978-3-030-45843-0_20.

Lemieux, Christopher J., Elizabeth A. Halpenny, Trevor Swerdfager, Mu He, A. Joyce Gould, Don Carruthers Den Hoed, Jill Bueddefeld et al. 2021. Free Fallin'? The Decline in Evidence-Based Decision-Making by Canada's Protected Areas Managers. *Facets* 6 (1): 640–664. https://doi.org/10.1139/FACETS-2020-0085.

London, Jonathan K., and Jill Lindsey Harrison. 2021. From Environmental Justice Activist to Agency Staff: Implications for Agencies, Movement Organizations, and These Insider Allies. *Environmental Justice* 14 (5): 338–344. https://doi.org/10.1089/env.2021.0011.

Peterson, Tarla R. 2018. Keynote Address: Paradox of Trust in Unsettled Times – Can Scientists "Speak Truth to Power"? In *Understanding the Role of Trust and Credibility in Science Communication: Proceedings from the 6th Iowa State University Symposium on Science Communication*, edited by K.P. Hunt. Iowa State University. https://doi.org/10.31274/sciencecommunication-181114-10.

Reed, Betsy. 2020. The Value of Allies, Advocates and Partners. In *Communicating Social and Environmental Issues Effectively*, 119–142. Emerald Group. https://doi.org/10.1108/978-1-83867-467-020201015.

Reimer, Julie M. 2022. *Amplifying the Potential of Marine Spatial Planning for Conservation and Sustainability.* Memorial University of Newfoundland and Labrador.

Reimer, Julie M., Rodolphe Devillers, and Joachim Claudet. 2021. Benefits and Gaps in Area-Based Management Tools for the Ocean Sustainable Development Goal. *Nature Sustainability* 4 (4): 349–357. https://doi.org/10.1038/s41893-020-00659-2.

Reimer, Julie M., Rodolphe Devillers, Rachel Zuercher, Pascale Groulx, Natalie C. Ban, and Joachim Claudet. 2023. The Marine Spatial Planning Index: A Tool to Guide and Assess Marine Spatial Planning. *npj Ocean Sustainability* 2 (1): 1–8. https://doi.org/10.1038/s44183-023-00022-w.

Said, Alicia, and Brice Trouillet. 2020. Bringing "Deep Knowledge" of Fisheries into Marine Spatial Planning. *Maritime Studies* 19 (3): 347–357. https://doi.org/10.1007/s40152-020-00178-y.

Satterthwaite, Erin V., Valeriya Komyakova, Natalia G. Erazo, Louise Gammage, Gabriel A. Juma, Rachel Kelly, Daniel Kleinman et al. 2022. Five Actionable Pillars to Engage the Next Generation of Leaders in the Co-Design of Transformative Ocean Solutions. *PLOS Biology* 20 (10): 1–14. https://doi.org/10.1371/journal.pbio.3001832.

Sienkiewicz, Marta, and David Mair. 2020. Against the Science–Policy Binary Separation: Science for Policy 1.0. In *Science for Policy Handbook*, edited by the European Union, 2–13. Elsevier. https://doi.org/10.1016/B978-0-12-822596-7.00001-2.

Slawinski, Natalie, Bruna Brito, Jennifer Brenton, and Wendy K. Smith. 2023. Rapid Problem Formulation for Societal Impact: Lessons from a Decade-Long Research-Practice Partnership. *Journal of Business Venturing Insights* 19 (April): e00390. https://doi.org/10.1016/j.jbvi.2023.e00390.

Smith, Hillary, and Xavier Basurto. 2019. Defining Small-Scale Fisheries and Examining the Role of Science in Shaping Perceptions of Who and What Counts: A Systematic Review. *Frontiers in Marine Science* 6 (May). https://doi.org/10.3389/fmars.2019.00236.

Trouillet, Brice. 2020. Reinventing Marine Spatial Planning: A Critical Review of Initiatives Worldwide. *Journal of Environmental Policy and Planning* 22 (4): 441–459. https://doi.org/10.1080/1523908X.2020.1751605.

University of Kansas. 2023. Recognizing Allies. In *Organizing for Effective Advocacy*. The Community Tool Box. https://ctb.ku.edu/en/organizing-effective-advocacy.

Voyer, Michelle, Genevieve Quirk, Alistair McIlgorm, and Kamal Azmi. 2018. Shades of Blue: What Do Competing Interpretations of the Blue Economy Mean for Oceans Governance? *Journal of Environmental Policy and Planning* 20 (5): 595–616. https://doi.org/10.1080/1523908X.2018.1473153.

Wall, Tamara U., Elizabeth McNie, and Gregg M. Garfin. 2017. Use-Inspired Science: Making Science Usable by and Useful to Decision Makers. *Frontiers in Ecology and the Environment* 15 (10): 551–559. https://doi.org/10.1002/fee.1735.

Werle, Dirk, Paul R. Boudreau, Mary R. Brooks, Michael J.A. Butler, Anthony Charles, Scott Coffen-Smout, David Griffiths et al. 2018. Introduction: The Future of Ocean Governance and Capacity Development. In *The Future of Ocean Governance and Capacity Development: Essays in Honor of Elisabeth Mann Borgese (1918–2002)*, edited by the International Ocean Institute, 1–4. Brill. https://doi.org/10.1163/9789004380271_002.

Wisz, Mary S., Erin V. Satterthwaite, Maree Fudge, Mibu Fischer, Andrei Polejack, Michael St. John, Stephen Fletcher and Murray A. Rudd. 2020. 100 Opportunities for More Inclusive Ocean Research: Cross-Disciplinary Research Questions for Sustainable Ocean Governance and Management. *Frontiers in Marine Science* 7 (August): 1–23. https://doi.org/10.3389/fmars.2020.00576.

Wright, Glen, Kristina M. Gjerde, David E. Johnson, Aria Finkelstein, Maria Adelaide Ferreira, Daniel C. Dunn, Mariamalia Rodriguez Chaves, and Anthony Grehan. 2021. Marine Spatial Planning in Areas Beyond National Jurisdiction. *Marine Policy* 132: 103384. https://doi.org/10.1016/j.marpol.2018.12.003.

Yet, Maggie, Patricia Manuel, Monica DeVidi, and Bertrum H. MacDonald. 2022. Learning from Experience: Lessons from Community-based Engagement for Improving Participatory Marine Spatial Planning. *Planning Practice and Research* 37 (2): 189–212. https://doi.org/10.1080/02697459.2021.2017101.

Young, Louise, and Per Vagn Freytag. 2021. Beyond Research Method to Research Collaboration: Research Co-Production Relationships with Practitioners. *Industrial Marketing Management* 92: 244–253. https://doi.org/10.1016/j.indmarman.2020.02.016.

Zuercher, Rachel, Nicole Motzer, Rafael A. Magris, and Wesley Flannery. 2022. Narrowing the Gap Between Marine Spatial Planning Aspirations and Realities. *ICES Journal of Marine Science* 79 (3): 600–608. https://doi.org/10.1093/icesjms/fsac009.

15 Rethinking cost-benefit analysis for sustainable marine spatial planning

Ibrahim Issifu, Ilyass Dahmouni, Iria García-Lorenzo and U. Rashid Sumaila

Introduction

The increasing threats posed by climate change (Sumaila et al. 2019, Cheung et al. 2021), marine pollution (Abbott and Sumaila 2019, Issifu and Sumaila 2020), overfishing (Pauly et al. 2002), and illegal, unreported, and unregulated fishing (Sumaila et al. 2006, Sumaila et al. 2019) have significantly impacted marine biodiversity and habitats globally. These challenges necessitate the implementation of comprehensive management strategies to ensure the sustainability of marine resources. One such strategy is marine spatial planning (MSP), which has emerged as a widely adopted approach to mitigate damage to marine environments while enhancing the well-being of people whose livelihoods depend on these areas. MSP involves the spatially and temporally explicit allocation of scarce marine spaces, resources, and services to competing uses, and a governance framework for the design, implementation, and monitoring of these allocations (Ehler and Douvere 2009, Issifu et al. 2024). Policymakers adopt MSP for various reasons, including environmental, biological, political, socioeconomic, and national security concerns. MSP has been rapidly adopted worldwide as a response to these environmental pressures. This chapter delves into the economic dimensions of MSP decision-making, offering an exploration of how economic considerations are integrated into MSP initiatives. The chapter investigates the practical application and use of economic data in guiding MSP decisions, highlighting the critical role that economic information plays in this process. In addressing this gap in the literature regarding the incorporation of economic information in MSP, the chapter examines several key areas. These include the quantitative analysis of value-added aspects of MSP, the assessment of contributions from various MSP sectors such as employment and income generation, and the evaluation of spatial and temporal allocations of marine resources. Through this comprehensive approach, we provide valuable insights into the economic dimensions of MSP decision-making, enhancing our understanding of this complex and important field.

Economics, marine spatial planning and ocean management

We argue that integrating economics into MSP is crucial for effective ocean management for several key reasons. First, MSP inherently involves the allocation of limited marine spaces and resources among competing uses, which requires a thorough understanding of the economic implications of different allocation decisions. By incorporating economic analyses, policymakers can evaluate the trade-offs between various activities such as fishing, tourism, renewable energy, and conservation. This would ensure that the benefits derived from marine resources are optimized while minimizing potential conflicts and negative impacts on the environment (Ehler and Douvere 2009).

Economic tools such as cost–benefit analysis (CBA) and trade-off analysis enable the assessment of the economic viability and sustainability of different marine uses (Issifu et al. 2024). For example, the World Bank (2022) highlights that enhanced CBA is instrumental in assessing whether the economic benefits of a proposed marine activity outweigh its costs. This evaluation includes considering environmental and social impacts, as demonstrated in studies by Sumaila et al. (2012) and Teh and Sumaila (2020) on rebuilding depleted fish populations. This facilitates informed decision-making that supports long-term sustainability goals (White et al. 2012).

Moreover, integrating economics into MSP helps attract financing and investment by demonstrating the economic value of marine resources and the potential returns on investment. This is particularly important for securing funding for conservation projects and sustainable development initiatives. By quantifying the economic benefits of preserving marine ecosystems such as tourism revenue (see, for example, Cisneros-Montemayor and Sumaila 2010), fisheries values (Sumaila 2021), and coastal protection (Spalding et al. 2014), comprehensively-carried-out MSP can make a compelling case for investment in marine conservation (Sumaila et al. 2022).

Economic considerations also play a crucial role in fostering stakeholder buy-in and participation. By highlighting the economic benefits of MSP, such as job creation, income generation, and enhanced livelihoods, policymakers can garner support from local communities, industries, and other stakeholders. This collaborative approach ensures that MSP is more inclusive and considers the needs and aspirations of all relevant parties (Ehler and Douvere 2009).

Furthermore, incorporating economic analyses into MSP helps align marine management strategies with broader economic and social objectives, such as poverty reduction, food security, and social equity. By addressing the economic dimensions of marine resource use, MSP can contribute to achieving the United Nations Sustainable Development Goals (SDGs), particularly SDG 14 (Life Below Water), while also supporting other interconnected goals like decent work and economic growth (SDG 8) and reduced inequalities (SDG 10) (United Nations 2015).

Also, integrating economics into MSP in a way that mitigates the current shortcomings of CBA is essential for effective ocean management. It enables the evaluation of trade-offs, supports sustainable decision-making, attracts investment, fosters stakeholder participation, and aligns marine management with broader economic and social objectives. By incorporating economic considerations, MSP can ensure the sustainable and equitable use of marine resources, thereby enhancing the long-term health and productivity of ocean ecosystems.

Reimagining cost-benefit analysis for long-term marine spatial planning

As we delve deeper into MSP, it becomes increasingly clear that traditional economic tools may not be sufficient to address long-term and intergenerational challenges. One such tool is CBA, which, while useful, often falls short in the context of MSP's extended time horizons and complex environmental interactions. A fundamental issue with conventional CBA is its tendency to prioritize short-term private benefits over long-term societal outcomes. This is exacerbated by standard discounting practices, which significantly reduce the perceived value of future benefits. Consequently, projects or policies with immediate economic gains are often favored over those offering substantial but distant environmental or social benefits.

To address these shortcomings, we need to reconsider how CBA is applied within MSP. While the core elements of CBA—consideration of prices, costs, and discounting—should be retained, the approach must be modified to more effectively accommodate the long-term nature of marine ecosystem processes and the intergenerational impacts of our decisions.

Intergenerational cost-benefit analysis

The Icelandic case study explored in more depth below introduces the concept of intergenerational CBA, offering a fundamentally new approach to valuing long-term benefits. This method acknowledges that the majority of benefits from marine restoration and conservation efforts will accrue to future generations. Instead of discounting these future benefits from the current generation's perspective, intergenerational CBA proposes discounting from the perspective of each benefiting generation (Sumaila 2004, Sumaila and Walters 2005, Sumaila 2021, Jongbloed et al. 2021).

There are several advantages to this approach. First, it captures the real value of long-term ecosystem services more transparently, as perceived by those who will actually enjoy them. Second, it levels the playing field between very-short-term economic projects and long-term conservation efforts. Lastly, it provides a more ethical basis for decision-making by acknowledging our responsibility to future generations.

Applying intergenerational CBA to MSP could ensure more balanced and sustainable decisions. It would likely advocate for projects and policies that guarantee the long-term health of ecosystems, even if they do not provide immediate returns. This aligns with the concept of the "Infinity Fish," which emphasizes the infinite benefits of sustainable ocean use (Sumaila 2021).

In summary, intergenerational CBA offers a more equitable and forward-thinking approach to evaluating MSP projects. By valuing long-term benefits from the perspective of future generations, it supports sustainable decision-making that prioritizes the enduring health and resilience of marine ecosystems.

Social cost-benefit analysis

The Netherlands' approach to MSP in its North Sea Exclusive Economic Zone (EEZ), also explored in more depth below, introduces a critical modification to conventional CBA: the use of social cost–benefit analysis (SCBA). This adjustment accounts for the broader societal impacts of decisions in MSP, revealing the true costs and benefits of these decisions (World Bank 2022, Jongbloed et al. 2021). Social costs in MSP may relate to local communities, changes in ecosystem services, impacts on cultural heritage, and long-term environmental effects. Including these factors in CBA calculations helps balance economic development with social and environmental well-being. This is particularly relevant for the blue economy, where the relationship between the economy and the seas is complex and far-reaching. Explicitly accounting for social costs provides a clearer understanding of the real trade-offs (Dasgupta 2021) involved in different MSP scenarios.

Implementing these modified CBA approaches in MSP requires adaptation to the reality of the marine area as a valuable resource for future generations. This new era would involve more comprehensive data collection, interdisciplinary collaboration, and possibly new modeling techniques. However, the potential benefits are considerable. By adopting intergenerational CBA and including social costs, we can create MSP that are economically viable, socially just, and environmentally sustainable. These methods align well with the increasing recognition of the need for ecosystem-based management within marine environments. They provide a framework for quantifying and comparing the diverse values derived from marine ecosystems, from fisheries production and carbon sequestration to cultural significance.

While conventional CBA has its merits, it requires revisiting to adequately prepare practitioners for MSP. Intergenerational perspectives and broader conceptions of costs and benefits will lead to more robust and sustainable MSP. These approaches pave the way toward realizing the vision of Infinity Fish, ensuring that marine resources are available for all future generations (Sumaila 2021, Armstrong and Sumaila 2000

The value of integrating economics into marine spatial planning

In this section, we examine case studies of the Icelandic marine ecosystem and the Netherlands' North Sea through the lenses of intergenerational CBA and SCBA methodology, respectively. The Dutch EEZ in the North Sea successfully balanced the deployment of offshore wind farms against the need for sustainable food (primarily fisheries) and nature conservation (World Bank 2022), while the Icelandic model resulted in the rebuilding of fish stock (Sumaila 2021). These case studies provide practical insights into the application of enhanced CBA in MSP, illustrating innovative methodologies and sustainable marine resource management.

Case study: modeling the marine ecosystem of Iceland

The Icelandic marine ecosystem is home to various marine animals, exhibiting complex relationships, including predator–prey dynamics (Flaaten 1991) and instances of cannibalistic behavior (Armstrong and Sumaila 2000; 2005). Additionally, numerous fishing fleets operate different types of vessels and gear within this ecosystem.

The Icelandic marine ecosystem model we reference is based on the International Council for the Exploration of the Sea (ICES) fishing area covering 376,766 sq km, focusing on the year 1997 (Asberr and Buchary 2001). This model divides the ecosystem into 25 distinct "functional groups" and is subject to exploitation by 14 different fleet types (Asberr and Buchary 2001). These functional groups are categorized based on similarities in taxonomy, size, growth, mortality rates, and diet.

To compare the benefits of restoration, two scenarios were developed: "status quo" and "restoration." In the status quo scenario, the model is run for 50 years into the future using the present-day fleet structure, and the stable equilibrium outcomes are then projected for another 50 years, providing a total 100-year time horizon for the analysis (Asberr and Buchary 2001). In the restoration scenario, the model operates with various fleet configurations and sizes to select a restoration strategy. This involves closing the "lines and gillnetters," "bottom trawlers," and "capelin seines" fleets for the first 25 years, while allowing the remaining 11 fleets to fish based on their 1997 effort levels (Asberr and Buchary 2001). From the 26th year, 50 percent of the previously removed capacity is reinstated (Asberr and Buchary 2001). This approach is justified as cod, primarily harvested by lines, gillnetters, and bottom trawlers, rely on capelin, mainly caught by seines, as their main prey (Sumaila 1997).

The simulated catches are valued by applying prices per unit of the functional group landed. From this, the costs of catching and landing the fish, assumed to be about 40 percent of the price per unit weight, are subtracted to focus on purely market values (Asberr and Buchary 2001). This Icelandic approach to MSP exemplifies how ecosystem modeling can be coupled with economic valuation techniques.

The Icelandic case study is particularly instructive due to its comprehensive nature, breaking the ecosystem into 25 functional groups and considering the impact of 14 different fleet types (Asberr and Buchary 2001). This complexity is crucial for assessing the potential impacts of various management decisions. A striking feature of the Icelandic approach is the comparison between the "status quo" and "restoration" scenarios over a 100-year horizon. This long-term perspective is essential to understanding the benefits of ecosystem restoration (Asberr and Buchary 2001). The restoration scenario, with a 25-year fleet closure followed by partial reopening, reflects a balanced approach to conservation and sustainable marine resource use (Asberr and Buchary

2001), aligning well with the Infinity Fish concept, which promotes the view that ocean benefits are infinite and should be available perpetually.

The economic valuation component is another compelling aspect. By applying prices to simulated catches and accounting for fishing costs, the potential economic benefits of different management approaches are expressed in monetary terms. Focusing solely on market values demonstrates that restoration can often be justified on economic grounds alone, without considering non-market values. Perhaps the most innovative feature of the Icelandic case study is the examination of intergenerational CBA. This method is more equitable, considering benefits across multiple generations and discounting from each generation's perspective (Sumaila 2021). This rectifies a major weakness of conventional CBA, which heavily discounts future benefits. Sensitivity analysis on discount rates further strengthens the findings, showing that intergenerational CBA supports restoration efforts even at higher discount rates where conventional CBA would not.

This result has significant implications for MSP and ecosystem restoration worldwide. The Icelandic case study provides a robust framework for integrating ecological modeling with economic analyses, offering valuable insights for jurisdictions facing similar challenges. The long-term perspective and consideration of intergenerational equity are particularly noteworthy.

Case study: marine spatial planning of the North Sea by the Netherlands

The Netherlands' approach to MSP in its North Sea EEZ provides a compelling case study on balancing competing interests within a complex marine environment. This approach uniquely integrates economic analysis with ecological concerns for sustainable development and environmental protection (Jongbloed et al. 2021). Additionally, it supports the achievement of the United Nations SDG 14: Life Below Water.

Effective MSP requires understanding economic and ecological impacts. The Dutch MSP began with a detailed cost–benefit assessment of different spatial plans for the North Sea, emphasizing an ecosystem-based approach. This aligns with a global trend toward holistic marine management.

In 2015, the maritime spatial plan for the Dutch EEZ ambitiously allocated large areas for various uses, particularly focusing on renewable energy projects like offshore wind farms (World Bank 2022). This focus reflects broader European and global strategies to transition to cleaner energy sources and combat climate change. The revised MSP aims to accommodate additional sectoral policy needs while balancing ecological considerations.

The methodology included an SCBA to assess economic and ecological costs and benefits under different planning scenarios. This provided a quantitative basis for comparing options and understanding their potential impacts. Interestingly, the CBA revealed that the economic impacts of different spatial planning variants were relatively small, mainly due to minor variations in wind farm site locations. This suggests limited economic trade-offs between planning options and highlights other relevant factors beyond immediate economic impact for MSP decisions. One strength of the Dutch approach was acknowledging knowledge gaps and further research needs. The preliminary assessment and stakeholder engagement process identified areas where information was lacking, highlighting the importance of addressing uncertainty in a dynamic, often data-poor marine environment. The Dutch example also demonstrates the need for flexibility and continuous assessment in MSP planning. This adaptive strategy allows for revisions based on new information or changing circumstances, essential given the long time frames of many MSP decisions.

A key lesson from the Dutch experience is the integration of economic development with ecological sustainability (World Bank 2022). By considering both economic and ecological elements in their CBA and broader planning process, Dutch policymakers could more effectively balance decision-making. This approach recognizes that long-term economic prosperity in marine sectors is intertwined with the health and resilience of marine ecosystems. The case study also underscores the necessity of developing practical tools for MSP. While the CBA was constructive, the Dutch case shows the need for more advanced ecosystem modeling, better stakeholder engagement techniques, and new methods for valuing ecosystem services to fully understand the complexities of MSP.

In summary, the Dutch approach to MSP in the North Sea offers valuable lessons for other jurisdictions: combine robust economic analysis with ecological considerations, adapt planning processes, and consistently build up research and tools. This approach provides a model for reconciling offshore wind farms with the needs of sustainable food production and nature conservation while safeguarding long-term marine ecosystem health. Such integrated and balanced approaches are imperative for meeting the sustainable use of marine resources for generations to come, fulfilling the vision of an Infinity Fish future.

Conclusion

From the case studies presented herein, several solutions emerge for improving CBA in MSP. First, adjusting discount rates by lowering them can give more weight to future benefits, ensuring that long-term environmental and social outcomes are not undervalued (World Bank 2022). This adjustment would better reflect the true value of sustainable marine resource management over extended periods. Second, incorporating non-market values into CBA, such as ecosystem services, biodiversity, and cultural significance, can provide a more comprehensive assessment of the benefits and costs associated with MSP. This broader perspective ensures that the full range of environmental and social impacts is considered in decision-making. By rethinking and adapting the application of CBA in MSP, we can better address the long-term and intergenerational challenges inherent in managing marine ecosystems, supporting more sustainable and equitable outcomes for both present and future generations.

The inclusion of intergenerational perspectives and social costs in CBA represents a significant advancement in MSP methodologies. Future research should explore integrating these approaches more broadly, ensuring that MSP is both environmentally sustainable and socially equitable (Issifu et al. 2023). This synthesis of case study insights paves the way for more robust and sustainable marine resource management strategies.

References

Abbott, J. Kent, and Sumaila U. Rashid. 2019. Reducing Marine Plastic Pollution: Policy Insights from Economics. *Review of Environmental Economics and Policy* 13 (2): 167–341. https://doi.org/10.1093/reep/rez007.

Ainsworth, C.H. and Sumaila, U.R. (2005). Intergenerational valuation of fisheries resources can justify long-term conservation: a case study in Atlantic cod (Gadus morhua). *Canadian Journal of Fisheries and Aquatic Sciences*, 62, 1104–1110.

Asberr, Natoumbi Mendy, and Eny Buchary. 2001. Constructing an Icelandic Marine Ecosystem Model for 1997 Using a Mass-Balance Modelling Approach. In *Fisheries Impacts on North Atlantic Ecosystems: Models and Analyses*, edited by Sylvie Guénette, Villy Christensen, and Pauly Daniel, 182–197. Fisheries Centre, University of British Columbia.

Cheung, W. William, Thomas L. Frölicher, Vicky W.Y. Lam, Muhammed A. Oyinlola, Gabriel Reygondeau, Sumaila, U. Rashid Colette C. Wabnitz et al. 2021. Marine High Temperature Extremes Amplify the Impacts of Climate Change on Fish and Fisheries. *Science Advances* 7 (40): eabh0895. https://doi.org/10.1126/sciadv.abh0895.

Cisneros-Montemayor, M. Andrés, and Sumaila, U. Rashid. 2010. A Global Estimate of Benefits from Ecosystem-Based Marine Recreation: Potential Impacts and Implications for Management. *Journal of Bioeconomics* 12: 245–268. https://doi.org/10.1007/s10818-010-9092-7.

Dasgupta, Partha. 2021. *The Economics of Biodiversity: The Dasgupta Review.* London: HM Treasury.

Ehler, Charles, and Fanny Douvere. 2009. *Marine Spatial Planning: A Step-By-Step Approach Toward Ecosystem-Based Management.* Intergovernmental Oceanographic Commission and Man and the Biosphere Programme. IOC Manual and Guides No. 53, ICAM Dossier No. 6. Paris: UNESCO.

Flaaten, Ola. 1991. Bioeconomics of Sustainable Harvest of Competing Species. *Journal of Environmental Economics and Management* 20 (2): 163–180.

Issifu, Ibrahim, Ilyass Dahmouni, E. Worlanyo Deffor, and Sumaila, U. Rashid. 2023. Diversity, Equity and Inclusion in the Blue Economy: Why They Matter and How Do We Achieve Them? *Frontiers in Political Science* 4 (12): 1067481. https://doi.org/10.3389/fpos.2022.1067481.

Issifu, Ibrahim, Ilyass Dahmouni, Iria García-Lorenzo, and Sumaila, U. Rashid. 2024. Economics in Marine Spatial Planning: A Review of Issues in British Columbia and Similar Jurisdictions. *Sustainability* 16 (3): 1210. https://doi.org/10.3390/su16031210.

Issifu, Ibrahim, and Sumaila, U. Rashid. 2020. A Review of the Production, Recycling and Management of Marine Plastic Pollution. *Marine Science and Engineering* 8 (11): 945. https://doi.org/10.3390/jmse8110945.

Jongbloed, Ruud, Piet Gerjan, Peter Roebeling, and Sander van den Burg. 2021. Netherlands Case Study: Assessing the Economic and the Ecological Impacts, Costs and Benefits of Spatial Plans for the North Sea. In *Study on Integrating an Ecosystem-based Approach into Maritime Spatial Planning*, 6–52. European Commission.

Pauly, Daniel, Villy Christensen, Sylvie Guénette, J. Tony Pitcher, Sumaila, U. Rashid. J. Carl Walters, Reg Watson, and Dirk Zeller. 2002. Towards Sustainability in World Fisheries. *Nature* 418 (6898): 689–695. https://doi.org/10.1038/nature01017.

Spalding, D. Mark, Susan Ruffo, Carmen Lacambra, Imen Meliane, Lynne Zeitlin Hale, Christine C. Shepard, and Michael W. Beck. 2014. The Role of Ecosystems in Coastal Protection: Adapting to Climate Change and Coastal Hazards. *Ocean & Coastal Management* 90: 50–57. https://doi.org/10.1016/j.ocecoaman.2013.09.007.

Sumaila, U. Rashid. 1997. Strategic dynamic interaction: The case of Barents Sea fisheries. *Marine Resource Economics* 12, 77-94.

Sumaila, U. Rashid. 2004. Intergenerational Cost–Benefit Analysis and Marine Ecosystem Restoration. *Fish and Fisheries* 5 (4): 329–343.

Sumaila, U. Rashid. 2021. *Infinity Fish: Economics and the Future of Fish and Fisheries.* Cambridge: Academic Press.

Sumaila, U. Rashid, Jackie Alder, and Keith Head. 2006. Global Scope and Economics of Illegal Fishing. *Marine Policy* 30 (6): 696–703. https://doi.org/10.1016/j.marpol.2005.11.001.

Sumaila, U. Rashid, William Cheung, Andrew Dyck, Kamal Gueye, Ling Huang, Vicky Lam, Dirk Zeller et al. 2012. Benefits of Rebuilding Global Marine Fisheries Outweigh Costs. *PLOS One* 7 (7): e40542. https://doi.org/10.1371/journal.pone.0040542.

Sumaila, U. Rashid, Travis C. Tai, Vicky W. Lam, William W. Cheung, Megan Bailey, Andrés M. Cisneros-Montemayor, Li A. Chen, Sumeet S. Gulati. 2019. Benefits of the Paris Agreement to Ocean Life, Economies, and People. *Science Advances* 5 (2): eaau3855. https://doi.org/10.1126/sciadv.aau3855.

Sumaila, U. Rashid, Melissa Walsh, Kelly Hoareau, Ibrahim Issifu, Dana Miller, Louise Teh, Junjie Zhang et al. 2022. Financing a Sustainable Ocean Economy. *Nature Communication* 12 (3259). https://doi.org/10.1038/s41467-021-23168-y.

Sumaila, U. Rashid, and Carl Walters. 2005. Intergenerational Discounting: A New Intuitive Approach. *Ecological Economics* 52 (2): 135–142.

Teh, S. Louise, and U. Rashid Sumaila. 2020. Assessing Potential Economic Benefits from Rebuilding Depleted Fish Stocks in Canada. *Ocean & Coastal Management* 195 (1): 105289. https://doi.org/10.1016/j.ocecoaman.2020.105289.

United Nations. 2015. *Transforming Our World: The 2030 Agenda for Sustainable Development.* Available at: https://sdgs.un.org/2030agenda.

White, Crow, Benjamin S. Halpern, and Carrie V. Kappel. 2012. Ecosystem Service Tradeoff Analysis Reveals the Value of Marine Spatial Planning for Multiple Oceans Uses. *PNAS* 109 (12): 4696–4701. https://doi.org/10.1073/pnas.1114215109.

World Bank. 2022. *Applying Economic Analysis to Marine Spatial Planning.* Available at: https://documents1.worldbank.org/curated/en/099515006062210102/pdf/P1750970bba3a60940831205d770baece51.pdf.

16

Evaluating climate risk at the right scale: local lessons from the Climate and Ocean Risk Vulnerability Initiative (CORVI)

Sally Yozell, Tracy Rouleau, Natalie Fiertz and Carolyn Gruber

The problem

Climate change threatens coastal communities. Historically, Small Island Developing States (SIDS) and coastal Least Developed Countries (LDCs) have contributed little to greenhouse gas emissions yet are enduring some of the worst effects of climate change. SIDS and LDCs are together responsible for less than 5 percent of global greenhouse gas emissions, according to UN Development Programme reports published in December 2022 (Keo and Jo 2022a, 2022b). Yet SIDS and LDCs are widely recognized as being the most vulnerable because they rely more directly on the oceans' resources, they are more severely impacted by climate-related health threats, and their lower socioeconomic status does not leave any buffer for recovery after a climate disaster (Keo and Jo 2022a, 2022b). For coastal communities across the Global South, the climate "future" that scientists have long warned about has already arrived (Lam et al. 2020).

Rising seas threaten freshwater supplies, leaving less water available for drinking supplies, sanitation, industrial use, and the growing of crops. Storm surge and king tides[1] inundate agricultural lands in island states like Tuvalu, Kiribati, and the Marshall Islands, and saltwater intrusion threatens already very limited sources of fresh drinking water (Salem 2020).

Record-breaking storms are destroying livelihoods, homes, and infrastructure. The longest-lasting tropical cyclone on record crossed the entire Indian Ocean in early 2023 before dropping six months' worth of rain on Malawi in six days. The storm killed more than 1,200 people and destroyed critical sanitation infrastructure in a country already suffering from its worst-ever cholera outbreak (World Health Organization Africa 2022).

Increasing ocean temperatures are causing shifts in the distribution of fish stocks as they seek cooler waters, and coral reefs are bleaching at record rates, imperiling the food and economic security of fishing-dependent communities. Fishers in

Madagascar, for example, are taking their vessels out further to sea, for longer periods of time, and facing dangerous and sometimes deadly ocean conditions to find the fish that used to be inshore (UN News 2024).

In 2023, the highest sea surface temperatures on record (see Figure 16.1) coalesced for months around Jamaica. This resulted in the worst coral reef bleaching and mortality event recorded across the entire Caribbean (National Oceanic and Atmospheric Administration 2023a, 2023b).

More than 2 billion people live along the world's coastlines, and populations continue to increase, particularly in low-lying coastal cities (Reimann et al. 2023). Risk is a function of hazard, exposure, and vulnerability.

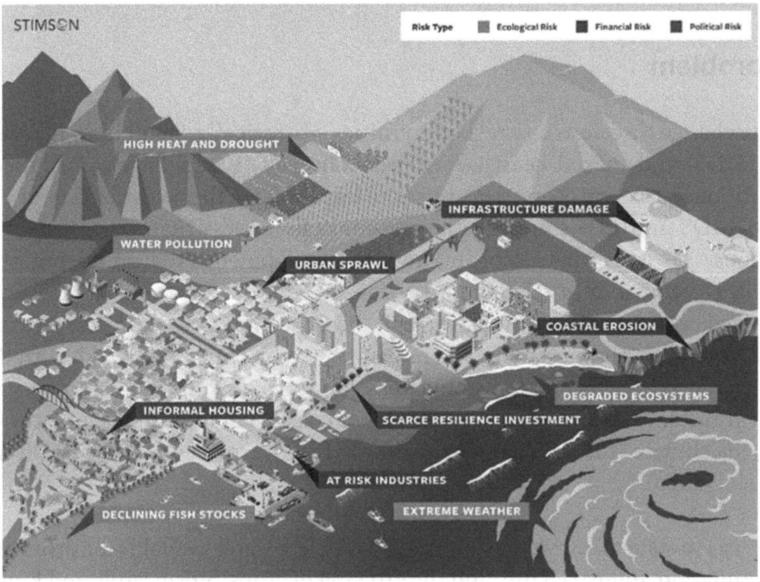

Note: This infographic shows a variety of ecological, financial, and political risks and how they might interact and affect a coastal community.

Source: Authors' own.

Figure 16.1 Compounding risks for coastal communities

Box 16.1 Calculating climate risk

$\text{Risk}_x = f(\text{Hazard}_x, \text{Exposure}_x, \text{Vulnerability}_x)$

Climate risk is a function of hazards, exposure, and vulnerability. For climate risk, a "hazard" is a natural phenomenon that may cause loss of life, injury, property damage, social and economic disruption, or environmental degradation. Examples of hazards include hurricanes, heatwaves, and sea level rise. "Exposure" is the people, infrastructure, housing, and other tangible assets that could be lost to a hazard. "Vulnerability" is the conditions which increase the susceptibility of exposed people, communities, and assets to the impacts of hazards. Examples of vulnerability include whether a shoreline is protected from storm surge by a seawall or mangroves or is unprotected, or whether a community has widespread air conditioning it can use in the event of a heatwave.

Frequent exposure to climate hazards that are increasing in severity threatens their economic security. Critical coastal infrastructure like the roads, ports, and energy and water utilities that support homes and businesses are vulnerable. Further, the ecosystems that have traditionally provided protection from storms and flooding, and served as habitat for fisheries, are degraded or have been developed, further perpetuating the cycle of risk. Blue economies—including fisheries, trade, and tourism—that support coastal communities are expected to sustain losses of $8.4 trillion (about half the size of China's entire economy) over the next fifteen years without immediate and drastic action (World Wildlife Fund 2024). Coastal communities face a set of interconnected and compounding risks that demands holistic, locally tailored climate risk assessment and action (see Figure 16.1).

The need

While the broad spectrum of risks faced by SIDS and coastal LDCs is well understood, the specific risks for specific coastal communities, however, are much more difficult to define, prepare for, and adapt to. It is critical that coastal communities understand their multidimensional climate risk to efficiently allocate resources and enact effective adaptation strategies (Ruth 2010).

Risk is a function of hazard, exposure, and vulnerability. While data on climate and ocean hazards and exposure is becoming more widely available, data on the vulnerability of coastal populations remains limited. When this data does exist, it is often poorly managed and stored in silos that make it difficult to access and use, even for city government officials (Hardoy and Pandiella 2009). This is especially true for social data (Cartwright et al. 2013, Ziervogel et al. 2014) which is critical for understanding how climate impacts will manifest for specific communities and populations and the ways in which disadvantaged communities are likely to bear the brunt of the impacts.

Decision-making for climate change adaptation requires an integrated and cross-sectoral approach to adequately capture the complexity of interconnected systems (Olazabel et al. 2018). To do this, decision-makers in coastal cities need a methodology that enables them to consider all three dimensions of climate risk—hazards, exposure, and vulnerability—across ecological, economic, and social systems to develop a comprehensive picture of climate risk for their city.

The Climate and Ocean Risk Vulnerability Initiative

To provide a holistic understanding of current and future climate impacts for a coastal community, the Stimson Center created the Climate and Ocean Risk Vulnerability Initiative (CORVI). The CORVI program analyzes a diverse set of risks to produce a comprehensive climate risk assessment and recommendations for action.

The methodology

There is a well-documented need for local climate vulnerability assessments at the city level or across a small island state, particularly in LDCs and SIDS. These assessments are most effective when setting climate hazards in the context of broader social, economic, and political vulnerabilities. To do this effectively, engaging a broad range of stakeholders at the subnational level is essential. A CORVI assessment[2] encompasses more than 100 indicators of risk across ten categories, grouped under ecological, financial, and political risk, as shown in the CORVI Wheel (see Figure 16.2).

Coastal cities are heavily dependent on both terrestrial and marine environments for their safety and economic security. Ecological risks, such as ecosystem health, the

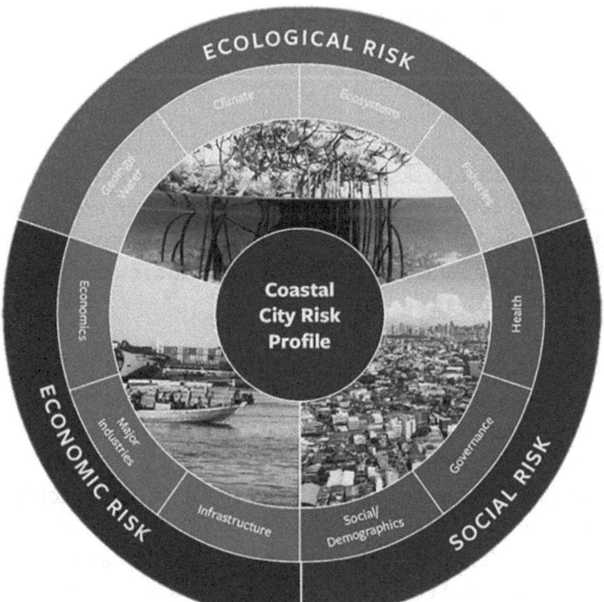

Note: The CORVI Wheel is a visual representation of the types of risks included in a CORVI assessment.

Source: Authors' own.

Figure 16.2 The CORVI Wheel

state of near and offshore fisheries, and geological factors like coastal erosion, provide important metrics to understand the environmental changes faced by coastal cities and communities. In CORVI assessments, the ecological risk area encompasses fisheries, ecosystems, climate, geology, and water resources in the selected study area.

Climate change represents a threat to major industries such as tourism, fishing, and shipping, as well as coastal infrastructure, including seaports, airports, housing, and public utilities. The economic risk area also encompasses the economic vulnerability of residents by assessing their ability to adapt to and recover from slow-onset changes such as migrating fish stocks, as well as rapid-onset events like extreme weather events. In CORVI assessments, the economic risk area encompasses infrastructure, major industries, and economics in the selected study area.

A community's social and political systems are at the heart of how cities and small island states experience and respond to climate risk. The social risk category includes government institutional capacity, demographic and population patterns, and poverty levels. The intersection of social and political risks with environmental and economic pressures can drive social instability. Limited political capacity can also constrain the effectiveness of responses to the threats posed by the climate emergency. In CORVI assessments, the social risk area encompasses demography, governance, and health in the selected study area.

The ten categories of risk—fisheries, ecosystems, climate change, geology/water, infrastructure, major industries, economics, demography, governance, and stability—are made up of more than 100 indicators (see Table 16.1a–c). These indicators reflect a range of issues, such as the vulnerability of critical infrastructure, the health of marine ecosystems, and urbanization dynamics. To ensure that the CORVI indicator scores provide a holistic risk rating, each indicator assesses current, past, and expected trends; the rate of change of the risk; and the impact of this risk on the coastal city or island state.

Box 16.2 Acknowledging the impacts of climate change on human health

The CORVI methodology is flexible; adjustments to the risk indicators are made based on locally specific concerns. For example, the risk indicators to show the impacts of climate change on human health were added after the COVID-19 pandemic as health vulnerabilities received greater recognition and were more explicitly linked to climate change. The 2024 CORVI assessment in Belize City is the first CORVI assessment to evaluate (1) food security and undernutrition (food insecurity), (2) impact on mental health (mental health disorders and stress-related disorders), (3) cardiovascular disease and respiratory disease (noncommunicable diseases), (4) heat-related morbidity and mortality, and (5) health worker density and distribution. These indicators were added to existing climate-health indicators, including the incidence of vector-borne disease and access to healthcare, in response to feedback from local partners during previous CORVI assessments, and increasing evidence of the importance of including public health actors in climate adaptation planning processes (Sheehan et al. 2022).

Table 16.1a The CORVI indicators: ecological

CORVI category	Indicator list
Geology/water	Percent of metro area at risk of flooding Percent of landscape that is arable land Degree of soil salinity in arable lands Projected change in sea level rise Rate of coastal erosion Degree of saltwater intrusion in coastal aquifers Piped water supply continuity Percent of bodies of water with high water quality Level of geophysical risk of landslides
Climate	Total number of hurricanes/tropical cyclones Total number of flood events Total number of extreme heat events Total number of droughts Total number of people affected by extreme weather events Total number of wet days Change in sea surface temperature
Ecosystems	Level of mangrove coverage Level of coral reefs coverage Level of sea grass bed coverage Health of existing mangroves Health of existing coral reefs Health of existing sea grass beds Rate of occurrence of harmful algal blooms Incidences of invasive species
Fisheries	Nearshore fish stock status Offshore fish stock status Fish consumption per capita Level of unreported catch estimate Percent of fisheries managed sustainably Capacity of fisheries enforcement institutions Number of fisheries access agreements with foreign nations Number of incidents of foreign vessels fishing in Exclusive Economic Zone

Source: Authors' own.

Table 16.1b The CORVI indicators: economic

CORVI category	Indicator list
Economics	National gross domestic product (GDP) per capita National youth unemployment rate Debt ratio Income inequality Urban unemployment rate Level of informal economy Market losses from extreme weather events Percent of GDP generated in coastal cities
Infrastructure	Percent of low-income housing in relation to flood zones Percent of people living below 5 meters above sea level Level of commercial infrastructure damage from extreme weather events Level of housing damage from extreme weather events Level of shoreline development Level of informal or unplanned settlement Level of grid resilience Renewable energy share in total energy consumption Level of water distribution infrastructure resilience Proportion of wastewater safely treated Percent of population with adequate access to electricity Effectiveness of solid waste management procedures Level of resilience for roads Level of resilience for airports Level of resilience for ports and shipping
Major industries	Percent of national economy based in agriculture Percent of national economy based in nearshore fishing industry Percent of national economy based in offshore fisheries Percent of national economy based in tourism industry Percent of national economy based in port and shipping industries Percent of people employed in agriculture Percent of people employed in tourism Percent of people employed in port and shipping industries Percent of people employed in commercial fishing Percent of people employed in artisanal and subsistence fishing

Source: Authors' own.

Table 16.1c The CORVI indicators: social

CORVI category	Indicator list
Governance	Level of perceived transparency within government Capacity of ethics enforcement bodies Voter turnout Civil society participation National Climate Adaptation Plan Rule of law Capacity of current disaster response Investment in climate-resiliency development projects Number of incidences of civil unrest or instability
Social/demographics	Urban population density Percent of population below the poverty line Percent of international migrants living in country Urban population (% of total population) Percent of urban population below 30 years of age Urbanization rate Dependency ratio Percent of population achieving proficiency in literacy and numeracy Percent of adult citizens living outside of the country Level of tension between social groups
Health	Mortality attributed to heat Mortality rate attributed to non-communicable diseases Cases of infectious diseases Percent of population at risk of mental health disorders and stress-related disorders Percent of population experiencing moderate or severe food insecurity Access to healthcare Health worker density and distribution Mortality rate attributed to unsafe water, unsafe sanitation, and lack of hygiene

Source: Authors' own.

CORVI combines a quantitative assessment of risk and vulnerability based on an in-depth survey methodology of structured expert judgment (SEJ) with qualitative insights gathered from semi-structured interviews with local stakeholders. This data collection process is essential to measuring climate impacts in data-sparse environments. With this invaluable, highly localized input, CORVI can help inform and prioritize specific, effective, and integrated policy solutions.

Box 16.3 Applying structured expert judgment to fill local-level data gaps

To overcome data gaps, the CORVI methodology relies on local experts to collect data that is otherwise unavailable. This primary data[3] is combined with secondary data[4] using structured expert judgment (SEJ) to produce a relative risk score for each indicator.[5] SEJ is a well-established social science technique that seeks to quantify risk when preexisting secondary data is inadequate. Through surveys, as well as a series of weighting procedures to ensure that data is accurate, SEJ allows researchers to fill data gaps and quantify key risks. To apply SEJ to CORVI, subject matter experts across academia, government, civil society, and the private sector are identified through stakeholder mapping and extensive outreach in the target communities. These experts then refer the project team to other experts and stakeholders using "snowball" or chain-referral sampling.

The process

The "core" of CORVI is community-focused research. The typical CORVI assessment begins with extensive preliminary background research, followed by a series of interviews and surveys, bookended by two in-country visits. An essential player in this work is a sponsor within the local or national government who can support and maintain community buy-in. Each CORVI study involves surveying and interviewing more than 60 local experts—from academia, government ministries, and business sectors like agriculture or transportation—on the 100 different risk indicators (see Table 16.1a–c). Throughout the CORVI process, the support of a local project partner organization is critical, especially for the surveys and interviews. These local project partners typically lead the in-country data collection and are situated on the ground

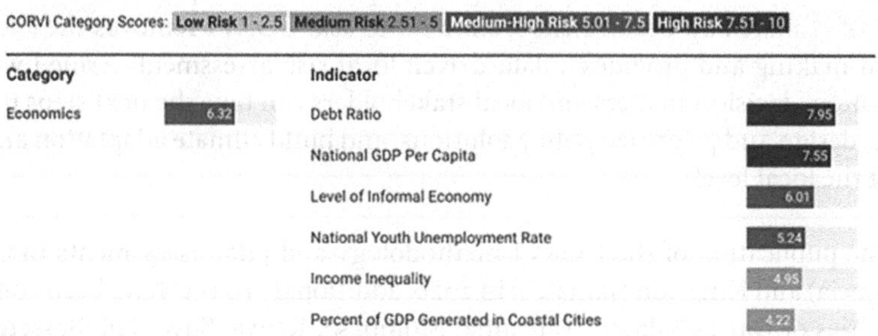

Note: This figure shows the detailed indicators for one of the ten risk categories; in this case, economic risk with respect to major industries.

Source: Authors' own.

Figure 16.3 Sample CORVI indicator scores

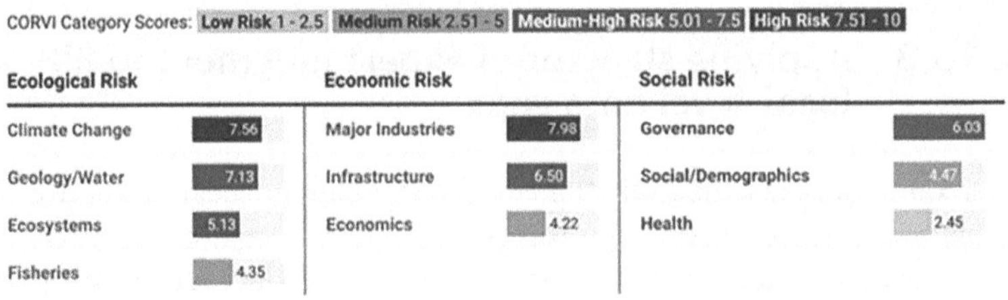

Note: This figure shows an example of what the scores may look like across each of the ten categories, as grouped into ecological, economic, and social risks.

Source: Authors' own.

Figure 16.4 Sample CORVI category scores

so that they can engage regularly with stakeholders. Once all the surveys have been completed, scores for each of the 100 indicators (see Figure 16.3) included in the ten categories (see Figure 16.4) of risk are produced. These scores, which range from low, medium, and medium-high to high, serve as the foundation of a customized Climate Risk Report. The Climate Risk Report includes locally specific findings and concrete recommendations to help the CORVI champions and government sponsors prioritize resilience activities. A second in-country visit offers an opportunity to translate the Climate Risk Report into action.

The outcomes

Located at the interface between land and sea, coastal cities are at the nexus of climate change impacts and climate adaptation efforts. Resilience planning in coastal cities and across small island states must be based on integrated systems thinking. The CORVI risk assessment process is designed to provide a comprehensive and holistic picture of climate and ocean risks from land to sea. CORVI removes the silos from decision-making and provides a data-driven local risk assessment. Armed with this information, decision-makers and local stakeholders can take the next steps to access finance, design and prioritize policy solutions, and build climate adaptation and resilience at the local level.

Since the publication of the CORVI methodology and pilot assessments in Castries (Saint Lucia) and Kingston (Jamaica) in 2020, additional projects have been completed in the cities of Dar es Salaam, Tanzania; Mombasa, Kenya; Suva, Fiji; Basseterre, St. Kitts and Nevis; Chattogram, Bangladesh; and Dagupan, Philippines. At the time of publication, there are ongoing assessments in Belize City, Belize; Toamasina, Madagascar; and for the island nation of Aruba.

Case study: Castries, Saint Lucia

Built on reclaimed land and located on the west coast, Castries is the capital of Saint Lucia and its largest city. Castries faces heatwaves, droughts, floods, and hurricanes, undermining a tourism-dependent economy characterized by high unemployment and inequality. Our research on the ground in Castries revealed degraded wastewater and solid waste infrastructure that resulted in clogged drainage canals and inland flooding. Informal housing poses a significant challenge to the supply and dissemination of freshwater. Unregulated tourist settlement construction and pollution from a lack of effective waste management has negatively affected coastal ecosystems, such as coral reefs, mangroves, and sea grass beds.

The CORVI assessment for Castries identified three priority areas for action:

1. *Improve city adaptation planning.* Adaptation planning in Saint Lucia is generally undertaken at the national level; there is a need to enhance local risk management and planning capabilities. Empowering the Castries Constituency Council or establishing new city-level agencies to address adaptation and planning is crucial to effectively address local issues, such as erosion and flooding; even minor rainfall can lead to flooding in Castries. Increased local funding and capacity can inform accurate zoning maps and regulations to reduce city-specific vulnerability.
2. *Diversify economic output.* With more than 1.2 million visitors in 2019, Saint Lucia must balance the expansion of its tourism industry against the industry's negative impacts, poor waste management, and the destruction of important ecosystems, including coral reefs and mangroves. The growth of the tourism sector also leaves Saint Lucia vulnerable to any shocks that might interrupt "sun, sea, and sand" tourist activities. To diversify its economy, Saint Lucia should consider channeling public and private funding to new service and industrial sectors, including light manufacturing, agricultural crops, and finance.
3. *Build climate-resilient infrastructure.* The vulnerability of Castries' critical tourism, transportation, energy, and water infrastructure depends on factors such as building materials, design, maintenance, and past damage. A detailed vulnerability analysis of selected critical infrastructure could identify risk hotspots and inform strategies to build resilience, such as updated building regulations, retrofitting, and nature-based solutions.

Case study: Chattogram, Bangladesh

In Chattogram, Bangladesh, the CORVI assessment identified a suite of compounding risks connected to rapid unplanned urbanization. Rapid urbanization drives the expansion of informal settlements and uncollected solid waste, with both resulting in blocked drainage channels that exacerbate waterlogging. Untreated wastewater from residential sources and from the city's major industries, such as shipbreaking and garment making, enters the city's key waterways. This wastewater harms human health and the health of key coastal and marine ecosystems—ecosystems already under threat from development to accommodate the city's growth—and their degradation reduces coastal protection and endangers the blue economy.

The CORVI assessment identified three priority areas for action:

1. *Improve and expand flood adaptation and waste management.* This could include adopting a multilayered plan to reduce solid waste, which may involve public collection, performance-based contracts for private providers, financial support for and facilities for informal waste pickers to use, and waste-to-energy projects. This should be accompanied by clearing drainage channels, expanding green spaces, and restoring water bodies.
2. *Improve urban climate-resilience implementation and invest in climate-smart infrastructure.* The national government, the local government, civil society, and international partners should work together to reduce fragmented governance and improve project implementation. This work should draw on international best practices and explore emerging sources of finance to help resource climate-resilience implementation, including climate-resilient debt clauses, debt-for-nature swaps, resilience bonds, and new insurance initiatives.
3. *Implement a sustainable shoreline development strategy.* Integrating development with sustainable environmental management will promote resilient economic growth that sustainably alleviates poverty in Chattogram. This strategy could include expanded marine zoning coupled with stronger enforcement of existing protected areas, improving the treatment of residential and industrial wastewater by passing and enforcing pollution standards, facilitating housing development in low-risk areas of the city, and supporting the integration of rice agriculture with other crops, including the use of salt-tolerant rice varieties.

The impact

CORVI assessments can be used for four essential next steps to build climate resilience: (1) support short- and long-term local planning, (2) identify locally specific shovel-ready projects, (3) develop local policy solutions, and (4) unlock financing mechanisms to support the implementation of projects and policy solutions in the near, medium, and longer time frames. In Saint Lucia and Chattogram, CORVI has supported local climate-resilience efforts in different ways.

In Saint Lucia, the CORVI assessment recommendations produced in 2021 align with the Saint Lucia Blue Bond Framework that was drafted in 2023. Blue and green bonds[6] are an innovative financing effort that offers an opportunity for Saint Lucia to sustainably leverage its ocean-based resources to support its post-pandemic recovery and economic diversification. The Saint Lucia Blue Bond Framework describes how the Government of Saint Lucia can deliver environmental, social, and economic benefits in return for financing. With this financing, Saint Lucia plans to build and support its economic growth and resilience by strengthening the sustainability and competitiveness of two critical and interconnected sectors—tourism and fisheries—and expand its infrastructure for waste management.

In Chattogram, the outputs of the CORVI analysis informed the Chattogram city master plan. In line with CORVI recommendations, the Chattogram city master plan will address stormwater drainage and flood control, support a long-term development strategy for the communication and transportation system, and establish an environmental management plan. In addition, the CORVI analysis is supporting the ongoing implementation of the Bangladesh Delta Plan 2100 and can be used to help access international technical and financial assistance. The key goals of the Bangladesh Delta Plan 2100 align directly with the CORVI indicators and recommendations, particularly around ensuring water and food security, fostering climate-resilient economic growth, and improving environmental sustainability.

From policy recommendations to practical resilience

With sixteen CORVI assessments completed or in progress, there is now a wealth of information available that can paint a clear picture of climate risk and resilience in these coastal communities. The goals of CORVI are to fill data gaps, identify cascading and compounding climate risks, support informed decisions, avoid costly mistakes, and take advantage of opportunities for sustainable growth. But the true value of CORVI analysis is the vast amount of local data and information it can collect, curate, and connect. As we have learned through the CORVI program time and again, climate risks are inherently local; the best, most effective solutions will be designed with locally specific data and implemented collaboratively where it matters most—at the community level.

There is always more to do.

The fragmented nature of climate vulnerability data at the city level hinders coordination and collaboration among different stakeholders, such as government agencies, non-profit organizations, and private sector actors. This can result in duplicated efforts, wasted resources, and ineffective strategies for adapting to climate change. CORVI uses SEJ and semi-structured interviews to integrate local and traditional knowledge regarding key social, economic, and ecological vulnerabilities into policy recommendations. We need continued advancements and innovations in the use of expert elicitation techniques, such as SEJ, to develop more culturally sensitive and relevant strategies for building climate resilience.

In each of the completed CORVI assessments, sector-specific concerns have emerged as an important area for follow-up. Adapting the CORVI methodology to identify opportunities for sustainable growth in these sectors and industries will support climate-resilient blue economies in coastal communities. Building on the foundations of a full CORVI assessment, a sector-specific CORVI assessment could identify and assess high-priority risks that are likely to affect a specific industry—like tourism, shipping, or fisheries—that are essential to coastal economies.

Using the CORVI assessment to access and unlock funding to support climate resilience is easier said than done. According to the United Nations (2024), the global economic growth rate for 2024 is at its lowest point in decades. When combined with mounting national debt, this compounds the climate impacts facing coastal communities. To respond to these challenges, coastal countries and island states are seeking to build climate resilience, develop their sustainable blue economies, and stabilize their economy by focusing on sustainable tourism, sustainable fisheries, and renewable energy. Yet the gap between the available funding for climate adaptation and what is needed to adapt to the impacts of climate change is growing; needs are ten to eighteen times as great as current funds (United Nations Environment Programme 2023). Island states and coastal nations need an accessible mix of long-term and flexible financing, including from governments, multilateral development banks, the private sector, and philanthropic funding. Instead, they face a complex financing landscape and complicated funding application requirements, and struggle to bridge the gap between the information they have and the information funders need. A post-CORVI finance module will help local CORVI champions access the climate adaptation funding they need to implement practical solutions to address the risks that the CORVI assessments identify as the highest priority.

The complexity and urgency of today's ocean and climate challenges require a shift in our approach to research. We need to consider environmental, social, economic, and political factors concurrently to be effective and achieve sustainable outcomes. Dynamic questions require dynamic answers; a holistic and multidisciplinary research agenda will better serve the clear need for solutions. As we apply this new research agenda, using research methods supported by local knowledge and expertise will be critical. Collaborating with local experts to measure what matters not only adds these essential perspectives to the broader adaptation toolkit, but also helps fill data gaps and make important linkages between datasets.

Notes

1. "King tide" is a term used to describe exceptionally high tides that are typically associated with a new or full moon or with regionally specific seasons.
2. For a peer-reviewed analysis of the CORVI methodology, see Rouleau et al. (2022).
3. Primary data is information collected first-hand for a specific research purpose. It is original and provides new insights into the research objectives.
4. Secondary data is derived from primary data and is collected by others. Examples of secondary data include app data like GPS coordinates, information from government websites, and journal articles.
5. For an introduction to structured expert judgment, see Cooke (1991) and Colson and Cooke (2017).

6. A blue (or green) bond is a debt instrument issued by governments, development banks, or others to raise money from impact investors to finance projects that have positive environmental, economic, and climate benefits.

References

Cartwright, Anton, James Blignaut, Martin De Wit, Karen Goldberg, Myles Mander, Sean O'Donoghue, and Debra Roberts. 2013. Economics of climate change adaptation at the local scale under conditions of uncertainty and resource constraints: The case of Durban, South Africa. *Environmental Urbanization* 25 (1): 139–156.

Colson, Abigail R., and Roger M. Cooke. 2017. Cross validation for the classical model of structured expert judgment. *Reliability Engineering & System Safety* 163: 109–120.

Cooke, Roger. 1991. *Experts in Uncertainty: Opinion and Subjective Probability in Science.* Oxford: Oxford University Press.

Hardoy, Jorgelina, and Gustavo Pandiella. 2009. Urban poverty and vulnerability to climate change in Latin America. *Environmental Urbanization* 21: 203–224.

Keo, Kalyan, and Yoona Jo. 2022a. *The State of Climate Ambition: Snapshot – Small Island Developing States (SIDS).* New York: United Nations Development Programme.

Keo, Kalyan and Yihong Liu. 2022b. *The State of Climate Ambition: Snapshot – Least Developed Countries (LDCs).* New York: United Nations Development Programme.

Lam, Vicky W.Y., Edward H. Allison, Joanna D. Bell, Jessica Blythe, William W.L. Cheung, Thomas L. Frölicher, Maria A. Gasalla, and U. Rashid Sumaila. 2020. Climate change, tropical fisheries and prospects for sustainable development. *Nature Reviews Earth & Environment* 1 (9): 440–454.

National Oceanic and Atmospheric Administration. 2023a. *Caribbean Coral Reef Watch*, Vol. VIII, Issue IV. Available at: https://rcc.cimh.edu.bb/caribbean-coral-reef-watch-vol-viii-issue-iv-september-december-2023/.

National Oceanic and Atmospheric Administration. 2023b. *Caribbean Coral Reef Watch*, Vol. VIII, Issue V. Available at: https://rcc.cimh.edu.bb/caribbean-coral-reef-watch-vol-viii-issue-v-october-2023-january-2024/.

Olazabel, Marta, Aline Chiabai, Sebastien Foudi, and Marc B. Neumann. 2018. Emergence of new knowledge for climate change adaptation. *Environmental Science & Policy* 83: 46–53.

Reimann, Lena, Athanasios T. Vafeidis, and Lars E. Honsel. 2023. Population development as a driver of coastal risk: Current trends and future pathways. *Cambridge Prisms: Coastal Futures* 1: e14.

Rouleau, Tracy, Jack Stuart, Maia Call, Sally Yozell, Nagisa Yoshioka, Miko Maekawa, and Natalie Fiertz. 2022. The climate and ocean risk vulnerability index: Measuring coastal city resilience to inform action. *Frontiers in Sustainable Cities* 4.

Ruth, Matthias. 2010. Economic and social benefits of climate information: assessing the cost of inaction. *Procedia Environmental Science* 1: 387–394.

Salem, Salam. 2020. Climate change and the sinking island states in the Pacific. *E-International Relations.* Available at: www.e-ir.info/2020/01/09/climate-change-and-the-sinking-island-states-in-the-pacific/.

Sheehan, Mary C., Fay Khudairi, Gurtejandeep S. Swaich, William Hines, Shivani Mehta, and Mary A. Fox. 2022. Urban climate-health governance: Charting the role of public health in large global city adaptation plans. *PLOS Climate* 1 (3): e0000012.

United Nations. 2024. *World Economic Situation and Prospects 2024.* New York: UN.

United Nations Environment Programme. 2023. *Adaptation Gap Report 2023: Underfinanced. Underprepared. Inadequate Investment and Planning on Climate Adaptation Leaves World Exposed*. Nairobi: UNEP.

UN News. 2024. Fishers in Madagascar adapt to deadly seas due to climate change. Available at: https://news.un.org/en/story/2024/04/1148496.

World Health Organization Africa. 2022. Tropical storms, flooding and Cholera: Malawi faces cholera emergency amidst severe climate events. Available at: www.afro.who.int/photo-story/tropical-storms-flooding-and-cholera-malawi-faces-cholera-emergency-amidst-severe/.

World Wildlife Fund. 2024. Navigating ocean risk: Shaping the transition to a sustainable blue economy. Available at: https://value-at-risk.panda.org/#intro.

Ziervogel, Gina, Mark New, Emma Archer van Garderen, Guy Midgley, Anna Taylor, Ralph Hamann et al. 2014. Climate change impacts and adaptation in South Africa. *Wiley Interdisciplinary Review: Climate Change* 5: 605–620.

17 Understanding the ocean within the aquatic system for sustainable fisheries

Shehu Latunji Akintola, Isa Olalekan Elegbede, Abdulwakil Olawale Saba, Olanrewaju Femi Olagunju, Akinkunmi Sunday Ojo, Isaac Kofi Osei and Denis Worlanyo Aheto

Introduction

Humans are at a crossroads in the sustainable use of Earth's resources, requiring genuine collaboration and co-production of knowledge to promote a truly globally sustainable and resilient society. It is desirable to implement fair research partnerships, mutual capacity-building, and technology co-development between the Global North and South. An agenda for sustainable fisheries means that there is a need to evolve away from *Homo socius* and *Homo economicus* to *Homo sustinere*—as a knowledge domain in fish and fisheries production and consumption. Fisheries knowledge reflects a social-ecological system (SES), and the interaction between social and ecological processes must be emphasized (Ostrom 2009). The silos must be broken down, as reflected by Sumaila (2024) and the integrated view of fisheries from Kelvin (Cochrane 2017).

Our understanding of the ecosystem dynamics of the ocean is relatively superb in terms of basic food webs. It can be said that there has been a good understanding of the fundamental structure of marine food webs, including the roles of phytoplankton, zooplankton, fish, and larger marine animals. However, continuous monitoring and research to better understand ocean health is imperative. This includes the complementary use of both biotic and abiotic indices in ecological risk assessments, the importance of sentinel species in the early detection of the ecological impact of both natural and anthropogenic stressors, and the role of less abundant or non-representative (indicator) species for food web integrity considering both trophic and non-trophic interactions.

The tension between small- and large-scale fisheries in the Global South for space would benefit from further research to promote a better understanding and sustainable use of fish and fisheries for social and economic developments. In Nigeria, Ghana, and Gambia, the fisheries sector faces diverse challenges in the adoption of management and conservation principles to deal with topical issues in fisheries. These include co-management, marine spatial planning (MSP), neoliberalism, gender equality, Individual Transferable Quotas (ITQs), Territorial Use Rights for Fisheries (TURFs), and illegal, unreported, and unregulated (IUU) fishing. Additionally, accounting for estuarine and lagoonal fisheries by collecting data on landings and methods of exploitation to drive their conservation and development on national and regional scales is needed. Experience from the Global North in the transition of small-scale fisheries to industrial fisheries would be interesting for the Global South.

The 1982 United Nations Convention on the Law of the Sea (UNCLOS) provided the foundation for the peaceful resolution of conflicts over fish and marine resources. Other governance instruments have been developed or evolved from UNCLOS but have faced the challenges of either no ratification by states or, when ratified, slow or no implementation. The slow ratification or implementation of governance instruments meant to achieve sustainable fisheries management, such as the World Trade Organization (WTO) Agreement on Fisheries Subsidies, guidelines for small-scale fisheries, and various conservation tools, slows down progress toward sustainable oceans.

The Treaty on Biological Diversity Beyond National Jurisdiction (BBNJ Agreement) offers another moment for the fisheries sector to deal with the twin challenges of fishing and conservation when it comes into force. It should facilitate equitable exchange and collaboration between states. However, there are issues that researchers must unpack given the often-neglected externalities in fisheries as well as the associated complex nexuses such as issues of food, climate change, and biodiversity, among others.

This chapter presents potential avenues for future research to advance sustainable ocean management policies. These potential research areas include advancing our understanding of the ecosystem dynamics of the ocean, small-scale versus large-scale fisheries issues, integrated aquatic systems, governance instruments in the management of the aquatic system, and externalities in balancing fishing and conservation under the BBNJ Agreement.

Ecosystem dynamics of the ocean

The health of the world's oceans depends on a range of factors, each playing a vital role in shaping marine ecosystems. Recognizing this interconnectedness is crucial for maintaining resilience and sustainability amidst environmental changes. Physicochemical factors such as temperature and ocean currents are fundamental. Temperature affects the distribution and metabolism of marine life, while currents transport nutrients, gases, and organisms over long distances. These interactions influence primary productivity, biodiversity, and nutrient cycling. Sustainable fisheries management depends on maintaining these interconnected systems.

Conversely, human activities and their associated consequences—pollution, overfishing, climate change, habitat degradation, rising temperatures, and ocean acidification—disrupt marine environments, posing threats to ocean health (Shaffer et al. 2023). Continuous monitoring and research to understand these waters' status are critical to fisheries conservation and management. In this respect, some recent studies have demonstrated critical issues for further research in the assessment of ocean health (Table 17.1). This includes the complementary use of both biotic and abiotic indices in ecological risk assessments (Thabet et al. 2024), the importance of sentinel species in the early detection of the ecological impact of both natural and anthropogenic stressors (Razak et al. 2024), and the role of less abundant or non-representative (indicator) species for food web integrity considering both trophic and non-trophic interactions (Stratmann et al. 2024).

The marine ecosystems of Africa and the Global South, in particular, face challenges due to human activities and natural factors, threatening their health and sustainability despite their rich biodiversity. Recognizing the interconnectedness of these environments, ecosystem-based fisheries management (EBFM) is seen as a comprehensive approach to fisheries management in these regions. However, EBFM relies on robust scientific data and information to inform decision-making processes. Data gaps and limited scientific knowledge about marine ecosystems within the Global South pose significant challenges to implementing EBFM practices. In response to data limitations in fisheries management, simple, cost-effective methods have been developed for stock assessment in data-limited fisheries. Their capabilities include estimation of population size without catch data, relying on length frequency data or genetics-based

Table 17.1 Data-limited approaches for stock assessment

Number	Stock assessment methods/tools for data-limited fisheries	Reference(s)
1.	Rejection sampling methods and agent-based models	Carrella et al. 2024
2.	Catch Maximum Sustainable Yield CMSY++, an improvement on CMSY+ and Bayesian Schaefer Model (BSM); CMSY-BSM Model; and Catch-MSY method	Froese et al. 2017, 2023
3.	Abundance Maximum Sustainable Yields (AMSY)	Froese et al. 2020
4.	Length-based Bayesian Biomass Analysis (LBB)	Froese et al. 2018
5.	Close-Kin Mark-Recapture (CKMR)	Bravington et al. 2016
6.	Length-Based Spawning Potential Ratio (LB-SPR)	Hordyk et al. 2015a
7.	Froese's Length-Based Indicators (LBIs) for sustainable fishing	Froese 2004

Source: Authors' own.

approaches, and using indicators like the percentage of mature fish or specimens with optimal length, while some feature the use of artificial neural networks (ANN).

General Research Considerations

i. Due to the possibility of using both quantitative and qualitative data in filtering and the agent-based method, the methodology could be explored further in data-limited fisheries where parameter estimates have broad uncertainty.
ii. The extensions and refinements of CMSY++ should be explored to incorporate additional sources of uncertainty, such as environmental variability and structural model uncertainty, and to evaluate its performance in data-limited fisheries contexts.
iii. CKMR's immense potential for monitoring populations of low-density and highly mobile species needs to be explored.
iv. The simplicity of length-based methods and the Catch MSY could be used in extremely data-limited situations, and more applications of the LBB method should be considered for invertebrate species.
v. The strengths of different methods should be leveraged in applying them to multi-species assessment.

Large and small-scale fisheries in Nigeria

The Nigerian fisheries sector faces diverse challenges, including co-management, MSP, neoliberalism, gender equality, ITQs, TURFs, and IUU fishing. These issues, as listed in Table 17.2 and spanning socio-economic, environmental, and policy dimensions, threaten both large-scale and small-scale operations.

Effective co-management systems, MSP, scrutiny of neoliberal policies, and gender equality promotion are imperative. Enhanced surveillance, governance frameworks, and international cooperation are needed to combat IUU fishing. Embracing innovative governance approaches can enhance sustainability, resilience, and community well-being.

Co-management

Co-management systems are essential for the effective governance of fisheries resources in Nigeria. Challenges such as governance gaps, insufficient stakeholder participation, and inadequate enforcement mechanisms hinder the success of co-management initiatives. Strengthening stakeholder engagement, building local community capacity, and fostering adaptive management approaches are crucial steps to enhance co-management effectiveness.

Marine spatial planning

The absence of comprehensive MSP in Nigeria poses challenges for sustainable resource management and conflict resolution in coastal areas. Effective MSP requires stakeholder engagement, data-driven decision-making, and integration of ecological,

Table 17.2 Issues and research focus of fisheries governance in Nigeria

Number	Issue	Agenda	Reference(s)
1	Co-management	Implement co-management strategies that involve collaboration between government and local stakeholders to equalize power dynamics among stakeholders, integrate local and scientific knowledge, and empower local communities	Aguión et al. 2021
2	Marine spatial planning	Develop and implement MSP frameworks to regulate activities in marine areas sustainably	Yatim et al. 2016
3	Neoliberalism	Promote alternative governance models, emphasize community-based management, foster collaboration	Bresnihan 2019
4	Gender-based issues	Promote gender equality, empower women, enhance awareness, support women's participation	Gustavsson et al. 2021
5	Individual Transferable Quotas	Evaluate the effectiveness of ITQs and consider adjustments to ensure sustainable fish stock management	Branch 2009
6	Territorial Use Rights for Fisheries	Ensure TURFs are of sufficient size and design to effectively manage fisheries resources	Viana et al. 2019, Aceves-Bueno et al. 2017
7	Illegal, unreported, and unregulated fishing	Enhance surveillance and monitoring, improve governance and enforcement, promote transparency and traceability, engage communities, foster international cooperation, and embrace technological innovation	Agnew et al. 2009, Leonardo and Deeb 2022

Source: Authors' own.

social, and economic considerations. Implementing MSP can balance competing interests, ensure sustainable resource use, and promote ecosystem health in Nigerian fisheries.

Neoliberalism

Neoliberal policies have reshaped fisheries management in Nigeria, emphasizing privatization, profit-driven motives, and market penetration. This change in basic assumptions has altered relationships between fishers, communities, and the marine environment, often overlooking local knowledge and practices. Addressing neoliberalism's negative impacts requires promoting alternative governance models, empowering local stakeholders, and fostering collaboration between government agencies and fishing communities.

Gender-based issues

Gender disparities persist in Nigerian fisheries, with women facing limited resource access, unequal pay, and diminished decision-making power. Traditional gender roles marginalize women in small-scale fisheries, while discrimination impedes their leadership participation in large-scale fisheries. Addressing gender-based issues requires promoting gender equality, empowering women through training and capacity-building programs, and integrating gender considerations into fisheries policies and programs.

Individual transferable quotas

The implementation of ITQs in Nigerian fisheries necessitates careful consideration of context-specific challenges and stakeholder engagement. ITQs can promote sustainable fishing practices and equitable resource access but may exacerbate inequities, especially for small-scale fishers. Addressing concerns about equity, enforcement, and ecosystem impacts is crucial for the successful implementation of the ITQ program in Nigerian fisheries.

Territorial use rights for fisheries

Challenges facing TURFs in Nigeria include governance gaps, enforcement issues, stakeholder conflicts, and sustainability concerns. Strengthening stakeholder engagement, capacity-building, adaptive management, and ecosystem-based approaches can enhance the effectiveness of TURF governance in Nigerian fisheries.

Illegal, unreported, and unregulated fishing

IUU fishing poses significant challenges to fisheries governance in Nigeria, leading to economic losses, environmental degradation, and threats to food security. Combating IUU fishing demands enhanced surveillance, governance frameworks, and international cooperation. Implementing seafood traceability systems, strengthening enforcement mechanisms, and engaging local communities are essential strategies for addressing IUU fishing in Nigerian waters.

To address key issues in fisheries management, a comprehensive approach involving various strategies is essential. Table 17.2 outlines the issues and actions needed to combat these challenges.

Nigeria's fisheries face multifaceted challenges demanding coordinated solutions. Co-management initiatives must bridge governance gaps, enhance stakeholder involvement, and strengthen enforcement. MSP is vital for sustainable resource use and ecosystem health. Neoliberal policies stress privatization, urging equitable governance models, but the SSF Guidelines do not mention any market-oriented policies and are considered largely inequitable in small-scale fisheries. Gender equality and empowerment are crucial. Implementing ITQs and TURFs requires equity and ecosystem considerations. Combating IUU fishing necessitates surveillance and international cooperation. Integrated approaches can ensure long-term viability, benefiting coastal communities and marine ecosystems.

Integrated aquatic systems

The ocean acts as a large sink into which all the water bodies and land inundations empty. This implies that the health of the world's oceans is impacted by the state of the adjoining water bodies (including riverine and lacustrine systems), especially coastal ecosystems like estuaries and lagoons. According to King (2007), primary production in coastal waters is often much higher due to the nutrients derived from terrestrial sources. In the same vein, the productivity of the coastal waters can be negatively impacted if the ecological services (especially provisioning, regulating, and supporting services) are undermined through overexploitation and pollution, among other issues. In the Global South, unsustainable fishing practices and methods have led to the decline of many important commercial fisheries, which could be attributed to ineffective governance systems, poor policy conception and implementation, and the incoherence of national policies with global instruments and best practices.

A recent publication by Chuku et al. (2022) has brought to the fore how women-led estuarine mangrove shellfisheries have taken the initiative of enhancing food and nutrition security as well as improving livelihoods through rights-based co-management in West Africa. Two women-led resource user groups from Gambia and Ghana have championed and spearheaded a co-management policy with the involvement of stakeholders, including government officials, traditional authorities, research/academic institutions, and non-governmental organizations/civil society organizations, to exploit shellfisheries rationally and sustainably. In Ghana, for instance, it has been documented that the oyster fishery is a profitable resource, supporting the livelihood of women (Osei et al. 2020), although less considered.

The rights-based co-management approach stimulates a sense of ownership in resource users, which motivates fishers to take management and conservation measures seriously by carrying out biodiversity enhancement and pollution-free campaigns in estuarine systems, thereby promoting a healthy marine ecosystem.

There is a need for coastal countries in the Global South to account for estuarine and lagoonal fisheries by collecting data on landings and methods of exploitation to drive their conservation and development on national and regional scales. To enhance the yield of these neglected but important fisheries, there is surging interest in cultivating some of the fisheries to optimize yield and provide fish year-round, as opposed to their seasonal production in the wild, while ensuring a safe aquatic environment through the enforcement of sound environmental policies and laws.

The following are three approaches to shaping sustainable ocean governance:

1. To effectively manage estuarine fisheries, there is a need to adopt the EBFM approach by modeling the system with a focus on multi-species and their interactions with fishing gears, as well as environmental processes in the marine, coastal, and freshwater systems.
2. The biology and ecology of key fisheries and candidates for culture must be studied extensively to guide policy toward sustainable management.
3. Investigate the culturability of highly commercial estuarine fishes (including bivalves, gastropods, crustaceans, and finfish) in order to move into the cultivation of the species, taking into consideration its biotic and abiotic factors.

Overview of fisheries policy and governance issues

Global fisheries governance is crucial as we face increasing environmental threats and seafood demands. Understanding ecosystem services and their implications for governance structures is essential for effective resource management strategies. Inclusive governance frameworks are needed to accommodate socio-economic variations and combat IUU fishing (Thoya et al. 2022). The global community must continue to build international collaboration, which is essential for monitoring and enforcement efforts, with trust, continuous funding, and incentives being critical components.

Governance difficulties in attaining sustainability stem from intricate governance arrangements, and adaptive governance systems are needed to manage maritime resources effectively (De la Torre-Castro 2012). Interactive governance theory can enhance resilience in community-based small-scale fisheries management, emphasizing the importance of incorporating social dimensions into governance strategies (Jentoft and Chuenpagdee 2022). Government reforms are needed to bolster resilience in small-scale fishing communities across Africa and Asia.

Climate change presents a significant challenge to fisheries governance globally, necessitating the adoption of adaptive management strategies and multilateral approaches to mitigate risks and enhance resilience. Institutional arrangements are pivotal in shaping outcomes in ocean governance, emphasizing inclusivity, equity, and regulatory resources in decision-making processes, with deliberate communication promoted among stakeholders. Gender considerations must be integrated into analyses to avoid repeating past neglect of gender issues.

Indigenous approaches to fisheries oversight are essential for sustainability and equity. It is important to tailor management actions at the site level and prioritize Indigenous history in oyster reef restoration, extraction, and management. Similarly, Reeder-Myers et al. (2022) advocate for the active involvement of Indigenous communities in collaborative processes related to oyster reef restoration, extraction, and management, underscoring the critical integration of social and cultural perspectives into fisheries governance to promote equity, resilience, and sustainability.

The UNCLOS agreement, UN fish stocks agreement, the WTO Agreement on Fisheries Subsidies, and similar agreements have been mostly delayed during implementation, posing threats to ocean resource management. The WTO Agreement on Fisheries Subsidies, ratified in 2022, promotes ocean sustainability but has only been ratified by 62 members due to delays caused by several nations (Figure 17.1). Apart from Europe, which has demonstrated the strongest commitment since the European Union ratified the agreement, North America records the highest percentage of countries in agreement, followed by Asia, South America, and Africa, while Oceania records the lowest. The Committee on Fisheries' endorsement of the SSF Guidelines in 2014 was a success, but not all countries have fully implemented it, putting the Global South at a disadvantage.

African nations are implementing fisheries governance mechanisms like fisheries acts, ministerial decrees, and executive orders to address challenges. Often, these mechanisms struggle to control the industrial fisheries sector and limit small-scale fisheries. IUU fishing impacts food security and livelihoods. Balancing industrial and small-scale marine fisheries is crucial for sustainable resource management and protecting small-scale fishers' livelihoods.

Ocean governance is a complex system of regulations and strategies aimed at managing the effects and demands on the marine ecosystem. It involves transforming economic and social systems to support a thriving relationship between humans and the ocean (Haas et al. 2021). Ocean governance is centralized under the UNCLOS and regional fisheries management organizations, enforced by various stakeholders including governments, businesses, non-government groups, and the public. Marine fish stocks, which are categorized as 'transboundary,' require collaboration between coastal governments and high seas fishing states (Stier et al. 2020). International

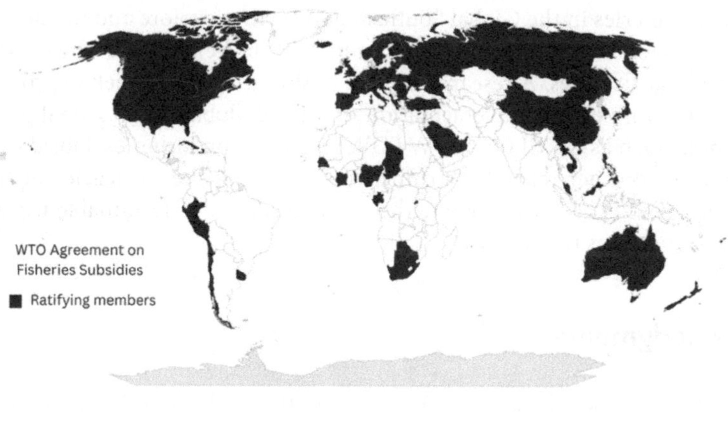

Source: Adapted from WTO website (https://www.wto.org/english/tratop_e/rulesneg_e/fish_e/fish_acceptances_e.htm).

Figure 17.1 WTO Agreement on Fisheries Subsidies ratification status

fisheries law regulates international collaboration on marine fisheries, but ensuring sufficient regulation under national jurisdiction is challenging due to the transboundary nature of marine biodiversity (Mukwele 2024). Regional cooperation is crucial for effective governance in areas beyond national jurisdiction, particularly in developing countries.

Externalities

Fishing and conservation as economic and human development activities have both unintended negative and positive impacts, which economics refers to as externalities. The BBNJ Agreement addresses the two objectives of conservation and sustainable use of the sea, accounting for 95 percent of the global ocean. The BBNJ allows states that have not ratified UNCLOS to ratify it, enhancing opportunities to bring more states on board with the regime and to meet the 60-state requirement for the agreement's entry into force by 2025. States need to prioritize the implementation of other legal instruments that deal with conservation and sustainable use of aquatic resources generally. This is important since different externality types (i.e., stock, crowding, technological, and ecological) influence aquatic systems in conjunction. There is also a need to investigate the complexity and diversity of the nexuses of these different externalities in the BBNJ Agreement.

Conclusion

Research toward sustainable fisheries will benefit from continuous efforts to better understand the ocean's health through collaboration and the co-production of knowledge across the globe. This research should investigate research methods on biotic and abiotic indices in ecological risk assessments, among other areas. Research into sustainable fisheries in the Global South should further explore and unpack concepts such as neoliberalism, co-management, and MSP to help reduce tensions between small and large fisheries. A research agenda in this area should seek to provide a better understanding of the implementation of related global and regional governance frameworks, such as UNCLOS, the WTO's Agreement on Fisheries Subsidies, the SSF Guidelines, and other related instruments. Unpacking the intricacies of the BBNJ Agreement would further accelerate the twin objectives of sustainable use and conservation of fisheries resources.

Acknowledgments

We acknowledge the efforts of all who will contribute to solidifying our views and help in promoting a better knowledge of the ocean.

References

Aceves-Bueno, Elizanda, Javiera Cornejo-Donoso, Shannon Miller, and Steven Gaines. 2017. Are Territorial Use Rights in Fisheries (TURFs) Sufficiently Large? *Marine Policy* 78: 189–195. https://doi.org/10.1016/j.marpol.2017.01.024.

Agnew, David J., John Pearce, Ganapathiraju Pramod, Tom Peatman, Reg Watson, John Beddington, and Tony Pitcher. 2009. Estimating the Worldwide Extent of Illegal Fishing. *PLOS One* 4(2): e4570. https://doi.org/10.1371/journal.pone.0004570.

Aguión, Ana, Elena Ojea, Lucía García-Flórez, Teresa Cruz, Javier Garmendia, Denis Davoult, and Gonzalo Macho. 2021. Establishing a Governance Threshold in Small-Scale Fisheries to Achieve Sustainability. *Ambio* 51(3): 652–665. https://doi.org/10.1007/s13280-021-01606-x.

Branch, Trevor A. 2009. How Do Individual Transferable Quotas Affect Marine Ecosystems? *Fish and Fisheries* 10(1): 39–57. https://doi.org/10.1111/j.1467-2979.2008.00294.x.

Bravington, Mark V., Hans J. Skaug, and Eric C. Anderson. 2016. Close-Kin Mark-Recapture. *Statistical Science* 31(2): 259–274. https://doi.org/10.1214/16-STS552.

Bresnihan, Patrick. 2019. The (Slow) Tragedy of Improvement: Neoliberalism, Fisheries Management and the Institutional Commons. *World Development* 120: 210–220. https://doi.org/10.1016/j.worlddev.2017.09.017.

Carrella, Edoardo, James Powers, Stephanie Saul, Robert M. Bailey, Nicole Payette, Kristen A. Vert-pre, Arvind Ananthanarayanan et al. 2024. Rejection Sampling and Agent-Based Models for Data Limited Fisheries. *Frontiers in Marine Science* 11. https://www.frontiersin.org/articles/10.3389/fmars.2024.1243954.

Chuku, Elimma O., Ebenezer Effah, Joseph Adotey, Stephen Abrokwah, Rebecca Adade, Isaac Okyere, Daniel W. Aheto et al. 2022. Spotlighting Women-Led Fisheries Livelihoods Toward Sustainable Coastal Governance: The Estuarine and Mangrove Ecosystem Shellfisheries of West Africa. *Frontiers in Marine Science* 9: 884715. https://doi.org/10.3389/fmars.2022.884715.

Cochrane, Kevin L. 2017. An Integrated View of Fisheries: Tunnelling Between Silos. ICES *Journal of Marine Science* 74(3): 625–634. https://doi.org/10.1093/icesjms/fsw198.

De la Torre-Castro, Maricela. 2012. Governance for Sustainability: Insights from Marine Resource Use in a Tropical Setting in the Western Indian Ocean. *Coastal Management* 40(6): 612–633. https://doi.org/10.5455/jfcom.20190528122752.

Froese, Rainer. 2004. Keep It Simple: Three Indicators to Deal with Overfishing. *Fish and Fisheries* 5(1): 86–91. https://doi.org/10.1111/j.1467-2979.2004.00144.x.

Froese, Rainer, Nadir Demirel, Gianluca Coro, Katharine M. Kleisner, and Henning Winker. 2017. Estimating Fisheries Reference Points from Catch and Resilience. *Fish and Fisheries* 18(3): 506–526. https://doi.org/10.1111/faf.12190.

Froese, Rainer, Henning Winker, Gianluca Coro, Nadir Demirel, Athanassios C. Tsikliras, Danai Dimarchopoulou, Giuseppe Scarcella et al. 2020. Estimating Stock Status from Relative Abundance and Resilience. *ICES Journal of Marine Science* 77(2): 527–538. https://doi.org/10.1093/icesjms/fsz230.

Froese, Rainer, Henning Winker, Gianluca Coro, Nadir Demirel, Athanassios C. Tsikliras, Danai Dimarchopoulou, Giuseppe Scarcella et al. 2018. A New Approach for Estimating Stock Status from Length Frequency Data. *ICES Journal of Marine Science* 75(6): 2004–2015. https://doi.org/10.1093/icesjms/fsy078.

Froese, Rainer, Henning Winker, Gianluca Coro, M.L. Deng Palomares, Athanassios Tsikliras, Danai Dimarchopoulou, Kyriakos Touloumis et al. 2023. New Developments in the Analysis of Catch Time Series as the Basis for Fish Stock Assessments: The CMSY++ Method. *Acta Ichthyologica et Piscatoria* 53: 173–189. https://doi.org/10.3897/aiep.53.e105910.

Gustavsson, Madeleine, Kyriaki Frangoudes, Lis Lindström, Maria Álvarez, and Maricela Castro. 2021. Gender and Blue Justice in Small-Scale Fisheries Governance. *Marine Policy* 133: 104743. https://doi.org/10.1016/j.marpol.2021.104743.

Haas, Berit, Mary Mackay, Chloe Novaglio, Lauren Fullbrook, Maricris Murunga, Chiara Sbrocchi et al. 2021. The Future of Ocean Governance. *Reviews in Fish Biology and Fisheries*. https://doi.org/10.1007/s11160-020-09631-x.

Hordyk, Adrian R., Ken Ono, Keith J. Sainsbury, Neil Loneragan, and Jeremy Prince. 2015a. Some Explorations of the Life History Ratios to Describe Length Composition, Spawning-Per-Recruit, and the Spawning Potential Ratio. *ICES Journal of Marine Science* 72(1): 204–216. https://doi.org/10.1093/icesjms/fst235.

Hordyk, Adrian R., Ken Ono, Sebastian Valencia, Neil Loneragan, and Jeremy Prince. 2015b. A Novel Length-Based Empirical Estimation Method of Spawning Potential Ratio (SPR), and Tests of Its Performance, for Small-Scale, Data-Poor Fisheries. *ICES Journal of Marine Science* 72(1): 217–231. https://doi.org/10.1093/icesjms/fsu004.

Jentoft, Svein and Chuenpagdee, Ratana. 2022. Blue Justice in Three Governance Orders. In *Blue Justice: Small-Scale Fisheries in a Sustainable Ocean Economy*, edited by Svein Jentoft, Ratana Chuenpagdee, Amalfa B. Said, and Moenieba Isaacs, 17–32. Cham: Springer Nature. https://doi.org/10.1007/978-3-030-89624-9.

King, Michael. 2007. *Fisheries Biology, Assessment and Management*, 2nd ed. Oxford: Blackwell Scientific Publications.

Leonardo, Adin, and Najmaddin Deeb. 2022. Illegal, Unreported and Unregulated (IUU) Fishing in Indonesia: Problems and Solutions. *IOP Conference Series Earth and Environmental Science* 1081(1): 012013. https://doi.org/10.1088/1755-1315/1081/1/012013.

Mukwele, Samuel K. 2024. Enforcing Ocean Governance Cooperation Through Transboundary Marine Protected Areas: Establishing Opportunities and Overcoming Challenges. In *Governing Oceans*, edited by Catherine Jones, 154–168. Cheltenham, UK and Northampton, MA: Edward Elgar Publishing.

Osei, Isaac K., Kwasi Yankson, and Eric A. Obodai. 2020. Demographic and Profitability Analyses of the West African Mangrove Oyster (*Crassostrea tulipa*) Fishery in the Densu Delta, Ghana. *Journal of Fisheries and Coastal Management* 2: 12–22.

Ostrom, Elinor. 2009. A General Framework for Analysing Sustainability of Social-Ecological Systems. *Science* 24: 419–422. https://doi.org/10.1126/science.1172133.

Razak, Fardila, Wai Y. Lua, Nor H. Abd Rasid, Nurul H. Aziz, Ismail M. Repin, Xiong-Zhi Xue, Muhammad Ashraf et al. 2024. Adopting Marine Spatial Planning (MSP) Using Coral Health Assessment as Indicator: A Case Study in Pulau Redang Marine Park, Malaysia. *Ocean & Coastal Management* 248: 106943. https://doi.org/10.1016/J.OCECOAMAN.2023.106943.

Reeder-Myers, Leslie, Todd J. Braje, Catherine A. Hofman, Emily A. Elliott Smith, Caitlin J. Garland, Megan Grone, and Carla S. Hadden et al. 2022. Indigenous Oyster Fisheries Persisted for Millennia and Should Inform Future Management. *Nature Communications* 13(1): 2383. https://doi.org/10.1038/s41467-022-29818-z.

Shaffer, Morgan, Susan Mariott, Kathleen A. Lewis, John Buszowski, and Kim de Mutsert. 2023. Action Science in Practice: Co-Production of a Decision Support Tool Visualizing Effects of Nutrient and Hypoxia Reduction Goals on Fisheries Species. *Marine and Coastal Fisheries* 15(6): e10262. https://doi.org/10.1002/mcf2.10262.

Stier, Adrian C., Alice O. Shelton, Joshua F. Samhouri, Blake E. Feist, and Phillip S. Levin. 2020. Fishing, Environment, and the Erosion of a Population Portfolio. *Ecosphere*, 11(11): e03283. https://doi.org/10.1002/ecs2.3283.

Stratmann, Tobias, Francisco J. Murillo, Manuel K. Sacau, Maximiliano K. Alonso, and Ellen Kenchington. 2024. Role of Astrophorina Sponges (Demospongiae) in Food-Web

Interactions at the Flemish Cap (NW Atlantic). *Marine Ecology Progress Series* 729: 99–116. https://www.int-res.com/abstracts/meps/v729/p99-116/.

Sumaila, U. Rashid. 2024. Reflections on Breaking Down Silos in Fisheries Science. *Fisheries* 49: 205–210. https://doi.org/10.1002/fsh.11076.

Thabet, Wessam M., Ahmed A. Moneer, Omar Abdelwahab, H. Hoda Ahdy, Mohamed Khedawy, and Nashwa A. Shabaan. 2024. Ecological Risk Assessment of Metal Pollution in the Surface Sediments of Delta Region, Egypt. *Environmental Monitoring and Assessment* 196: 351. https://doi.org/10.1007/s10661-024-12481-w.

Thoya, Peter, Michael A. Owuor, Moritz von Thenen, and John O. Omukoto. 2022. Variations in Community Perceptions of Ecosystem Services Within the Tana River Estuary, Kenya: Implications for Ocean Governance. *Western Indian Ocean Journal of Marine Science* 1/2022: 47–57.

Viana, Daan, Sergio Gelcich, Elizanda Aceves-Bueno, Brian Twohey, and Steven Gaines. 2019. Design Trade-Offs in Rights-Based Management of Small-Scale Fisheries. *Conservation Biology* 33(2): 361–368. https://doi.org/10.1111/cobi.13208.

Yatim, Mohamed, Aznan Omar, Nazirah Abdullah, and Nursyazwana Hashim. 2016. Institutional Mapping Towards Developing a Framework for Sustainable Marine Spatial Planning. *The International Archives of the Photogrammetry Remote Sensing and Spatial Information Sciences* XLII-4/W1: 159–166. https://doi.org/10.5194/isprs-archives-XLII-4-W1-159-2016.

18 Toward sustainable ocean governance: research for inclusive and equitable development in Indonesia

Umi Muawanah, Zamroni Salim and Agus Eko Nugroho

Current ocean governance

The government of Indonesia has committed to protecting 30 percent of its marine areas by 2045, encompassing about one million sq km of its waters (Ministry of Marine Affairs and Fisheries [MMAF] 2024). These efforts aim to safeguard biodiversity and preserve the ocean's ecosystem services. A key factor in achieving this is the effective implementation of good governance across various aspects of the blue economy (Sumaila 2012), which can lead to the sustainable conservation of marine ecosystems. Since the 2000s, Indonesia's National Medium-Term Development Plan (RPJMN) has highlighted the critical role of effective ocean management in achieving sustainable development goals. It is anticipated that the blue economy will be pivotal in shaping Indonesia's second long-term development agenda from 2025 to 2045.

In 2021, the government of Indonesia launched the national blue economy development framework (BAPPENAS 2023), which aims to enhance economic benefits from ocean sectors such as the seafood industry, sea transportation, coastal marine infrastructure, marine tourism, the salt industry, and ocean energy. Sustainability and an equitable ocean economy are crucial for Indonesia, the world's largest archipelagic nation. The country must ensure its blue economy initiatives benefit not only large-scale enterprises but also coastal communities and marine ecosystems (Bennet et al. 2019). For instance, marine ecotourism is vital for sustainable development due to Indonesia's biodiversity-rich ecosystems (Tegar and Gurning 2018). For marine and fisheries sector development, the MMAF has developed a roadmap for a blue economy, which is central to Indonesia's economic planning. This roadmap establishes five key pillars for blue economy development: conservation, sustainable fisheries managed through a quota system, sustainable aquaculture, sustainable development of coastal and small island areas, and effective marine debris management.

Indonesia has also collaborated with numerous international and regional organizations, actively participating in platforms such as the High-Level Panel for a Sustainable Ocean Economy and the AIS (Archipelagic and Island States) Blue Economy Hub, as well as engaging in bilateral cooperation with Sweden on blue economy initiatives. These collaborations enhance both national and global interests, with a strong emphasis on the health of ocean ecosystems and the ocean as a public good. For example, the cooperation between Indonesia and Sweden aims to improve the well-being of coastal communities and conserve marine resources through the development of a blue economy model (Oktaviani and Iqbal 2023).

The objective of this chapter is to offer insights for future research to better understand blue economy models based on Indonesia's ongoing research and development. The next section examines existing findings and theoretical insights on blue economy models. Subsequently, we identify research gaps related to practical challenges in ocean governance in Indonesia. Finally, we discuss potential theoretical and methodological approaches for future research into the development of blue economy models.

Current research findings and theoretical insights on ocean governance in Indonesia

This section explores findings and theoretical insights in the evolving field of ocean governance, which could stimulate future research and development to address sustainability challenges. The innovative findings and theoretical insights discussed in this chapter highlight the dynamic nature of sustainable ocean governance and the importance of interdisciplinary research collaboration (Sumaila 2024). By integrating empirical evidence with theoretical frameworks, scholars and policymakers can develop innovative governance solutions that promote the long-term health and resilience of marine ecosystems while supporting human well-being and economic prosperity. Addressing gaps in research is essential for tackling emerging challenges and advancing toward a more sustainable future for ocean governance.

Sustainable ocean governance has recently become a critical area of research due to the growing recognition of the importance of marine environmental and ecosystem stability, which contributes to the socio-economic wealth of nations. Since the establishment of Indonesia's Ministry of Marine Affairs and Fisheries in the 2000s, there has been an increased focus on ensuring that the use of marine resources not only benefits the broader community but also maintains ecological sustainability. Contemporary studies on ocean governance encompass a wide range of research that delves into interconnected aspects of marine-related legal frameworks, policy formulation, institutional setups, socio-economic activities, and environmental preservation efforts. These aspects are increasingly linked to emerging real-world problems such as climate change, biodiversity loss, and environmental degradation. Given this complexity, insights are often derived from interdisciplinary approaches, discussions with policymakers, the policy-making process, and engagement with industries and communities in the field. This has enriched the breadth of research in marine science, environmental studies, socio-economics, and public policy.

To identify the state of the art in previous studies on the blue economy and ocean governance in Indonesia, a systematic literature review (SLR) was conducted using the English-language Scopus publication database. Over the last decade (2013–2023), a total of 73 documents were obtained using keywords such as *ocean economy, blue economy, fisheries trade, Indonesia, ocean conservation, fisheries conflict, social equity, ocean sustainable development, ocean governance, ocean fisheries human capital, governance coordination, ocean research and development, fisheries institutions, tools and methods in ocean governance*, and *ocean knowledge integration*. During this period, a positive trend in publications was observed, increasing from just two papers in 2013 to 14 in 2023, with the highest number recorded in 2020 at 17 papers. The growing number of studies on the blue economy and ocean governance is closely linked to the European countries' planning project to promote maritime sustainability, which started in 2020 and will continue for 15 years (2020–2035) (Martínez-Vázquez et al. 2021).

Prior to 2017, marine research topics mainly revolved around environmental protection, natural resource use, and governance approaches. From 2018 to 2019, the focus shifted toward marine biodiversity, fisheries, forest management, sustainable development, ocean governance, climate change, and the ocean economy. In 2020, the emphasis was on fisheries management, sustainable fisheries, ecosystems, tourism development, and sustainability. By 2021, research topics had specifically shifted toward the blue economy, tourism, ecosystem services, sustainable tourism, livelihoods, stakeholders, and renewable energy.

Extended analysis of the SLR through density visualization shows the emergence of several less-discussed research topics, particularly in areas such as fisheries management, tourism, oceanography, ecosystem services, commerce, and sustainable tourism. Research themes on the blue economy and ocean governance are still largely confined to collaboration between authors within the same clusters or similar scientific disciplines, with limited multidisciplinary research collaboration. Therefore, future studies could benefit from increased inter-cluster collaboration to further develop global perspectives on ocean governance.

Significant research gaps in ocean governance in Indonesia

From the SLR on the blue economy and ocean governance in Indonesia, we identify research gaps in three main areas: the blue economy, ocean governance, and sustainable development. Currently, research interest in these areas remains limited in both scope and depth of analysis. By focusing on these core issues in Indonesia as the locus of study, several research topics can be developed to better understand the real-world problems associated with marine resource use. Addressing these research gaps in ocean governance requires interdisciplinary methodologies, incorporating disciplines such as marine science, environmental studies, socioeconomics, and more. We present here some challenging practical research topics and developments that may attract attention for deeper investigation into real cases of ocean governance:

Sustainable fisheries management and the agenda of achieving sustainable development goals

Sustainable fisheries management critically depends on the interplay of forces within fisheries resource utilization, exploring potential scenarios of merging, converging, and co-evolving governance processes across involved institutions (Garcia et al. 2014). Achieving sustainable fisheries management involves addressing key concerns related to ocean ecosystems, biodiversity, and climate change within the broader context of ocean governance. The institutional aspects of fisheries management must be examined through social, cultural, and historical lenses, particularly concerning property rights and the unequal access to coastal resources that promote sustainable marine development (Chuenpagdee and Song 2012). These governance pathways significantly influence both fisheries ecosystems and biodiversity conservation.

In terms of development, ocean governance prioritizes the pursuit of best practices to meet the Sustainable Development Goals (SDGs) and the objectives of the United Nations (UN) Ocean Decade (Haas et al. 2022). However, efforts to sustain fisheries management within the framework of ocean governance remain limited in achieving the SDG agenda. This research is particularly interesting when related to blue economies, knowledge economies, and digital technology. Integrating knowledge on effective environmental governance, both broadly and specifically in relation to oceans, requires comprehensive analysis from legal, political science, and anthropological perspectives. The findings of this research highlight the need for tools, approaches, and methods to facilitate knowledge integration in ocean governance (Poto et al. 2022).

The ocean and fisheries sector contributes approximately 2.6 percent to Indonesia's gross domestic product (GDP) (Thomas 2019). While this contribution is lower compared to sectors like mining and other resources, it provides jobs and livelihoods for about 7 million households directly dependent on ocean resources (FAO 2000). However, there remains a significant disparity in the distribution of benefits between large industries and small-scale fishers. For instance, poverty rates in coastal areas are higher than in non-coastal areas and significantly exceed global poverty rates (Tobey and Torell 2006, Barbier 2015). Long-term development plans include leveraging the blue economy and ocean resources as key drivers of economic growth. Several initiatives focus on adding value to marine products, such as those in the seaweed industry (Trade Policy Research and Development Agency 2015).

Ecosystem-based management of ocean governance

Recent research highlights the importance of adopting an ecosystem-oriented approach to ocean governance, emphasizing the interdependence of marine ecosystems and the need for comprehensive management strategies. Innovative studies have identified key ecological indicators and thresholds essential for successful ecosystem-centered governance, providing valuable insights into preserving marine biodiversity and ecosystem functions. Marine ecosystem-based management (EBM) is a holistic approach that considers the interconnected components, structures, and functioning of ecosystems alongside human activities (Fluharty 2018, Haugen et al. 2024). EBM is recognized as the optimal method for managing diverse ocean uses and their respective sectors, directly addressing the trade-offs among them.

EBM emerged in response to concerns over declining biodiversity, fish populations, and their habitats, and the inadequacies of sector-focused governance structures in preventing environmental degradation (World Economic Forum 2023). It advocates for prioritizing ecosystems, including ocean ecosystems, fisheries, and their biodiversity. EBM requires a comprehensive approach that considers the social, ecological, cultural, and economic implications of various uses and stressors. This integrated perspective ensures that ecosystem health and resilience are maintained while balancing human needs and activities.

Integrated coastal zone management

Integrated coastal zone management (ICZM), also referred to as integrated coastal management (ICM), highlights the necessity of integrating land and sea interactions, involving stakeholders, and employing adaptable governance mechanisms. ICM is an ongoing decision-making process aimed at sustainably using, developing, and protecting terrestrial and marine coastal areas along with their resources (Cicin-Sain et al. 1995, Hong and Lee 2001). Recent research underscores the importance of ICZM in enhancing resilience to climate change impacts, mitigating coastal risks, and improving socio-economic sustainability in coastal regions. The adoption of the ICM framework by numerous coastal cities and municipalities across East Asia has led to the successful implementation of strategies to counteract environmental degradation caused by significant human activity (Chou et al. 2021).

ICM can strengthen environmental and societal resilience against the added pressures of climate change by ensuring the robust coordination of scientifically informed management actions supported by widespread stakeholder agreements. Coastal cities implementing ICM are better equipped to tackle emerging challenges like climate change due to their proactive efforts to address the interconnected issues of environmental and societal concern (Chou et al. 2021).

Blue economy strategies for ocean governance

The concept of the blue economy has emerged as a crucial strategy for achieving sustainable ocean governance, focusing on the responsible use of marine resources while preserving ecosystem health. Recent studies in the blue economy have highlighted innovative business models, such as ecosystem-based tourism and sustainable fishing practices, that maximize economic benefits while minimizing environmental damage. The blue economy and ocean governance are rapidly expanding research areas that encompass economic activities reliant on the sea, frequently interconnected with sectors such as tourism, maritime transportation, energy, and fishing (Martínez-Vázquez et al. 2021). These areas focus on the sustainable growth of maritime and marine industries, recognizing oceans and seas as vital drivers of the global economy with significant potential for innovation and progress.

Sustainable development and ocean governance provide evidence-based strategies to foster sustainable development and effective management of ocean and coastal areas in the Asia-Pacific region (Morgan et al. 2022). This includes exploring governance frameworks, strategic planning, sectoral management, and risk mitigation strategies. Moreover, it involves innovative financial models designed for ocean preservation and approaches to address the impacts of climate change and unsustainable activities on communities and sectors reliant on ocean and coastal ecosystems.

Carbon credits and carbon markets in the ocean

Recently, the increase in extreme weather events has underscored the reality of climate change. The prolonged hot and drought seasons over the past five years have convinced many of us of its occurrence. A recent study on the impact of climate change on Indonesia's oceans and tourism revealed that fish production could potentially decline by up to 25 percent if no action is taken. This would threaten both national and regional food security, as Indonesia exports many of its seafood products. Additionally, rising ocean temperatures are predicted to significantly alter the distribution of fish, as well as the coverage of seagrass and coral reefs (MMAF et al. 2023).

The potential of blue carbon credits and markets is attracting investors and companies that traditionally struggle to reduce their emissions (Friess et al. 2022). Despite the government's plan for the Indonesia Blue Carbon Strategy Framework (IBCSF), several key challenges persist, including policy and regulation coherence; reliable technology for measuring carbon storage or absorption; funding gaps in establishment, verification, and maintenance; and coordination among relevant institutions at the national and local levels (Sidik et al. 2023).

The lack of coordination and low trust from other stakeholders in government agencies increases the uncertainty of IBCSF implementation. Non-government actors in the blue carbon sector should provide knowledge to policymakers and foster network trust (Ayostina et al. 2022).

Sustainable marine tourism

The connection between the blue economy and sectoral studies requires precision in identifying which sectors are closely related to ocean governance. One sector that has garnered significant attention is the tourism industry. In Indonesia, the rapidly growing tourism industry in coastal areas raises environmental issues, particularly due to the substantial influx of people, which directly or indirectly affects the ocean environment. The issue of human waste and pollution adversely impacting marine resources can lead to various socioeconomic problems, including inequality and the welfare of coastal communities that depend on marine resource sustainability. Therefore, social fairness within ocean governance is crucial and is shaped by the governance structure. This fairness is an integral component of both national and international commitments that need to be promoted (Crosman et al. 2022).

On the governance front, inter- and intra-agency coordination and a shared understanding of managing ocean resources remain challenging, leading to silos and ineffective management. Overlapping or disjointed authorities between national agencies are evident. For example, marine tourism dominates tourism in Indonesia. The tourism sector contributes 8 percent to the national GDP (Sutrisno 2021), a significant figure given Indonesia's archipelagic nature. However, the Ministry of Tourism has less concern over marine conservation, and the authorities rely on the MMAF. This issue is further exacerbated by some marine parks' authorities and management under the Ministry of Forestry and Environment.

Justice and equity issues

The overlapping interests and competition between large and small industries in ocean exploration for economic growth are prevalent. In Indonesia, large players dominate seafood production, accounting for about 80 percent of the total catch with just 10 percent of the big fishing vessels (Ayunda et al. 2017). Conversely, small boats make up nearly 90 percent of the total fishing vessels, contributing only about 20 percent to the national catch annually (California Environmental Associates 2018). This disparity has created significant challenges in ocean resource management, both at the national level for total quota allocation and at the local government level for specific quota distribution.

Conflicts and disharmony are evident within and between agents and institutions involved in marine governance. For example, there are conflicts between different agents in the fishery sector, such as seaweed farmers and fishers. Fishers passing through seaweed farming areas can damage the seaweed. Similarly, on Karimunjawa Island, there is ongoing conflict between aquaculture farmers and fishers. Semi-intensive and intensive fish farming in coastal areas often discharges water into the sea, polluting the nearshore waters and killing fish, leading to complaints from fishers.

Digital technology and ocean governance

Furthermore, the connection with the economy can be extended toward a digital economy, particularly through the role of e-commerce in supporting ocean governance—an area that has not been extensively studied. Emerging practical topics include downstream maritime industries and advanced technologies such as machine learning and artificial intelligence (AI). A recent World Bank report highlights the significant potential of Indonesian seaweed in producing biodegradable plastics to replace conventional plastics in the short term (World Bank 2023). Advanced biotechnologies present an emerging field in Indonesia, offering various benefits from the blue economy. Examples include seaweed products like animal feed, bio-stimulants, green plastics, and nutraceuticals (World Bank 2023). The ocean ecosystem also contains genes for biological compounds that can be developed into high-value products.

The growth of start-ups could significantly boost the blue food sectors. Analyzing the gap between the current condition and the ecosystem needed for the use of digital technology by 2045 is an area for strategic research. Additionally, the role of new technologies (AI and machine learning) in supporting the blue food industry, including their readiness level and applicability, is crucial. AI has been used for weather prediction apps, monitoring water quality, and overall ocean conditions. It can also be trained to predict fish schools, greatly benefiting small-scale fishers by providing access to technology, financing, and markets. Identifying suitable technology platforms, their innovations, and their applicability to increase fish farming efficiency is of utmost importance for aqua farmers today.

Digital platforms can leverage technology to overcome the geographical barriers faced by coastal communities (Peddle 2007). For instance, Aruna is an Indonesian start-up that markets high-quality seafood products from producers or groups of fishers directly to consumers. By using its app, fishers can predict demand for seafood products and sell them more efficiently, resulting in rapid and significant resource changes (Cooke et al. 2021). Advances in fishing and processing technology have led to a substantial increase in seafood production globally since the late 1980s.

To maximize benefits, adding value and shortening the supply chain are key solutions. Fishery start-ups like Aruna in Indonesia have successfully shortened the supply chain, bringing fishers and customers closer together. Aruna offers an integrated digital platform that connects the entire process from farm to plate. It includes a tracker device and fishers' app, a midstream enterprise resource planning (ERP) dashboard, and market connections through e-commerce, Aruna wholesale e-commerce, and a reseller app. Fishers working with Aruna have seen their incomes increase by about 50 percent compared to non-Aruna fishers (Aruna 2022). This study also finds that Aruna fishers experience greater financial inclusion.

Theoretical and methodological approaches

Effective ocean governance necessitates a nuanced understanding of complex systems and multifaceted challenges. Various theoretical and methodological frameworks provide the analytical tools necessary to navigate and address these complexities. This section delves into three pivotal approaches: polycentric and transformative approaches to ocean governance, social-ecological systems (SES) in ocean governance, and interdisciplinary approaches and potential interlinkages on ocean governance (Figure 18.1).

Polycentric and transformative approaches to ocean governance

Polycentric and transformative approaches offer innovative pathways for enhancing the resilience and adaptability of ocean governance systems. Polycentric governance emphasizes the importance of multiple, overlapping decision-making centers, each with its own autonomy yet operating under a coherent framework. This model fosters collaboration, enhances accountability, and allows for more tailored responses to local conditions. Theoretical models like polycentric governance offer valuable insights into the complex nature of ocean governance systems, acknowledging the diversity of actors, scales, and institutions involved. Polycentric governance models

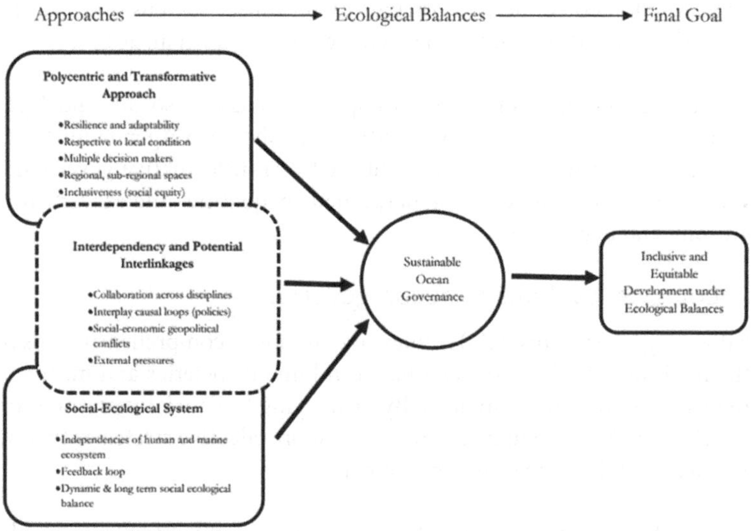

Source: Authors' own.

Figure 18.1 Theoretical and methodological approaches on ocean governance

illustrate how individuals pursue their policy objectives by navigating institutional complexities to enhance collective well-being and adaptive capacities (Lubell and Morrison 2021). This approach also presents a novel method for addressing the multifaceted challenges posed by climate change induced by greenhouse gas emissions (Ostrom 2009).

By decentralizing decision-making power and encouraging multi-level governance frameworks, polycentric approaches support adaptive management and enhance the resilience of marine ecosystems against global changes. The importance of regional and subregional dimensions in global ocean governance is gaining increased recognition. Additionally, regional and subregional multilateral agreements, including Indigenous agreements formulated by countries within those regions, merit consideration in constructing comprehensive regional ocean governance (Mahon and Fanning 2019).

Meanwhile, transformative governance perspectives emphasize the need for fundamental changes in institutional setups and principles that negatively impact the integrity of marine life and the welfare of both human and non-human beings dependent on a thriving ocean (Erinosho et al. 2022). By promoting innovation, inclusiveness, and self-awareness, transformative governance methods facilitate the shift toward fairer and more environmentally robust ocean governance systems and address the root causes of environmental degradation and social inequities, paving the way for more robust and dynamic governance systems. Fragmented governance indirectly contributes to the decline in ocean biodiversity by failing to provide coordinated solutions to simultaneously address various direct causes such as overfishing, pollution from both land and sea, and climate change (Erinosho et al. 2022).

Transformative governance of the ocean spans ecological, social, and legal fields to respond to the UN's call for change outlined in the 2030 Agenda for Sustainable Development (Lombard et al. 2023). Additionally, transformative governance must address economic growth models that perpetuate inequalities and exacerbate conflict and environmental degradation.

Social-ecological systems in ocean governance

The social-ecological systems (SES) framework provides a comprehensive lens through which the intricate interdependencies between human societies and marine ecosystems can be understood and managed. By identifying feedback loops, trade-offs, and synergies within SES, policymakers can design more effective strategies that promote long-term sustainability and ecosystem integrity.

The theory of SES provides a robust framework for understanding the dynamic interactions between human communities and marine ecosystems. SES theory integrates social and ecological dimensions, recognizing that sustainable ocean governance requires a balance between human needs and ecological health. This approach emphasizes adaptive management, resilience, and the capacity to respond to environmental changes and uncertainties. Transboundary marine SES are complex and continually evolving systems (Tuda et al. 2021). By integrating both social and ecological dimensions into governance processes, as guided by SES theory, it becomes possible to identify feedback mechanisms, trade-offs, and mutual benefits crucial for sustainable ocean management. Achieving sustainability in such systems requires adaptive governance supported by polycentric frameworks. Governing transboundary marine SES poses challenges due to significant differences in institutional structures for resource management and adaptive governance capacities. SES illustrate the intricate connections between social and environmental components within systems. Effective ocean governance must comprehend and embrace this complexity to foster and facilitate adaptation to unforeseen events or changes within the system (Lombard et al. 2023).

It is essential to recognize the systemic complexity and multifaceted impacts of environmental issues on the governance and management of shared resources or ecosystem services, as well as the surrounding territories. Ocean governance, particularly within coastal SES, is complicated due to the multitude of stakeholders with varied interests, the ever-changing environment, and frequently overlapping and sometimes conflicting legislation and policies. Therefore, evaluation methods that account for the interconnected and causal relationships between the environment and society, incorporating various scales and processes within a social-ecological system, are crucial for addressing the challenges of sustainable development across its three interrelated dimensions: ecological, economic, and socio-cultural (Gonçalves 2020, Celliers et al. 2023).

Interdisciplinary and potential interlinkages

Interdisciplinary approaches are crucial for addressing the multifaceted nature of ocean governance challenges. Understanding the interlinkages and causal relationships between different factors—such as policy decisions, resource conditions, economic activities, and external pressures like climate change and geopolitical dynamics—requires a holistic perspective.

By fostering collaboration across disciplines, interdisciplinary approaches enable a more comprehensive and nuanced analysis of governance issues, leading to more innovative and effective solutions. These approaches enhance our understanding of complex systems and facilitate the development of integrated policies that address ocean governance's diverse dimensions. Understanding the interplay and causal loops among policies, natural resource conditions, extraction activities, economic activities, and exogenous factors such as extreme climate events and geopolitics is essential for comprehensive studies.

Integrating geospatial and geopolitical economic conflicts into ocean governance is an immediate need. Conflicts of interest among ocean users typically have negative impacts on marine resource quality. For example, coastal nickel mining benefits industrialization but can deteriorate water quality, negatively affecting the tourism industry. Different industry sizes can create conflicts over marine resource uses; for example, coastal mining and tourism industries compete for space: marine tourism relies heavily on high marine quality, while mining can lead to pollution and sedimentation along shorelines. Additionally, high political will and global pressure for climate-responsive action are likely to impact blue economy activities, potentially increasing the use of emerging technologies such as AI to boost economic productivity.

Interdisciplinary approaches and potential interlinkages of ocean use and governance in Indonesia warrant further study. Through these scientific efforts, the goal of sustainable ocean governance can be achieved, fostering inclusive and equitable development in Indonesia. Moreover, these findings and strategies can be applied and expanded not only within Indonesia but also to other countries around the world.

References

Aruna. 2022. Dampak Sosial Ekonomi dan Strategi Pengembangan Pasar Laporan Akhir Lembaga Penyelidikan Ekonomi dan Masyarakat, Fakultas Ekonomi dan Bisnis, Universitas Indonesia LPEM FEB UI.

Ayostina, Ines, Lucentezza Napitupulu, Barakalla Robyn, Cynthia Maharani, and Daniel Murdiyarso. 2022. Network analysis of blue carbon governance process in Indonesia. *Marine Policy* 137: 104955.

Ayunda, Nisa, Mariusz R. Sapota, and Anna Pawelec. 2017. The Impact of Small-scale Fisheries Activities Toward Fisheries Sustainability in Indonesia. In Interdisciplinary Approaches for Sustainable Development Goals, eds. Tymon Zielinski, Iwona Sagan, and Waldemar Surosz, 147–167. Berlin: Springer Nature.

BAPPENAS. 2023. Ekonomi Biru Berbasis Sains dan Teknologi Terhadap Strategies Pembangunan Ekonomi Indonesia. Presentation slides by Leonardo A.A. Teguh Sambodo, Direktur Industri, Pariwisata, dan Ekonomi Kreatif, Kementerian PPN/ BAPPENAS. Webinar Ekonomi Biru di Indonesia: Paragidma Pembangunan Ekonomi Nasional berbasis Sains dan Inovasi, Jakarta, 13 February 2023.

Barbier, Edward. 2015. Climate change impacts on rural poverty in low-elevation coastal zones. *Estuarine, Coastal and Shelf Science* 165: A1–A13. https://doi.org/10.1016/j.ecss.2015.05.035.

Bennett, N. J., Cisneros-Montemayor, A. M., Blythe, J., Silver, J. J., Singh, G., Andrews, N., ... & Sumaila, U. R. 2019. Towards a sustainable and equitable blue economy. *Nature Sustainability* 2 (11), 991–993.

California Environmental Associates. 2018. Trends in Marine Resources and Fisheries Management in Indonesia: A 2018 Review. Available at: https://www.ceaconsulting.com/wp-content/uploads/Indonesia-Report-2018_Executive-Summary-compressed.pdf.

Celliers, Louis, Lena Rölfer, Nina Rivers, Sérgio Rosendo, Meredith Fernandes, Bernadette Snow, and María Mãnez Costa. 2023. Stratification of stakeholders for participation in the governance of coastal social-ecological systems. *Ambio* 52(9): 1418–1430.

Chou, Loke-Ming, Thia-Eng Chua, and Danilo Bonga. 2021. Integrated Coastal Management Enhances Coastal Resilience to Climate Change: The East Asia Experience. In *Climate Change Science*, edited by David S.-K. Ting and Jacqueline A. Stagner, 59–79. Elsevier. https://doi.org/10.1016/B978-0-12-823767-0.00004-5.

Chuenpagdee, Ratana, and Andrew M. Song. 2012. Institutional thinking in fisheries governance: Broadening perspectives. *Current Opinion in Environmental Sustainability* 4(3): 309–315. https://doi.org/10.1016/j.cosust.2012.05.006.

Cicin-Sain, Biliana, Robert W. Knecht, and Gregory W. Fisk. 1995. Growth in capacity for integrated coastal management since UNCED: An international perspective. *Ocean & Coastal Management* 29(1–3): 93–123. https://doi.org/10.1016/0964-5691(96)00028-2.

Cooke, Steven J., Paul Venturelli, William M. Twardek, Robert J. Lennox, Jacob W. Brownscombe, Christian Skov, Kieran Hyder et al. 2021. Technological innovations in the recreational fishing sector: Implications for fisheries management and policy. *Reviews in Fish Biology and Fisheries* 31: 253–288.

Crosman, Katherine M., Edward H. Allison, Yoshitaka Ota, Andrés M. Cisneros-Montemayor, Gerald G. Singh, Wilf Swartz, Megan Bailey et al. 2022. Social equity is key to sustainable ocean governance. *npj Ocean Sustainability* 1(1): 4. https://doi.org/10.1038/s44183-022-00001-7.

Erinosho, Bolanle, Hashali Hamukuaya, Claire Lajaunie, Alana Lancaster, Mitchell Lennan, Pierre Mazzega, Elisa Morgera, and Bernadette Snow. 2022. Transformative Governance for Ocean Biodiversity. In *Transforming Biodiversity Governance*, edited by Ingrid J. Visseren-Hamakers and Marcel T.J. Kok, 313–338. Cambridge University Press.

Fluharty, David. 2018. Ecosystem-Based Approaches to Ocean Management in the United States: Weaving Together Multiple Strands. In *The Ecosystem Approach in Ocean Planning and Governance*, edited by David Langlet and Rosemary Rayfuse, 371–412. Brill. https://doi.org/10.1163/9789004389984_013.

Food and Agriculture Organization of the United Nations. Fisheries Department. 2000. *The State of World Fisheries a Aquaculture, 2000*, Vol 3.

Friess, Daniel A., Jen Howard, Mark Huxham, Peter I. Macreadie, and Finnley Ross. 2022. Capitalizing on the global financial interest in blue carbon. *PLOS Climate* 1(8): e0000061.

Garcia, Serge M., Jake Rice, and Anthony Charles. 2014. Governance of Marine Fisheries and Biodiversity Conservation: Convergence or Coevolution? In *Governance of Marine Fisheries and Biodiversity Conservation: Interaction and Coevolution*, edited by Serge M. Garcia, Jake Rice, Anthony Charles, 18–36. Wiley.

Gonçalves, Leandra R., Mayara Oliveira, and Alexander Turra. 2020. Assessing the complexity of social-ecological systems: Taking stock of the cross-scale dependence. *Sustainability* 12(15): 6236. https://doi.org/10.3390/su12156236.

Haas, Bianca, Mary Mackay, Camilla Novaglio, Liam Fullbrook, Michael Marunga, Carla Sbrocchi, Jan McDonald. 2022. The future of ocean governance. *Reviews in Fish Biology and Fisheries* 32: 253–270. https://doi.org/10.1007/s11160-020-09631-x.

Haugen, Janne B., Jason S. Link, K. Cribari, Alida Bundy, Mark Dickey-Collas, Heather M. Leslie, J. Hall et al. 2024. Marine ecosystem-based management: Challenges remain, yet solutions exist, and progress is occurring. *npj Ocean Sustainability* 3(1): 7. https://doi.org/10.1038/s44183-024-00041-1.

Hong, Seoung-Yong, and Chan-Wen Lee. 2001. Coastal Zone Management. In *Encyclopedia of Ocean Sciences*, edited by John H. Steele, 496–499. Academic Press. https://doi.org/10.1006/rwos.2001.0497.

Lombard, Amanda T., Jai Clifford-Holmes, Victoria Goodall, Bernadette Snow, Hannah Truter, Patrick Vrancken, Peter J.S. Jones et al. 2023. Principles for transformative ocean governance. *Nature Sustainability* 6(12): 1587–1599. https://doi.org/10.1038/s41893-023-01210-9.

Lubell, Mark, and Tiffany H. Morrison. 2021. Institutional navigation for polycentric sustainability governance. *Nature Sustainability* 4(8): 664–671. https://doi.org/10.1038/s41893-021-00707-5.

Mahon, Robin, and Lucia Fanning. 2019. Regional ocean governance: Polycentric arrangements and their role in global ocean governance. *Marine Policy* 107: 103590.

Martínez-Vázquez, Rosa María, Juan Milán-García, and Jaime de Pablo Valenciano. 2021. Challenges of the blue economy: Evidence and research trends. *Environmental Sciences Europe* 33(1): 61. https://doi.org/10.1186/s12302-021-00502-1.

Ministry of Marine Affairs and Fisheries, World Bank, University of British Columbia, David & Lucile Packard Foundation, and ProBlue. 2023. *Hot Water Rising: The Impact of Climate Change on Fisheries and Coastal Communities*. MMAF et al.

Morgan, Perter J., Michael C. Huang, Michelle Voyer, Diminique Benzaken, and Atsushi Watanabe. 2022. *Blue Economy and Blue Finance: Toward Sustainable Development and Ocean Governance*. Asian Development Bank Institute.

Oktaviani, Jusmalia, and Firdaus Muhamad Iqbal. 2023. The interplay of interest between Indonesia and Sweden in blue economy cooperation. *Nation State: Journal of International Studies* 6(1): 49–70.

Ostrom, Elinor. 2009. A polycentric approach for coping with climate change. Available at SSRN 1934353.

Peddle, Katrina. 2007. Telehealth in context: Socio-technical barriers to telehealth use in Labrador, Canada. *Computer Supported Cooperative Work (CSCW)* 16: 595–614.

Poto, Margherita Paola, Annegret Kuhn, Apostolos Tsiouvalas, Kara K. Hodgson, Montoya Valentina Treffenfeldt, and Christine M. Beitl. 2022. Knowledge integration and good marine governance: A multidisciplinary analysis and critical synopsis. *Human Ecology* 50: 125–139. https://doi.org/10.1007/s10745-021-00289-y.

Sidik, Frida, Anissa Lawrence, Tonny Wagey, Franky Zamzani, and Catherine E. Lovelock. 2023. Blue carbon: A new paradigm of mangrove conservation and management in Indonesia. *Marine Policy* 147: 105388.

Sumaila, U. Rashid (2012). Seas, oceans and fisheries: A challenge for good governance. *The Round Table: The Commonwealth Journal of International Affairs* 101(2): 157–166.

Sumaila, U. Rashid (2024). Reflections on breaking down silos in fisheries science. *Fisheries* 49 (5): 207–210.

Sutrisno, E. (2021). Strategi Pemulihan ekonomi pasca pandemi melalui sektor UMKM dan pariwisata. *Jurnal Lemhannas RI* 9(1): 167–185.

Tegar, Dimas, and Raja Oloan Saut Gurning. 2018. Development of marine and coastal tourism based on blue economy. *International Journal of Marine Engineering Innovation and Research* 2(2). https://doi.org/10.12962/j25481479.v2i2.3650.

Thomas, Jason. 2019. Indonesia's fisheries not managed efficiently. *The ASEAN Post*. 11 September. Available at: https://theaseanpost.com/article/indonesias-fisheries-not-managed-efficiently.

Tobey, James, and Elin Torell. 2006. Coastal poverty and MPA management in mainland Tanzania and Zanzibar. *Ocean & Coastal Management* 49(11): 834–854.

Trade Policy Research and Development Agency. 2015. *Seaweed Commodity Info*. Ministry of Trade of the Republic of Indonesia.

Tuda, Arthur Omondi, Salit Kark, and Alice Newton. 2021. Polycentricity and adaptive governance of transboundary marine socio-ecological systems. *Ocean & Coastal Management* 200: 105412. https://doi.org/10.1016/j.ocecoaman.2020.105412.

World Bank. 2023. *Global Seaweed: New and Emerging Markets Report 2023*. ProBlue and the World Bank Group.

World Economic Forum. 2023. The importance of ecosystem-based management in protecting the ocean. June 9. https://www.weforum.org/agenda/2023/06/ecosystem-based-management-protecting-ocean/.

PART VI

Emerging themes

19 Bringing visitors to the ocean world? Emerging issues in deep sea exploration and tourism

John Hannigan and Greg Richards

On June 18, 2023, the submersible *Titan* operated by OceanGate Expeditions imploded in the North Atlantic, 500 miles off the coast of Newfoundland. There were five victims: Stockton Rush, the CEO of OceanGate; Hamish Harding, a British aircraft broker and adventurer; Shahzada Dawood, vice-chairman of one of Pakistan's largest conglomerates, and his 19-year-old son Suleman; and Paul Nargeolet, a French explorer and submariner. Of the five, the latter four had paid $250,000 each to descend to the wreck of the *Titanic*, the iconic ocean liner that sank after striking an iceberg on April 15, 1912.

The loss of the *Titan* rapidly became a cautionary tale in many circles, a story about the arrogance of "rich tourists" who foolishly think money can buy them access to "extreme destinations" (Weibel 2023). There is currently no binding regulation of deep-sea tourism, and the *Titan* could therefore use innovative, but in retrospect risky, technology involving a carbon fiber hull. According to Smith (2023), deep-sea adventures such as the *Titan* voyage appeal to thrill-seekers looking for danger, prestige, and authenticity.

Weibel (2023) compares the *Titan* expedition to recent developments in space travel:

> It's not necessarily coincidental that commercial passengers on spaceflights and deep-sea descents have a lot in common; in fact, the two groups overlap much more than might be imagined. A voyage to the bottom of the ocean is every bit as 'alien as a trip into space, requiring a specially designed vehicle to resist the dangers on the other side of the hatch and taking passengers into environments that are incompatible with human life.

Another parallel lies in the blurring between the roles of tourist and researcher. Space tourists add to existing medical knowledge by participating in on-board medical tests and experiments. On the *Titan*, the passengers were also participating in citizen science. Paul Nargeolet, for example, was a French diver who was an acknowledged expert on the *Titanic.*

Finally, there is an overlap between oceanauts and astronauts. Hamish Hardin, who perished in the *Titan* accident, was previously a passenger on the fifth suborbital flight of Jeff Bezos' Blue Origin NS-21 mission and became a leading advocate of space tourism. Kathy Sullivan, the first American woman to walk in space for NASA (National Aeronautics and Space Administration), is an oceanographer who sits on the board of EYOS corporation, which conveys tourists on the submersible *Challenger Deep* to the Mariana Trench, the lowest point on Earth. A number of these elite adventurers are linked through membership in the Explorers Club, a New York-based society that celebrates expeditions at the frontiers of knowledge.

There has been more research on the potential of space tourism than on deep-sea tourism to date (e.g., Kim, Hall, and Kwon, 2023). One reason for this is the high profile of space expeditions, and the investment of billionaires such as Elon Musk and Jeff Bezos in rocket technology.

The development of adventure tourism

Wright (2023) reports that there has been substantial growth in adventure tourism in recent years, and travelers are becoming increasingly interested in visiting undiscovered destinations. As Buckley (2006) outlined, adventure tourism has undergone three basic phases: the age of adventurers "discovering" new lands, followed by the growth of unadventurous mass tourism, and finally the rise of commercially provided adventure experiences.

Demand has also been stimulated by destinations developing adventure products, and also thanks to advocacy by the industry. According to the Adventure Travel Trade Association (ATTA), adventure tourism provides "much sought-after escapes as well as ecological, cultural and economic benefits to destinations. These benefits include attracting high-value customers, the encouragement of sustainable practices, and support of local economies due to low economic leakage" (ATTA 2016).

The ATTA defines adventure tourism as a trip that includes at least two of the following three elements: physical activity, natural environment, and cultural immersion. This is a broad definition, which supports an estimate of industry size as $324.9 billion in 2023, or 8 percent of the global leisure tourism market (Statista 2024). It also seems to lack any real sense of "adventure."

A more realistic estimate of potential market size might come from the concept of thrill-seekers—people who are looking for some degree of danger as a mark of authenticity. Janowski et al. (2021) argue that risk and danger, the natural environment, thrill and excitement, challenge, and physical activity are at the core of adventure travel. In safe modern societies, risk and danger are often relatively rare in everyday life, causing a desire for "safe danger" (Hannigan 2005). Adventure tourism seems to offer the possibility of safe consumption of dangerous experiences by tourists.

This makes adventure tourism attractive for many, particularly as mainstream tourist experiences are now relatively devoid of danger. This matches Boorstin's (1962) critique of tourism as replacement of authentic adventures undertaken by heroic figures by inauthentic "pseudo-events" created purely for tourist consumption. Boorstin's (1983) book *The Discoverers* was billed "An original history of man's [*sic*] greatest adventure: his search to discover the world around him." This included the navigation of the oceans and the exploration of the deep. In his earlier book *The Image*, Boorstin (1962) attacks the tourist for venturing out over the surface of the water in the relative safety and comfort of a cruise ship, rather than braving the elements unprotected, as true explorers did in the past. Now we are seeing the cocoon of the cruise ship being extended to the ocean depths through the production of diving vessels and undersea platforms that allow for leisurely perusal of the oceanscape. Li, Zhang, and Shi (2023) report on a semi-submersible platform (900 meters by 600 meters), which can be used in waters up to 1200 meters deep. The development of this platform is linked by the authors to the development of China's maritime economy and its desire to exploit marine resources.

There is a continuing debate on the role of risk in adventure tourism. Rantala, Rokenes, and Valkonen (2018) identify a continuum of definitions, ranging from "soft" adventure tourism based on "shallow" adventure to the "deep-end, original adventures" involving relatively high levels of risk and thrill. Deep-sea tourism and space tourism currently lie at the extreme end of the hard adventure category.

In fact, this type of exploration may be linked to the idea of frontiers. Laing and Crouch (2011, 1516) argue that tourists in the modern era can visit more remote and exotic "frontier" locations, which may involve "the re-enactment of exploration myths through the retracing of famous historical journeys." They see the exploration myth as part of a Western cultural legacy that had its genesis in the exploits of Spanish and Portuguese explorers in the sixteenth century and which flourished in the eighteenth and nineteenth centuries with the voyages of explorers such as Captain Cook. Frontier tourism is therefore often linked to the desire for heroism. Frontier tourists "re-enact archetypal myths based on the epic tales of exploration and, in the process, contribute to the modern mythology of the heroic journey for a new generation of tourists" (Laing and Crouch 2011, 1534). Now that the coasts and shallow oceans have been mapped and extensively explored, the deep ocean (over 200 meters in depth) remains a relatively unexplored part of the planet.

Deep-sea tourism

Deep-sea tourism: a brief history

Maritime tourism has been established in one form or another since the late eighteenth century (Picken 2021, Rozwadowski 2005). In its early days, wealthy individuals such as Joseph Banks sponsored voyages of exploration, sometimes signing on as resident naturalists engaged in gathering and documenting new plant and animal species (Weibel 2023). This blurring of the roles of tourist and scientist has continued to the present day.

Deep-sea tourism was severely limited for a long time by the impossibility of humans descending to any great distance beyond the surface of the ocean. In the 1950s, a clutch of spectacular technological innovations opened the deep for the first time. Most importantly, the invention of the aqualung, a pressurized, self-contained underwater breathing device, by Jacques Cousteau and Emile Gagnan, permitted humans to swim underwater at depths previously considered out-of-bounds. Scuba diving clubs proliferated: there were 213 dive clubs in North America by mid-century (Rozwadowski 2013, 4). However, this was more of a recreational pursuit than a tourist activity. By 1982, at best only 1 percent of the American population was participating in the sport (*New York Times* 1982).

In its infancy, scuba diving was regarded as a form of extreme leisure. For example, the Afro-American diving club in the United States called itself the "Underwater Adventure Seekers" (Hannigan 2022, 119). As scuba became more established, diving vacations emerged, especially in the Caribbean. Scuba diving resorts walk a fine line between depicting the activity as safe and risky. According to data from the US Consumer Safety Commission on estimated average emergency room admissions, scuba diving (1,569) ranked well behind golf (36,616), snowboarding (19,706), and bowling (15,055) (Schofield 2021), although it should be noted that there are far more bowlers and golfers than there are scuba divers. Nonetheless, the dangers associated with scuba diving have a greater "dread factor" than the possibility of dropping a bowling ball on your toe, as well as a greater risk of severe injury and death.

In 1960, oceanographers Jacques Picard and Don Walsh descended for the first time to the Mariana Trench in the Pacific, the deepest known point on Earth, in a two-passenger bathyscaphe, the *Trieste*. They remained there for 20 minutes. It would not be for another five decades until this feat would be replicated in March 2012 by acclaimed Hollywood film director James Cameron. This opened the door to diving for dollars in the deep ocean. At the forefront of this has been EYOS Expeditions, a company that operates commercial expeditions to the sea floor. A seat on EYOS' "ultra-exclusive excursion" to Challenger Deep (the deepest point of the Mariana Trench) costs $750,000. The *Challenger Deep* descends to a depth three times that reached by the *Titan*. EYOS is partnered in this venture by Caladan Oceanic, a submersible builder and private undersea diving company piloted by Victor Vescovo, who holds the distinction of being the only person to have dived to all five of the world's deepest oceanic sites as well as flying into space with Blue Origin.

For those tourists who cannot afford submersible dives, there are a host of submerged hotels and aquariums. One popular variation is the underwater shark tunnel, an acrylic tube that passes through the aquarium and conveys sharks and other marine life. These structures are more or less safe; the only recorded death occurred in 2019 when a Louisiana man exited his undersea cabin in a resort off the east coast of Africa, swam up to the cabin with a sign proposing marriage to his fiancée, and drowned.

Deep-sea tourism as a "blue-growth strategy"

Deep-sea tourism can be seen as part of a wider "blue growth" strategy. The economic potential of blue growth is highlighted by Jobstvogt et al. (2014, 11). They report "A global valuation of...[the] annual...value for the marine environment (including coastal waters) of $20.9 trillion, or 63 percent of the value provided by all ecosystem services globally." Klinger et al. (2018) outline the potential of key sectors for "blue growth" including aquaculture, wind and wave power, seabed mining, and tourism. They report that marine tourism has been growing strongly in recent decades, and that this is likely to continue in the future.

For example, Jonas (2024) outlines the emerging opportunities in "blue tourism," or coastal and marine tourism, which has an estimated global value of $82 billion. Most activity and policy attention is focused on shallow coastal waters. For example, European Union policy on the sustainable blue economy highlights coastal tourism: "'In coastal regions, developing green infrastructure will help preserve biodiversity, coastal ecosystems and landscapes, strengthening the sustainable development of tourism and of the coastal regions' economy" (European Commission 2021). Jonas (2024) argues that "blue tourism" is a contemporary term covering traditional coastal and marine tourism concepts, with a strong focus on sustainability practices and the intentional application of conservation and preservation principles. Blue tourism incorporates oceanic exploration into the analysis of marine environments, adding new dimensions beyond purely recreational forms of tourism.

With underwater exploration, we are moving into the realm of "deep blue tourism," which potentially adds scientific motivations as well as thrill-seeking. This is likely to remain a niche within blue tourism, but the publicity value of relatively risky forms of frontier tourism may mean that it attracts a disproportionate amount of attention. The exploratory and arguably scientific nature of deep-sea tourism also means that it can contribute actively to Sustainable Development Goal 14: Life Below Water (United Nations Development Programme 2023).

However, virtual reality experiences in blue tourism already exist with 360-degree views of the world's top beaches being available from the comfort of your couch (Adaway 2021). This may have the added benefit of reducing the number of visitors to overcrowded beach areas, which would enhance the protection and conservation of sensitive coastal and marine environments. More remote and fragile beaches that should be off-limits to tourists could also form part of these virtual reality tours. Tsvetkov (2023) notes that additions can be made to tourist sites through augmented reality, such as using it with shipwrecks to illustrate what the ship looked like before it capsized or ran aground. This means that new technologies might in the future remove the need for tourists to be exposed to danger to "visit" deep-sea sites, but it is in fact the danger that attracts many adventure tourists.

Wright (2023) suggests that as more tourists participate in adventure travel, more people will seek novelty and greater adventure, and this could lead to more specialist travelers seeking increased risk through adventure travel. He also discusses future scenarios in which climatic challenges and disasters may force humans to seek new areas to live, including space and the ocean depths. In this case, he suggests, adventure travel may serve to develop the skill sets necessary to undertake such a transition. This mirrors in many ways discussions about the exploitation of fragile environments on land (Buckley 2000), and the concept of "last chance tourism" driven by disappearing habitats, species, and natural environments.

Travel to the fragile deep sea has so far been facilitated by a handful of pioneers. For example, Karl Stanley has been operating regular tourist dives to over 600 meters in Honduras since 1998. Stanley has operated more than 2,500 dives transporting three or four people for $1,200 per hour on trips lasting around four hours.

The cost of deep-sea tourism is clearly a limiting factor. A dive off the shore of Tenerife to undertake microplastics studies costs $1,955, and more expensive trips—for example, to study climate change in Antarctica or the origins of life at hydrothermal vents—can go up to $54,000. Submarine operator Scott Waters comments: "The people who want to travel in a submarine are adventurers and explorers who want to make a true impact on science" (Aguirre 2023).

Regulatory and governance challenges

In the wake of the *Titan* accident, concerns about the lack of governance and regulation of deep-sea tourism multiplied on the Internet. In a short piece entitled "The Titan Sub and the Dangers of Unregulated Deep-Sea Tourism," *TIME* reporter Simmone Shah (2023) cites Canadian professor Jon Heshka:

> The government won't regulate until there's a demonstrated need that industry has failed to self-regulate. If things are humming along and the activities are being administered, more or less incident free, and businesses are making money and clients are willing to shell out the coin, there is no need for the government to become involved.

To fully understand the issues and problems faced in the regulation of deep-sea tourism, it makes sense to cast our nets more broadly, both in the context of ocean governance and in comparison to the regulation of space tourism.

As should be evident to readers of this volume, sustainable ocean governance is both complex and uneven. Signed in 1982 and coming into force in 1994, the United Nations Convention on the Law of the Sea (UNCLOS) established a legal framework for maritime activity. UNCLOS has done much to codify what was previously a chaotic situation, but it has gaps. For example, it provides for the regulation of deep-sea mining but only on the seafloor.

Venancio (2023) points to a host of legal loopholes regarding underwater vehicles (UVs) as a reason for the lack of regulation of submarine tourism, the riskiest form of deep-sea travel. In the first instance, it remains unclear whether UVs qualify under the UNCLOS framework as ships/vessels; as a result, they are more or less free to operate without regulatory constraints. While national states may be able to impose restrictions on UVs engaged in marine scientific and/or mining activities in coastal waters and in their Exclusive Economic Zone (EEZ), this does not apply to submarine recreational exploration.

In the OceanGate case, the *Titan* fell between the regulatory cracks. As Venancio (2023) explains, OceanGate, Inc. is an American company legally registered in Washington; unfortunately, the United States does not require inspections for submersibles with six or fewer passengers. To further muddy the waters, OceanGate Expeditions, which led the dive, was based in the Bahamas. There is a greater degree of regulation in the Bahamas for crewed submarines, but these are restricted to UVs operated or launched in Bahamian waters; the *Titan* was launched by a Canadian vessel on the high seas off the coast of Newfoundland.

The legal situation is further confused as far as OceanGate uses an experimental design that cannot be judged by existing regulatory standards (Shah 2023). Rather than relying on ships specially outfitted with cranes and A-frame structures to lower the submersible into the water, OceanGate designed a custom trailer or platform named the *Ms. Lars* (Mobile Subsea Launch and Recovery System) to tow the sub. When it comes time to descend, *Ms. Lars* floods its flotation tanks with water, sinking 16 to 32 feet below the surface. This design is intended to bring down costs (Fecht 2017), but it strands *Ms. Lars* as a regulatory orphan, neither ship nor underwater vehicle. Maritime historian Salvatore Marcogliano uses the analogy of pulling a boat on a trailer: "The highway patrol has jurisdiction over the car and the trailer, but not over the boat. The boat is cargo" (Finley 2023).

In the wake of the *Titan* catastrophe, several media commentators noted that OceanGate declined to submit its submersible for safety certification. This requires some clarification. Maritime certification applies to commercial shipping. Certification societies, which offer this service, are non-governmental organizations that establish and maintain technical standards for the construction of ships and offshore structures (European Maritime Safety Agency 2024). The twelve leading societies are members of the International Association of Classification Societies (IACS), which acts as a consultant to the International Maritime Organization (IMO). Certification is not mandatory for submersibles, but it is normal practice. OceanGate's failure to certify the *Titan* was of special concern to the Marine Technology Society, a professional membership organization. In 2018, the manned underwater vessel (MUV) committee of the Marine Technology Society drafted a letter (it was never sent) to OceanGate warning that the experimental approach adopted by OceanGate could result in negative outcomes (from minor to catastrophic) that would have grave consequences for everyone in the industry.

One portal through which we can understand the governance of deep-sea tourism is to compare it with space tourism. Von der Dunk (2019) observes that space tourism needs to be regulated as a subset of private spaceflight activities. The major dilemma here is whether space tourism falls under the jurisdiction of aviation law or space law.

A further distinction is made between private *orbital* spaceflight (orbiting around the Earth) and private *suborbital* spaceflight (spaceflights *not* achieving or intending to reach Earth orbit). While the former clearly falls under the aegis of space law, the latter falls somewhere between air law and space law. Space law is premised on the involvement of a *space object* (e.g., booster and module), while international air law hinges on the presence of an aircraft. There is a parallel here with deep-sea travel where it is not clear whether the submersible is a ship or an object. Von der Dunk (2019) identifies the United States as "the only state that has thus far taken substantive steps to address private spaceflight including private suborbital spaceflight and space tourism" (p. 11). In doing so, it collapsed the space objects and aircraft into a single category but otherwise opted for a space law approach.

Another parallel between deep-sea tourism and space tourism pertains to liability. The Commercial Space Act and the Commercial Space Launch Competitiveness Act in the United States have adopted an "informed consent regime," meaning that there is no statutory obligation to accept liability on the part of spaceflight operators. Launch vehicles are not required to be certified as safe, only the launch itself. In short, space tourists like William Shatner travel entirely at their own risk. In the case of submersibles carrying paying guests, tourists sign waivers that essentially clear the operator from legal action if something goes wrong. The OceanGate waiver warns that guests would be "subject to extreme pressure" and that "any failure of the vessel could cause severe injury and death" (Finley 2023). This is not appreciably different from the liability waivers required of scuba divers.

Towards a research agenda for deep-sea exploration and tourism

Developing the research agenda for deep-sea exploration and tourism includes several key areas.

Oceanic exploration

The development of ocean exploration and frontier tourism is intricately linked to the search for raw materials and the technologies needed to support these efforts. Deep-sea tourism is likely to grow as commercial exploitation of the deep seas increases and the technology needed to reach great depths becomes more accessible. At the moment, little is known about the range and performance of submersibles available to tourists, or the development of the submarine hotel market. An inventory and categorization of deep-sea tourism opportunities and their distribution would help to provide an overview of deep-sea exploration and tourism potential. It is likely that there will be rapid advances in technology, also as a spillover from space exploration. This is also likely to stimulate new possibilities for mineral extraction, which in turn should stimulate advances in deep-sea tourism.

This chapter has also shown the close parallels between undersea tourism and space tourism, which is also a rapidly growing area of research (Cohen and Spector 2020). These similarities and overlaps deserve a more detailed consideration, analyzing the ways in which these forms of exploration have influenced each other. As commercial space travel takes off, will this leave the deep oceans looking like the final undiscovered frontier for tourism?

Motivations: why do people engage in journeys to the deep?

The thrill of venturing into the deep sea is assumed to be a prime driver of frontier tourism in the deep sea. But little empirical research exists on the motivations of (potential) deep-sea tourists. Research on the psychology of deep-sea tourism would be useful in distinguishing different participant profiles and motivations. Given the small number of current participants, it might also be useful to study the willingness to participate among the wider population as well; for example, through panel studies. In light of the high cost of deep-sea tourism, issues of equality and accessibility are also important to consider.

We have seen evidence that deep-sea tourism can blur the tourist and researcher roles. But again, detailed research on this is lacking. Motivational studies could also explore the willingness of deep-sea tourists to act as researchers and explore the potential to grow citizen science activity in the oceans. With research budgets being squeezed, enlisting erstwhile maritime explorers in data collection and analysis would add to our knowledge of the oceans.

Exploration, exploitation, and tourism

As a form of frontier tourism, deep-sea travel has strong links with the idea of exploration. This may be stimulated by a desire to emulate famous voyagers, as suggested by Laing and Crouch (2011), or simply to explore the unknown and to push personal boundaries. In the past, there has always been a close relationship between exploration and exploitation, with marine voyages often being stimulated by the search for novel resources. This also is an important aspect of contemporary marine exploration, particularly in the deep sea. It would be interesting to examine the extent to which deep-sea explorers see themselves as modern pioneers, and whether a maritime frontier mentality can be discerned, particularly among the entrepreneurs who often fund such exploration.

To what extent do (potential) deep-sea tourists share such a frontier mentality? As well as the personal risk involved in exploring the ocean depths, there are also potential personal and social benefits to be gained. How does the potential exploitation of the riches of the deep sea weigh against the potential costs, in terms of both individual risks and the social or cultural risks involved? The fact that 50 percent of moon landing missions fail does not seem to deter more launches (Iles 2023), although it does hurt national pride. Does the fact that most deep-sea exploration is privately funded mean it is less prone to public discussion about the cost–benefit ratio? The number of deep-sea dives is currently relatively small, but the indications are that deep-sea exploration and tourism are likely to grow significantly in the future. Such growth is likely to threaten fragile deep-sea ecosystems, and an evaluation of the risks is clearly needed.

Regulation of the deep

Finally, we need to better understand the regulatory roadblocks and possibilities accruing to deep-ocean tourism. One difficulty here is that the existing regulatory framework is directed at overseeing the exploration and exploitation of commodities: oil and gas, minerals, and bio-organisms. In this regard, Haas et al. (2022) argue that ocean governance currently faces three core risks: (1) the impacts of the overexploitation of marine resources, (2) the inequitable distribution of access to and benefits from marine ecosystem services, and (3) the inadequate or inappropriate adaptation to changing ocean conditions. Are these the same risks potentially posed by undersea tourism?

The guiding principle of the deep-seabed mining regime is what is called the Common Heritage of (Hu)Mankind (CHM). This posits that the resources of the deep seabed are not subject to national appropriation, but rather belong to all members of the international community. Thus, the International Seabed Authority (ISA), the chief regulatory institution for deep-sea mining, is not only tasked with issuing permits and contracts for exploration and exploitation and protecting the seabed and ocean floor from harmful environmental effects, but it also is expected to guarantee that land-bound nations, especially those in the Global South, share in the profits from undersea mining. Does the CHM apply to deep-sea tourism? This is especially salient insofar as "submersible tourism" is currently the province of the ultra-wealthy.

Conclusions

Ocean governance has been described as a "nebulous concept" (*World Ocean Review* 2015) lacking a universal definition and applicability. For example, there is no official definition of "marine scientific research," a term that is mentioned frequently in policy documents (*Superyacht News* 2022). Haas et al. (2022, 253) point out that "Inconsistencies in sectoral approaches, conflict between actors, jurisdictions with overlapping mandates, and poor communication among governance institutions have undermined the effectiveness of ocean governance."

The difficulties cited above are magnified in deep-sea tourism. It has been suggested that the problem lies centrally in the disjuncture between an industry that has been expanding rapidly and the lack of regulation. In this view, what is urgently needed are enhanced safety measures and stringent oversight. If so, where should this regulation be situated? Industry commentators recommend comprehensive certification by trusted bodies such as the marine certification societies. Another alternative is to expand the jurisdiction of international organizations such as UNCLOS. The latter would necessitate a new or revised international agreement regulating deep-sea tourism, no mean feat considering that the United States has yet to sign UNCLOS. As McCue (2022, 1113) observes for the prospects of a new international treaty in outer space: "the treaty will need the expertise of industry leaders, potential passengers and states to succeed."

As we have noted earlier in this chapter, a new safety and certification regime will most certainly enhance perceptions of security by tourists, but removing the sense of danger could strip the experience of its potential for hard adventure. Does extreme frontier travel, we might ask, thrive *despite* the risks or *because* of them?

References

Adaway, K. 2021. Hit the World's Best Beaches With These 360-Degree Virtual Experiences. https://www.thrillist.com/travel/nation/virtual-beach-vacations-tours.

Adventure Travel Trade Association. 2016. ATTA 2016 Industry Snapshot. https://learn.adventuretravel.biz/research/industry-snapshot-2016/.

Aguirre, Jessica Camille. 2023. Deep-Sea Tourism Is on the Rise. But Is It Safe? *Afar*, November 29. https://www.afar.com/magazine/deep-sea-tourism-is-on-the-rise-but-how-safe-is-it.

Boorstin, Daniel. 1962. *The Image: A Guide to Pseudo-Events in America*. New York, NY: Random House.

Boorstin, Daniel. 1983. *The Discoverers: A History of Man's Search to Know His World and Himself*. New York, NY: Random House.

Buckley, Ralf. 2000. Tourism in the Most Fragile Environments. *Tourism Recreation Research* 25(1): 31–40.

Buckley, Ralf. 2006. *Adventure Tourism*. Wallingford: CABI.

Cohen, Erik, and Samuel Spector. 2020. Space Tourism: Past to Future – A Perspective Article. *Tourism Review* 75(1): 136–139.

European Commission. 2021. A new approach for a sustainable blue economy in the EU: Transforming the EU's Blue Economy for a Sustainable Future. COM(2021) 240 Final. Brussels: European Commission. Available at: https://oceans-and-fisheries.ec.europa.eu/publications/putting-blue-green_en.

European Maritime Safety Agency. 2024. Classification Societies. https://www.emsa.europa.eu/inspections/90-classification-societies.html.

Fecht, Sarah. 2017. DeepSea Tourism Could Become a Thing Soon. *Popular Science*, April 17. https://www.popsci.com/deep-sea-tourism/.

Finley, Ben. 2023. Tourist Sub's Implosion Draws Attention to Murky Regulations of Deep-Sea Expeditions. *Associated Press*, June 23. https://apnews.com/article/titanic-sub-accident-laws-deep-sea-6d1e100f39a46091ae9895706adbcceb.

Haas, Bianca, Mary Mackay, Camilla Novaglio, Liam Fullbrook, Michael Murunga, Carla Sbrocchi, Jan McDonald et al. 2022. The Future of Ocean Governance. *Reviews in Fish Biology and Fisheries* 32(1): 253–270. https://link.springer.com/article/10.1007/s11160-020-09631-x.

Hannigan, John. 2005. *Fantasy City: Pleasure and Profit in the Postmodern Metropolis*. London, UK and New York, NY: Routledge.

Hannigan, John. 2022. *Rise of the Spectacular: America in the 1950s*. London, UK and New York, NY: Routledge.

Iles, Gail. 2023. Almost Half of Moon Missions Fail. Why Is Space Still So Hard? https://theconversation.com/almost-half-of-moon-missions-fail-why-is-space-still-so-hard-211914.

Janowski, Ingo., Gardiner, S., & Kwek, A. 2021. Dimensions of Adventure Tourism. *Tourism Management Perspectives*, 37, 100776. https://doi.org/10.1016/j.tmp.2020.100776.

Jobstvogt, Neils, Nick Hanley, Stephen Hynes, Jasper Kenter, and Ursula Witte. 2014. Twenty Thousand Sterling Under the Sea: Estimating the Value of Protecting Deep-Sea Biodiversity. *Ecological Economics* 97: 10–19.

Jonas, Lynn C. 2024. Emerging Opportunities in Blue Tourism. *Tourism in Marine Environments*. https://doi.org/10.3727/216901924X17117021040174.

Klinger, Dane H., Anne Maria Eikeset, Brynhildur Davíðsdóttir, Anne-Marie Winter, and James R. Watson. 2018. The Mechanics of Blue Growth: Management of Oceanic Natural Resource Use with Multiple, Interacting Sectors. *Marine Policy* 87: 356–362.

Kim, Myung J., Colin M. Hall, and Ohbyung Kwon. 2023. Space Tourism: Do Age and Gender Make a Difference in Risk Perception? *Journal of Hospitality and Tourism Management* 57: 13–17.

Laing, Jennifer H., and Geoffrey I. Crouch. 2011. Frontier Tourism: Retracing Mythic Journeys. *Annals of Tourism Research* 38(4): 1516–1534.

Li, Xiute., Zhang, Dingming, and Shi, Pei. 2023. Research on Energy Self-sustaining Tourism Platform Facing the Deep Sea. *Tourism Management and Technology Economy*, 6(5): 76–82.

McCue, Molly M. 2022. A Regulatory Scheme for the Dawn of Space Tourism. *Vanderbilt Law Review* 55(4): 1087–1116.

New York Times. 1982. Scuba Diving's New World. September 29, D-5. https://www.nytimes.com/1982/09/29/business/scuba-diving-s-new-world.html.

Picken, Felicity. 2021. The Future, the Devil and the Deep Blue Sea. *Science Fiction, Disruption and Tourism* 6: 30.

Rantala, Outi, Arild Rokenes, and Jarno Valkonen. 2018. Is Adventure Tourism a Coherent Concept? A Review of Research Approaches on Adventure Tourism. *Annals of Leisure Research* 21(5): 539–552.

Rozwadowski, Helen M. 2005. *Fathoming the Ocean: The Discovery and Exploration of the Deep Sea*. Cambridge, MA: Belknap Press.

Rozwadowski, Helen M. 2013. From Danger Zone to the World of Wonder: The 1950s Transformation of the Ocean's Depths. *Coriolis: The Interdisciplinary Journal of Maritime Studies* 4(1).

Schofield, Danielle. 2021. Is Scuba Diving Safe? *PADI* (Professional Association of Diving Instructors) Blog, December 4. https://blog.padi.com/scuba-diving-safe/.

Shah, Simmone (with Anna Gordon). 2023. The Titan Sub and the Dangers of Unregulated Deep-Sea Tourism. *TIME.com*, June 22. https://time.com/6289279/titanic-tourism-sub-deep-sea-regulation/.

Smith, Scott. 2023. Danger, Prestige and Authenticity Draw Thrill-seekers to Adventure Tourism. *The Conversation*, June 23. https://theconversation.com/danger-prestige-and-authenticity-draw-thrill-seekers-to-adventure-tourism-208353.

Statista. 2024. Leisure travel. https://www.statista.com/markets/420/topic/493/leisure-travel/#overview.

Superyacht News. 2022. Victor Vescovo: Exclusive Interview. May 13. https://www.superyachtnews.com/owner/victor-vescovo-exclusive-interview-.

Tsvetkov, T. 2023. Virtual reality in travel: 9 Applications for tours, destinations & activities. Regiondo, July 25. https://pro.regiondo.com/blog/virtual-reality-in-travel/.

United Nations Development Programme. 2023. *UNDP Annual Report 2023*. https://www.undp.org/publications/undp-annual-report-2023.

Venancio, Daiana S. 2023. Law of the Sea and the Titan Incident: The Legal Loophole for Underwater Vehicles. *EJIL: Talk!* (Blog of the *European Journal of International Law)*, July 14. https://www.ejiltalk.org/law-of-the-sea-and-the-titan-incident-the-legal-loophole-for-underwater-vehicles/.

Von der Dunk, Frans G. 2019. The Regulation of Space Tourism. In *Space Tourism: The Elusive Dream*, edited by Erik Cohen and Sam Spector, 177–199. Bingley: Emerald Group.

Weibel, Deana L. 2023. The Highs and Lows of Extreme Tourism: The Titan Accident and Commercial Expeditions to Space and the Deep Sea. *Space Review.* July 31. https://www.thespacereview.com/article/4630/1.

World Ocean Review. 2015. On the Difficulty of Governing the Sea. https://worldoceanreview.com/en/wor-4/politics-and-the-oceans/on-the-difficulty-of-governing-the-sea/.

Wright, Daniel W.M. 2023. The Future Past of Travel: Adventure Tourism Supporting Humans Living on the Edge of Existence. *Journal of Tourism Futures* 9(2): 151–167.

20 Identifying knowledge gaps in the politics of marine plastic pollution

Babet de Groot, Justin Alger and Peter Dauvergne

The annual amount of plastics polluting the ocean is set to more than double from 2016 to 2030, if trends continue (Borrelle et al. 2020). What makes plastics so useful—their lightness, durability, flexibility, and abundance—are the same qualities propelling this pollution crisis. Ocean currents transport plastics far from their place of origin to the open ocean or the shores of coastal nations. Over time, they break down into macroplastics, microplastics, and nanoplastics, with large quantities ending up in marine and human food systems (Ong et al. 2022, Ahmed Dar et al. 2024, Sun et al. 2024).

The ubiquity of plastics and their integration throughout global supply chains make plastics especially challenging to govern. A diverse and extensive network of decentralized actors contributes to generating plastic pollution. Fossil-fuel and petrochemical producers are primary beneficiaries of the externalization of the costs of marine plastic pollution, but manufacturers, banks, retailers, and consumers also benefit from the cheap production of materials, packaging, and products. Given how entrenched plastics are in global supply chains and the world economy, ocean plastics scholarship needs to develop a deeper, more holistic understanding of the institutions, interactions, and objectives involved in the global production and use of plastics.

This chapter outlines a research agenda for ocean plastics that aims to encourage researchers to move beyond conceptualizing the problem of ocean plastics as one of marine plastic debris. This terminology is problematic because it conceals the essential nature of ocean plastics as pollution. Plastics need to be framed as a toxic, hazardous environmental contaminant for marine life. Doing so is essential for keeping the policy focus on preventing upstream origins of marine plastics rather than on merely cleaning up plastics already in the ocean. More research into the *politics* underlying the overproduction of plastics, the profit-making of the plastics industry, and the global failures of plastics governance, we argue, is especially vital for developing effective solutions to escalating marine plastic pollution.

We begin with an overview of how the accumulation of plastics in the ocean gained attention, and the existing governance mechanisms to address it. We then turn to what we see as some key ontological and epistemological gaps in the literature.

Specifically, we see the need for more research on the agency of subnational actors and the power of norms within the fragmented, multilevel global governance of plastics. We further see value in greater epistemological diversity, especially more critical and reflective forms of inquiry into the causes and consequences of marine plastic pollution. Following this discussion, we turn to reflect upon the emerging global plastics treaty and some of the challenges and opportunities this presents for researchers. We conclude by identifying a few areas that we see as particularly worthy of further study. The scale and scope of the escalating global plastics crisis warrant an ambitious research agenda into the politics of marine plastic pollution. This chapter outlines just a few of the potential new avenues that scholars can explore to expand this research.

Governing ocean plastics

The proliferation of plastics in the ocean is relatively recent. Plastic production has increased from around 2 million tons a year at the start of mass production in the 1950s to over 450 million tons a year now. At least 19–23 million tons end up in aquatic ecosystems each year (Borrelle et al. 2020, 1515–1516). The first discovery of plastic accumulation in the ocean dates to at least the early 1970s, but it was Captain Charles Moore's 1997 discovery of the Great Pacific Garbage Patch that revealed the scale of the problem (Collins 2023). Despite Moore's discovery, the international community has been slow to respond with coordinated action.

The scale and severity of ocean plastics began to gain the full attention of the international regulatory community in the 2010s. Media coverage played an important role, such as a 2015 viral video of biologist Christine Figgener dislodging a plastic straw from the bleeding nostril of a sea turtle (Bailey 2022). Plastics washing up on beaches further captured public attention but had the consequence of framing plastics in the ocean as a tangible and therefore manageable problem (Heath and Cotton 2022, Chertkovskaya et al. 2023). Unlike problems such as climate change and biodiversity loss, solving the plastics problem seemed a simple matter of removing wayward debris. As knowledge and public awareness grew, nongovernmental organizations (NGOs) emerged around the world with the mandate to combat ocean plastics, with campaigns centered on inspiring individual action through beach cleanups. A more informed and galvanized public increased the pressure on national governments and regulatory agencies to act, and by the early 2020s efforts were underway to strengthen the global governance of ocean plastics (Linhares and Cavadas 2021, Rotter et al. 2022).

Nonetheless, the initial lack of action to combat ocean plastics is consistent with broader ocean governance. The ocean has historically been considered a convenient disposal site for the refuse of human activity, including sewage, garbage, and industrial waste. Based on the assumption that any effluent emitted was "a drop in the ocean," nation-states and corporations exercised their implicit "right to pollute" (Mendenhall 2019, 31).

The devastating and visible impact of oil spills on ocean ecosystems helped raise awareness of the limits of the ocean to absorb pollution, leading to an upswell in global action to combat the sources of marine pollution. Initial efforts focused on sea-based sources. The 1958 Convention on the High Seas established rules to prevent the discharge of oil and radioactive waste. In 1982, the United Nations Convention on the Law of the Sea (UNCLOS) created a foundation for ocean governance (coming into force in 1994). Specialized organizations have also been important, including the International Maritime Organization (IMO) to regulate shipping and the International Seabed Authority (ISA) to regulate seabed resources. Through the IMO, states negotiated the 1972 London Convention on the Prevention of Marine Pollution by Dumping of Wastes and Other Matter and the 1973/78 International Convention for the Prevention of Pollution from Ships (MARPOL). UNCLOS itself also remains central to sustainable ocean governance because it requires states to address ocean pollution and impose penalties for ships contributing to it (Cremean and Techera 2012).

Pollutants originating from land-based sources are primarily the responsibility of individual states. Voluntary guidelines have been employed to try to improve global governance of these pollutants, including the 1995 Global Programme of Action for the Protection of the Marine Environment from Land-based Activities (GPA) and the 2012 Global Partnership on Plastic Pollution and Marine Litter (GPML). The GPML operates in conjunction with the Regional Seas Programme (RSP) as a coordinating and capacity-building institution for coastal management (Kimball 1995, Jacques 2020). Insufficient international regulation of land-based pollutants is a significant weakness in global marine governance, and there is a need for more scholarly research into the consequences for ocean life.

Existing research on plastics governance and ocean pollution

Scholarship has provided key insights into the politics and efficacy of international state-based and treaty-centric approaches to marine plastic pollution, including UNCLOS, the IMO, and soft law instruments such as the GPA, GPML, RSP, Agenda 21, and the Honolulu Strategy (e.g., Vince and Hardesty 2017, Kirk and Popattanachai 2018, Mendenhall 2019, 2023, Ferraro and Failler 2020, Diana et al. 2022, Stoll et al. 2022, Cowan et al. 2023, Landrigan et al. 2023, Aanesen et al. 2024). Scholarship has also offered deep insights into the consequences of national and subnational politics on the governance of marine plastic pollution. Research has revealed the wide-ranging influence of Indigenous peoples, poor communities, and developing countries on the formation, diffusion, and uptake of anti-plastics norms (Clapp and Swanston 2009, Winston 2018, Behuria 2021, Pathak 2023a, 2023b), and how these norms in turn are shaping global environmental governance (Dauvergne 2023a). It has shown the power of grassroots organizations, digital social movements, and transnational advocacy networks to strengthen anti-plastic sentiments and spur government bans on single-use plastics, such as bags, straws, and Styrofoam (Shipton and Dauvergne 2022, Dauvergne and Islam 2023). It has documented the power of industry to weaken governance, delay action, and disseminate misinformation on the ecological and health risks of plastics (Mah 2021, 2022). It has demonstrated the vital importance of the principles of justice and equity for effective multilevel governance of plastics (Stoett 2022, Dauvergne 2023b). And it has uncovered how the organizing structure of the world economy, and the pursuit of corporate profits and economic growth, are propelling unsustainable production and consumption of plastics (Jacques 2023, Tilsted et al. 2023).

There is still considerable potential, however, for scholars to dig even deeper into the complex, multisided politics of the causes of, and solutions to, marine plastic pollution. Understanding global plastics governance as multilevel, fragmented, and constantly contested will help here (Biermann et al. 2009, Biermann and Pattberg 2012, Stoett 2022). Earth system governance (ESG) provides a valuable lens to study the politics of ocean plastics. It conceives of global governance as a complex, multilayered system of institutions interacting with one another and their environments (Biermann 2014). ESG encourages the exploration of crosscutting themes such as "norms," "knowledge," "architecture and agency," "justice and allocation," "democracy and power," "adaptiveness and reflectivity," and "anticipation and imagination" (Burch et al. 2019).

Future research could also valuably build upon the scholarship on the constitutive power of global norms for governing plastics, especially single-use plastics. Clapp and Swanston (2009), for example, show the power of the anti-plastic bag norm, which, as they document, diffused through a "multi-scalar," "non-networked," "South to North" trajectory. Dauvergne (2018a) demonstrates the importance of an anti-microplastics norm for the uneven global phasedown of microbeads from personal care products. Examining the norm dynamics of these and other cases, Loges and Jakobi (2020) reveal how anti-plastic norms revolve around different ideas, values, and behaviors that are unlikely to produce "coherent" governance. This fragmentation of environmental norms is common and a considerable challenge in advancing anti-plastics norms (Alger and Dauvergne 2020). Constructivist analyses of international environmental norms, such as these, broaden the understanding of the translocal politics shaping the governance of marine plastics pollution.

There is also considerable potential for reflective and post-positivist epistemologies to further enrich plastics research. This might include, for instance, assuming social systems are unstable or shifting and understanding meaning as contingent. Through the method of deconstruction, a post-structural approach could help unravel the contested meanings of terminology, including the problem definition of the global plastics crisis itself. In a similar vein, feminist and decolonial perspectives remain underexplored in plastics research (with important exceptions; e.g., Hanson 2016, 2017, Farrelly et al. 2021, Liboiron 2021, Fuller et al. 2022, Peryman et al. 2024). The global plastics crisis disproportionately affects women, whose reproductive health is adversely impacted by endocrine-disrupting chemicals (Shipton and Dauvergne 2022). It also disproportionately impacts racialized and marginalized peoples, who are inundated with pollution transported by ocean currents or the global plastic waste trade and are more likely to work as informal waste pickers (Farrelly et al. 2021, Stoett 2022, Bennett et al. 2023, Dauvergne 2023b). Drawing even more from reflective theories and concepts articulated in environmental justice and discard studies, the study of the politics of marine plastic pollution could further diversify its knowledge foundations.

The politics of the global plastics treaty

A recurring theme in the social science literature on plastic pollution is the potential value of a multilateral agreement on plastics. Stoll et al. (2022, 1130) argue that tackling the plastics crisis is going to require "a comprehensive, systems-level approach," with strong measures to prevent pollution and vigorous support to engage stakeholders. This is echoed by many others who emphasize the potential of a well-designed plastics treaty to improve governance (Borrelle et al. 2017, Tessnow-von Wysocki and Le Billon 2019, Cowan and Tiller 2021, Tiller et al. 2022, Landrigan et al. 2023, Aanesen et al. 2024, Brandon et al. 2023). Cremean and Techera (2012) propose an overarching treaty for ocean pollution, contending that a single instrument to govern both land- and ocean-based pollution could help reduce regulatory overlap, confusion, and conflict. Barrowclough and Birkbeck (2022) agree that effective global plastics governance is going to require much stronger integration of international environmental law and far more cooperation among a great diversity of states and civil society groups. Additional recommendations to support better global governance of plastic pollution include the creation of specific, trackable, and time-bound targets; the inclusion of scientific expertise and community knowledge; the development of robust market mechanisms; and, above all, measures to support high levels of international cooperation (Borrelle et al. 2017, Vince and Hardesty 2017, Dauvergne 2018b). These insights collectively underscore the urgency of a global plastics treaty to address the global plastics crisis.

States responded to this call to action. In 2022, the United Nations Environment Assembly (UNEA) committed to developing, by the end of 2024, a legally binding international instrument to address the plastics crisis. Despite a strong consensus on the value of a global plastics treaty, further research is critical to ensure its practicability and effectiveness. The negotiation of this treaty, ongoing at the time of writing in 2025, provides several intriguing and crucial avenues for future research. Specifically, drawing on the lead author's participant observations during the negotiating sessions in Punta del Este (2022), Paris (2023), Nairobi (2023), and Busan (2024), we see a need for further research into the geopolitical tensions shaping the negotiating process, the effects of stakeholder engagement, and mechanisms for transparency. Addressing knowledge gaps in these areas would not just inform scholarship but also be of use to negotiators, policymakers, and practitioners.

As with other multilateral negotiations, the contemporary geopolitical context plays an important role in shaping the content and eventual implementation of the plastics treaty. The first intergovernmental negotiating session commenced in November 2022, just six months after the Russian invasion of Ukraine and one year before the severe escalation of the Israel–Palestine conflict, both of which have sown divisions.

Part of the challenge geopolitical tensions pose to cooperation on plastics is the close connection between geopolitical aims and fossil fuels. Petro states and plastics producers have a vested interest in the perpetuation of a global plastics industry. These interests materialized concretely in the form of the Like-Minded Group—a coalition including states such as Bahrain, China, Cuba, Iran, Russia, and Saudi Arabia. It was briefly known as the Global Alliance for Plastics Sustainability, but this name was ultimately (and ironically) discarded due to a lack of consensus. Further analysis of the political motivations of key states in the negotiations is needed to better understand the ways through which the intersection of geopolitics and the political economy of plastics ends up shaping a global plastics treaty. As in other issue areas, the sanitized discourse of diplomacy can mask a lack of genuine commitment to addressing the plastics crisis.

Nonstate actors are also playing an important role in shaping the global plastics treaty. Understanding how they pursue their goals throughout the negotiating process can yield further insights into the politics of plastics governance. The UN Stakeholder Engagement Mechanism facilitates the participation of stakeholders in intergovernmental negotiations, including NGOs, industry, Indigenous peoples, women, youth, scientists, and several other impacted communities. The Intergovernmental Negotiating Committee (INC) to develop the plastics treaty did not, however, include this provision in its rules of procedure, which were adopted from the Minamata Convention on Mercury. To overcome this shortcoming, the INC Secretariat held a one-day multistakeholder forum prior to INC-1 in 2022 and then communicated key messages from the forum to member states. This was met with considerable backlash by state negotiators who emphasized that the INC is a state-based process, not a stakeholder one. Further research could valuably examine how stakeholders have pursued goals through the INC process absent the Stakeholder Engagement Mechanism. This is just one aspect of much-needed research into the role of nonstate actors in global plastics governance. The influence of corporations and NGOs in shaping plastics governance is multifaceted, dynamic, and consequential. Further research into their interests, strategies, and power can all enrich the literature on plastics governance.

Finally, transparency is imperative for the efficacy of a global plastics treaty and warrants further study. The value of transparency spans global plastics governance, including within the treaty negotiating process, across the global plastic value chain, and through the regulation of plastics. Plastics industry representatives have routinely gained access to the INC process through national delegations, obscuring the influence of private actors. This influence has the potential to weaken international regulation of plastics. A better understanding of the role of transparency throughout the life cycle of plastics is also needed. The decentralized nature of the global plastics value chain shrouds critical aspects of its environmental impact, such as the chemical composition of feedstocks, the pathways of the global plastic scrap trade, and scientifically questionable approaches to waste management.

Research highlighting precautionary approaches to governance can reveal the ways in which incomplete knowledge of the plastics life cycle is hazardous to human health and the environment. Further study of the importance and integration of measures of transparency to advance best practices would also be welcome. Many questions remain about mechanisms for monitoring, reporting, and accountability in plastics governance. Examining transparency in more depth would not only enhance our understanding of accountability in the global plastics treaty (and plastics governance more broadly), but also promote more inclusive and effective strategies to mitigate, prevent, and manage plastic pollution on a global scale.

Conclusion

The global plastics crisis is not only a marine pollution issue, but also a threat to planetary health. The scale and pace at which these pollutants are entering the environment could fundamentally reshape the Earth systems that we depend on. In our judgment, it is a crisis on par with the climate crisis in terms of its potential planetary harm. This chapter has highlighted several ways to advance research into the politics of governing ocean plastics, but it only scratches the surface of potential research avenues.

Many questions could be investigated further. How are political, corporate, and civil society discourses about plastics shaping how policymakers are conceptualizing the problem of plastic pollution? To what extent are the oil and gas, petrochemical, and retail industries profiting from marine plastic pollution and influencing global governance, including treaty negotiations? What is the role of banking and financial institutions in thwarting efforts to impose a global cap on plastic production? What are the political dynamics shaping industry "solutions" to plastic waste? What can a rights-based approach contribute to improving marine plastic pollution, given the impact of plastics on marginalized peoples around the world? What does a just transition away from plastics look like, and how will a transition impact those within the plastics industry, from producers to waste pickers? How can Indigenous knowledge advance sustainable plastics governance? By exploring these questions, among others, scholars can contribute to a more holistic, comprehensive understanding of what is going to be necessary to rein in marine plastic pollution.

References

Aanesen, Margrethe, Julide C. Ahi, Tenaw G. Abate, Farhan R. Khan, Frans P. de Vries, Hauke Kite-Powell, and Nicola J. Beaumont. 2024. Insights from International Environmental Legislation and Protocols for the Global Plastic Treaty. *Scientific Reports* 14 (1): 2750. https://doi.org/10.1038/s41598-024-53099-9.

Ahmed Dar, Afzal, Zhi Chen, Muhammad Fahad Sardar, and Chunjiang An. 2024. Navigating the Nexus: Climate Dynamics and Microplastics Pollution in Coastal Ecosystems. *Environmental Research* 252 (July): 118971. https://doi.org/10.1016/j.envres.2024.118971.

Alger, Justin, and Peter Dauvergne. 2020. The Translocal Politics of Environmental Norm Diffusion. *Environmental Communication* 14 (2): 155–167. https://doi.org/10.1080/17524032.2019.1665567.

Bailey, Ian. 2022. Media Coverage, Attention Cycles and the Governance of Plastics Pollution. *Environmental Policy and Governance* 32 (5), 377–389. https://doi.org/10.1002/eet.1977.

Barrowclough, Diana, and Carolyn Deere Birkbeck. 2022. Transforming the Global Plastics Economy: The Role of Economic Policies in the Global Governance of Plastic Pollution. *Social Sciences* 11 (1): 1–26. https://doi.org/10.3390/socsci11010026.

Behuria, Pritish. 2021. Ban the (Plastic) Bag? Explaining Variation in the Implementation of Plastic Bag Bans in Rwanda, Kenya and Uganda. *Environment and Planning C: Politics and Space* 39 (8): 1791–1808. https://doi.org/10.1177/2399654421994836.

Bennett, Nathan J., Juan José Alava, Caroline E. Ferguson, Jessica Blythe, Elisa Morgera, David Boyd, and Isabelle M. Côté. 2023. Environmental (In)Justice in the Anthropocene Ocean. *Marine Policy* 147: 105383. https://doi.org/10.1016/j.marpol.2022.105383.

Biermann, Frank. 2014. *Earth System Governance: World Politics in the Anthropocene.* Cambridge, MA: MIT Press.

Biermann, Frank, and Philipp Pattberg. 2012. Global Environmental Governance Revisited. In *Global Environmental Governance Reconsidered*, edited by Frank Biermann and Philipp Pattberg, 1–24. Cambridge, MA: MIT Press. https://doi.org/10.7551/mitpress/9232.001.0001.

Biermann, Frank, Philipp Pattberg, Harro Van Asselt, and Fariborz Zelli. 2009. The Fragmentation of Global Governance Architectures: A Framework for Analysis. *Global Environmental Politics* 9 (4): 14–40. https://doi.org/10.1162/glep.2009.9.4.14.

Borrelle, Stephanie B., Chelsea M. Rochman, Max Liboiron, Alexander L. Bond, Amy Lusher, Hillary Bradshaw, and Jennifer F. Provencher. 2017. Why We Need an International Agreement on Marine Plastic Pollution. *Proceedings of the National Academy of Sciences* 114 (38): 9994–9997. https://doi.org/10.1073/pnas.1714450114.

Borrelle, Stephanie B., Jeremy Ringma, Kara Lavender Law, Cole C. Monnahan, Laurent Lebreton, Alexis McGivern, Erin Murphy et al. 2020. Predicted Growth in Plastic Waste Exceeds Efforts to Mitigate Plastic Pollution. *Science* 369 (6510): 1515–1518. https://doi.org/10.1126/science.aba3656.

Brandon, Anja, Kumar Raja Vanapalli, Olwenn V. Martin, Hanna Dijkstra, Gabriel Enrique De la Torre, Nanna B. Hartmann, Michael A.R. Meier et al. 2023. Charting Success for the Plastics Treaty. *One Earth* 6 (6): 575–581. https://doi.org/10.1016/j.oneear.2023.05.022.

Burch, Sarah, Aarti Gupta, Cristina Y.A. Inoue, Agni Kalfagianni, Åsa Persson, Andrea K. Gerlak, Atsushi Ishii et al. 2019. New Directions in Earth System Governance Research. *Earth System Governance* 1 (January): 100006. https://doi.org/10.1016/j.esg.2019.100006.

Chertkovskaya, Ekaterina, Jacob Hasselbalch, and Johannes Stripple. 2023. Plastic Turbulence: Illusions of Containment, Clean-up, and Control, and the Emergent Promise of Diverse Economies. In *Global Environmental Politics in a Turbulent Era*, edited by Peter Dauvergne and Leah Shipton, 25–36. Cheltenham, UK and Northampton, MA: Edward Elgar Publishing. https://doi.org/10.4337/9781802207149.00009.

Clapp, Jennifer, and Linda Swanston. 2009. Doing Away with Plastic Shopping Bags: International Patterns of Norm Emergence and Policy Implementation. *Environmental Politics* 18 (3): 315–332. https://doi.org/10.1080/09644010902823717.

Collins, Alex. 2023 (January 9). Plastics in Oceans. *Witness History: History as Told by the People Who Were There.* [Podcast]. BBC. https://www.bbc.co.uk/sounds/play/w3ct3bzx.

Cowan, Emily, and Rachel Tiller. 2021. What Shall We Do with a Sea of Plastics? A Systematic Literature Review on How to Pave the Road toward a Global Comprehensive Plastic Governance Agreement. *Frontiers in Marine Science* 8: 798534. https://doi.org/10.3389/fmars.2021.798534.

Cowan, Emily, Rachel Tiller, Thea Lurås Oftebro, Mimmi Throne-Holst, and Anne Katrine Normann. 2023. Orchestration Within Plastics Governance: From Global to Arctic. *Marine Pollution Bulletin* 197: 115635. https://doi.org/10.1016/j.marpolbul.2023.115635.

Cremean, Damien, and Erika J. Techera. 2012. Marine Pollution Law. In *Routledge Handbook of International Environmental Law*, edited by Shawkat Alam, Md Jahid Hossain Bhuiyan, Tareq M.R. Chowdhury, and Erika J. Techera, 277–293. New York, NY: Routledge.

Dauvergne, Peter. 2018a. The Power of Environmental Norms: Marine Plastic Pollution and the Politics of Microbeads. *Environmental Politics* 27 (4): 579–597. https://doi.org/10.1080/09644016.2018.1449090.

Dauvergne, Peter. 2018b. Why is the Global Governance of Plastic Failing the Oceans? *Global Environmental Change* 51: 22–31. https://doi.org/10.1016/j.gloenvcha.2018.05.002.

Dauvergne, Peter. 2023a. Governing Plastics: The Power and Importance of Activism in the Global South. *Environmental Science and Policy* 147: 147–153. https://doi.org/10.1016/j.envsci.2023.06.011.

Dauvergne, Peter. 2023b. The Necessity of Justice for a Fair, Legitimate, and Effective Treaty on Plastic Pollution. *Marine Policy* 155: 105785. https://doi.org/10.1016/j.marpol.2023.105785.

Dauvergne, Peter, and Saima Islam. 2023. The Politics of Anti-Plastics Activism in Indonesia and Malaysia. *Cambridge Prisms: Plastics* 1 (1e): 1–9. https://doi.org/10.1017/plc.2023.3.

Diana, Zoie, Tibor Vegh, Rachel Karasik, Janet Bering, Juan D. Llano Caldas, Amy Pickle, Daniel Rittschof, Winnie Lau, and John Virdin. 2022. The Evolving Global Plastics Policy Landscape: An Inventory and Effectiveness Review. *Environmental Science & Policy* 134: 34–45. https://doi.org/10.1016/j.envsci.2022.03.028.

Farrelly, Trisia, Sy Taffel, and Ian Shaw, eds. 2021. *Plastic Legacies: Pollution, Persistence, and Politics*. Athabasca: Athabasca University Press.

Ferraro, Gianluca, and Pierre Failler. 2020. Governing Plastic Pollution in the Oceans: Institutional Challenges and Areas for Action. *Environmental Science & Policy* 112: 453–460. https://doi.org/10.1016/j.envsci.2020.06.015.

Fuller, Sascha, Tina Ngata, Stephanie B. Borrelle, and Trisia Farrelly. 2022. Plastics Pollution as Waste Colonialism in Te Moananui. *Journal of Political Ecology* 29 (1): 534–560. https://doi.org/10.2458/jpe.2401.

Hanson, Anne-Marie S. 2016. Women's Ecological Oral Histories of Recycling and Development in Coastal Yucatán. *Gender, Place & Culture* 23 (4), 467–483. https://doi.org/10.1080/0966369X.2015.1013445.

Hanson, Anne-Marie S. 2017. Women's Environmental Health Activism Around Waste and Plastic Pollution in the Coastal Wetlands of Yucatán. *Gender & Development* 25 (2), 221–234. https://doi.org/10.1080/13552074.2017.1335450.

Heath, Abigail, and Matthew Cotton. 2022. Responsibility, Engagement, and Policy Strategy for Ocean Plastic Waste Management: A Q-method Study of Stakeholder Perspectives. *Journal of Environmental Planning and Management* 65 (13): 2412–2435. https://doi.org/10.1080/09640568.2021.1971954.

Jacques, Peter. 2020. International Regulation of Ocean Pollution and Ocean Fisheries. In *Oxford Research Encyclopedia of International Studies*. Oxford: Oxford University Press. https://doi.org/10.1093/acrefore/9780190846626.013.240.

Jacques, Peter. 2023. Stages of Capitalist Development and Maximum Marine Plastic Pollution. *Cambridge Prisms: Plastics* 1: E5. https://doi.org/10.1017/plc.2023.1.

Kimball, Lee A. 1995. An International Regime for Managing Land-Based Activities that Degrade Marine and Coastal Environments. *Ocean & Coastal Management* 29 (1–3): 187–206. https://doi.org/10.1016/0964-5691(96)00006-3.

Kirk, Elizabeth A., and Naporn Popattanachai. 2018. Marine Plastics: Fragmentation, Effectiveness and Legitimacy in International Lawmaking. *Review of European, Comparative & International Environmental Law* 27 (3): 222–233. https://doi.org/10.1111/reel.12261.

Landrigan, Philip, Christos Symeonides, Hervé Raps, and Sarah Dunlop. 2023. The Global Plastics Treaty: Why Is It Needed? *The Lancet* 402 (10419): 2274–2276. https://doi.org/10.1016/S0140-6736(23)02198-0.

Liboiron, Max. 2021. *Pollution is Colonialism*. Durham, NC: Duke University Press, 2021.

Linhares, Elisabete, and Bento Cavadas. 2021. "Bad Plastics-Oceans Free of Plastic": The Role of Education. In *Handbook on Teaching and Learning for Sustainable Development*, edited by Walter Leal Filho, Amanda Lange Salvia, and Fernanda Frankenberger, 62–74. Cheltenham, UK and Northampton, MA: Edward Elgar Publishing. https://doi.org/10.4337/9781839104657.00006.

Loges, Bastian, and Anja P. Jakobi. 2020. Not More than the Sum of Its Parts: De-Centered Norm Dynamics and the Governance of Plastics. *Environmental Politics* 29 (6): 1004–1023. https://doi.org/10.1080/09644016.2019.1703385.

Mah, Alice. 2021. Future-Proofing Capitalism: The Paradox of the Circular Economy for Plastics. Global Environmental Politics 21 (2): 121–42. https://doi.org/10.1162/glep_a_00594.

Mah, Alice. 2022. *Plastic Unlimited: How Corporations Are Fuelling the Ecological Crisis and What We Can Do About It*. Cambridge: Polity.

Mendenhall, Elizabeth. 2019. The Ocean Governance Regime: International Conventions and Institutions. In *Climate Change and Ocean Governance: Politics and Policy for Threatened Seas*, edited by Paul G. Harris, 27–42. Cambridge: Cambridge University Press. https://doi.org/10.1017/9781108502238.002.

Mendenhall, Elizabeth. 2023. Making the Most of What We Already Have: Activating UNCLOS to Combat Marine Plastic Pollution. *Marine Policy* 155: 105786. https://doi.org/10.1016/j.marpol.2023.105786.

Ong, Hooi-Theng, Hayati Samsudin, and Herlinda Soto-Valdez. 2022. Migration of Endocrine-Disrupting Chemicals Into Food from Plastic Packaging Materials: An Overview of Chemical Risk Assessment, Techniques to Monitor Migration, and International Regulations. *Critical Reviews in Food Science and Nutrition* 62 (4): 957–979. https://doi.org/10.1080/10408398.2020.1830747.

Pathak, Gauri. 2023a. "Plastic Pollution" and Plastics as Pollution in Mumbai, India. *ethnos* 88 (1): 167–186. https://doi.org/10.1080/00141844.2020.1839116.

Pathak, Gauri. 2023b. Plastic Politics: Industry Stakeholders and the Navigation of Plastic Control Policy in India. *Environmental Politics* 32 (1): 135–156. https://doi.org/10.1080/09644016.2021.2025301.

Peryman, Matt, Romilly Cumming, Tina Ngata, Trisia A. Farrelly, Sascha Fuller, and Stephanie B. Borrelle. 2024. Plastic Pollution as Waste Colonialism in Aotearoa (New Zealand). *Marine Policy* 163: 106078. https://doi.org/10.1016/j.marpol.2024.106078.

Rotter, Ana, Ernesta Grigalionyte-Bembič, Katja Klun, and Rachel Tiller. 2022. Microplastics Pollution: A Thriller with Many Leading Roles and an Unknown Ending. In *Plastic Pollution and Marine Conservation*, edited by Giuseppe Bonanno and Martina Orlando-Bonaca, 275–306. Cambridge, MA: Academic Press. https://doi.org/10.1016/C2019-0-03607-2.

Shipton, Leah, and Dauvergne, Peter. 2022. Health Concerns of Plastics: Energizing the Global Diffusion of Anti-Plastic Norms. *Journal of Environmental Planning and Management* 65 (11): 2124–2144. https://doi.org/10.1080/09640568.2021.1957796.

Stoett, Peter. 2022. Plastic Pollution: A Global Challenge in Need of Multi-Level Justice-Centered Solutions. *One Earth* 5 (6): 593–596. https://doi.org/10.1016/j.oneear.2022.05.017.

Stoll, Theresa, Peter Stoett, Joanna Vince, and Britta Denise Hardesty. 2022. Governance and Measures for the Prevention of Marine Debris. In *Handbook of Microplastics in the Environment*, edited by Teresa Rocha-Santos, Mónica Costa, and Catherine Mouneyrac, 1129–1151. Cham: Springer.

Sun, Xiaoping, Ruiping Yang, Jing Ji, Zebin Zhu, Jason C. White, and Yu Shen. 2024. An Evaluation of Microplastic Contamination in the Marine Waters and Species in the Coastal Region of the South Yellow Sea, China. *Journal of Hazardous Materials* 469 (May): 134018. https://doi.org/10.1016/j.jhazmat.2024.134018.

Tessnow-von Wysocki, Ina, and Philippe Le Billon. 2019. Plastics at Sea: Treaty Design for a Global Solution to Marine Plastic Pollution. *Environmental Science and Policy* 100 (October): 94–104. https://doi.org/10.1016/j.envsci.2019.06.005.

Tiller, Rachel, Andy M. Booth, and Emily Cowan. 2022. Risk Perception and Risk Realities in Forming Legally Binding Agreements: The Governance of Plastics. *Environmental Science & Policy* 134: 67–74. https://doi.org/10.1016/j.envsci.2022.04.002.

Tilsted, Joachim Peter, Fredric Bauer, Carolyn Deere Birkbeck, Jakob Skovgaard, and Johan Rootzén. 2023. Ending Fossil-based Growth: Confronting the Political Economy of Petrochemical Plastics. *One Earth* 6 (6): 607–619. https://doi.org/10.1016/j.oneear.2023.05.018.

Vince, Joanna, and Britta Denise Hardesty. 2017. Plastic Pollution Challenges in Marine and Coastal Environments: From Local to Global Governance. *Restoration Ecology* 25 (1): 123–128. https://doi.org/10.1111/rec.12388.

Winston, Carla. 2018. Norm Structure, Diffusion, and Evolution: A Conceptual Approach. *European Journal of International Relations* 24 (3): 638–661. https://doi.org/10.1177/1354066117720794.

Index